THE FLIGHT OF THE IOLAR

The Aer Lingus Experience 1936–1986

Eamon de Valera, as President of Ireland, presenting to Michael Dargan, then General Manager, Aer Lingus, a globe which he had acquired to assist him in advancing the cause of Shannon as the transatlantic terminus. 'To get a rough idea of Europe', he wrote to Dargan on 3 December 1968, 'I thought the simplest and quickest way was to get a large globe, and with a thin piece of twine or thread to determine the distances of the various continental points . . . When I was Taoiseach I always kept it in my office in Government Buildings, and when I was elected President my successor, Mr Lemass, let me have it here at Aras an Uachtaráin.'

THE FLIGHT of the IOLAR

The Aer Lingus Experience 1936-1986

Bernard Share

GILL AND MACMILLAN

Published in Ireland by
Gill and Macmillan Ltd
Goldenbridge
Dublin 8
with associated companies in
Auckland, Dallas, Delhi, Hong Kong,
Johannesburg, Lagos, London, Manzini,
Melbourne, Nairobi, New York, Singapore,
Tokyo, Washington

7171 1457 0
Print origination by
Wellset Ltd, Dublin 1
Printed by
Criterion Press Ltd, Dublin

Pour Elizabeth,
qui a dû tout supporter

Contents

Acknowledgments

AMONG the very many people with Aer Lingus associations or with a special interest in the airline who made their knowledge and experience available to me, I would particularly like to thank those who consented to be interviewed at some length: Sean Braiden; Donal Brennan; Terry Byrne; Alistair Campbell; Margaret Coyne; M. J. Dargan; G. P. Dempsey; Finbarr Donovan; Tommy Dunne; Desmond Fennell; Garret FitzGerald; Frank Fitzpatrick; C. J. Haughey; David Kennedy; Tom Kennedy; Brendan McGann; Conor McGrath; Neil McIvor; Terry McManus; Paddy MacNamara; Dick Murphy; Mícheál Ó Riain; Louis Slater; Arthur Walls; Niall Weldon; R. N. White; Bill Yeoman. I must also acknowledge the assistance of some others who have preferred to remain anonymous. I am indebted to Aer Lingus for permission to make use of interviews conducted by John O'Donovan and Bill Maxwell with the following: Thekla Beere; Packy Bourke; P. J. Brennan; Michael Cusack; Frank Delaney; J. F. Dempsey; Nuala Doyle; Neil Gleeson; Oliver Hone; Muriel and Jim Hughes; Patrick Lynch; Tommy McKeown; T. J. O'Driscoll; Diarmuid Ó Riordáin; W. J. Scott; Paddy Tierney; Aidan Quigley and Stanley Williamson.

For advice and assistance in specific areas I would wish to thank Ann Barry; Tommy Crannitch; Norman Edwards; Tom Hanley; Michael Keating; Mrs Betty O'Connor and family; Eamonn Power, Oonagh Reynolds, F. Glenn Thompson, Niall Weldon and Commandant Peter Young. Bert Keenan, Phil Newport and Mícheál Ó Riain bore the brunt of identifying, selecting and preparing the photographic content.

For permission to quote from two novels by Francis Stuart I am indebted to Victor Gollancz. The quotation from *Where the River Shannon Flows* is reproduced by permission of Dundalgan Press.

Finally, to my colleagues in *Cara* I owe a particular debt of gratitude for the forebearance they have shown towards an over-preoccupied editor.

Introduction

THERE are changes in the air. The next decade will very possibly see the return of the propeller with the unducted fan engine and perhaps a reorientation of the airline structure in Europe. Noel MacMahon, Secretary of the Department of Communications, speaking in Washington in his capacity as President of the European Civil Aviation Conference (ECAC) in April 1985 told his audience: 'The discussions within the EEC are proceeding on the basis of guidelines recently approved by Transport Ministers on the basis of work done during Ireland's presidency of the European Community in the second half of 1984. Somebody recently commented on the fact that during this period Ireland simultaneously held the Presidency of the European Community and of ECAC, and that IATA . . . was under the Presidency of the Aer Lingus Chief Executive, David Kennedy.'

'That Ireland is enabled to play a role out of all proportion to its size is attributable in a large measure to the achievement and reputation of its national airline over a period of fifty years. In the world of aviation,' wrote Knut Hammarskjöld, Director-General of IATA, 'Ireland, through its national airline, Aer Lingus, has come to make contributions to the worldwide integrated air transportation system which go far beyond what could be explained by its size and relative importance.' It is against this background that I have attempted to trace the development of Aer Lingus from the beginnings to the present day.

Anyone who has been involved, however peripherally, with the fortunes of our State-sponsored bodies cannot but have become aware of the marked ambivalence towards them on the part of the public at large — an uneasy amalgam of reluctant pride and smouldering resentment. This is not a condition that has manifested itself solely within recent years: the Shannon Scheme was summarily appended to the national herd of white elephants well before the ink was dry on the plans and, of course, jokes and jibes at the expense of Bord na Móna and Córas Iompair Éireann are as old as those institutions themselves. If such attitudes may be attributed in part to the natural propensity towards begrudging, a more fundamental explanation is to be sought in the attitude of successive governments and of several generations of civil servants who have neglected to come to terms with the full implications of the rule of the state sector in the economy. Crises, such as the Irish Shipping debacle, produce renewed calls for greater accountability; but the guiding principle, developed more from expediency than from any political philosophy, that State-sponsored bodies should be let run their own affairs and that the relevant minister cannot interfere, has so far withstood major challenges since it was first enunciated, in relation to the conduct of Aer Lingus, by Seán Lemass in the late 1930s.

The wider ramifications of these equivocal relationships are fascinating: but I have not in this book set out to write a political or economic history. The reasons should be obvious: any work dealing with matters as recent as those of the day before yesterday cannot hope to lay claim to the degree of objectivity necessary to place such issues in perspective. I have therefore endeavoured to present the first fifty years of the development of Aer Lingus largely as seen through the eyes of those immediately and principally involved, in the hope that in so doing the structure and balance of the narrative would not vary significantly as between what might be termed the historical era and the events of more recent times.

It will be apparent — and particularly and perhaps painfully apparent to those with close Aer Lingus connections — that there are many who played a role who do not appear in these pages; equally that there are areas of activity which receive limited treatment. To those who feel that they have been ignored either personally or in relation to their occupational interest I offer my apologies in the context of the guiding principle I have adopted of attempting to set the airline, its function and achievement within a broad national and international context in the interests of a wide and non-specialist audience.

The task could not have been undertaken without the full and unreserved co-operation of the present management of the airline and of a very large number of its employees and associates past and present. To all these I owe my thanks and their individual contributions are, I hope, adequately acknowledged elsewhere. I owe a particular debt of gratitude to David Kennedy and Mícheál Ó Riain for their patience and forebearance in the face of what must at times have seemed my obstinate refusal to see the wood for the trees. Both read the drafts many times and offered invaluable criticism and comment. In no respect, however, did they or any other individual attempt to coerce me into views which I could not in honesty sustain or to include material for patently cosmetic reasons. I make this assertion in the knowledge that there will be some who will view my current tenure of the editorship of *Cara,* the inflight magazine of Aer Lingus, as inhibiting my objectivity in dealing with matters of policy and internal politics. In this regard I feel it necessary to point out that I am not, and never have been, a full-time employee of Aer Lingus and that my work under contract for the airline is in a category totally different from that represented by this book.

It must also be said in this connection that there are, inevitably, matters of very recent history, particularly as affecting relationships between the airline and its Shareholder, which cannot in the nature of things be ventilated as fully as those relating to earlier periods. I have, nevertheless, been afforded access to all such material of a sensitive nature and am satisfied that nothing has been abridged that would have materially affected the accuracy and balance of the presentation. Finally it must be stressed that the concept, structure, treatment and analysis are the responsibility of the author and of no one else.

Aer Lingus has been fortunate in the quality and commitment of those who have guided its evolution over the past half century, and in none more than in J. F. Dempsey, whose experience is almost as old as that of the airline itself. When I invited him to make a comment for inclusion in this introduction his first point was that it is through its people that Aer Lingus continues to remain 'one of the great bulwarks in our national economy'. 'At the commencement', he recalled, 'we were in no way equipped to deal with the technical side of the business but we learned quickly. We were a small group who understood that life itself was about people. We were fortunate in the laying of the foundations of the Company that we had people who were dedicated to the ideal of service to one's fellows as an essential element in everyday life, and were prepared to sacrifice self in so doing. One of my most treasured early memories is that of an unsolicited tribute from one of our passengers, and I quote: "Yours is the airline with a heart — an airline with a human personality." We were also motivated by a high degree of idealism in that we were privileged through this new vehicle in the transportation business of introducing our country to the outside world and becoming an integral part of it. And of course we saw in it the opportunity of taking the sting out of emigration and of becoming one of the main props in the development of tourism. I hope and I sincerely believe that we have justified our existence. What is more important, I hope our shareholders in this community share my view.'

For David Kennedy, the present Chief Executive, satisfaction at having completed fifty years of service to the community 'must be tempered by the sober realisation that there are plenty of difficulties and potential pitfalls ahead of us. The future challenges for Aer Lingus are immense. It would be a dangerously facile assumption to believe that because currently Aer Lingus is making higher levels of profit than at any previous time in its fifty year history therefore all is well. In fact given the enormous capital expenditure which the airline will face over the next ten years for fleet replacement our current levels of profit are totally inadequate.' David Kennedy fears that the industry as a whole will repeat its former mistakes by adding capacity in excess of market needs, resulting in reduced load factors, renewed price wars and a slide back into heavy financial losses. For Aer Lingus, he suggests, the implications are clear: it has to become more competitive both in terms of the quality of service it provides and, even more importantly, the cost of producing that service. 'We are competing in a tough and demanding industry and the going will be all the more difficult in the years ahead.'

That is for the future. In the Spring of 1952 I was summoned to London to attend an interview for an university post in Australia. I was booked on the last Aer Lingus flight of the day, and decided for pressing reasons of economy to take not the airline bus from Cathal Brugha Street but the 41A from Eden Quay. Somewhere beyond Santry the bus came to a sudden and unsignalled halt. Both driver and conductor descended and peered with no degree of urgency into the engine whilst, on the top deck, I had visions of flight, interview and job receding into the realms of what might have been. After a decorous interval, however, the crew resumed its position and the reluctant power unit was coaxed back into life. On our eventual arrival at the airport terminal building I was greeted by a uniformed individual with some degree of impatience. 'We've been waiting for you', he admonished me sternly, and whisked me past customs men and idle bystanders out onto the ramp where the steps were just being removed from the departing DC3.

I got the flight — and, incidentally, the job. And if it was not my first experience of Aer Lingus it was one which, perhaps, had some small influence on my decision to embark upon this narrative.

1

A Day at the Races

IRISH Aviation Day, held in the Phoenix Park, Dublin, on Sunday 10 May 1936, attracted an attendance of upwards of four thousand people; the fortunate individual who had secured from the Irish Aero Club the sole rights to the management of the Bicycle Park must have been well satisfied with the day's work. Not everybody, however, arrived on bicycles. Flight-Lieutenant Tommy Rose, who had recently broken the record for a flight from London to the Cape of Good Hope and back, flew in with his wife in his Miles Falcon monoplane. Miss Lily Dillon came from Germany in her Klemm Swallow for the dinner and dance on the preceding Friday; Mrs Levington arrived from India where she had been flying with her two sons. Another visitor, Mrs Crosseley, an aerobatic pilot, was perhaps somewhat taken aback at the extent of the local feminine rivalry in her chosen field: but the sport of aviation knew no sex barriers. On 2 May a French airwoman, Mlle Vivienne Elders, had been reported missing in the Sahara. Between the dinner and dance and the dawn of Irish Aviation Day in Dublin, Mrs Amy Mollison had beaten Tommy Rose's record to the Cape, completing the journey in three days, six hours and twenty-six minutes — of which she spent just six hours asleep.

The winner of the first event in the Park was, however, Mr J. W. Weldon, who flew Sir Osmond Grattan Esmond's Gipsy Moth from Athlone to gain first place in the 'arrival' competition. He landed in the Fifteen Acres behind the United States Legation, a site which had been mentioned as suitable for a permanent aerodrome. 'In front of the main enclosure Mr C. W. A. Scott's fleet is drawn up,' wrote Colonel Charles Russell in his magazine *Aviation*: 'the massive tri-engined Airspeed Ferries towering over the light Cadets, Lynx, Mongoose and the diminutive autogiro... further up the line are grouped some curiosities of the air, a ridiculous-looking Flying Flea and a graceful Douglas Drone, both making their first appearance in Ireland.' The Minister for Defence, Frank Aiken, was introduced to the crowd by Seán Ó hUadhaigh, solicitor and Chairman of the Irish Aero Club. 'And here we get the first sign of the undercurrent which seems to run through Aviation Day this year,' wrote Russell: 'The popular Chairman of the Aero Club has always been noted as an unquenchable optimist, but even he seems to feel the effect of years of frustrated hopes. He will only commit himself to stating that if the long-promised Anglo-Irish service does not materialise this summer he will be very much disappointed.'

'In Ireland it would be a little unfair to say that the growth of aviation has been ignored,' commented *The Irish Times* the next day: 'The truth is rather that the growth has been unperceived, and that few people have grasped what it might mean to this country in the future.' There were those, however, who were already planning ahead. Commandant O'Sullivan, representing the Government, was in the Shannon Estuary area at the the beginning of May in company with Major Banks of Imperial Airways, carrying out investigations into the possible establishment of a transatlantic air base. This and subsequent visits to the area during the month were shrouded in considerable secrecy. On Friday, 15 May, the proposal to site an 'air base' at Merrion Strand was debated by the Dublin Port and Docks Board, which had had the suggestion under consideration for some time. The idea had originally been put forward in an article in the Jesuit review *Studies* in 1935 and the Board's renewed interest stemmed from a visit it had just paid to Belfast, where the new city airport was in course of development of Sydenham. Desmond McAteer, a consulting engineer, had based his argument on two fundamental points: 'firstly, that facilities for air travel are necessary for Dublin; secondly, that existing aerodromes in the neighbourhood of Dublin are not suitable for a municipal airport'. On 22 May *An Roinn Cosanta,* The Department of Defence, wrote to the Acting Officer Commanding the Air Corps at Baldonnel requesting, on behalf of the Department of Industry and Commerce, an urgent report on the technical feasibility of the Phoenix Park for a civil airport.

Other possibilities were under consideration. 'Either Collinstown or Kildonan could be developed as the Terminal Airport of Dublin, though neither would be quite suitable in view of their distance from the centre of the city', the report of the Departmental Committee established by the Minister for Defence to enquire into Civil Aviation in Saorstát Éireann had concluded in December 1935. Kildonan, in Finglas village some eight kilometres north of the city, had been established by Hugh Cahill in 1931 as Ireland's first commercial airport. His company, Iona National Flying School and Motor Engineering Works ('Any make of aeroplane supplied') was based at Cross Guns Bridge in Phibsboro and the legend 'Iona National Air Taxis and Flying School' appeared on the fuselage of his first aircraft, a Desoutter Mark II, registered as EI-AAD on 10 October 1930. Kildonan was acquired in 1933 by Everson Flying Service, owned jointly by Lady Kathleen Nelson and George Everett, and again taken over in February 1935 by Lady Mary Heath and her second husband James, who renamed the operation Dublin Air Ferries. On 3 May, 1936 at Kildonan demonstrations took place of a new 40 hp cabin monoplane which had been acquired as a trainer by the reorganised company which, in common with several others, had ambitions to open scheduled air services to Britain and Europe.

On 30 April Major F. L. Crilly of Crilly Airways, London, described as 'the only Irishman managing an airline', had arrived in Cork by air from Galway to survey the possibility of linking that city into a network of planned services between Ireland and Britain. 'We have the goods', he told an interested audience, 'and are ready to start tomorrow if the people of Cork want such a service. The time has arrived for Ireland to come into the air business.' Crilly's backers included Lord Inchiquin, and on 21 May the Galway Chamber of Commerce passed a motion assuring him of its willingness to back him 'financially and otherwise' in the establishment of a Galway–London service which would carry mails landed at the port by Cunard and North German Lloyd, who had already promised support. On Friday 22 May, the indefatigable Major was in Cork again in company with Colonel Charles Russell, late Officer Commanding the Air Corps, and T. J. Kenny, Chairman of the Irish Tourist Association. 'This is the first real step to form an Irish transport service,' said Crilly, proposing a daily link between Cork and London. 'The idea', explained Russell, 'is the achievement of an Irish national air transport service, entirely owned and manned by Irishmen.'

But time was running out for Major Crilly. Essential to his plans was the approval of the Government under the Air Navigation (International Lines) Order of 1935, which provided for the Minister's prior authorisation to the establishment of 'any international airway between Saorstát Éireann and any other country with a view to the limitation or regulation of competition as may be considered necessary in the public interest'. And on 5 May Crilly had received a letter from his Dublin solicitors who had been informed that the Minister was 'unable to entertain his proposals'. The reason given was the Government's intention to set up a national airline 'at the earliest possible date'.

As part of his submission to the Minister for Industry and Commerce, Major Crilly had gone as far as offering to establish an aircraft factory. However — as Senator Fitzgerald told him bluntly in Cork — there was no future for him under the new legislation which had been in preparation for several years (a slight political exaggeration) and which was shortly to be placed before the Dáil in the form of the Air Navigation and Transport Bill 1936. 'A scheme has been under consideration for some time past', the Minister had told deputies the previous November, 'for the establishment of a national air transport company in the Saorstát.' Those plans were now on the verge of accomplishment.

They had been some years in the making. On 11 April 1928 Captain Hermann Koehl, Günther Freiherr von Hünefeld and Major James Fitzmaurice had taken off from Baldonnel, county Dublin, in the Junkers W33

Bremen on what was to prove to be the first east–west crossing of the Atlantic. Fitzmaurice and his companions became international celebrities; but no sooner had the Irish officer resumed his duties as Officer Commanding the Air Corps than he was looking for new worlds to conquer. 'My enthusiasm to render the State still further service remains undaunted,' he wrote in his autobiography, 'and my energies became directed towards the establishment and development of commercial aviation linking Ireland with the British Isles and the Continent. My old friend and service comrade, Colonel Charles Russell, came to my assistance in this matter to which we devoted our full attention. Our efforts were, however, fruitless as the Government of the day showed not the slightest interest. Bitterly I came to the conclusion that our stay-at-home compatriots lacked the high qualities of enterprise and endeavour which stood their brothers in such good stead in their activities abroad . . . Ireland seemed to me to be a land in which only the gombeenman could make good. I felt, somehow, I had had enough.'

A committee appointed by Patrick McGilligan, the Minister for Industry and Commerce, had in fact reported in 1928 that a nationally-operated air service would require financial assistance in its early years, and the Government had decided to take no action. Fitzmaurice resigned his Air Corps commission in disgust, but his interest in civil aviation continued: in 1934 he persuaded Irish Hospital Sweepstakes to sponsor his entry for the Macrobertson Trophy Air Race from London to Melbourne. In this he was to suffer another disappointment. A few hours before the race was due to begin he and his Ballanca aircraft, EI–AAZ *The Irish Swoop* were disqualified following a disagreement over the amount of fuel permitted. 'My shabby treatment in this great international event reflected nothing but the greatest discredit on each and every member of the Race and Stewards' Committee,' he concluded bitterly: 'so much for British sportsmanship when the question of the prestige of an industry is involved.' (His aircraft was American.) On 10 May 1936 one of the co-organisers of Irish Aviation Day was C. W. A. Scott, winner of that Mildenhall to Melbourne event of two years previously. But Fitzmaurice had by this time left for America.

Before Desmond McAteer advocated his Merrion Strand scheme in *Studies,* Sir John Purser Griffith had made use of the same medium to promote the advantages of Galway as a sea and air port. His article appeared in September 1929, some two years before the setting up of the ambitiously-titled Irish Transatlantic Air Corporation, the moving spirit behind which was C. H. Glendining. He was told in November of that year by Patrick McGilligan, on behalf of the Cumann na nGaedheal Government, that the scheme would receive their goodwill provided Irish interests were adequately protected. A site was selected in Galway, and in 1933 the new Fianna Fáil Minister, Seán Lemass, expressed interest, as did German aviation circles: the British, on the other hand, were markedly unenthusiastic. In 1934 the company was granted 934 acres at Sydney, Nova Scotia, by the Canadian Government, but apart from a visit to Cork by the promoter in April 1936 nothing more was heard of the proposal.

One of those who had been invited to comment on Sir John Purser Griffith's article in the same issue of *Studies* was the solicitor Arthur Cox, who described himself as a director of Irish Airways Limited. This company was formed 'with a view to commencing, with the assistance of a government subsidy, a civil aviation service between Ireland and England and also within Ireland'. The plans of this group came to nothing; neither did those of Iona National Airways, who in 1932 had made some demonstration flights with a Fox Moth, EI-APP, with the intention of establishing a Dublin–London–Berlin route with feeder services to Cork and Galway. It was ultimately to fall to a Scottish company, Midland and Scottish Air Ferries, to claim the distinction of operating the first commercial passenger services between Ireland and Britain. Midland and Scottish were represented in Ireland by Captain H. J. Hosie of Athy, a director of Industrial Vehicles (Ireland) and distributor for De Havilland aircraft. Operations commenced on Monday 13 August 1933 with a flight from Hooton, near Liverpool, to Baldonnel via Speke, and continued on a daily basis, Sundays excepted. On 30 September they ceased for good, probably on account of poor loads, but also because the Department had informed Hosie that he would have to form an Irish company to continue to operate the service, and to include in any such company a representative of the Great Southern Railways. Midland and Scottish had, however, opened a route from Glasgow (Renfrew) to Belfast (Aldergrove) on 30 May 1933 which was to continue to operate successfully. On 20 August 1934 it conveyed its first bag of mail to Belfast and became known as 'the Royal Mail Route'. On 24 May 1934 Seán Lemass told the Dáil: 'The question of a Free State Air Navigation Company . . . is being dealt with. We hope to have brought matters to the point that these services can be inaugurated at the beginning of next year.'

His forecast proved optimistic; but on the ground there were clear signs of progress. On Tuesday 19 May 1936 a new radio station, to be known officially as DUBLIN AERADIO and unofficially as 'the little tower', opened at Baldonnel Aerodrome with the W/T (wireless telegraphy) callsign LIJ. It was operated by the Department of Posts and Telegraphs for the new Marine and Civil Aviation section of Industry and Commerce on a frequency of 348 kilocycles and was to be in service from 08.45 to 16.45 daily. 'We had to build up a radio communications service and the Chief Engineer of the Post Office did a fantastic job,' recalled T. J. O'Driscoll, who had been Private Secretary to John Leydon, Secretary of the Department of Industry and Commerce, and who was now to head the Marine and Civil Aviation section. Three days later, on 22 May, Aer Lingus Teoranta was formally incorporated 'To carry on and foster the business and pursuit of aviation in all its forms, both within and without Saorstát Éireann . . . To make, build, assemble, buy, hire or otherwise acquire, and to equip and furnish, work and use, and to improve, repair, maintain, tend, cleanse, store and warehouse, and to supply, sell, let, lend or otherwise dispose of, and generally to deal in aircraft of every description. . . . '

The first board meeting of the new company was held on Monday, 25 May at 11.00 at 57 Upper O'Connell Street, Dublin. The directors present were Seán Ó hUadhaigh, solicitor, in the chair; Augustus P. Reynolds, accountant; John O'Leary, company director; William H. Morton, Manager, Great Southern Railways; and Thomas J. Flynn, civil servant. The Board decided upon the name 'Irish Sea Airways' for the new service. On Wednesday 27 May at 09.00 a De Havilland DH84 Dragon carrying the registration EI-ABA and the name *Iolar* (Eagle) took off with five passengers from Baldonnel bound for Bristol. *The Irish Times'* editorial, together with the main news columns of all the Dublin newspapers of the day, was devoted to the maiden voyage from Southampton, England, of the new luxury liner *Queen Mary*.

2

Vision in the Pragmatic Sense 1928–36

ABROAD, the rumblings in Europe were ominous. At home the economic war with Britain continued to drain both resources and initiative: it was not a time for visions. 'No one in Ireland was interested in having a proper Irish airline,' T. J. O'Driscoll remembered: 'the State had to put up the money.' The issue, however, was not quite so clear cut. There were individuals, as has been seen, very anxious to enter the area: and the Government view was ambivalent. Industry and Commerce, in the persons both of its Minister, Seán Lemass, and its Secretary, John Leydon, became convinced of the necessity and the role of a national airline. J. J. McElligott, of Finance, claimed that a highly successful airline was being run in Sweden on a private enterprise basis. It was to be first of a continuing series of disagreements between the two departments in matters of airline policy.

Leydon saw the airline as a national asset, and he had a marked facility for quiet and persuasive negotiation. Seán Lemass possessed the same vision in the pragmatic sense: he saw the necessity for the country to be in control of its external communications and he conceived of a national airline in terms of a second line of defence in any emergency. He also foresaw circumstances in which foreign airlines might choose not to serve Ireland and the effect this would have on trade and tourism. 'Strategic considerations were a prime consideration of Lemass,' in the view of Patrick Lynch, who was to become chairman of Aer Lingus in 1954 on the invitation of John Leydon, acting for his Minister: 'He regarded it as essential for the sovereignty of the country that it should have an independent airline.'

Lemass's approach, though well-disposed, was cautious. 'The decision to enter the field of civil aviation,' he wrote on the occasion of the twenty-first anniversary of Aer Lingus in 1957, 'was one of the many difficult decisions which have had to be made by the State in the course of the past quarter century.' The difficulties were rooted as much in the genesis of the concept as in the estimates of its success.

The Cork Harbour Commissioners' Report on Aerodromes for Aeroplanes and Seaplanes, dated 10 October 1928, recommended that 'For Aeroplanes, the site that best fulfils the requirements is the large field of flat land south of the railway, just east of Little Island Railway Station.' Some three years later a representative of the Dutch airline KLM arrived in Cork to evaluate the possibilities of a transatlantic air base in the harbour. He was highly interested, but complained in his report of the slowness of the authorities in furthering the project. There was one individual, however, who was determined that Cork should have both its airport and its international air services. This was Richard F. O'Connor, Cork County Surveyor, a man with a wide-ranging and inventive mind and deeply interested in all forms of transport. On 4 July 1933 he presented his proposed scheme for Cork Terminal Airport to a group of interested Cork people. A fortnight later *Flight*, the British aviation journal, commented: 'The unique geographical position of Cork Harbour as the most westerly harbour in Europe, situated on the track of the North Transatlantic steamship routes and equipped to accommodate large liner traffic makes it the obvious site for the North European terminal airport. Cork Harbour is already established as a port of call for transatlantic liners ... Sir Eric Geddes, chairman of Imperial Airways, recently stated that the crossing of the Atlantic by seaplane services will become an accomplished fact.... It is, however, material that Cork Airport should be set up at once if advantage is to be taken of the present liner traffic....'

Richard F. O'Connor, who proposed an international airport for Cork in 1933

The well-planned location of the airport was a tidal mudflat at Belvelly, situated between Great Island, Little Island and the mainland. The project would necessitate the reclamation of 460 acres and the site had already been surveyed both from the air and at ground level by several experienced airmen, including Colonel Charles Russell. 'All agreed', reported *Flight*, 'as to the great possibilities of the site as likely to form the safest landing ground in Europe.' R. F. O'Connor proposed four initial routes: Cork-Dublin-Belfast-Glasgow; Cork-Rosslare-Pembroke-London; Cork-Dublin-Liverpool and Cork-Cherbourg direct — the latter to be operated by seaplanes. The airport was to cater for both transport modes on a single site, a concept which, in the eyes of several of the aspiring transatlantic operators, offered exciting prospects for development. Imperial Airways, in a letter to O'Connor, expressed the view that as far as what they described as 'internal air services within the confines of these islands' were concerned, Cork to London was unquestionably one of the most attractive routes that could be operated from the point of view of saving time compared with surface means of transport.

'We have lost control over all shipping lines using Irish ports, but there is now a real opportunity of gaining full control of airways,' O'Connor told a meeting in Cork the following April. In the intervening months he had been enthusiastically advocating his scheme, which was exhaustively prepared and researched. He had sought quotations for site and drainage works and for electrical and other equipment and had meticulously costed all aspects of the project. Events, as he was to discover, were moving fast, if not perhaps in the direction he anticipated. On 1 May 1934 he wrote to his uncle, Christopher Musgrave, Bt: 'Since I saw you last I have been trying to move heaven and earth to get our local people to build my aerodrome at Belvelly . . . the result is

The proposed Belvelly airport. From 'Flight', 20 July 1933

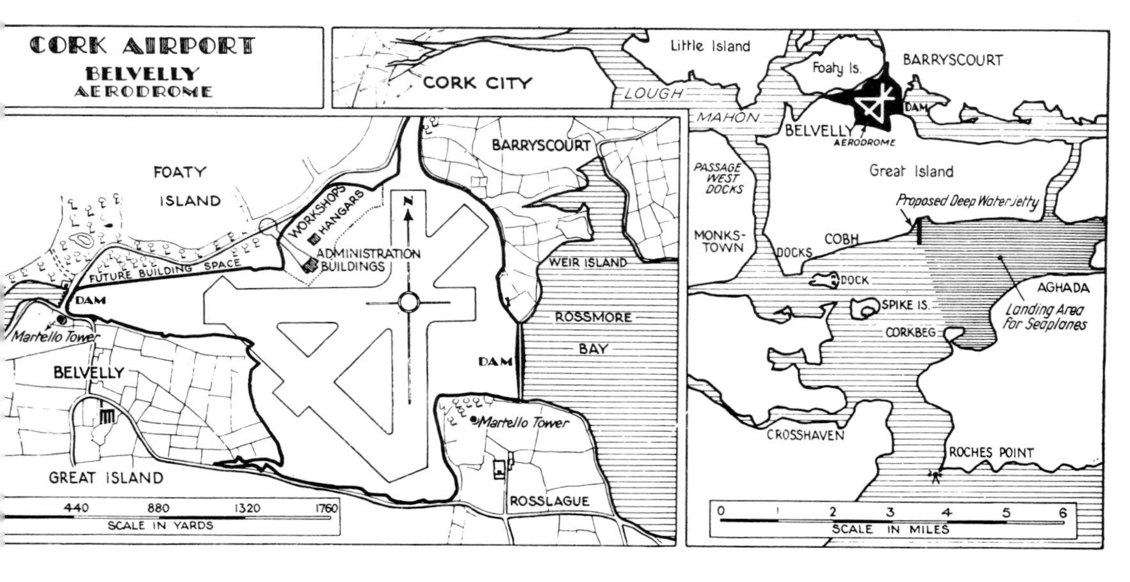

that a joint committee of our local supporters is to meet shortly "to consider the question of Cork Airport". I can manage this crew alright and get them to cough up the money for building the airport. The next step is to get up a Company to carry on the flying business. I was inadvertently dragged into the promotion of such a company and have now come to realise that this is the one and only object of my existence while the building of the airport is only a sideline.'

The first meeting of the Cork Airport Joint Local Authorities Committee was held on 21 May and it had before it an offer from the Government to provide £20,000 by way of a Relief Grant provided that an equivalent sum were forthcoming from the Authorities themselves. Whilst the Councillors were arguing over the money for Belvelly, O'Connor was finding the other, and in his view the more important part of the plan, anything but plain sailing. His partners in the airline scheme were C. P. McCarthy, a chartered accountant, and Captain W. P. Delamere, Officer Commanding the Air Training School at Baldonnel. It was not long before he learnt that a rival scheme was being prepared in Dublin by Colonel Charles Russell and E. J. Smyth, who had latterly retired from the Marine and Transport Branch of the Department of Industry and Commerce. Russell and J. J. O'Leary, founder of the printing house of Cahill and an aviation enthusiast, were seeking the support of Lady Mary Bailey, a leading Irish aviator. Lady Mary, only daughter of the Fifth Lord Rossmore of Monaghan, had gained her pilot's licence in 1927 and became the first woman to fly across the Irish Sea. In 1928, aged thirty-eight and the mother of five children, she flew to Capetown in a DH Moth, making the return journey the following year. In 1934 she was living in England. R. F. O'Connor stole a march on his rivals by inducing her to visit him at his home in Mallow to discuss his own project. She had expressed keen interest and promised assistance but in June he had bad news for her. 'Our flying business is in a hopeless muddle,' he wrote. They had, as he saw it, three options; to drop the whole business and let the Dublin people muddle through; to get Cork people onto the Board of Russell's company; or to get Cork businessmen to support his own venture. A few days later came further bad news: the Department of Defence had refused permission to Captain Delamere to serve on the board of a private company. O'Connor, understandably, suspected political intrigue. He talked the matter over with Hugo Flinn who lived in Cobh and was Parliamentary Secretary to the Minister for Finance. 'Would you believe it,' he wrote to Lady Mary, 'but Mr Flinn and other businessmen who have lived near Cork Harbour all their lives cannot see, until after hours of bitter argument, that there may be something to be said in favour of using aircraft to pick up mails from liners at Cork Harbour, and fly them to Berlin. No wonder I feel rather jiggy. I shall go away and live on an Island.'

Colonel Charles Russell's proposal for the formation of a public company, Irish Air Transport Limited, had been forwarded to E. J. Smyth, still at the time employed by the Marine and Transport Branch, on 12 April 1934. He told Smyth in his covering letter that he had approached the railway companies with a view to their providing half of the capital and nominating directors 'in an equal number to those put forward by the promoters' but had been unsuccessful. He did not, however, believe that this represented the railways' final word on the matter: 'If it were possible to secure the Minister's approval of the proposals as set out in the enclosed Memorandum, it would appear that the Railway Companies are disposed to approve of and co-operate in a National Aviation Development Scheme along these lines.' In the light of the parallel moves by O'Connor's group the last paragraph of Russell's letter is not without interest: 'Regarding the representation of aviation interests on the Board of the proposed Company, you may assume, so far as the promoters are concerned, that the participation of all genuine National Aviation interests will be welcome. They must, however, be genuine interests, and capable of providing a portion of the capital required by the Company.'

Russell's proposed company 'would enjoy the full and exclusive support of the Government, financial and otherwise, for a period of five years. The company in return would accept on its Board such representation and such restrictions as are deemed necessary by Government to ensure that its programme is properly carried out and that Government funds . . . are correctly expended and accounted for.' The first objective was to be 'the operation of a Dublin/London Daily Service in each direction throughout the year and the provision of an aerodrome at Dublin with the necessary meteorological and wireless organisation. Experience would doubtless show that a twice daily service would be justified during certain months of the year.' This service would be extended to Cork and Galway during the tourist season. Subsequent objectives, in order of priority, were the establishment of airports at Cobh and Galway 'with a view to the development of Trans-Atlantic traffic at these ports'; the provision of landing grounds and fuelling centres at various unspecified points throughout the country; the operation of a regular mail service between Cobh and Paris and a 'branch air line' off the Dublin-London service to Hamburg. The capital cost of all this, excluding the Cobh airport, for which no estimates had been prepared, was put at £250,000.

Russell envisaged close co-operation with the existing military air organisation, including the employment of 'only reserve or retired Military air pilots and mechanic personnel', and assumed that Baldonnel would be made available for the Dublin–London service together with the provision, free of charge, of 'directional wireless and meteorological service'. 'Doubtless many schemes for an air service between Dublin and London have been put forward,' he continued somewhat disingenuously: 'and the amount of the subsidy required has varied considerably. Here is it desired to point out that the type of service which these proposals cover is one comparable in every way with the best of the European services. The service operated by Royal Dutch Airlines between London and Amsterdam may be taken as the standard aimed at.' The route, he believed, 'calls for the use of large multi-engined aircraft capable of maintaining the service with safety and on schedule in the meteorological conditions likely to be encountered from time to time . . . the geographical features on the routes, which include a 65 miles sea crossing, call for the greatest care in the maintenance of aircraft . . . this is not possible in the case of a service operated by a Company utilising unsuitable or obsolete machines.' He proposed the utilisation of a fleet of four fifteen-seater, three-engined aircraft (make unspecified) operating at an average speed of 125 miles per hour over ground.

Having provided estimates of costs, traffic and revenue, Colonel Russell turned to the provision of the necessary capital: 'National Air Transport, if it is to be really National and retained as such, must be owned and controlled by the Irish people. These proposals, therefore, include as part of the assistance asked for from Government, such financial guarantees as are necessary to obtain Irish capital. Also such legislation as is necessary to prevent the transfer of Irish capital interests in the Company to foreign interest is asked for.'

Whilst O'Connor and Russell were seeking to further their separate interests, a new element was introduced into the situation which was to prove decisive. O'Connor was a member of the Irish Aero Club based at Baldonnel (and became president of the Cork Aero Club when it was set up in 1934) and knew its chairman, Seán Ó hUadhaigh. A solicitor in the firm of Little, Ó hUadhaigh and Proud of 12 Dawson Street, Dublin, Ó hUadhaigh was a personal friend of the Taoiseach, Eamon de Valera and influential in political circles. On 24 May 1934 Ó hUadhaigh had written to O'Connor to tell him that he had been asked by the Minister for Industry and Commerce to use his good offices to try to bring together the two groups 'who are trying to start a Saorstát air transport Company, with a view to avoiding dissipation of strength and energy on the promotion of rival schemes.' The two groups met in Dublin on 6 June and again on 13 June. At the latter encounter — 'a proper dogfight' in O'Connor's estimation — the Cork group was 'virtually wiped out'. The judgment was premature: on 21 June Ó hUadhaigh again wrote to O'Connor to tell him that he had just had a meeting with Seán Lemass who had expressed himself as unsatisfied with Russell's scheme and wanted to see the Cork project. He was, added Ó hUadhaigh, prepared to grant the concession to a united group. O'Connor responded to the challenge. By the beginning of July he had completed the prospectus of his proposed airline company. The name he had chosen was *Aerlingus Éireann Teoranta.*

The document was a report rather than a company prospectus in the legal sense. It proposed the issue of £56,000 in five shilling (25p) shares out of a nominal capital of £100,000. The principal object in establishing Aerlingus Éireann, the report stated, was to secure for an airline company, controlled and eventually manned by Irishmen, a share of the most paying portion of transatlantic transport by taking advantage of the geographical position and political circumstances of Ireland. 'It will be noted . . . that Bulgaria and Ireland are at present the only countries [of Europe] which do not possess their own National Airline Company. It will also be noted that each Country's Airline Company is given a distinctive name in the language of the country.'

Richard O'Connor was many things but had few pretensions towards being a Gaelic scholar. Having decided that the name of his new company should be in the Irish language, he enlisted the assistance of Mícheál Ó Cuill of *Comhaltas um Oideachas Gairme Beatha* (the Vocational Education Committee) in Cork who, in May 1934, had forwarded a list of suggestions: *Aer Raoin Teoranta; Aer Roda Teoranta; Aer Róid Éireann; Aer Bhóithre Éireann; Aer Reim Éireann; Aerdacht Éireann; Aereamhlacht Éireann.* Ó Cuill put forward the names of a couple of other people who might be able to help should none of these prove acceptable. Whether O'Connor followed that suggestion or not, by the date of the first meeting with Russell's group, 6 June, the name *Aerlingus Éireann* was a reality.

The name derives from *Aer*, air and *loingeas*, a fleet, and is thus the exact equivalent of *Aeroflot*. The corruption of *loingeas* to the more immediately accessible *lingus*, a word not found in the Irish dictionary (the closest is *lingeach*, springy), argues the publicist rather than the scholar; it is difficult not to suspect the involvement at some stage of Seán Ó hUadhaigh who appeared on the first Aer Lingus letterhead with the explanatory qualification 'formerly John K. Woods', and who gave his address as Gleann Caorthainn, Dalkey.

If O'Connor's own project never literally got off the ground (he suggested that flying should commence from Baldonnel in 1935 pending completion of 'The Great Airport of Cork') his vision and foresight finds some small if largely unrecognised acknowledgement in the name borne by the national carrier under its eventual state-sponsored identity. O'Connor's own design for an insignia — spread wings bearing in the centre a harp and the letters, in Gaelic script, AE — also found an echo in the first Aer Lingus emblem; and if one might regret the loss of the harp, replaced by a shamrock, it might have proved a little difficult to establish a version that infringed neither Government prerogative or that of a not inconsiderable Dublin brewery.

O'Connor had a meeting with Lemass early in July 1934 and took the opportunity to emphasise the transatlantic dimension of his scheme, which he felt the latter had not until then properly appreciated. He learned that Russell's proposal had definitely been rejected, and it was further hinted that Russell was not regarded as a reliable man. Be that as it may, the Colonel became chairman of the proposed board of the joint Russell–O'Connor project, which was to be known as *Aerlingus Éireann.* The other members, as of September 1934, were to be O'Connor, T. J. Kenny of Galway, Chairman of the Irish Tourist Association and a nominee of the Great Southern Railways. Ó hUadhaigh was acting as secretary and drafting a Memorandum and Articles based on those of Imperial Airways of London.

A meeting of the provisional board was held at 12 Dawson Street on 12 October. It had before it a letter from John Leydon to the effect that the Minister had not yet come to a decision in the matter of commercial aviation. On 30 October Ó hUadhaigh wrote to O'Connor to tell him that he had had an interview with Lemass 'and he told me that he was not going on any further with aerial developments until he gets an inter-departmental committee set up'. 'I take it that our happy little band of pioneers is dissolved in thin air,' O'Connor replied: 'at least until the Minister's inter-departmental committee has issued its report'. On 9 November *The Irish Times* carried a report of its Air Correspondent's interview with Colonel Charles Russell. 'It is understood', it said, 'that the committee [of inquiry] will consider whether or not a Government subsidy is necessary for the carrying out of an air transport service.' The meetings would be in private and 'present and former members of the Irish Aero Club's council are among those being invited'. The committee would be nominally responsible to the Department of Industry and Commerce, though the Department of Defence was also concerned. 'The decision to hold a formal inquiry into Civil Aviation in the Free State is attributable to a scheme put forward by *Aerlingus Éireann Teoranta* (Air Fleets of Ireland Ltd) for the operation of a state-aided air service between the Free State and Great Britain.'

The interview 'appears to have been Charlie Russell's own idea,' Ó hUadhaigh wrote to O'Connor on 13 November: 'I am afraid Charlie has finished himself with the Minister and all his officials by this very injudicious publication which involved a disclosure to the public of the fact that the committee was being set up, which was intended to be confidential.' 'Since I saw you last I got mixed up with some people who appeared to be equally keen,' O'Connor wrote to Captain Hosie on 15 January 1935: 'but regret to say my experience was most disheartening. There are more petty jealousies among aviators than among ballet girls.'

Though the future of the airline would seem to have passed beyond his control, O'Connor had by no means given up his scheme for the Great Cork Airport. He had aroused the interest of another major carrier, Deutsche Lufthansa, and on 17 October 1934 its Dornier Wal Do 18 flying-boat

Tornada, registered D–ADYS, visited Cork. The first commercial flying-boat to be fitted with heavy-oil engines, it moored at a British Admiralty buoy off Cobh. Aboard was W. E. Schmitt-Rex, London Manager of Deutsche Lufthansa, and the welcoming party included Captain Kelly, the Cork Harbour-master, the Chairman and General Manager of Cork Harbour Commissioners and, of course, the County Surveyor. Another air survey of Belvelly was undertaken by C. W. A. Scott's Flying Display of London at a cost of £14.10s. (£14.50p) and on 6 March 1936 the London *Sunday Express* was reporting that 'a vast airport is being constructed close to Queenstown(Cobh) and Atlantic liners will call there. On arrival the passengers will be transported by plane and spread like a spray over Europe. . . . So soon in Ireland we will have a country which will be outside the range of war but easily reached in air liners.' This totally misinformed report was a sad irony, for by then Belvelly had been added to the lengthening list of Irish aviation might-have-beens.

W. H. Morton, Seán Ó hUadhaigh, J. J. O'Leary and A. P. Reynolds, the newly-appointed members of the Air Transport Advisory Committee, attended at the office of the Minister for Industry and Commerce on 18 May 1935. Also present were John Leydon, Secretary of the Department, and an assistant secretary, T. J. Flynn. Seán Lemass explained that a number of schemes for air services, private chartering facilities and aerodrome development had been submitted for the approval of the Government in the past few years, but that none of them had been sufficiently complete or satis-

The Dornier Wal DO 18 moored off Cobh, 17 October 1934

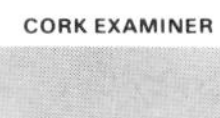

CORK EXAMINER

factory in every respect to command the fullest confidence. 'The object', he said, '... was the establishment of a first-class undertaking, capable of operating services up to the best European standard, and designed to enter substantially into the business of (*a*) air transport connections for mails, passengers, and the more valuable merchandise, between transatlantic steamer and — later — air services, on the one hand and European centres of population (including London) and the trunk European air services based on them, on the other hand; (*b*) services between Dublin and Northern Ireland and Great Britain; (*c*)services wholly within the Saorstát. Certain co-operation might also be possible between the new Company and Pan-American Airways in regard to transatlantic air services.'

The operation of services to and from other countries by the proposed Company involved reciprocal facilities for air transport services of the other countries, said the Minister, and 'as it was desirable to reduce competition to a minimum, the possibility of co-operating with foreign companies in the ownership and control of subsidiary joint operating companies seemed to be worth investigating. Certain progress had already been made in tentative negotiations for a joint operating company for cross-channel services with Great Britain.'

Lemass told the committee that they had been chosen, not for their association with any of the previous proposals, but because of their general association with aviation and their experience in business. He suggested that some of them might, in due course, be associated with the new company. Mr Flynn, he said, would act as their chairman.

The 'tentative negotiations for a joint operating company for Cross-Channel services' were, in fact, by then reaching an advanced stage. At the beginning of March, John Leydon had received a letter from Sir Alan Cobham, KBE, DFC, with an address at Trafalgar Square, London. 'For a long time I have been interested in Aviation in Ireland,' he wrote: 'It has been my privilege to conduct my Air Display on a Tour around the Irish Free State during which time we received the full support of the people and in return did our utmost to popularise flying.... However, the time has come when as a result of the increased confidence in Aviation the public are now ready for Air Transport, and I am gradually transferring my activities in that direction. I should like to make it clear at this point that although my financial backing is considerable and secure I am in no way connected with any combine, trust or group, but stand absolutely clear of any entanglements. I very much wish to be associated with an Air Transport Development between Dublin and London and I should be quite prepared to collaborate with any selected Company in such work.'

Cobham went on to outline a somewhat complicated general scheme based upon the opening, by him, of a temporary service between Dublin and

Liverpool and Dublin and London 'for a period of four to five months or until such time as the Irish company could be established'. This latter reference was to a proposed Irish holding company whcih would take up a 50 per cent interest in Cobham's eventual operating company 'Dublin-London Airlines Ltd'.

This initial approach was followed by a discussion in Dublin on 14 May with T. J. Flynn and on 17 May by an amplified proposal. 'I have always been under the impression', Sir Alan wrote, 'that it was the intention of the Authorities of the Irish Free State to form a big, substantial Irish Aviation operating company, and that it is still their intention to do so. The main work of this company would be to operate services in Ireland, and to co-operate with other companies in the operation of services to Great Britain.' He continued to advocate a fifty-fifty arrangement on the Irish Sea, and suggested a daily service London–Dublin and a return, together with a twice-daily operation on the Liverpool route, beginning on 1 July 1935. The London service, he suggested, should leave Dublin at 15.00 and arrive Croydon or Heston at 17.30 'so that passengers would have ample time for dinner and a show in town in the evening'. He advocated the use of four new, twin-engined 240 HP Lynx Envoys. 'I have particular experience of these aircraft,' he wrote, 'having them in operation on my London-Guernsey air route. They leave nothing to be desired as far as passenger comfort, reliability and controllability are concerned. All pilots admit they are a beautiful aeroplane to fly.' Cobham was confident that 'after say nine months' operation with the experimental service as outlined . . . everybody in the Irish Free State will be ready for the big scheme. . . . If I am permitted to operate the experimental service, it would be on the understanding that I should be the first to be asked to collaborate in the formation of the big scheme.' After suggesting that should the final choice fall upon some other operator he would feel himself entitled to reimbursement, he concluded: 'Before leaving Mr Flynn, I discussed with him the possibility of collaborating with Mr Olley on the question of the service between Dublin and the Isle of Man. And I informed Mr Flynn that Mr Olley was a very old friend of mine, of some sixteen years' standing, and that I should be only too happy to work with Mr Olley in this respect, and consequently interviews have been arranged regarding this matter.'

The Advisory Committee met on 28 May and agreed on a draft authorisation in favour of Sir Alan Cobham which incorporated a number of substantive amendments to his proposal. Most significant was an insistence that the shareholding in the Irish Sea company would be in the ratio of 'Saorstát 51 per cent, British 49 per cent'. The committee also made it clear that Cobham's role would be restricted to the Irish Sea routes only. 'It must be indicated to Cobham', said J. J. O'Leary, 'that the cross-channel proposal is only one of three divisions — internal, cross-channel, and continental services. ... We may, or may not, seek his co-operation afterwards on internal and continental. I suggest that a Saorstát Company should be formed which would be the Crosschannel Company. The Irish public would hold no share in the cross-channel Company, only in the Parent Company to be formed.'

The authorisation to Sir Alan Cobham referred to 'temporary and experimental' services only, the committee envisaging that the establishment of air services between the Saorstát and Great Britain should proceed on the basis: '(i) That steps should be taken to secure the operation [of services] for a limited period of 12 months from the date of commencement, such services to commence early in the Summer of this year [1935]; (ii) that steps be taken to form a Saorstát Company from the Saorstát groups whose proposals have already been received by the Minister for Industry and Commerce ... ; (v) The proposals of Sir Alan Cobham are preferred to those of Railway Air Services [British] and Captain Olley as offering greater possibilities for the eventual development of air services under Saorstát control free from association with already established British transport interests.'

Sir Alan was again in Dublin on Saturday 1 June to discuss his proposals with the committee. On 6 June the latter expressed the opinion 'that it would be preferable in the National interest that the cross-channel Operating Company owned 51/49 per cent by Saorstát and British interests respectively, registered here and owning and operating Saorstát aircraft, should be formed at once rather than allow Sir Alan Cobham to come on the experimental service with British owned machines from the start, even for a limited period. We see no difficulty in forming the Company with a small capital, to be financed by Sir Alan Cobham for the present by a loan in machines, other stock and cash.'

The full Air Transport Scheme as outlined by the committee had now taken the form of four separate but related companies: 'Company A: Principal Saorstát Air Transport Company. One of its functions would be to hold the Saorstát interest in Company B; Company B: Saorstát Company for permanent air services with Great Britain embracing Saorstát and British interests on equal terms, so far as practicable; Company C: The British financing and holding Company proposed by Sir Alan Cobham to finance the temporary services and hold the British interest in Company B: Company D: The Company proposed by Sir Alan Cobham for the operation of the temporary services'.

On 22 June T. J. Flynn wrote to Cobham at the direction of the Minister enclosing the Heads of an Agreement relating to the operation of 'preliminary air transport services'. 'Upon the required sanction [by Parliamentary Vote] being obtained and the necessary legal formalities completed, the Minister will be prepared to grant authorisation to yourself or a company promoted by you, and to a Saorstát group, to establish and operate regular air services for the commercial carriage of passengers, mails, and merchandise, or any of them, in both directions between Saorstát Éireann, on the one hand, and the United Kingdom of Great Britain and Northern Ireland, the Channel Islands and the Isle of Man, on the other... for a period of one year from 1st July, 1935.' 'The Minister agrees in particular', wrote Flynn, 'with the object of the combination of interests, viz: the elimination of competition.'

On 26 June John Leydon wrote to Seán Ó hUadhaigh inviting him to act as chairman and as one of the first directors of the proposed Saorstát Company. He replied that he would make every endeavour to see the job through. On 15 July the Chairman-designate wrote to Sir Alan Cobham: 'to tell you how sorry I am personally that, as far as I can learn from Industry and Commerce, our collaboration in setting up the Dublin–London air line appears to have fallen through. I hope that they are taking a pessimistic view of the matter, and that it will turn out that either you or some combination in which you will take a leading part will co-operate with us in establishing this service.'

Ó hUadhaigh was to be disappointed. Cobham, in his reply dated 16 July, made it clear that it was a matter of money: 'For your own information, I would like you to know that I was personally let down three times in succession on a point of finance. While I was prepared to do the thing myself, my financial advisers and solicitors would not permit me to do it as they insisted I was placing too many eggs in one basket. Your offer of assistance is very greatly appreciated indeed, and I am doing all I can to persuade Mr Olley to carry on with the work where I left off.' 'I am very sorry that the thing is working out as it is,' Ó hUadhaigh wrote on 18 July: 'I believe that Mr Olley will be communicated with and invited to come over and discuss that matter of starting a line.... I am in hopes, anyhow, that the job will be done this time and not merely talked about....'

On 16 September 1935 John Leydon sent Seán Ó hUadhaigh a copy of the Heads of an Agreement 'to be made between a Saorstát Air Transport Company, to be formed, and Olley Air Service, Limited, in relation to the establishment and operation of Air Transport Services', informing him at the same time that it was now necessary to take steps to establish the Saorstát Company.

Muriel Hughes, who became Captain Gordon Olley's secretary and first employee in 1934, recalled that the Heads of Agreement were originally set out on the back of a Shelbourne Hotel, Dublin, menu. Olley was backed by Cyril Cunliffe-Owen, chairman of British American Tobacco and promoter of an odd aircraft know as the 'Flying Wing', who took part in the negotiations together with J. W. S Comber, later head of Isle of Man Air Services. Lemass told the Dáil at the end of November 1935 that the arrangement with Olley had reached the state where parliamentary authority was necessary to enable commitments to be entered into in advance of the full scheme which was to be dealt with by contemplated legislation. The Irish Sea operations, he stressed, were to be strictly on commercial lines, and the first services would be between Dublin and Liverpool and Dublin and Bristol, connecting with express trains serving those ports, with Dublin–London and Cork–London also in prospect. The liabilities for the first year of operation were not to exceed £20,000.

In December a Departmental Committee established by the Minister for Defence to review proposed civil aviation schemes in the light of military considerations expressed the view that the proposed Anglo-Irish service 'provides the Saorstát with the best opportunity of initiating external services with the minimum of delay. The Committee would prefer to see such a service operated by an exclusively Irish Company, but presume that the Department of Industry and Commerce have examined this in detail and are satisfied that it is not practicable.' It also noted a scheme put forward by Pan American which was to represent an extension of that company's proposed transatlantic services. It was to be entirely US-controlled and required a monopoly of Ireland–United States traffic for fifteen years, together with free landing facilities. Pan Am planned to build and maintain their own aerodromes. The Committee felt that this scheme was 'of such importance to Irish aviation that it should be encouraged as far as possible'.

On 10 January 1936 a meeting took place at 14 St Stephen's Green in Dublin between representatives of Olley Air Services and representatives of 'Air Lingus [*sic*] in process of formation'. The agreements were still being drafted from the Heads agreed but there were immediate matters to be discussed. It was recognised that it would not be practicable to commence services before 1 March and that a telephone would be necessary for the Station manager at Baldonnel. Captain Olley proposed that, at the outset, one of his newest aircraft should be transferred to the Saorstát Company. This would be a De Havilland six-seater Dragon, with lavatory, with a cruising speed of 110 miles per hour. It had cost £2,900 and would, of course, be depreciated adequately. This was a two-engined machine. He had on order two fourteen-seater De Havilland 86A four-engined machines, with lavatory, with a cruising speed of 150 miles per hour. He thought that these would shortly be required on the service and he would propose to transfer one of them to the Saorstát Company when it would be found necessary. The timetables would not be based on high speeds. It was always better, he said, to have a margin in hand than frequently to exceed scheduled times.

A general discussion took place on the giving of information to the press, Olley expressing the view that to withhold such information might militate against the according of publicity when most desired. It was not necessary, he suggested, that the items to be communicated should contain anything very definite. The cautious press release that ensued prompted, nevertheless, a large volume of applications for positions in the new company from people with a wide variety of background and experience: P. A. Sheehan, managing editor of *The Garda Review*, made application for 'the publicity work that will be necessary in connection with the New Air Service'. Seán Ó hUadhaigh expressed reservations about possible publicity regarding a survey flight from London to Dublin via Bristol which had been arranged for 10 March. 'Although I do not like publicity personally,' he wrote to Olley, 'and the Department of Industry and Commerce have been very strongly against it up to now, I am inclined to think that it would be for the good of the business itself that we should have the amount of publicity which will follow letting the press know when we are arriving, so that they will be on the scene with their cameras, reporters and other paraphernalia, with which I am sure you are only too painfully familiar.'

At a meeting of the two contracting parties on 14 February the Irish company had been referred to in the minutes as 'Saorstát Air Transport'. On Wednesday 18 March a meeting was held 'of the Directors elect of *Aer Lingus Teoranta*': the name had finally stuck. It was agreed that a copy of the Memorandum and Articles, as amended by Mr Ó hUadhaigh and Mr Flynn, should be forwarded for the immediate printing of twelve galley proofs for the Directors.

Writing on 'The Economist and Public Policy' in 1953 Patrick Lynch quoted Keynes: 'The important thing for government is not to do the things which individuals are already doing, and to do them a little better or a little worse, but to do those things which are at present not done at all.' Seán Lemass, though his prime intent may have been 'to convert the Irish public service into a fountainhead for entrepreneurial development corporations', as Brian Farrell put it, was by no means a committed or even consistent advocate of the key role of state-sponsored bodies. 'If they are to fulfil their proper role in the national economy,' he wrote in 1959 after a lifetime of experience, [they] 'require to be kept under continuous pressure, from inside and outside, to revise their procedures and costs in a continuous effort to maintain their efficiency.... The performance of a State corporation depends, in our experience, on the capacities of the individual holding the chief executive post.' His broad position might be fairly expressed in terms of the comment in the 1967 Report on Full Employment prepared by the National Industrial Economic Council: 'There is no need to come to any doctrinaire judgment. Against the Irish background particularly, it would be more sensible to view private and public enterprise as complementary rather than competitive sources of national development.' Where air transport was concerned Lemass, having examined the alternatives, was left in no doubt as to the necessity of a State role.

The task of putting together the substantive legislation, The Air Navigation and Transport Bill 1936, fell to T. J. O'Driscoll, who was fortunate, he said, in that a similar bill had just gone through the House of Commons in London: 'I must say I took large chunks out of the debates.' Lemass congratulated him on his substantial brief, and the second reading took place in the Dáil on 8 July 1936. Seán Lemass was ill, and two members of the Government party, Fianna Fáil, out of a possible seventy-six listened to Thomas Derrig, substituting for him, describe air transport as 'the special expression of the spirit of the age, the spirit of practical achievement'. On a more down-to-earth level he stressed the importance of the Saorstát being in a position to utilise the advantage of its geographical location on the fringe of Europe to establish its claim to routes in which it was interested. Lemass had previously explained to deputies that though he wished to minimise competition on economic grounds, he recognised that no one country could hope to reserve to its own nationals the whole of the air transport between its own territory and that of another country.

The thinking behind the bill, which enshrined the position of the State as sole international carrier, had been influenced by European developments. KLM had been set up in 1919, Lufthansa in April 1926 and Air France in 1933: all State entities benefiting from official restriction of competition. The Irish legislation was to establish a national company 'to centralise the administration of all future aerial development in or through the Irish Free State', thus covering both internal and external services. 'We feel that it is absolutely essential at this stage', Mr Derrig told his sparse audience, 'that we should utilise any opportunities we have to the very fullest in developing our geographical position and putting this country on the map as a really international centre to which different countries would send their ships [*sic*], and that we should establish the enterprise in such a way that this country would be well regarded on the Continent of Europe as one which has definitely taken up the air attitude. . . .'

For the Opposition, Patrick McGilligan attempted to needle the acting-Minister regarding certain people who had wanted to inaugurate air services and had had their applications refused, whilst James Dillon wondered whether the Minister's investment in the shares of the company was to be by way of State socialism or State capitalism. Did the Government propose to run this enterprise for profit? Or did they intend to run it as a public service, setting up ideal conditions of employment, regarding solvency as a matter of minor importance, giving extravagant services for the minimum rates, and calling on the Exchequer to make up any deficiency in operating costs? Mr Dillon's questions were to prompt a number of conflicting answers over the course of the subsequent fifty years. He also returned to the matter of private participation, suggesting that a number of proposals had been received from individuals prepared to operate both internal and external services without State assistance. Mr Derrig agreed that such proposals had been received, though in each case a State subsidy had been sought.

The acting-Minister went on to explain the facts behind the premature birth of Aer Lingus. It had been set up, he said, with a nominal share capital of £100,000 to operate Ireland–Britain services in a joint working arrangement with Blackpool and West Coast Air Services, which was a subsidiary of Olley Air Services. It was presently being financed by the issued debentures which had been taken up by the British company and it would be necessary for the national company — to be established by the bill — to discharge any liabilities incurred which remained unsatisfied. Provision had been made in the capital of the holding company for capitalising Aer Lingus, the investment being by way of share capital. Aer Lingus, under the legislation, would start off with a clean sheet.

The Bill designed to bestow *post-facto* legitimisation on the airline made its measured progress through Dáil and Seanad. 'The intention is to set up a national company which shall invest in shares in the Joint Operating Company responsible for operating the transatlantic air service, but in addition to representing us in the Joint Operating Company, this national aviation company will have other functions. It will concern itself with aviation generally. It will control Aer Lingus and possibly other subsidiary companies running other services. . . . ' Aer Rianta, the national company referred to, was finally set up in April 1937. The Minister for Finance was empowered to take up shares to a nominal value not exceeding one million pounds and the company was authorised, with the Minister's consent, to lend to Aer Lingus Teoranta sums sufficient to discharge any liabilities which it might have incurred and which remained unsatisfied. In May 1937 Aer Rianta wrote to Aer Lingus requesting an estimate of such liabilities and was told that they were within the region of £30,000 to £35,000.

'Empiricism, not a grand design, should be the objective,' wrote Patrick Lynch of the role of state-sponsored bodies in 1963. The policy, said the arch-empiricist, Seán Lemass, in February 1937, 'will aim, amongst other things, at making the Saorstát the international juction for air traffic between Europe and North America, not only by direct services by air, but also by providing air connections at Saorstát ports with transatlantic shipping. It should, we think, be feasible in time to establish air services connecting the Saorstát directly with all the principal countries.'

At this time Aer Lingus were operating two small aircraft on two routes out of three temporary structures at a military aerodrome virtually in the middle of nowhere.

3

Clondalkin 39
1936–45

IN March 1936 Lieutenant E. F. Stapleton of the Air Corps gave a series of lectures on aerodrome control to his fellow officers at Baldonnel, county Dublin. Together with his assistant lecturer, Lieutenant M. Comiskey, he had attended a course in Britain in the techniques, then new to Ireland, of handling civilian air traffic; both men were subsequently to serve at the new Collinstown Airport in Dublin and at the seaplane base at Foynes on the Shannon. At this time, before the opening of the Aer Lingus service, civilian traffic was confined to small private planes and an occasional visiting foreign airliner, but the military were not entirely happy with the way the situation was developing. 'I feel that a certain amount of friction has arisen between the Departments,' [of Defence and Industry and Commerce], Major M. Brennan, Chief of Staff, had written to his Minister in December 1935: 'which, if allowed to develop, will seriously interfere with the efficient running of the Civil Aviation Scheme. Aviation in all its branches is recognised in every country as definitely linked up with the country's defences and it is essential that we ensure from the outset that our scheme of civil aviation fits into the general defensive scheme of the State.' In June of the following year B. A. Mulcahy, commanding the Air Corps, was moved to write to the Secretary of the Department of Industry and Commerce pointing out that military officers could not carry out the same range of inspection duties as their civilian counterparts and suggesting training some of the latter preparatory to the opening of Collinstown.

Baldonnel, some fifteen kilometres from Dublin (it was not infrequently spelt with an extra 'l') had been established under the British regime as a training base for the Royal Flying Corps in Ireland at the close of the 1914-18 war. The birth of the Irish Air Corps anticipated the withdrawal of all British units from the country in 1922, and it commenced operations with one non-military aircraft, a five-seater Martynside; this was acquired in Britain by Commandant-General McSweeney and Captain (later Colonel) Charles Russell at the time of the Anglo-Irish treaty negotiations with a view to spiriting Michael Collins out of England, should the talks fail. Known appropriately as 'The Big Fella' it was flown to Baldonnel on 19 June 1922 and was the first aircraft to carry the then new Irish tricolour. It was joined in July by the State's first strictly military aircraft, a Bristol Freighter F2B which had been in service with the Royal Air Force. In the same year Captain Russell was appointed Director of Civil Aviation with a view to establishing a school of flying.

The Defence Forces Regulations of 1932 noted that Ireland was the only nation that had thrown its military aerodromes open for the unrestricted use of civil aircraft, and this was still the position as arrangements were being completed for the inauguration of the Aer Lingus service. In November 1935 Major F. Leo Crilly ('an Ulsterman who committed the indiscretion of being born in England') had written to the aerodrome manager, Baldonnel, from his London office requesting the schedule of landing charges. These ranged from 2 shillings (10p) for 'a small type, less than 500 sq.ft.' to £1.10s. 0d. (£1.50) for a 'large type with more than two engines'. Olley Air Services were also London-based, with offices at 7b Lower Belgrave Street. They operated from Croydon. Captain Olley had served with Imperial Airways, who generously gave him three months' leave without pay to start his own charter air company. His ambition, however, was to run a scheduled airline. Since for this Government approval was necessary, he sought and found an acceptable solution in his agreement with Aer Lingus. This was noted by the Board of the new company at its second meeting on 3 June 1936 as having been sealed with both Olley Air Services and its subsidiary Blackpool and West Coast Air Services. A contemporary advertisement, prepared by McConnell's advertising agency, proclaimed: 'We are proud .... born of our association with the progress of our country. Éire has always held her place among the nations in Art, Drama and Literature — now she is in the Air. Her scattered sons look homewards, proudly conscious of the Motherland's achievements in many spheres — not least her position in international transportation. Now are the "Wild Geese" linked more closely with Eire, not only in spirit, but in fact.'

'Just up and over' was the slogan employed by Irish Sea Airways in the same advertisement: but the journey began with a somewhat extended incursion by road into rural Ireland. Though Baldonnel had the advantage of being a fully-functional airport, it was not exactly adjacent to the city of Dublin, and Aer Lingus reached an agreement with Dublin United Tramways to operate a bus service from Aston Quay for the convenience of passengers. The airline's administrative office was at 39 Upper O'Connell Street but it also instituted a night booking office, telephone Dublin 43533, at the LSE Motor Company's premises in Parnell Street. Its 'terminal' at Baldonnel — telephone Clondalkin 39 — was erected by the Office of Public Works and consisted of a wireless hut and a passengers' hut containing a waiting room as well as pilots', control officers' and managers' rooms. One of these temporary structures was still standing and in use as a storeroom in 1985.

The elements of this minimal infrastructure were barely in place when the passengers and distinguished guests arrived for the first flight. They were met by the entire Aer Lingus Baldonnel staff of three: Station Superintendent J. J. Hurley, the former commander of a cruiser in the Chinese customs service; his Deputy M. J. Finnegan, and Booking Agent E. A. Rafter. Tickets were purchased immediately prior to departure.

Wednesday 27 May 1936. One of the interested spectators was the writer, surgeon, aviator and Senator, Oliver St John Gogarty, who in July 1933 had himself crash-landed at Baldonnel, running into a flock of sheep. He commented at the time: 'When the principal aerodrome in the country is let as a sheep ranch, and at a time when there is not much sale for sheep, it is more than a foregone conclusion that in an accident one of them is killed.' *Iolar,* blessed by Army Air Corps chaplain the Reverend William O'Riordan, suffered no such mishap. The five passengers who took off for Bristol on the somewhat ostentatiously enumerated Route No. 800 were W. H. Morton, Director of Aer Lingus and Manager of the Great Southern Railways; Mr and Mrs T. Fitzherbert of Dublin; T. J. O'Driscoll and Mrs Seán Ó hUadhaigh, who held Aer Lingus ticket number 1. The pilot was Captain Oliver Eric Armstrong, a Dubliner then in the employment of Olley. The only freight carried was a parcel of *The Irish Times* destined for London. For one interested spectator, Seán Lemass, the occasion must have been one of quiet satisfaction.

The passengers were welcomed at Bristol by a delegation which included Alderman A. A. Senington, Chairman of the Airport Committee, and F. Blunden, Bristol Manager of Blackpool and West Coast. W. H. Morton told a local reporter that the crossing was 'calm and pleasant'. Mr and Mrs Fitzherbert left the plane at Bristol but the others returned with the incoming service, arriving some thirty-five minutes behind schedule at 15.05. On the

The 'Iolar' at Baldonnel, 1936

AER LINGUS

AERLINGUS, TEÓRANTA. 59
AERPORT ÁṪA CLIAṪ, BAILE DOṀNAILL.
DUBLIN AIRPORT, BALDONNEL.

Uimir (Number)
Seirbís (Service)
Dáta (Date)

Ainm (Name) HORGAN
Ó (From) DUBLIN 09.00 · 6.7.36
Go (To) BRISTOL Luaċ (Fare) £ 1 :10:0·
Áiteanna Túirlingṫe ar an aontuiġeaḋ (Agreed Stopping Places)
Maiṫ go dtí (Valid until)
Tugṫa amaċ ag (Issued by) Sa
(At) Dublin
Dáta a tugṫa amaċ (Date of Issue) 6.7.36
Ticéad bagáiste Uimir (Baggage Ticket No.)
Fá na Coinġeallaċa Iomċarta Lastall.
(Subject to Conditions of Carriage on Back).

An early ticket, dated 6 July 1936 AER LINGUS

same day a Blackpool and West Coast service from Liverpool via the Isle of Man, piloted by Dubliner G. E. B. Stoney, arrived with no passengers but left Baldonnel again with six bound for Liverpool. It was a modest beginning.

On the same day, 27 May, Captain Olley wrote to Seán Ó hUadhaigh expressing his regret that he was not able to travel to Ireland for the opening of the service. 'My great worry was to get the machine away to you last night from de Havilland's and to see that everything was in order from this end.' His concern was not misplaced. Ó hUadhaigh replied on 28 May: 'The machine only left de Havilland's ultimately at 7 p.m. and did not land in Baldonnel until after dusk. Unfortunately the wireless set was defective from the receiving point of view and caused a good deal of trouble on the first run to Bristol. The only passengers who would be likely to talk about this were Mr Fitzherbert and Mrs Fitzherbert, she being the daughter of Mr Joseph X. Murphy who is a director of the Great Southern Railways Co. and of the Bank of Ireland. They were friends of Mr Morton, General Manager of the Great Southern Railways Co. who was also travelling in his capacity as one of our directors. I understand from Mrs Ó hUadhaigh however that they were quite pleased although they were fifty-five minutes late in arriving at Bristol, and of course lost their train to London. The other passengers on board with the exception of Mrs Ó hUadhaigh were not paying passengers, namely Mr Morton and Mr O'Driscoll. . . . They will not talk and the Press were crowded out which was just as well. Of course the Bristol newspapers knew about the late arrival, and I believe know why it occurred. The radio operators were aware of the fact that they could not get into communication with the machine. . . . This morning there are no bookings outwards on either line, nor so far as I know tomorrow, but we could fill two machines on Saturday I understand to the island [Isle of Man].'

A report on the Dublin–Bristol service dated 30 June 1936 stated that it had operated every day except one, 'when a landing wire fitting snapped while taxying [*sic*] to take off at Bristol. It was found necessary to cancel the 1215 hrs. Service that day, also the 0900 hrs. Service from Dublin next day. . . . Fortunately this did not cause any inconvenience to passengers as there were no bookings. With regard to weather the route generally is difficult, cloud invariably covering the hills making it necessary for the crossing to be made very high to get above the clouds. The average operating height being between 7,000 and 8,000 ft . . . On two occasions ice formed on the wings and wires whilst climbing through the clouds. . . On another occasion the Aircraft became so thickly coated with ice that while still trying to climb it lost height, and had to turn back and descend, both air speed indicators and turn indicators being put out of action. . . . '

The first report was compiled by the airline's chief pilot, Captain Armstrong. A return of passenger traffic for the period 27 May to 6 July revealed that 171 passengers travelled between Baldonnel and the Isle of Man, on which service there were 490 seats available. Comparable figures for the other sectors were: Isle of Man–Liverpool, 240 seats, 41 passengers; Baldonnel and Bristol, 400 seats, 49 passengers. Taking the total of the three sectors the percentage of passenger miles to seat-miles was a modest 19.80.

Pending the enactment of the enabling legislation, the finance for the first Aer Lingus aircraft, EI–ABI, had come from Olley. The DH86 was valued at £2,000, and the Board issued six debentures value £3,000 to Blackpool and West Coast to cover it and other equipment. In July 1936 the Board heard, no doubt with some relief, that their directors' fees had been sanctioned by Industry and Commerce: £300 per annum for the Chairman; £200 for the two representatives on the Joint Committee of Management (Flynn and Ó hUadhaigh) and £100 for the others. The Department refused remuneration to the members for what they described as the 'promotional period' from September 1935 to May 1936. On 30 May the company opened its own service to the Isle of Man — a route already being operated by Olley — and in August increased the baggage allowance from 30 to 33 pounds (15 kilogrammes). A second aircraft, a DH86A, was purchased on 14 September, registered EI–ABK and named *Éire,* and on the same day the Dublin–Bristol service was extended to London. Whilst *Éire* was London bound, carrying Alderman Alfie Byrne, Lord Mayor of Dublin, and again piloted by Captain Armstrong, *Iolar* was en route to Liverpool via the Isle of Man to inaugurate

AER LINGUS

The cockpit (left) and passenger cabin of a DH 84. The actual aircraft shown is a sister ship of 'Iolar', EI-AFK, restored and with original markings and registration (EI-ABI) for use in the Aer Lingus Golden Jubilee celebrations, 1986.

AER LINGUS

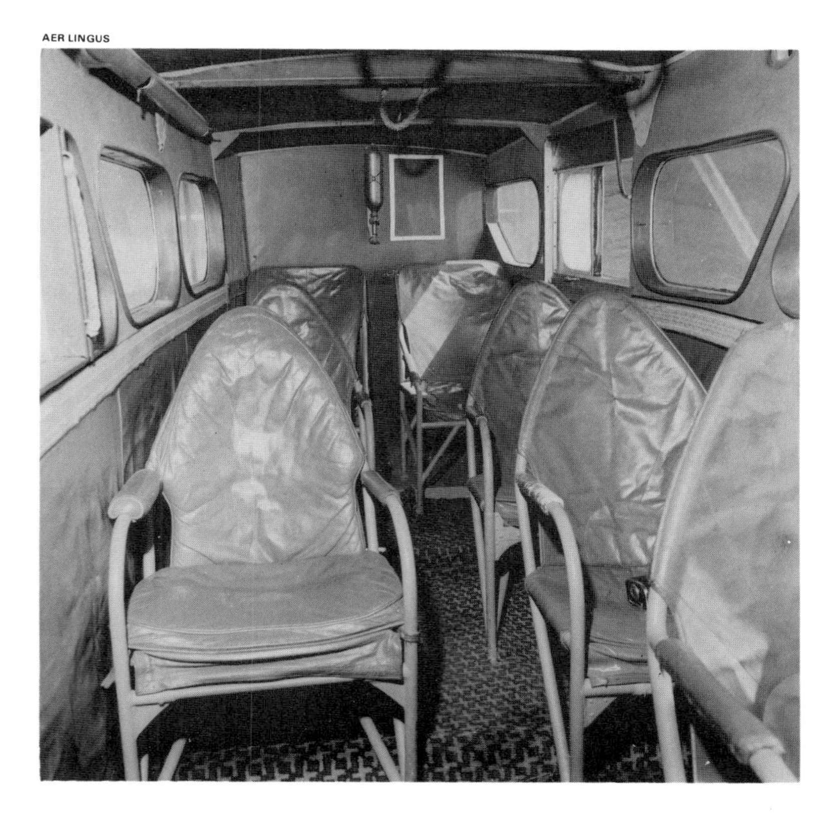

another new service. The London fare was £7.00 for a four-day return, £11.00 otherwise.

For the control officer at Baldonnel, the working day began at 07.30 when he sent out, in code and by telegram, a report on the local weather to 'Weather Telex' London. At 08.15 he received route weather in code from London which he had to decode and have ready for the Aer Lingus pilot at 09.55. At 08.30 he received weather in 'Q' (wireless telegraphy) from Croydon and at the same time similar information from Bristol. At 08.35 the circuit flag was hoisted and at 09.00 the aircraft took off en route for Bristol and Croydon. Information was telegraphed as to its time of departure and load and recorded on departure slips and on a map by means of flags.

James Dillon TD, found the service reasonably efficient in the wake of his initial strictures, but felt it left room for improvement. 'At the present time,' he observed, 'if you take an aeroplane from Baldonnel to London you will find that, when you get to Croydon, you are obliged to go the the nearest railway station and wait for 25 to 35 minutes for a local train to make your way to Victoria station. . . . I have arrived in Croydon at the same time as Imperial aeroplanes coming in from Paris and the Continent. The passengers coming off the two services were carefully segregated, the sheep from the goats. The sheep, who came by Imperial Airways, were put into a comfortable conveyance and carried into London, while the lone goat was sent to the local railway station and taken on one of these local trains to London simply because he had come by the local Aer Lingus Teo. service. . . .' It was a pattern of segregation which Aer Lingus passengers to London were to continue to experience.

In June 1937 Jeremiah F. Dempsey, who was then employed by the accountancy firm of Kennedy, Crowley and Company, was appointed Secretary-Accountant of Aer Lingus in a temporary capacity. 'The reservations could be kept on a little notebook, the sort the dairyman of the day delivering loose milk made use of,' he remembered. 'To keep faith with the timetable we did on occasions fly empty over and back. We would get a call at maybe four o'clock in the afternoon from our friends in West Coast Air Services and we'd be asked "have you any passengers for tomorrow's flight?" and we'd say no. And they'd say "well, we've nothing out of here — let's scrub it". And we'd say no: the goods are in the shop window. The shop window is the timetable and we must keep faith with the timetable.'

The profit motive was, understandably, pre-eminent in Olley's thinking. The Aer Lingus concept, in Dempsey's view, was both different and wider. At the first meeting which he attended in his temporary capacity, on 26 June 1937, he learnt that the airline was to be considered for membership of the International Air Transport Association, proposed by Imperial Airways, seconded by KLM. Two months later, however, when his appointment was made permanent, he was obliged to minute the Board's displeasure at the employment by John Maher, The Chief Ground Engineer, of three boys and its anxiety to know whether the company could really teach them their trade as then organised. In any event, the Board suggested, a fee ought to be paid either by them or their parents. On a more positive commercial note, the Board spent ten guineas (£10.50) on a window display, designed by Fergus O'Sheehan, for the new offices in O'Connell Street, from which the buses for Baldonnel were now to depart.

At Baldonnel itself there had been evidence of some operational disorganisation and some friction between civil and military interests. In June 1936 Seán Ó hUadhaigh had complained about restrictions in access to the camp and, following negotiations, it was arranged that Aer Lingus staff would be issued with passes. There were other problems: in October 1937 it was reported that the London–Dublin service had recently been operated by an aircraft of the Olley fleet which was without lavatory accommodation, resulting in severe embarrassment to one of the passengers. In January 1938 the Board concluded that the position with regard to West Coast accounts was highly unsatisfactory. It decided to take over Captain Armstrong from Olley and appoint him Chief Pilot and Air Superintendent at a salary of £1,000 for seven years.

The 1937 summer service, with three flights daily to the Isle of Man and Liverpool and two to London, one of which called at Bristol, had been taxing the manpower resources of the young company. Not all the pilots recruited had proved satisfactory, and eyes turned naturally to the Air Corps which had already provided a ground engineer in the person of 16067 Company Sergeant Maher, J.R. The Corps, for its part, manifested itself as co-operative in principle but wary in practice. In April 1936 Seán Ó hUadhaigh wrote to Major Mulcahy, Officer Commanding Baldonnel, to the effect that he was being strongly urged by the directors of Aer Rianta to do something substantial towards increasing air-mindedness, and that he was proposing to institute a series of Sunday pleasure flights from Baldonnel and back, taking in the more picturesque parts of Dublin city and environs. It was one thing, however, in the military mind to cater for a known number of civilians boarding scheduled flights; quite another to be required to exercise control over Sunday trippers. They agreed, subject to there being strict supervision (one NCO and three men were assigned to assist the control officer) and there was to be no wandering. 'Any person found in any other part of the camp is liable to be called upon to give an account of his movements,' ran a draft Aer Lingus notice, later modified in the interests of public relations: 'and to be taken into military custody'.

Pleasure flights, from Baldonnel's point of view, were bad enough, but when Ó hUadhaigh followed up with a request for 'a small number of round tables and chairs near the company's office for people to watch flying, also a caterer with a small tent from which to serve tea, coffee and cakes', Mulcahy wrote to the Chief of Staff suggesting, with some emphasis, that Aer Lingus should forego such moneymaking amenities until the new Dublin Airport was made available: 'It would be most unsatisfactory and a source of abuse and danger, to allow portion of the camp to be used as a public pleasure resort.' He was overruled, and Seán Ó hUadhaigh got his tables — tea, cakes and all!

On a more fundamental level the company had been conscious for some time of the need for an experienced general manager. On 4 May 1938 the Board was considering a list of candidates which included Erskine H. Childers, a future Minister for Transport and Power and President of Ireland, when a cable arrived from a man they had already approached, the pioneer North American aviator Robert Logan: REFERENCE PREVIOUS COMMUNICATIONS I WISH TO APPLY FOR POSITION MANAGER AIRLINES ON BASIC SALARY £1500 NET YEARLY PLUS TRAVELLING EXPENSES SELF AND WIFE STOP COULD ARRIVE DUBLIN BY JUNE 1ST VIA NEW YORK IF ADVISED BY CABLE. Logan was appointed and duly arrived, but within weeks was asking for clarification of his position, complaining that the policy of the Board and the objectives to be attained were not clear to him. He asked to have placed on record the fact that he did not agree entirely with what had been done in the past and pointed out that in many particulars radical alteration was necessary. His list of complaints was a long one: 'In order to accept this appointment I resigned from two important positions, one as Consultant and Special Representative of the largest Air Transport Company in the Western Hemisphere, the other as Vice-President and Managing Director of a gold mining company. . . . Am I supposed to be General Manager of this company or am I supposed to be a dummy figurehead without any real objective, authority or responsibility?' He complained that after six weeks he still had no clear instructions, that working conditions were poor. He thought even less of the Baldonnel bus service 'demanding a fare from passengers who ride in company with labourers in a cloud of smoke' and had hard things to say about Baldonnel itself — an inadequate terminal building, chaotic conditions at departures, fire hazards, no reserve plane for the Dublin-London route, no qualified second pilot, no second wireless telegraph operator. He was particularly incensed by 'the case of the Chief Pilot who claims to hold a contract with the company effective for seven years as Chief Pilot and Operations Manager, including charge of maintenance, yet who holds neither the necessary navigation certificate nor British validation of his pilot's certificate and who has declined to obtain them, and who had little time to supervise operations or maintenance due to being absent about 11 hours per day'. He recommended the immediate purchase of new aircraft, together with the immediate employment of an experienced pilot and sufficient experienced men for two crews. The fleet stood at two, *Iolar* having been sold in February 1938 and replaced by a DH89 Dragon Rapide, registered EI-ABP and named *Iolar II;* in October another aircraft, a DH86B registered EI-ABT and named *Sasana* was bought secondhand from Imperial Airways for £5,000. A tractor for towing aircraft at Baldonnel was ordered, and intending smoke-wreathed passengers were no longer charged bus fares. Then it was back to the Air Corps.

On 14 November 1938 there was a meeting in Dublin at which were present T. J. Flynn and Robert Logan, representing the airline, Major Mulcahy and two colleagues representing the Department of Defence, and T. J. O'Driscoll of Industry and Commerce. Mulcahy agreed that he could make Air Corps personnel available subject to the conditions offered by Aer Lingus being sufficiently attractive. A scheme of short-service, three year commissions was awaiting approval, but the trainees under that scheme would not be available until 1942. He suggested that in the meantime Aer Lingus should take an officer on probation for three months: up to the end of that period he could have the option of remaining on in civil employment and severing his connection with the Air Corps (except the reserve) or of returning without loss of seniority or army rights.

Logan responded the following month with a definite offer of a job for a co-pilot: 'Any pilot we employ, whether from military or civil life, must be an experienced pilot on multi-engined aeroplanes. He should have been flying for at least two years and should have done at least 600 hours solo flying, of which at least 100 hours should have been solo flying on aeroplanes having two or more engines. Preferably he should have an air navigator's certificate, 2nd class, and should know something about wireless...'

There were five applicants: J. Devoy, T. J. Hanley, M. Higgins, J. K. Johnston and A. C. Woods. On 2 January 1939 Lieutenant T. J. Hanley took up the appointment: the first of a long line of Air Corps pilots to enter the service of Irish civil aviation.

A joint meeting of the Boards of Aer Rianta and Aer Lingus, held to discuss a development plan covering the next five years, had concluded in November 1938 that there was no immediate prospect of commercial aviation in Ireland operating without subsidies, and felt that it should therefore indicate to the Government what in its opinion was reasonably practicable, with estimates of capital costs and annual subsidy; and that as it was for the government to provide the money, it should retain the right to the ultimate decision. The development plan was nothing if not ambitious. In Year 1 (April 1939 to March 1940) it envisaged extending the Dublin-London route to Paris or Amsterdam. Year 2 (1940-41) was to see a Cork-Paris route in pool with Air France (though there was as yet no functioning Cork airport). A Shannon-Oslo mail service was also to be opened, depending upon the serviceability of Rineanna, the planned transatlantic airport, which would also be linked with Birmingham, Amsterdam and Warsaw in pool with other carriers. Year 3 (1941–42) was earmarked for the inauguration of either Dublin–Paris or Dublin–Amsterdam — whichever had been relegated from Year 1. As for years 4 and 5: 'It is difficult to foresee developments so far ahead', the plan admitted, 'when there are so many incalculable variants.' The biggest incalculable variant was, of course, to be World War Two: and it is interesting, if unprofitable, to speculate as to the future of the airline had it succeeded in putting that ambitious route network into place. All other things being equal, it would have been unlikely that the resources could have been found to finance so dramatic an expansion. Introducing an Order for a supplementary sum of £37,000 for transport and meteorological services early in 1939 Lemass admitted that the experience of the companies to date had made it clear that there was no prospect of securing rapid development in commercial aviation without substantial Government support. Though the number of passengers flown had increased from 1,130 in 1936 to 4,987 in 1938 and aircraft miles from 151,600 to 385,533 in the same period, the services were being operated at a loss: £4,824 in 1936–37; £7,330 in 1937–38; and an estimated £14,235 in 1938-39. The percentage represented by the subsidy in relation to receipts (60.8 per cent) compared favourably, on the other hand, with that returned by other airlines: Air France 61.2 per cent; Czechoslovakian 66.97 per cent: Polish 70.73 per cent; only Lufthansa (40.63 per cent) and Sabena (34.43 per cent) were significantly better. It remains an untriguing speculation as to whether the proposed pool mail service with Norske Luftfartselskap would have effectively altered the course of subsequent developments in Irish aviation.

In December 1938 orders were placed for two new Lockheed 14 aircraft, each capable of carrying nine passengers. Frank Delaney, who joined the company in the following March as an aeronautical engineer, having served with both the Air Corps and the British Air Force, collected them off the boat in Southampton in England. The Lockheed was the first all-metal aircraft in the Aer Lingus fleet. Robert Logan was, however, still unhappy, and John Leydon, Chairman of Aer Rianta, applied to the Department of Defence for the full-time services of Commandant G. J. Carroll of the Air Corps as his successor; Logan was to be released from his contract at the end of the first year to return to Canada. Before that he was again seeking pilots from the Air Corps. 'As you are aware', Mulcahy, now promoted to Colonel, told him: 'this Corps is very short of pilots and it is only with great difficulty that we are carrying out our expansion programme. We can ill afford to lose the services of any pilot at the moment. However, bearing in mind the necessity for cooperation between military and civil aviation, we will continue to assist as far as we possibly can.'

In the event neither the Lockheeds nor the putative pilots were to be put to the use intended for them. The outbreak of what was described as war outside Ireland had an almost instantaneous effect on the fortunes and prospects of the airline. The General Manager told the Joint Boards on 3 October, a rate month after the commencement of hostilities, that the staff had been reduced to a minimum. The routes to Bristol and London and the Isle of Man and Liverpool had ceased to operate, and the Boards of both Aer Rianta and Aer Lingus agreed to place their resignations in the hands of the Minister for such action as he might consider necessary in the circumstances prevailing. But in October the route to Liverpool was reinstated on a once-daily basis, the British having decided it was in their interests to keep open an air link with their neutral neighbour. Seán O'Connell, the Publicity Assistant, whose position had been terminated, was reinstated on a month-to-month basis. By the middle of November the volume of traffic necessitated the duplication of services, which were being operated jointly with West Coast, on Mondays, Wednesdays and Fridays. The London, Midland and Scottish Railway agreed to stop their 08.30 ex Euston, London, at Mossley Hill, close to Speke Airport, to permit through travel from London to Dublin in one day.

In London, Muriel Hughes in the Olley office found herself having to record the names and addresses, and telephone numbers if any, of all passengers, and her unfamiliarity with Irish place names led her to the conviction that most of those offered could only be fictitious. Traffic continued to grow. During the five months from 23 October 1939 to 31 March 1940 a total of 2,893 travelled on the Dublin- Aer Lingus service, as compared with 760 on the Dublin-Bristol-London service in the previous twelve months. On 12 December 1939 the company received sanction from the Department of Finance to buy a Douglas DC3 aircraft to handle the new business. Flights were interrupted between 21 January and 12 February because Liverpool was unusable as a result of air attacks. Two days before the suspension, the first Aer Lingus passenger service had taken off from the new Dublin Airport at Collinstown.

As far back as June 1935 the Lord Mayor of Dublin, Alfie Byrne, had asked Seán Lemass to consider providing an airport for the city as an urgently needed relief scheme and to consider Collinstown for that purpose. The sense of urgency did not appear to communicate itself at that juncture to Lemass, who pointed out that under the Air Navigation Act of 1930 the provision of aerodromes was primarily a matter for the municipal authorities. Collinstown, an old British military air base, was in any case only one of the possible sites that were being generally discussed. Desmond McAteer's plan for Merrion Strand was both far-seeing and ambitious, involving extensive land reclamation, an 'aerodrome' over a mile square, housing and recreational areas and very easy access to the Great Southern Railway system at Booterstown. The whole project was costed at £1,500,000, a formidable sum at the time, but 'When considering a matter like the establishment of a National Airport.' wrote McAteer 'it could be well to get away from the idea of providing capital after the manner of a company formed to construct and operate a factory. The construction period of the work could be spread over five years, and in each of those years the Government and Corporation could contribute sums which would defray the whole of the expenditure. Apparently the only objection to this method is that the present generation would be doing something for posterity which had done nothing for it.'

Of the other possibilities, the Phoenix Park, though used for air displays, was not seriously considered for both legal and technical reasons, though the rumours were sufficient to prompt James Dillon in late 1936 to seek an assurance that no such idea was in the Government's mind. He was told that it was 'most unlikely'. In the 1930s the extensive suburb of Finglas was a small village with one hilly street, and Kildonan airport, two kilometres further out on the main road, was sited on private property owned by a family called Fitzpatrick. Katherine Butler, who gained her private licence there, recalled that 'a path by the side [of the house] led to a field with a hangar, some aircraft, a clubhouse, a petrol pump, a windsock — the Kildonan Aerodrome'. Captain Armstrong, later to become Aer Lingus Chief Pilot, had crash-landed at Kildonan in fog in 1933 whilst returning from Aintree with pictures of the Grand National, the first to be published in an Irish newspaper the morning after the race. In spite of the important role it was playing in private flying, it was not seriously considered as the site for Dublin's permanent airport. By the end of 1936 the Government had made its choice.

The proposed airport for Dublin. From 'Studies', March 1935

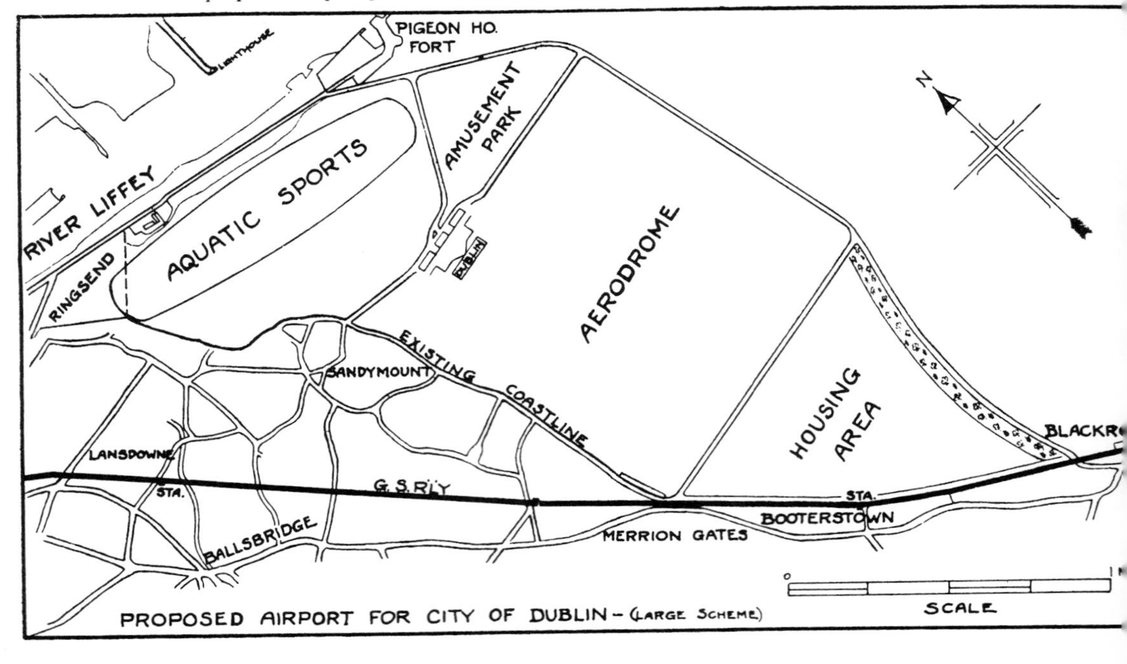

Collinstown under construction

AER LINGUS

Saving the hay, Dublin Airport

Collinstown, some nine kilometres north of the city centre, had been selected as a British airforce base in 1917 by Major Sholto Douglas of the Royal Flying Corps who was later to become, on the nomination of British European Airways, a member of the Board of Aer Lingus. The base had been the scene of an audacious arms raid during the war of independence. Following the Treaty and the British withdrawal, it fell into disuse and reverted to farmland — which character it retained until well into the Aer Lingus period. On 13 March 1941, for example, the General Manager was recommending to the Board that twenty-three acres of land at the airport should be cultivated for the purpose of growing oats, and these and other rural activities continued to make a contribution to airline revenue throughout the Emergency period.

The official announcement of the choice of Collinstown was made on 9 December 1936. It was planned to develop a total of 717 acres, some 258 of which were already owned by the State through the Office of Public Works. Development costs were estimated at £150,000, and after a certain amount of anxious political bargaining it was agreed that this was to be apportioned between the Government, Dublin Corporation and Dublin County Council, with the State paying half and the Corporation £58,000. Levelling and draining work provided much-needed employment, though there were bitter complaints, to be echoed by those engaged in a similar capacity at Rineanna, at the level of payment by the contractors: unskilled workers were earning 29 shillings (£1.45) per week, well below trade union rates. The first of the four grass runways was ready for use by late 1937 and was tested by the Air Corps. Meanwhile the terminal building, to the design of Desmond FitzGerald, brother of the future Taoiseach and sometime Aer Lingus employee, was in course of construction. This outstanding building, predictably categorised as a white elephant well before it opened, stood for some years as the only really satisfactory example of contemporary architecture in Ireland and, with its marked over-capacity in 1940s terms, as a testimony to the faith of those who foresaw a serious future for civil aviation.

The official opening, suitably muted in response to prevailing conditions, took place on Friday 19 January 1940 when one of the Lockheed 14s left on its regular flight to Liverpool from the new base. Packy Bourke, who had joined the airline from the Air Corps a month or so previously, was delegated to be at the airport at 06.00 to put heaters under the aircraft as insurance against a false start. The role of airport management had been assigned to Aer Rianta operating through its Aer Lingus subsidiary — a curious arrangement which was to prove a source of difficulty in later years. Board meetings were now normally held on a joint basis and in December 1941 both were reorganised with identical membership, John Leydon becoming overall Chairman.

After the modified euphoria of the airport opening, Aer Lingus had to face the fact that its fleet was far too large for the extent of its operations which, as far as anyone could judge, were likely to be restricted to the Liverpool route for the foreseeable future. On 30 January the DH89, EI-ABP, was sold to Australia for £2,800 and delivered to Speke airport. A further, though involuntary, reduction took place in March when the DH86, EI-ABK, made a forced landing at Malahide, some seven kilometres north-east of Dublin Airport as the crow flies. Paddy Tierney, who had joined the company in 1938, was one of those sent to try to recover the aircraft. 'Down on the island at Malahide it was like working in the desert,' he recalled: 'On a windy day the eyes were cut out of you with sand and on a wet day you were destroyed.' The nose had been badly damaged and Frank Delaney devised a tubular replacement which he covered with fabric. The DH86 was able to take off and return to Collinstown where a new nose had to be built since, under war conditions, replacements were no longer obtainable from the manufacturers. The overhauls at this time were carried out in a small temporary hangar which was later to become a cargo building. This modest overhaul facility initially employed about sixteen craftsmen: sprayers, fitters, sheetmetal and fabric workers, carpenters and painters. Working hours were long and unpredictable. Paddy Tierney would work all night, bicycle home to Walkinstown on the other side of the city for breakfast and bicycle back again.

EI-ABK remained out of service until October 1941. In April 1940 the two Lockheeds were sold to Guinea Airways for £52,500. The same month the *S. S. Westernland* docked in Antwerp from the United States with the disassembled components of the first Aer Lingus DC3. 'We collected the aeroplane off the boat and the wings off another boat,' said Frank Delaney, 'and brought it through Antwerp at half two in the morning when there was no traffic.' It was rebuilt at Deurne military airfield by Fokker, with whom an order for a second aircraft was placed, and then flown to Brussels where an Aer Lingus delegation consisting of the General Manager, Commandant G. J. Carroll, flight engineer Delaney, radio officer Synott and the pilot, Captain B. Blythe, were waiting to receive it with some anxiety, since the German advance into the Netherlands was drawing uncomfortably close. With little time to spare the DC3 took off, painted orange and displaying the Irish flag, for Dublin via Britain. 'There can't be any bigger than this,' Paddy Tierney said to himself as he watched its arrival.

The new aircraft, EI-ACA, entered service on the Liverpool route on 7 May. The question of employing 'stewardesses' was discussed, but it was decided to postpone any appointment for the present. In June, following a drop in traffic, the DC3 was replaced by the DH86 and a month later the second DC3, which had been ordered but not delivered, was sold to Pan American with the assistance of the Irish Consul-General in New York. EI-ACA was back on the route two days a week early in 1941, the balance of

IRISH

The first and the last. The delivery (above) of the first DC3. The group includes J. F. Dempsey (extreme left); John Leydon (holding hat, left); J. J. O'Leary (sixth from left); Seán T. O Ceallaigh (centre, with paper); Seán Lemass (on O Ceallaigh's left); Seán McEntee (tweed coat); Seán O hUadhaigh (plus-fours). Below: the last DC3, with names removed, sold to Royal Nepal Airlines in July 1964 with a farewell group

AER LI

the flights being operated by a West Coast DH86. On 19 April the DC3 was damaged on landing at Barton airport, Manchester, which had become the alternative destination when Liverpool was unserviceable, sliding and hitting a post. A recovery team, which included Delaney and Tierney, was sent over, and every morning when they went to work on the fuselage they found the grass round it burnt by incendiary bombs. The aircraft was taken apart and shipped back to Dublin on the *Lady Kilkenny* on 1 June. When it was reassembled not one nut or bolt was missing. There was a long delay, however, in acquiring spares to repair the crash damage and the aircraft did not return to service until August 1942.

In September 1942 a service between Dublin and Shannon was inaugurated with the DC86, leaving at 14.00 and arriving at 15.00 with the return flight at 15.15. The service operated three days a week, but the traffic, which it was intended would feed into the transatlantic operations out of Foynes, did not come up to expectations and the route was discontinued after the end of October. Though it was in a sense a special case, as operating between two established airports with a specific traffic in mind, Dublin-Shannon was seen in the context of a network of internal services anticipated in the 1936 Bill, which envisaged internal and external developments proceeding hand in hand. Under the legislation Aer Lingus had been granted sole operating rights in both areas, but internal developments had been inhibited both by lack of facilities and by the unlikelihood of such services ever breaking even. In the summer of 1942 revenue estimates and operational costings were prepared in respect of services between Dublin and Cork, Waterford, Shannon and Galway, and the General Manager visited Cork to look for a suitable site for an airport, finding nothing that satisfied him within thirty kilometres of the city. Draft timetables were, nevertheless, prepared the following year and submitted with estimates to Industry and Commerce. Under Emergency conditions and with the inability to obtain either new aircraft or spares for the existing fleet (De Havilland had informed the company in May 1942 that they could accept no further orders for airframe spares), it was unlikely that any developments could have been set in train, even had Government finance been available.

Operations on the Liverpool route continued, subject to the hazards of war. Jim Hughes joined Aer Lingus in 1942 after serving in the radio station at Foynes and following a brief spell in the traffic department (two contemporaries were Godfrey Quigley, the future actor, and Con Ryan, author of *A Bridge Too Far*); he was assigned as a radio officer. On the DH86 he sat among the passengers with a little curtain round his head, dependent on a code which had been supplied by the office of the British Representative, Sir John Maffey, in Dublin. 'Your clearance into Britain was without radio,' said Frank Delaney: 'You took the code in an envelope that was sealed and you opened it half way across the Channel. And from that code you were able to decipher the weather at Speke Airport. You had to circle a lighthouse at Anglesey. Sometimes the fella was in bed and he came out in his pyjamas, and sometimes if it was raining he came out with the umbrella. You were not allowed to go inland until he literally gave you the green light with an Aldis lamp.' There was always the danger of collision in cloud. The British tended to fly low where they could be easily identified whereas Aer Lingus would operate at around 5,000 feet. Once or twice they found themselves in the presence both of the Royal Air Force and the Luftwaffe: 'The DH86 was so slow it couldn't get out of its own way,' said Jim Hughes. There were fortunately no casualities as a result of belligerent action, though several 'incidents' remained unreported.

The aircraft were blacked-out and camouflaged and the passengers were either businessmen or others with good reasons for travelling: travel permits, issued by the British, were not easy to obtain. Amongst those permitted to fly regularly was a strong contingent of British cattle buyers who would come over to Dublin on a Tuesday, drink in the pubs near the cattle market all night, and return on the 10.00 flight on Wednesday. They would play poker all the way back, and the compulsive movements round the cabin of the little DH86 would frequently play havoc with the trim. Jim Hughes was at the time engaged in wooing his future wife with sausages and eggs from Findlater's in O'Connell Street and *A Winter's Tale* sherry. The suitcase he carried over came back filled with white loaves. The customs men at Liverpool didn't like it, but when he explained that he was simply doing it to help the British war effort, there was little they could say.

The administration of the airline was still based in what were described on the letterhead as 'temporary' premises in Dublin city, water and other facilities being still limited at the airport which closed every day after the last arrival at 17.30. There was no public transport and the staff went home on a bus with disembarking passengers. In 1943 there were 159 applications for the position of manageress of the new café — there had been no refreshment service up till then — which offered £3 a week. A lounge bar was opened by the Chairman later in the year and patrons could observe both the aircraft movements and those of the 460 sheep which grazed safely between arrivals and departures. There were some staff problems: in the same year the airport superintendent was found guilty of larceny of petrol and oil, precious commodities in Emergency Ireland, and falsification of records. Seamus Fitzgerald resigned his directorship on being elected to Dáil Éireann and J. J. O'Leary was appointed in his place. In March 1944 Seán Ó hUadhaigh, one of the men to whom the airline owed its existence, tendered his resignation from both Boards. He was, however, subsequently reappointed.

A significant and far-reaching development in the administrative area was the appointment, in January 1943, of J. F. Dempsey as Manager of both companies. He retained his position as Secretary as well as acting, by dispensation of the Boards, as Secretary of Irish Shipping, the State company which had been established by Seán Lemass to carry essential supplies into the country. A year later he took part, with John Leydon, in discussions in London on post-war aviation initiated by British Airways. Several European airlines were involved and an informal committee was set up. Dempsey pointed out to the Boards that the overnight allowance of 25 shillings (£1.25) was totally inadequate for London.

With the prospect of peace drawing closer, plans and conferences multiplied. In September 1944 Aer Lingus accepted an invitation to join the Conference of International Air Transport Operators which was being sponsored by North Eastern Airways of the United States. A more pressing invitation was, however, received from the Government of that country to attend an international civil aviation conference which had been convened for Chicago on 1 November 1944. The delegation was headed by the Irish Minister in Washington, Robert Brennan, and included John Leydon in his dual capacity of Secretary of the Department of Industry and Commerce and Chairman of the airline boards, and T. J. O'Driscoll, Principal Officer in the Aviation and Marine Division of Industry and Commerce. The Chicago conference established the Provisional International Commission on Air Organisation: the fifty-four signatories of the agreements represented only nations which had either fought on the Allied side during the war or had remained neutral. 'In one way or another every airline is an instrument of national policy,' said J. F. Dempsey in a lecture to the Institute of Transport in London in 1965: 'Even the private enterprise airlines are deply affected by the civil aviation policies of their respective governments.' In March 1945 the Department of Industry and Commerce had received through the British Trade Commissioner in Dublin a questionnaire on the development of post-war air traffic between Ireland and Britain and that autumn the Minister, Seán Lemass, went to London to discuss that matter with Lord Winster, the Minister of Civil Aviation.

Traffic on the sole Aer Lingus route, which had been showing a steady decline, ceased completely on Saturday 15 April 1944 at the 'request' of the British authorities: massive air and sea movements were in progress in preparation for the imminent invasion of mainland Europe. The British West Coast services were still permitted to operate but the loads were very small. Aer Lingus resumed services on 9 September and almost immediately met heavy demand: the DC3 had to be operated in addition to the DH86. Regulations requiring the blacking-out of windows were withdrawn and some of the habitual passengers, looking up from their poker games, were terrified by their first clear view from an aircraft at height. In March 1945 camouflage became a thing of the past and the following month, the last of the war in Europe, Aer Lingus traffic reached record proportions. The company's aircraft were now permitted to fly directly over Dublin city both arriving and departing from the airport, where work was in progress on laying concrete runways. An application had been made, through the United States' Minister in Dublin, for three war surplus DC3s. A new day was dawning.

4

The Place of the Birds 1936–48

IT is an appealing derivation: from *rinn,* a point or headland, and *éan,* a bird, and it appealed to, amongst others, T. J. O'Driscoll. It is a pity that it is wrong. The Four Masters offer the more accurate, if less avian origin: *Rinn eanaigh,* the point of the marsh. 'The Board of Works did a fantastic job,' said O'Driscoll: 'the place was open marshland.' The realist in him prevailed.

There was uncertainty also about Rineanna's anglicised spelling, the name appearing at first as Rhynana — more Welsh than Irish. The contractors who had the task of draining the marsh paid their workers 27 shillings (£1.35) a week, when the prevailing rate offered by Clare County Council was all of 35 shillings (£1.75). Conditions were so bad that the workers came out on strike on 21 February 1938. 'From a purely constructional aspect there is no element of urgency in having this strike settled,' said Seán Lemass. The original estimate for the airport works was £10,000, with another £6,000 for meteorological services. 'Aer Lingus, to survive, must have a western arm,' J. F. Dempsey was in the habit of saying. The ground was being prepared.

The question of transatlantic services had been under serious consideration since 1929 when Pan American had instigated an examination of possible routes. In 1932 a company called Transamerican Airlines planned a service from Denmark to North America via Ireland and Greenland. The following year Colonel Charles Lindbergh made a survey flight which brought him to Ireland on 23 October to investigate possible sites for a seaplane base. His itinerary included both Belvelly in Cork Harbour and Galway Bay. There were other interested parties: in 1935 Colonel F. C. Spelmerdine, director of British civil aviation at the Air Ministry, visited Dublin for exploratory discussions with the Secretaries of the Departments of External Affairs and Industry and Commerce, J. P. Walshe and John Leydon. From this and subsequent discussions there evolved the concept of an Irish base for transatlantic operations on a multinational level. Four countries — Britain, Canada, Ireland and Newfoundland (then an independent British dominion) met in Ottawa in November 1935 and agreed arrangements for survey flights and an experimental mail service. A Joint Operating Company was to be set up with a shareholding of 24.5 per cent in respect of Saorstát Éireann, 51 per cent for Britain and 21.5 per cent for Canada. Britain was to be in control of technical and operational matters and its nominated company, Imperial Airways, was to undertake the experimental flights. It was also agreed that Pan American were to be offered reciprocal landing rights. Ireland, for her part, was to provide all the necessary facilities both for flying-boats and land machines, to be constructed and owned by the State. What was described as 'a suitable proportion' of the joint operating company's aircraft would be registered in Saorstát Éireann, and the new airport was to be established and recognised as the first European port of call for westbound aircraft.

In view of post-war developments, when the large number of surplus land-planes available swung the balance between land-plane and flying-boat operations on the North Atlantic, it is of interest that Rineanna from the outset was conceived as a dual-role installation. The initial development, however, was concerned with the establishment of a seaplane base. The team of experts which investigated possible sites in 1935 under conditions of some secrecy included Juan Trippe of Pan American and Charles Lindbergh, who was to describe Ireland in the aviation context as 'one of the four corners of the world'. Locations examined included Cork, Loughs Carrib, Ree and Derg, Kenmare Bay, Tralee Bay, Valentia Island and the Shannon Estuary. On 16 December 1935 *The Irish Times* announced that Foynes had been selected as the base for the proposed transatlantic service, but there was no official confirmation until 19 October 1936 when Limerick Harbour Board met the Minister for Industry and Commerce in Dublin to discuss the establishment of 'The Kilconry International Airport' (a name which would appear to have enjoyed a very limited currency) at Rineanna. During the summer and autumn an engineering survey had been carried out on the mudflats in the vicinity of Beigh Castle by the Office of Public Works. Reactions to the decision were mixed. 'If the airliners have their European centre in Ireland,' observed *The Irish Times,* 'the aerial traffic from that place will not by any means be confined to the Transatlantic crossing.' 'I venture to predict', said James Dillon, 'that in five years' time if you suggested that an express airliner from the United States to a point east of Ireland from their point of view would come down on the Shannon to take petrol, the pilot would break his heart laughing.' Both predictions were in their own way correct.

Foynes, on the Shannon Estuary some fourteen kilometres downriver from the Rineanna site, was chosen as a temporary base largely because it offered excellent natural facilities, including shelter for aircraft moored in the lee of Foynes Island. The only serious rival was Lough Erne, which was in fact used by the British military for flying-boat operations during the 1939–45 war; though Blacksod Bay near Belmullet in County Mayo was designated as an alternative. At Foynes a pier and fuel depot were already in existence and to this were added a pontoon jetty, a fleet of launches for ferrying and patrol work, and an embryonic radio and meteorological service consisting of a high-power shortwave transmitter, a medium wave transmitter and medium and shortwave direction finders. The staff to operate these services found temporary accommodation in Foynes village. The meteorological service had to be built up from nothing. 'We were given a man by the British Met. Office', T. J. O'Driscoll recalled: 'Austin Nagle became more Irish than the Irish themselves'.

Work was started at the same time on the 700-acre site at Rineanna selected for the aerodrome, and by January 1937 about a hundred men were employed. An existing embankment protecting it from high tides on the estuary had to be strengthened and an elaborate system of drainage installed to remove surface water which was to be pumped into the river: the three pumping stations were completed in 1938. An initial plan, envisaged four runways intersecting at an angle of 45 degrees, each approximately 1,800 yards in length, the runway in the direction of the prevailing wind (NE-SW) to be 40 yards wide and the others 20. The permanent flying-boat base was to adjoin the aerodrome on the south-west corner of Knockbeagh Point and was planned to consist of a circular basin lying between the Point and Dernish Island and protected by a semicircular embankment. The work involved was considerable and, in fact, was never completed, the Dutch contractors returning home at the outbreak of war in 1939. When hostilities ceased, the need for a flying-boat base no longer existed. The full scheme was well thought out and designed to cater efficiently for the development of traffic as it was envisaged in the immediate pre-war years. Control and management of Rineanna was vested directly in the Government, though Lemass stated early in 1937 that it might prove advantageous for it to be operated by the new national company, Aer Rianta — a development that was to hang fire for thirty years.

The first transatlantic proving flights took place in July 1937, operated simultaneously by Pan American eastbound and Imperial Airways westbound on behalf of the Joint Transatlantic Services Operating Company. The aircraft employed were the Sikorsky S42B and the Shorts S23 respectively, neither of which had any revenue load capacity once fuelled and carrying a full crew. Pan American quickly placed orders for a larger aircraft, the Boeing 314, whereas Imperial Airways tackled the problem by experimenting with the Mayo Composite aircraft, a combination of a small, heavily-loaded seaplane mounted on top of a larger flying-boat and launched from it in mid-air. *Mercury*, as the top component was called, made the first revenue flight from Foynes to New York via Montreal on 20-21 July 1938 carrying mail and newspapers. Air France Transatlantique had also received Government permission to carry out proving flights from Marseilles to Rineanna to survey possible airfields for a land-plane service, which the

French foresaw — albeit somewhat prematurely — as the likely mode of transatlantic flight.

On 27 August 1937 a discussion had taken place between Seán Ó hUadhaigh and Major P. A. Mulcahy on the provision of pilots and ground engineers for the transatlantic operation. Ó hUadhaigh pointed out that under the terms of the agreement with Britain and Canada, Ireland was entitled to 24.5 per cent of the appointments. Mulcahy agreed that there were suitable personnel within the Air Corps but said they were not in a position to train pilots for the mandatory First Class Certificate of Navigation, which would necessitate the sending of selected officers on a twelve-month course elsewhere. A month later Mulcahy was complaining to the Chief of Staff about a speech made by Ó hUadhaigh on the transatlantic service at a luncheon at Dublin's Gresham hotel: 'He is reported', he wrote, 'as making a reference to "their school" and "the Armstrong Hallmark". One can infer from these remarks that it is his intention to start a flying training school and to put the Chief Pilot of Aer Lingus in charge. If the inference is correct, then Mr Ó hUadhaigh did not disclose his mind to us at the conference of the 28/8/37 and I feel that such action on his part does not tend towards cooperation between his company and ourselves.'

On 21 December 1938 Ó hUadhaigh was again at the Gresham hotel, this time in the company of his Aer Lingus colleagues Robert Logan and J. F. Dempsey and a formidable body of educationalists which included professors from the University Colleges of Dublin, Cork and Galway, Trinity College, Dublin, the Queen's University, Belfast and representatives from the Department of Education, Kevin Street, Dublin, and the Irish Nautical

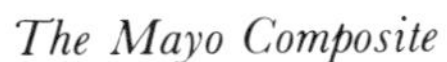
The Mayo Composite

College. The Company, he told them, was particularly anxious that suitable personnel would be available for posts which would be offering as soon as transatlantic air services were established.

Proving and experimental flights continued throughout 1938 and into 1939; by this time Imperial Airways had introduced their Shorts S30 Class (S23s modified for inflight refuelling and with Bristol Perseus engines), Pan American their Boeing 314, and American Export Airlines their Consolidated flying-boat (on a survey flight). 'If all goes according to plan,' the *Meccano Magazine* announced in its June 1939 issue, 'this month will see the beginning of the experimental air mail service across the Atlantic. The North Atlantic Division of Imperial Airways is under the management of Captain A. S. Wilcockson, who is also the commander of the *Maia,* the lower component of the Mayo Composite aircraft. The chief flying-boat commander of the division is Captain J. C. Kelly-Rogers...'

The *Caribou,* commanded by Kelly-Rogers, who was to become Deputy General Manager of Aer Lingus after the war, took off from Southampton on 5 August and was greeted on its arrival at Foynes by a large gathering which included the Taoiseach, Eamon de Valera. He accepted a flight in the *Maia* to watch the mid-air refuelling of the *Caribou* by a Harrow tanker aircraft, a technique which had recently been developed by Flight Refuelling of England, an organisation which maintained a base and equipment at Rineanna. The honour of completing the first transatlantic passenger service had, however, fallen to Pan American with the arrival at Foynes on 28 June of the Boeing 314 *Yankee Clipper* carrying eighteen passengers, a crew of eleven and sixty thousand letters. The sector from Botwood to Foynes, 1,993 statute

AER LINGUS

Forty years on: T. J. O'Driscoll (second from left) and J. C. Kelly-Rogers (second from right) celebrate the airline's anniversary in the Temporary Aviation Exhibition, at Dublin Airport, May 1976. Others in the picture are (left to right) Hostess Yvonne Colgan; Mícheál Ó Riain, Anne-Marie O'Neill.

miles, took thirteen hours thirty minutes at an average speed of 144 mph. The Clipper, with a wing span of 150 feet and a length of 106 feet was almost double the size of the Imperial Airways' flying-boat.

Richard Hayward, the Ulster author, recorded a conversation in a pub in Foynes in 1939, shortly after the introduction of the scheduled service:

'And then more people came into the bar, and I found that Foynes was fiercely divided between the merits of the British and American flying-ships.

"John Bull has only a bundle of scrap, that's all he has."

"America! Sure the most of the stuff they make you could buy in Woolworth's."

"I have no time for John Bull at all but, be God, he knows how to make a good machine."

"I'd sooner fly the bloody Atlantic on the end of the bed than trust my life to one of them British yokes."

The conversation dwindled, and then switched over to the question of the time taken on the flight from America, and I was impressed by the rapidity with which the human accommodates itself to new values. Two years ago these people would have been talking about a five-day trip between America and Ireland as a record; today if a flight occupies much more than twelve hours they look upon it as something very like a failure.

"John Bull, moryah! Sure the last time his bundle of scrap flew across didn't it take nearly fourteen hours. Dambut you could walk as fast."

And quickly came the answer, "And what about the American Clipper? Didn't she leave thirteen hours ago, as the man at the office told me, and won't be here for another three hours yet? Sure you could be there and back in the time if you were any good at all."

From the smoke and banter of the little pub we went down to the quay, where Captain Stapleton was waiting with the control launch, on which, by special permission of the department, we were privileged to travel. And then, just as we were talking about what we should do in the odd twenty minutes we had to wait, a deep-throated roar came from the heavens, and, like a beautiful silver bird high above the Cross of Foynes, we saw the American Clipper gracefully sweeping across the deep blue of a perfect summer sky.'

The summer skies clouded. The Emergency, otherwise the 1939–45 war, disrupted all the ambitious plans for civil aviation with Ireland as a distributor of transatlantic passengers to a wide range of destinations in Europe. Transatlantic flights continued, with interruptions as dictated by the exigencies of conflict. Imperial Airways, which had become British Overseas Airways Corporation, resumed via Foynes to Botwood, Montreal and New York on 3 August 1940 with the *Clare,* again commanded by J. C. Kelly-Rogers. When the Southampton–Foynes leg became too dangerous for flying-boats, feeder services using DH91s, Albatrosses, Ensigns and later Dakotas, were inaugurated by BOAC which flew them to secret British destinations. Pan American flying-boat services also continued, and on 5 May 1942 American Export Airlines were authorised by the Minister for Industry and Commerce to operate a transatlantic service with the proviso that no combatants should be carried and that space should be made available for priority passengers travelling in the national interest.

Arrivals were generally at dawn and departures at night. 'Although Foynes was remote from the war zone there was a risk of interception from German long range reconnaissance aircraft,' recalled Aidan Quigley, who joined the Air Corps in 1940: 'thus the protection of darkness was an added safety precaution. . . . One arrival at Foynes caused considerable concern to the control staff: the aeroplane did not alight near the flare path and was nowhere to be seen; and although the control officer was certain that it was safely down, the radio bearings indicated its position to be on land. The flying-boat had in fact been short of fuel, and with bad weather and limited visibility at Foynes the pilot decided not to waste time and alighted on the first suitable water surface that he saw in the area — a tiny creek off the Shannon. The captain taxied the huge machine across to a fisherman and explained his predicament; the man abandoned his own little craft and went aboard the flying boat to guide it home up-river to Foynes.'

The first land-plane to touch down at Rineanna, on 18 May 1939, had been an Air Corps Anson Mark I, and following the declaration of the Emergency the Corps established a permanent base at the airport, ousting from their accommodation Flight Refuelling Ltd who were found new accommodation by T. J. O'Driscoll, including space to pack and unpack their parachutes (they were charged 1s 9d — 8p approximately — for the use of the parachute room on each occasion). The first civilian flight into Shannon had been operated by the Belgian airline Sabena on 11 July 1939, but until the opening of the Aer Lingus Dublin–Shannon service in 1942 the land-plane traffic, apart from military movements, was largely confined to the shuttle service operated by BOAC. This company was also responsible for the handling of the transatlantic traffic, both on its own account and for the two other operating companies, Pan American and American Export. In 1943 they initiated discussions with the manager and secretary of Aer Lingus/Aer Rianta regarding the possibility of the State companies undertaking the work. J. F. Dempsey recommended to the joint Boards that as many as possible of the BOAC staff who had been recruited locally and who were unestablished should be re-employed, subject to suitability; and that two of the Dublin traffic staff, Messrs Bruton and Conway, should be transferred to Shannon to gain experience. The same Board meeting also discussed, somewhat optimistically, plans for post-war transatlantic services. It was agreed that the best interests of Aer Lingus would be served in preserving and implementing the Ottawa Agreement of 1935 which provided for Irish participation through the Joint Operating Company — which was never, in the event, to be formally constituted. The Boards felt that an independent service would not be practicable for many years to come, largely on account of the capital commitment involved in purchasing aircraft and the lack of suitably-trained personnel.

On 5 May 1943 an advertisement was placed in the newspapers seeking staff to handle traffic at Rineanna: the handling and catering services were taken over from BOAC on 7 June. Aer Lingus thereafter worked in close cooperation with Brendan O'Regan, the young organiser of the catering service which was to lead to the establishment of the world's first duty-free airport. In the short term, however, the move created serious problems for the airline. On 7 July an offer of £800 was made to T. J. Moran and Company, the firm responsible for constructing the runways, for a bungalow to house the traffic staff. A wireless set was to be purchased at a cost not exceeding £25 together with 'books of a semi-technical nature and aviation journals and magazines with a view to encouraging the staff in their studies.' The regime was to be spartan both spiritually and physically. A complainant in the Dáil alleged that the men were working for wages and bonus as low as £2.18s (£2.90) a week, from which a rental of 7s 6d (37.5p) was deducted for sleeping accommodation in an 'unsuitable wooden hut, in addition to which they had to provide their own bed linen'. Lemass's response was one which was to become the standard formula in the area of state-sponsored bodies: that this was a matter of the day-to-day running of the company and that he could not interfere.

In August 1943 there were only seven aircraft movements at Rineanna, and none at all in the period from mid-August to 22 October. Difficulties were experienced in recruiting a housekeeper for the bungalow and the wage offered had to be increased from 15 shillings (75p) to one pound per week. In October all the baggage porters were dismissed and traffic staff reduced to a minimum: the BOAC shuttle was being operated by flying-boats, following the crash of a Frobisher. No other land-planes were available. On 12 November all the Aer Lingus staff at Rineanna were withdrawn. They were back again the following February, the land-plane shuttle having resumed. A month later BOAC staff had to be brought back to take over the service following two dismissals: their stated role was to assist in training suitable Aer Lingus personnel. Traffic handling reverted to the State company on 1 August and movements began to increase with regular land-plane shuttles from Rineanna to Croydon, near London, and flying-boat services from Foynes to Poole on the English south coast.

As the war in Europe entered its final stages, plans were being considered for the future of transatlantic flying. At the international conference in

Chicago at the end of 1944 the Americans proposed four transatlantic routes, two of which would operate via Ireland. On 3 February 1945 a Bilateral Agreement was signed between Ireland and the United States in Washington which established the key role that Shannon was to play in the post-war development of the Atlantic. 'It is agreed in the Annex (to the agreement)', Lemass told the Dáil, 'that, in view of the long trans-oceanic flight and the still limited development of aeronautical science, all east-bound aircraft on the route specified in the Annex shall stop at the Shannon airport (the definite article was still current) as the first European port of call, and all west-bound aircraft on the same routes shall stop at the airport also.' 'We have a gold mine in Shannon if we go the right way about it,' said James Dillon, who went on to suggest a role for the airport as a freight centre and duty-free facility. He could see, however, no role for Irish services on the air routes of the world, apart from those to Britain, and even Lemass at this stage was not committing himself to an independent transatlantic operation. The rights of Irish companies to inaugurate such a service had, however, been fully safeguarded under the Bilateral Agreement which was in no sense exclusive. A permit had, in fact, been granted by the Government to BOAC, as successors to the now defunct joint operating company, to operate in and out of Ireland.

In April 1945 the Manager of Aer Lingus, J. F. Dempsey, attended an international aviation conference in Havana and reported that there had been informal discussions on shuttle services between Shannon — the name was now, sadly, displacing Rineanna on the world airline map — and the continent of Europe. BOAC and American Export Airlines announced that they were contemplating the use of land-planes on the transatlantic route. The other companies were not slow to follow. Thomas B. Wilson, Chairman of Transcontinental and Western Airways, now renamed Trans-World, visited Dublin on 12 September to conclude arrangements with Industry and Commerce and, following survey flights with Skymasters, regular passenger services began in October, closing one chapter at Shannon and opening another rich in promise. Lemass had no doubt as to the future importance of the airport to what he described as 'the blue ribbon route of air transport'. 'While our participation in the air transport operation over the Atlantic is contemplated at some stage, we have not at present the same degree of interest in advancing our rights as operators as we have in establishing our interests as air transport facility providers.' But events were to move faster than perhaps even the Tánaiste and Minister for Industry and Commerce was prepared to contemplate.

One of the decisions of the at-times acrimonious Chicago conference was to hold as soon as possible a number of regional conferences of the Provisional Civil Aviation Organisation which had emerged from those deliberations. During the Emergency Ireland had served as a base for the Transatlantic Air

Service Safety Organisation (TASSO), and working from this background, T. J. O'Driscoll was successful in securing the first North Atlantic area conference for Dublin. It was a diplomatic coup, in the opinion of Diarmuid Ó Riordáin, who was to become an Aer Lingus director in 1975 after serving as Secretary of the Department of Transport and Power: 'particularly as we were in the doghouse on account of our neutrality. At the end of that conference I got for the asking from the Department of Finance one hundred pounds to throw a party in Dublin Castle.' Delegates from thirteen nations were formally welcomed on 4 March 1946 by Seán Lemass in the temporarily converted Throne Room of the Castle, and there was general agreement that the event was an outstanding success, the rancour which characterised the Chicago meeting being notably absent. It was certainly successful from the Irish point of view, since from it emerged the recognition of Shannon as the air traffic control centre for the North Atlantic in the face of strong British pressure in favour of Prestwick. From it also emerged the conviction that the time was ripe for an Irish transatlantic service. Continental Europe, in the view of J. F. Dempsey, was not the immediate aim: after consolidating the position of Aer Lingus on the Irish Sea routes 'our thinking — certainly my thinking — was that we should look west where our kith and kin were'. His conclusion, after the Dublin conference, that 'we should give some thought to the Atlantic' was strongly supported by O'Driscoll and by John Leydon, who had an excellent working relationship with Lemass.

In April 1946 Paget McCormack, formerly of the Air Corps, was appointed Aer Lingus Chief Engineer. The day after he took up the post Captain W. J. Scott, who was then wearing three hats as chief pilot, airport manager and operations manager ('it was easy, because Aer Lingus ran the airport') was telephoned by J. F. Dempsey and invited to meet a Mr McInerney from Lockheed regarding the purchase of Constellations. It was the first Bill Scott had heard about the proposed transatlantic service. McInerney recommended that a technical man be sent out to the Lockheed plant in Burbank, California, as soon as possible. Paget McCormack was the only man with the necessary qualifications and though, in Scott's words, 'he had hardly got the office chair warm', he was despatched to supervise the delivery of the aircraft that Aerlínte Éireann, as the transatlantic company was to be called, had ordered for their planned service. Advertisements were placed in the newspapers for navigators and flight engineers. The delivery date of the new aircraft was estimated as April 1947.

On 2 July 1946 draft memorandum and articles of association were submitted to the Board of Aer Rianta for a new wholly-owned subsidiary to operate on the Atlantic. Aer Lingus, Aer Rianta and now Aerlínte: it was not only Dáil deputes who were confused as to the functions and relationship of the burgeoning State airline companies: the creation of Aerlínte as a separate company to operate on the Atlantic was, in fact, a response to opposition by BOAC to direct Aer Lingus involvement in the planned service. But though Aerlínte was to have its own board of directors, only two of them — D. Herlihy and J. P. Reihill — were not also on the board of Aer Lingus; and John Leydon was chairman of all three companies. Though many attempts were made to rationalise this situation in the years that followed and Aer Rianta eventually achieved autonomy as the airport authority, Aerlínte remained the company that officially operated on the Atlantic, though as far as the lay observer was concerned the distinction between it and Aer Lingus was to become imperceptible. On 11 November 1946 the Minister for Finance, Frank Aiken, told the Dáil that £174,000 of State capital had been invested in shares in the holding company, Aer Rianta, the previous March and that it was now proposed to provide a further £549,987. The five Constellations would cost $892,000 each and the cost of training forty-three people in the United States in connection with the new service would work out at some £45,000, of which £35,000 was to be paid in dollars — then in very restricted supply. For the Opposition, Liam Cosgrave had, ominously, considerable doubts as to the wisdom of embarking on a transatlantic service 'in order to maintain prestige'. In the meantime production difficulties had been encountered at Burbank, where Dermot Berry had become the company's plant representative, in the modification of the Constellations to Aerlínte requirements and the proposed opening date for the new service was put back to October 1947. This, as it transpired, was over-optimistic. Finally, on 20 September 1947, three aircraft reached Ireland. EI-ACS *St Patrick,* flown by Captain Stanley Williamson with Cyril Fortune as first officer, was the only one of the three to complete the journey to Dublin, where some twelve thousand people went out to Collinstown to witness the arrival. EI-ACR *St Brendan,* piloted by Captain T. Hanley, and EI-ADA *St Bridget,* flown by Captain R. Westlake, remained at Shannon.

EI-ADD *St Kevin* and EI-ADE *St Enda* were delivered shortly afterwards, and on 17 November, Constellations went into service on the Dublin-London route at a frequency of three return flights a week as a prelude to transatlantic operation. The general manager estimated that it would require a passenger utilisation of 60 per cent approximately to break even: they were achieving just 58 per cent. The cost was £125 per effective flying hour. On 28 November *St Enda* inaugurated the Dublin-Rome route. The flight was seen off by the Taoiseach, Eamon de Valera, with Seán Lemass among the passengers.

It was to be their last joint appearance in this particular context for some time. A new political party, Clann na Poblachta, had just won two bye-elections in Dublin County and South Tipperary, and de Valera decided to call a general election before it could capitalise on its success. In February 1948 Fianna Fáil was again returned as the largest single party, with 68 seats out of 147, but it had lost its overall majority. A new coalition government took office composed of Fine Gael, Labour, Clann na Poblachta, Clann na Talmhan and some independents. The new Minister for Finance was Patrick McGilligan, known for his acerbic style and his conservative economic views, and the new Minister for Industry and Commerce was Daniel Morrissey. On Saturday, 28 February it was reported that the Government had asked Aerlínte to postpone the inaugration of the transatlantic service, which had been scheduled for St Patrick's Day. Under the headline WESTWARD NO! *The Irish Times* leader-writer concluded that it had acted with prudence — the paper was pro-Government — in the difficult economic circumstances then obtaining.

J. F. Dempsey was addressing a group of aviation writers in New York when a man from the *New York Times* passed him a note which read: 'Dev out. Costello in. How now?'. He thought on his feet and replied that he was in business, not politics, and that even if Mr de Valera were not there on St Patrick's Day the *St Patrick* certainly would be. Back in Dublin the Secretaries of Departments, including of course the ambidextrous John Leydon, were called in to meet the new Government and its Ministers. Leydon, speaking as chairman of Aerlínte, courteously invited Mr McGilligan to participate in the first transatlantic flight.

'Mr Leydon,' replied McGilligan in his tight-lipped Ulster fashion: 'there won't be any first flight.'

Three Aerlinte Constellations at Shannon, 20 September 1947

CHAS E. BROWN

5

Hiberno-British Airways 1946–57

W. J. (BILL) SCOTT had just come from the war. He knew of the existence of Aer Lingus, but as a 'very, very tiny airline'. Its image, in the eyes of Aidan Quigley, who joined at about the same time from the Air Corps, was nil: an accurate enough reflection of the equipment, which stood at the cessation of hostilities at one DC3 and two DH86s, supplemented in May 1945 by the slightly eccentric purchase, for £4,000 including spares, of a Vickers-Supermarine Walrus amphibian and a Lockheed Hudson from the Air Corps, who no longer required them. In the following month the Board learned that they were sixty-seventh in the allocation list for United States' war surplus DC3s — there had been some inexplicable delay in registering the application. In June traffic on the single route to Liverpool broke all records, to be exceeded in July when in the week ending 28 July Aer Lingus carried 526 passengers and West Coast 117 on the combined service, involving two round trips with the DC3 per day and one with the DH86 for the Irish airline, and two with a DH86 for the British. The real pressure, however, was foreseen as likely to come from the US transatlantic airlines for feeder services out of Shannon and the assistance of TWA was requested to attempt to influence the American Government to release aircraft immediately. Captain Ray Wells, who was on loan from that company to Aer Lingus to assist with technical and traffic development, discovered at Hannau, Germany, an airfield strewn with C-47s (the cargo version of the DC3) and spares. He telephoned J. F. Dempsey: 'I can get you six of the best — nil hours on the clock, for around six thousand pounds apiece.' Washington agreed to the release of five which were converted to civilian use at Prestwick by Scottish Aviation. Of the first three aircraft delivered on 14 December 1945, one — EI-ACD — flew directly to Dublin in its unconverted form for use in pilot training, with the intention of its subsequently being cannibalised for spares. 'It was a beautifully-made aeroplane,' Frank Delaney remembered, 'because it was built at the Douglas works in Santa Monica and not at the Oklahoma City plant which turned out ten thousand — one every three hours.' Instead of scrapping it, Delaney and his team converted it for passenger use. 'Morrissey, who was Minister for Industry and Commerce, came out and saw the plane completed', said

Delaney, and asked, "why are we not in this business?" That was the start of doing things for ourselves.' The following February two new DC3s already carrying Aer Lingus registrations (EI-ACE and EI-ACF) arrived from California where they had been bought from Pacific Northern Airlines, and by July 1946 the fleet had expanded to ten DC3s, the two DH86s, the Walrus and the Hudson. Aer Lingus was a tiny airline no longer.

The route network had also been enlarged with the reinstatement, on 9 November 1945 of the Dublin-London service, operating between Collinstown and Croydon. Though work was proceeding with the laying of three concrete runways at Dublin, it was not complete by early February 1946 when torrential rain flooded the airport. The Liverpool services were operated from Baldonnel with the DH86s but, as the former Aer Lingus base was not suitable for regular DC3 operation, the service to London had to be suspended until 25 February when Collinstown was reopened. London flights had during this period been maintained by Ansons of the British Railway Air Services company on charter to West Coast, which had reopened the route with Aer Lingus.

The end of 1945 saw another radical increase in the company's resources, with which Bill Scott was closely involved. 'When I arrived in the airport the whole bottom concourse was absolutely full of girls. Ray Wells lined them all round the dining room. "I'll go round and pick the first twenty," he told me: "You go round and pick the next twenty. Eddie Newman can pick the next twenty and Harry Williams can see to the rest."' This was the second intake of some thirty hostesses following the initial appointment of Sheila Broderick, Angela Cogan and Maureen Fogarty, who took up duty on the London route

The passengers for the first Aer Lingus post-war flight from London at Croydon Airport
SUNDAY EMPIRE NEWS

on 26 December 1945. They had, in fact, been anticipated unofficially by Eva Toner of the publicity department, who had acted as a hostess on a Lockheed 14 flight to Liverpool at Christmas 1939, providing her own 'uniform' of a black ensemble to which she stitched a pair of pilots' wings. Stewards had been employed on the DC3 during the Emergency, but now in the atmosphere of post-war optimism and expansion, the number of applications for the job of hostess, following newspaper advertisements, was overwhelming: 'They had aristocrats' daughters, princesses, everybody applying,' said Nuala Doyle, one of the first ten: 'It was new.' Ray Wells made them walk straight to the door, 'looking for the wiggle, no doubt,' Scott commented. 'He asked us to raise our skirts above our knees,' said Nuala Doyle: 'and of course the Aer Lingus interviewers nearly fell off their chairs.' The pay was £3.10s (£3.50) to £5.00 per week according to qualifications.

In the autumn of 1945 when Seán Lemass went to London 'to explore the possibilities of initiating discussions in regard to air transport', the caution of the official statement made it clear that the Tánaiste had by no means gone with cap in hand. 'It was with reluctance', Patrick Lynch suggested, 'that he

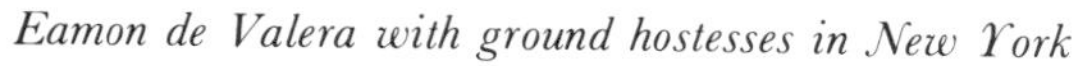

Eamon de Valera with ground hostesses in New York

AER LINGUS

EXIT
AER LINGUS
IRISH AIRLINES
TIMETABLE

The hostess uniform was to undergo many changes.

allowed British participation. And he was anxious to buy out the British interests as soon as feasible.' The visit was in the context of discussions that were proceeding in many places and at many levels on the whole future of peacetime civil air transport. Lemass believed that it was possible for Ireland to participate in the international sphere on a scale larger than the size of the population would indicate, and drew a comparison with pre-war Holland and KLM. There was no avoiding the fact, however, that as far as Aer Lingus was concerned the initial international development would take place on routes to Britain, and that for this the full co-operation of British European Airways would be essential. Lemass believed that any such co-operation should be negotiated to give the maximum advantage to Aer Lingus, whatever compromises had to be accepted in the process; it was in this vein that he revealed his thinking to the Dáil in the course of the debate on the Estimate for his Department in May 1946. The agreement which had been signed between Britain and Ireland the previous month would provide for the grant of reciprocal rights to Aer Rianta and BOAC in respect of transatlantic operations through Shannon. It also provided, he added almost as an afterthought, 'for the reconstitution of Aer Lingus as a joint company with the sole right to operate services between Ireland and Britain, together with rights to Shannon feeder services and fifth freedom rights in Britain' (the right to pick up passengers in that country for onward conveyance to other destinations). The shareholding was to be apportioned in the ratio of 60 per cent to Aer Lingus and 40 per cent to the British companies BEA and BOAC (30 per cent and 10 per cent respectively). All parties were to do their best to ensure that no one else should operate any scheduled services in competition.

The proposals were given the form of law under the Air Navigation and Transport Bill 1946. The nominal capital of Aer Lingus was to be increased from £100,000 to £1,000,000, 60 per cent held by Aer Rianta. The British were to nominate three directors out of seven. Aer Rianta's capital was at the same time to be increased from £1,000,000 to £2,000,000. Deputies confessed themselves still in some confusion as to the roles of Aer Rianta and Aer Lingus: 'Can the Minister', asked Liam Cosgrave, 'indicate the necessity, for the future, of maintaining both companies?' The Minister explained patiently that Aer Rianta was the senior company and was completely Irish-owned, with no private shareholders. Its role was to contribute capital to Aer Lingus, to manage Dublin Airport, and to operate transatlantic services (the creation of the third element in the confusing structure, Aerlínte, was not yet public knowledge). There was to be a new subsidy to Aer Lingus of £250,000 for five years.

The new Hiberno-British Aer Lingus was, in the view of Garret FitzGerald, who joined the company in 1949, a good idea: 'It meant that Aer Lingus got off the ground and was able to establish itself as a airline on a larger scale that would otherwise have been the case and reach a point where it could sustain the splitting of routes with the British.' It also gave the airline the valuable Fifth Freedom rights at a time when it would have been quite uneconomical to operate direct continental services. From the British point of view it left them free to concentrate on the routes which, in their eyes, were likely to prove most beneficial to them. They saw Aer Lingus essentially in terms of a 'domestic' feeder service with minimal extension further afield: a view which was in due course subjected to a somewhat painful revision.

At the beginning there was great admiration for Aer Lingus in the two British corporations, according to Oliver Hone, who himself joined from BOAC in 1947: 'firstly, surprise that the Irish could do it and, secondly, that they did it so well'. Old colonial attitudes die hard. There was undoubtedly an empathy. P. J. Brennan, who became Assistant Secretary of Aer Lingus and Aer Rianta in 1946, felt that the association with the British airlines was 'important on a much broader spectrum', particularly 'in relation to the association of the individuals concerned'.

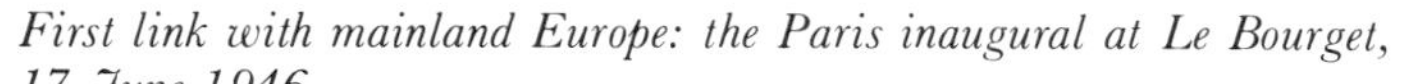

First link with mainland Europe: the Paris inaugural at Le Bourget, 17 June 1946

AER LINGUS

On 22 June 1946 there were present by invitation at a Board meeting in Dublin the three representatives of BEA and BOAC designated as the first British directors of Aer Lingus: Sir Harold Hartley, Conor Carrigan and J. W. S. Branker. On 1 July the London and Liverpool services were taken over completely by Aer Lingus — West Coast ceased flying and its other routes were taken over by BEA. On 17 June a new Aer Lingus route had been opened to Paris: Seán Lemass travelled on the inaugural flight, piloted by Captain W. J. Scott, head of Operations, and Captain Darby Kennedy, chief pilot. Kennedy had joined in 1939 and qualified as a senior pilot in 1943. Air France opened a reciprocal service in the following month. Dublin-Shannon had been reopened in May. It was on this route, on 18 June, that the company suffered its first serious accident involving passengers when the DC3 EI–ACA developed an engine fire on take-off and made a forced landing near Shannon Airport. Passengers and crew escaped with minor injuries but the damage to the aircraft was extensive. The airline was now, nevertheless, in process of acquiring what Seán Lemass described as 'a respectable fleet of suitable aeroplanes' and facing into a period of expansion and challenge. There were those, however, who remained unimpressed. 'Who is going to fly in all these airships?' asked a public representative from Wexford: It is only certain people with money, those who can pay £10, £15 or £25 to go to Paris or somewhere else.'

One of the complaints voiced against Aer Lingus was that there was not sufficient staff to handle the rapidly growing traffic and that the existing personnel was overworked and obliged to endure what would later be termed 'unsocial hours'. There were difficulties in booking seats. The rapid development of the airline had indeed imposed a severe strain on its infrastructure in spite of a substantial increase in its personnel and resources. When P. J. Brennan took up his appointment in the head office in O'Connell Street, his wife came in and did the typing for nothing for anybody who needed it: 'That was the spirit in those days.' They were starting from a very low base, said W. J. Scott, and climbing rapidly, which involved serious problems in handling the traffic increase. He was very impressed with J. F. Dempsey and John Leydon and with the degree of enthusiasm which was sustained for the first ten or fifteen years of his career with the airline. Garret FitzGerald had the same experience: 'When I was in Aer Lingus the enthusiasm of the staff and the dedication, especially at the managerial level, was very high. What gave us that enthusiasm was the fact that we were working for the country, not for private profit.'

This, from their point of view, was probably fortunate. Early in 1947 Lemass admitted that the company's operations were showing a bigger deficit than had been anticipated owing, he explained, to the non-delivery of the new aircraft (Vickers Vikings) for which crews had been employed and

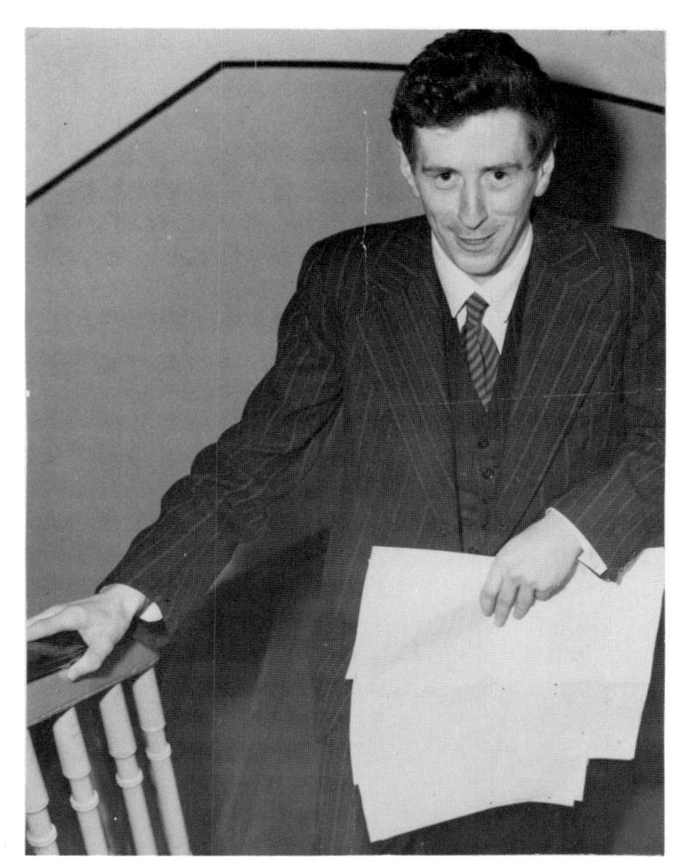

Garret FitzGerald in his Aer Lingus Dublin office in the early 1950s

AER LINGUS

trained. There were other major outgoings resulting from the airline's expansion. At the end of 1945 negotiations had been opened for the acquisition of premises in Cathal Brugha Street, Dublin, for a planned city terminal. In April 1946 Portland House, Limerick, was bought as a staff hostel for £4,550. In London, where Aer Lingus had been working out of the Irish Tourist Board offices in Lower Regent Street, a lease for twenty-one years was taken on premises at 221 Regent Street at £4,000 per annum plus rates. This was in June 1946. In the same month, in which a decision — later rescinded — was taken to buy Constellations for Aer Lingus as well as for Aerlínte, premises were acquired in Grafton Street and Upper Mount Street in Dublin. J. F. Dempsey was promoted to General Manager at £2,000 per annum. R. G. Pettite had come on loan from TWA as acting manager and it was now agreed that the permanent position should be offered to Max Stuart Shaw, who had been employed by BOAC at Shannon. He brought to the airline, in P. J. Brennan's words, 'a striving for perfection in serving the passenger'. In October 1946 the DH86A *Éire* had been sold, followed in November by the DH86B *Sasana*, breaking the last material link with the pre-war era. 'Easy to fly, easy to land — beautiful aircraft', was the opinion of a later Aer Lingus captain who had flown them elsewhere. 'It used to go everywhere at about 70 mph. If you flew through a very bad cloud the whole windscreen used to mist over. All you had was a wind-driven generator, so that when you were on the ground taxiing you couldn't go too far because your radio was starting to fail. You had to hustle along to get into the air to get the generator going.' To replace these veterans and to further modernise the fleet, it was decided in October 1946 to order seven long-nosed Vickers Vikings. Whilst delivery of these was awaited, BEA agreed to lease Aer Lingus an equal number of the short-nosed version — an offer that was not finally taken up.

With the active encouragement of Seán Lemass, more new routes were opened: to Amsterdam via Manchester in July 1947; to Brussels direct and to Glasgow via Belfast in July; Shannon-London in August; Dublin-Shannon-Paris and Dublin-Belfast-Liverpool in October; and Dublin-Rome, with the Aerlínte Constellations, in November. All this was, in Garret FitzGerald's view, grossly over-ambitious: 'The company launched into a massive expansion which there was no basis for in terms of traffic at that time. When I joined there were plans for services for which no research had been done whatever, on which it was quite evident they were going to lose large sums of money. In October we opened a route from Shannon to Paris which was supposed to connect with some transatlantic flight but never did. On 3 December I suggested that as no fare-paying passengers had travelled in either direction for two weeks it should be closed.' Quite apart from the non-materialisation of the transatlantic connection, it was quite impossible for ordinary Irish people to acquire the hard currency, in the economic conditions then obtaining, to travel to places like Rome, Brussels or Paris. Added to this was the fact that many of the services were inaugurated in the winter period when traffic in any event would have been at its least buoyant. One route which did not open, though it had been announced, was Dublin-Glasgow-Oslo-Stockholm. Norway and Sweden were, in 1985, still awaiting their direct air connection with Ireland.

From the point of view of the British members of the Aer Lingus Board these developments were not unwelcome, particularly since they involved the purchase of a new fleet of British-manufactured aircraft. The Viking was not the choice of the Irish Board members nor of the Aer Lingus technical experts, but the British applied extreme pressure. At one stage, Lemass said after the event, the argument reached a point when it seemed possible that the agreement of 1946 would be terminated, at which stage he held discussions with the Aer Lingus directors and indicated to them that he was not prepared to see it fall on the issue. So Aer Lingus got its Vikings — after a lengthy delay whilst they were grounded by the British Ministry of Civil Aviation to have certain defects in their construction remedied. They were a total disaster. The seat capacity was no greater than the DC3 and they had a fuel consumption of 98 gallons per hour as against 73 for the American aircraft. They were unstable in icing conditions. The first was delivered on 4 June 1947, registered EI–ADC and named *Ronan*; the last of the seven, EI–ADL *Feidhlim*, arrived in September. They survived barely a year in Aer Lingus service, and would have been gone even before that had there not been an acute shortage of potential buyers: 'everyone', said Captain R. N. (Dick) White, who had joined in 1946, 'was glad to see them go.' The decision to sell was actually taken in January 1948 when it was agreed that the fleet should be reduced to ten aircraft in addition to the Constellations hired from Aerlínte. In February an executive committee of the Board was set up with a view to securing the maximum economies: the estimated deficit for the year was £379,800.

The airline learnt a lesson from the imposition of the Vikings; but it was to have other unsuitable aircraft wished upon it, or to find its own preferences discounted, before securing freedom of choice — a freedom that was never to be absolute since the Government retained the power of final decision and on at least one occasion did not hesitate to employ it.

The political events of February 1948 had repercussions not only on the proposed transatlantic service. Aer Lingus came under severe scrutiny, and was firmly held to its own decision of the previous December to effect retrenchment and all-round economies. In the period from 1 January to 6

The first Vickers Viking, EI-ADF 'St Ronan'

AER LINGUS

June 1948, 259 Aer Lingus workers were laid off; and the routes which had been opened in a flood of optimism were closed one by one: Shannon-Paris in December 1947; Dublin-Rome in January 1948; Dublin-Belfast in March; Dublin-Brussels in June, together with the Dublin-London all-cargo service. The Constellations were taken out of service the same month and sold. At the end of 1947 fares had been increased by between 10 and 20 per cent. Shortly afterwards the free transport between the city and the airport in both Dublin and Limerick was withdrawn, the bus trip from Cathal Brugha Street now costing intending passengers one shilling (5p). New pay scales had been agreed for flight crew. A Senior Captain First Class now earned £1,400 per annum rising to a maximum of £1,500. The situation in which the airline found itself was a combination of miscalculations — a massive expansion which had no basis in terms of traffic, over-staffing, and the purchase of the completely uneconomic Vikings. The recovery from 1948 onwards was, in the circumstances, surprisingly rapid.

One of the advantages stemming from the agreement with the British was that Aer Lingus, having no partner on its routes, was completely free to develop its own promotional fare structure: 'one of the rare cases', commented Garret FitzGerald, 'where a monopoly led to cheaper fares'. He spent a week with KLM in November 1948 to learn from their experience and subsequently introduced the novel concept of Starflights and Dawnflights on the London route; they were less successful to Paris. Aer Lingus was the first airline, in 1949, to introduce reduced midweek fares, which were so well adjusted to the demand that they succeeded in raising the Tuesday and Thursday loads to the level of the Saturday peak. It was discovered that people were quite willing to change their contemplated day of travel provided they were offered a financial incentive. Major passenger surveys were undertaken in 1949 and again in 1954 which provided a solid basis for route planning. The sample employed — 15,000 — was large enough to ensure a high degree of accuracy, and all the routes until the late 1970s were opened in the order indicated by the results, with the exception of a service to Nice for which the French would not grant rights.

Air France's opening of a Paris-Dublin service in July 1946 had been followed by KLM (Amsterdam-Dublin via Manchester) in May 1947 and by Sabena (Brussels-Dublin) in June. Though the monopoly on Irish Sea routes was reserved to Aer Lingus, there were applications from British charter concerns to open services, the airline in all cases advising the Minister for Industry and Commerce against approval. One of these applications — from Cambrian to open a service to Cork — raised an old problem, that of internal services and the development of airports other than those established at Dublin and Shannon. It had been the view of Seán Lemass in 1945 that internal air routes would not be economically practicable, a view shared by

Aer Lingus: but the Cork lobby in particular was vocal and the Cambrian application lent it encouragement. In February 1949 Aer Lingus told the Department that it would not consider operating scheduled services to and from Cork with its present equipment and with existing facilities there, and that the Board considered it inadvisable to permit a service which would not preserve standards of operation and equipment similar to its own. The Cambrian proposal was ultimately refused by the Government on the grounds that the 1946 agreement 'did not contemplate that airlines other than Aer Lingus would operate scheduled services between the two countries'. Dissatisfaction, however, remained. Aer Lingus 'with its gorgeous title was doing its best to bypass Ireland as much as it could', claimed Con Lehane of Clann na Poblachta: he believed that 'the Minister should change the names of Aer Rianta and Aer Lingus to British Airways and let us know where we are'.

In spite of his disappointment over his airline project ('They have dropped my scheme but taken my name,' he told his family), R. F. O'Connor had still nurtured the hope of achieving an airport for Cork city. In February 1936 at a special meeting of Cork Corporation a notice of motion was tabled in the name of Eoin O'Mahony, BL (known then and thereafter as 'the Pope') proposing that a sum not exceeding £200 be expended for the making of a survey and providing a technical report on an airport for Cork. In August this report, commissioned from the British-based Air Commodore J. A. Chamier, recommended a site at Midleton at an estimated cost of £33,625. In October T. J. O'Driscoll, of Industry and Commerce, in a letter to O'Connor agreed that the Midleton site was the best that could be found within a reasonable radius of the city and saw no objection to the proposal to proceed with the provision of an aerodrome. 'The position regarding the water aerodrome is different,' the letter continued: 'From an examination of the maps and charts of Cork Harbour, this site does not conform to the minimum requirements for a first class water aerodrome.' The reference was to O'Connor's old proposal of Belvelly, but by this time there was, of course, another 'water aerodrome' under consideration elsewhere. In January 1937 O'Connor wrote to Hugo Flinn, TD: 'there will no doubt be a revival of interest in the Air Transport business when the Imperial Airways flying boat comes to Foynes shortly for experimental flights, and that should be the opportune moment to interest our Local Authorities in putting up money for the Cork Airport Project. Judging from press reports you are spending £150,000 at Collinstown for Dublin Airport and over £500,000 at Rynanna. It should be a small matter to raise £9,000 for Cork.' But O'Connor was privately far from optimistic. He wrote to E. J. MacLaughlin of the Office of Public Works in Dublin, the body responsible for the site development at Collinstown and Rineanna: 'At the moment our sub-committee is very pessimistic about the whole undertaking. We have no case to bring before our local authorities to show any return for an expenditure of £33,000 on building the Aerodrome, with the additional annual upkeep cost. There is no guarantee that if the Aerodrome is constructed the new National Transport Company will use it to its fullest advantage.' Understandably, he avoided using the name Aer Lingus.

Others were thinking on the same lines. Ó hUadhaigh, now Chairman of the national airline, wrote to Seamus Fitzgerald, the Cork-based director of Aer Rianta: 'There is no guarantee that there will be any traffic worth talking about at Cork for some time after the aerodrome has been established, and it is the establishment of the aerodrome and the offering of facilities that will bring the traffic.' Ó hUadhaigh was not totally unsympathetic: 'If Cork waits for its airport until the transatlantic services are in operation it may turn out that the marine operators will by then have found out that the share they retain of the total first-class traffic, in spite of air competition, is more than they at present apparently expect. In that case Cork's chance is lost, and lost permanently. Meantime public opinion will compel the aerodrome to be provided sooner or later. If it only serves local needs it must be much more of a burden on the public. . . .' He though that Aer Rianta would be prepared to undertake the management, or that a local representative appointed by Aer Lingus could undertake both jobs for some time to come. Ó hUadhaigh went to inspect the Midleton site at the end of 1937 and found that there was plenty of open space available, but that a good deal of levelling and cleaning required to be done.

Levelling and cleaning meant labour — and labour, from the standpoint of the Cork Local Authorities, was something they could not then afford on the scale required. The site was again considered in the early 1940s and a meteorological survey was carried out in 1946, but no further development was undertaken. Another site at Farmer's Cross, which had been used since July 1934 by the Cork Aero Club, was ruled out on the grounds that considerable improvements would need to be made, in particular the removal of part of an adjacent wood. This was done and in May 1948 the airstrip was opened under the ownership of the Cork Airways Company. It was to this minimal facility that Cambrian applied in the same year to open a service.

Other airlines were in this period equally unsuccessful in their intentions to serve Ireland. The Board agreed in June 1949, with reference to a proposal by Avio Linee to establish a route from Milan to Dublin via Paris, that no encouragement should be given to a company other than Air France to operate between Paris and Dublin. A similar reaction greeted the suggestion, a year later, that Linee Aeree Italiane should fly from Rome to Dublin, again via Paris: it was highly unlikely, of course, that the French would have assented to either proposal. In October 1950 the Minister for Industry and Commerce informed the Independent Air Transport Association of Britain that in his view Aer Lingus was providing adequate services between Ireland

and that country and that where additional services were justified the company would provide them in due course. One of the independents, Silver City, was proposing to start a car ferry from Liverpool, and Aer Lingus asked the Minister to 'protect the company's position' as they were considering the opening of a similar service on the route.

In these decisions the Irish and British Board members were broadly of one mind, since it was in the interests of both countries to maintain the Aer Lingus monopoly of traffic. There were changes in the British representation: Gerard D'Erlanger was appointed in the autumn of 1947 to be replaced at a special meeting on 8 April 1949 by Lord Douglas of Kirtleside. An adviser during the First World War on the choice of Collinstown as an airfield, he had become Air Vice Marshal Sir Sholto Douglas, with a distinguished war record, culminating in his appointment as Military Governor of Berlin in 1945. P. J. Brennan recalled him as a very colourful character, a very good chairman of BEA and with a real affection for Aer Lingus. At the same Board meeting the resignation was accepted of John Leydon who had been intimately involved with the fortunes of the airline, both as civil servant and Board member and Chairman, since its conception. He was succeeded as Chairman by E. T. McCarron.

The Hiberno-British concept was an unusual one in that it inevitably entailed the involvement of two sovereign governments, the interests of which were not always concurrent. In 1948 Aer Lingus addressed both of them on the financial implications of the fact that it held no mail contract from either; later in that year Lord Pakenham, the British Minister of Civil Aviation, asked that information on the airline's affairs should be furnished to him regularly as a matter of routine. The Board were unhappy with the request, agreeing that annual estimates, revised estimates and published annual accounts and traffic statistics should be supplied as long as 'the British Government have to provide monies for the British Corporations to enable them to meet their share of Aer Lingus losses', but that other information would be withheld. If there was unanimity, or at least a majority, on this course of action, the situation was very different when in 1952 the General Manager informed the Board that he had been unsuccessful in his attempt to acquire additional Fifth Freedom rights from the British Ministry of Civil Aviation in respect of a proposed service to Düsseldorf via a point in Britain. Lord Douglas explained the difficulty in which he found himself as Chairman of BEA, who felt that their traffic would be unfavourably affected by any extension of such rights to Aer Lingus. For this reason, he said, they would have no option but to oppose extensions of any Aer Lingus route which would involved a stop in Britain with Fifth Freedom rights. He added that in view of the consideration given to the claims of British independent operators, it might be advisable for Aer Lingus to agree to reasonable modifications to the

REX ROBERTS

Dublin Airport in the early 1950s

LENSMEN

bilateral and inter-company agreements as an alternative to negotiating new agreements which might prove less favourable. It was becoming clear that the 1946 agreement had largely outlived its usefulness. Negotiations aimed at its revision began in November 1953; and by then BEA were actively interested in securing a direct share of the growing traffic on the Irish Sea routes, particularly that between Dublin and London.

In May 1948 the company's premises in Argyll Street in London were relinquished. They were, recalled Niall Weldon who had joined in 1947, in a rather interesting location close to the London Palladium. Space was subsequently taken in Dorland Hall in Regent Street and it was there that Tommy Dunne went for the first of his series of interviews for the position of traffic clerk. He had been working in hospital administration and had been told by his wife that there was an advertisement in the paper by 'some Irish company'. He was interviewed successively by Weldon, Michael Dargan and Max Stuart Shaw — who completely overawed him — being summoned on each occasion by telegram. Having been given the job at £7.5s (£7.25) per week, he reported to Dorland Hall on Monday morning only to find nobody there. It was Easter Monday — a fact which had apparently escaped the notice of his new employers.

Aer Lingus were now operating into Northolt, a military aerodrome some eight kilometres north of the site of the future London Heathrow, then in course of development. The Aer Lingus station officer had the habit of meeting and greeting all the passengers off the incoming DC3; a similar atmosphere existed at Dorland Hall, where seat availability was chalked on a blackboard. It was impossible to book a return flight since all reservations were centralised in Dublin, but eventually Dunne and his colleagues secured an allocation of ten seats to offer to London passengers. It was a very cumbersome system, he remembered, and open to many forms of ingenious abuse. Also to human error; on warm summer days passenger record cards, flicked dextrously from desk to desk, used occasionally to take the wrong routing and depart through the window to be borne away on the roof of a number 9 bus.

The blackboard was in due course replaced by a steel equivalent with magnetic counters in different colours, then by a key and lamp unit — the first faint foreshadowing of electronics. When the offices moved from Dorland Hall to 174 Regent Street the staff telexed Dublin at 21.00: 'We are off the air,' and set out in a taxi with the three boxes which held the totality of the records. At 21.15 they were back on the air and ready for business. Later moves took them to Great Marlborough Street and thence, for a brief period, to Carnaby Street at the height of its fame. 'If you kept the windows closed you died of suffocation,' recalled Tommy Dunne: 'if you kept them open you were blasted by the Beatles!'

Aer Lingus in London had joined what was then a very limited Irish Representation. The High Commission became a full embassy following the passing of the 1949 External Relations Act and Bord Fáilte maintained a very small office, but as far as the Irish community at large was concerned, Aer Lingus was Ireland and a company representative was expected to be present at ethnic functions three or four nights a week. The non-Irish community knew little about the country and cared less: 'People had the impression of pigs in the kitchen and even up to the late 1950s,' said Dunne. There were times when he found it more than a job: 'The question of an hour's overtime never arose.' He became charter liaison officer for the Holy Year 1950, an event which marked the first really big Aer Lingus charter operation, for which extra aircraft were leased from the British independent airline, Hunting Clan.

In the same year the experimental Night Coach service, quickly renamed Starflights, was inaugurated. Explaining the thinking behind it, Garret FitzGerald wrote in the June 1950 issue of *Aerscéala*, the company magazine: 'In the first place, during much of the peak months of July, August and September the Company will be physically unable to carry, during daylight hours, all the passengers wishing to travel. . . . The second reason for the night services is the Company's anxiety to attract to air transport some of the millions who are willing and anxious to fly but cannot at the moment afford it.' The real innovation was that Aer Lingus were offering cheap *one-way* fares — £4.5s (£4.25) weekdays, £5 weekends — which compared favourably with surface transport: Dublin to London first class steamer, third class rail via Holyhead was £4.2s.10d. (£4.14 approximately). 'For the first time', wrote FitzGerald, 'we are really competing with surface transport at its own fare level. It will be interesting to see what happens.' It was.

Traffic across the Irish Sea continued to grow, and by 1957 services were operating from Dublin to ten British destinations: London (day, dawn and night flights); Birmingham; Cardiff; Bristol; Liverpool; Manchester (day and night flights): Glasgow; Edinburgh; the Isle of Man and Jersey. In the financial year 1956/57 they carried 411,966 revenue passengers.

On 31 August 1956 the Minister for External Affairs, Liam Cosgrave, and the British Ambassador to Ireland, Sir Alexander Clutterbuck, signed the Revision to the Bilateral Agreement of 1946. Under its terms Aer Rianta bought 285,000 or three-quarters of the BEA holding in Aer Lingus, giving it a total holding of 90 per cent, and it also undertook the liability to repay to BEA £473,160 in loan capital which the latter had contributed over a period of years. This, together with other loan capital advanced to Aer Lingus by Aer Rianta, amounted to £1,182,900 and was converted into share capital held by Aer Rianta. The British shareholding in Aer Lingus was reduced to 10 per cent and their representation on the Board to one director. British operators were given freedom to compete with Aer Lingus on the routes between

Dublin and Birmingham, Cardiff, Manchester, Liverpool and London and to operate a car ferry between Liverpool and Dublin. In return Aer Lingus secured Fifth Freedom rights through Manchester to several continental points. 'The intervention of other airlines on routes exclusively operated hitherto by Aer Lingus will probably mean that the volume of the company's traffic is unlikely to show significant increase this year,' wrote Patrick Lynch who had become Chairman of the Boards in July, 1954. 'Moreover, costs are rising and there is no immediate prospect of a compensating expansion of revenue.' BEA services were introduced on the London, Birmingham and Manchester routes in April 1957. In the same month Aer Lingus began flying to several new European destinations via Manchester, signalling, in Lynch's words, the second stage of its evolution.

The British withdrawal left one unwelcome legacy in the shape of another aircraft — the Bristol 170 Mark 1E freighter — which had also been more or less wished upon Aer Lingus against their better judgment. The first of the type, EI-AFQ *St Finbarr*, was delivered on 27 June 1952 with two more following in the same year. From the beginning they gave trouble with brakes, heating and de-icing and the decision was taken to dispose of them in 1954. A happier choice of machine had been made at the end of 1950 when a reservation was placed on four Vickers Viscounts, the first of which, V-707 EI-AFV *St Patrick*, was delivered in March 1954, followed closely by EI-AFW *St Brigid* and EI-AFX *St Brendan*. All three were to carry three names each before they were sold in 1960. The Viscount, aided by a powerful advertising campaign, caught the public imagination — Aer Lingus was the first non-British airline to operate them — and in 1985 there was still a pub on the airport road in north Dublin city named after them; though few patrons of the mid-1980s would have recognised the attribution. They offered new standards of comfort and service, the leading London designer, James Gardner, having been retained to work on the interiors. In January 1956

The arrival at Dublin of the first Viscount 707

LENSMEN

Before embarking on a round-Ireland Viscount demonstration flight: (from left) R. N. White; Owen MacAlinden; J. J. O'Leary; President Seán T. O Ceallaigh; Seán O hUadhaigh

The F27 Friendship

FOKKER

orders were placed for the large Viscount 800, capable of carrying up to sixty-five passengers, and for five Fokker F27 Friendships which were equipped with the same turboprop engine as the Viscount — the Rolls-Royce Dart. In this case the choice of aircraft was made by an independent special committee which evaluated all the feasible alternatives. Both the Viscount and the Friendship proved to be excellent choices. 'In the critical discussions about the future size and composition of the fleet the company has continued to receive the constructive support and encouragement of the Minister for Industry and Commerce and his department,' the 1956 annual report stated blandly. The implication was that the days of political considerations were a thing of the past — a conclusion that was to prove somewhat premature.

The Friendships were planned as a replacement for the long-serving DC3s, the total of which had been tragically reduced by the loss, on 10 January 1952 of EI-AFL, *St Kevin*, which crashed in Snowdonia, North Wales with the loss of all twenty passengers and three crew members. In November 1950 Aer Lingus had been awarded the Cumberbatch Trophy by the Guild of Air Pilots and Navigators for 'safety and reliability in operations'. This was the company's first fatal accident and one which deeply affected the whole nation. The aircraft came down in darkness and in bad weather in inaccessible mountain terrain. P. J. Brennan was assigned to the scene with Michael Dargan. 'I would have regarded myself as a rather squeamish person,' he said, 'and yet I found that because it was your job and your duty you could look at these pathetic human remains quite objectively.' The Jewish representatives amongst the religious of several faiths and denominations who attended were anxious to locate those of their persuasion for a separate burial service, but many of the coffins were buried empty. The company made an ex-gratia payment of one month's salary to staff dependants and avoided using the flight number, EI 165, for some considerable time. Commenting on the disaster, *The Irish Times* said: 'Tragically Aer Lingus had broken its fifteen-year old record of immunity from death.... Its history has been surprisingly free from blemish. Although for a service belonging to a small country it has flown a remarkable number of miles, it has flown them well, and has had every reason to congratulate itself on its immunity from accidents of any serious kind.... Yesterday evening's calamity is unlikely to impair, for any time, its reputation for trustworthiness....' In the following January another DC3, *St Kieran*, made a forced landing near Elmdon airport, Birmingham, but on this occasion there were, fortunately, no casualties. A public enquiry was held, as a result of which the licences of the captain and the first officer were endorsed so as to preclude them from acting as pilots in aircraft carrying passengers.

The early fifties, as Niall Weldon remembered them, were slow moving: 'We weren't doing an awful lot.' The heady expansionist days of the late forties were over and the airline was settling down to making a success of its services to Britain. In the first quarter of the previous year one passenger in six had crossed the Irish Sea on Aer Lingus services, which was believed at the time to be some kind of world record. The growth was, however, beginning to slow down. In January 1951 J. F. Dempsey warned that the company's half year profit of £115,000, earned during April to September 1950, had dwindled by almost half by December, and he was not optimistic that what remained would be sufficient to bridge the gap between revenue and expenditure in the last and most difficult three months of the financial year. Costs were rising under every head, he said, and the obvious move of increasing fares would not, in his opinion, increase gross revenue.

The long sought-for night mail service which had opened on 12 March 1951 between Dublin and Manchester made a valuable contribution to revenue in this difficult year, as well as markedly accelerating the movement of correspondence between the two countries. A profit of £92,000 was recorded on the 1951/52 operations, due in part to the bold expedient of introducing winter bargain fares. Max Stuart Shaw, the Commercial Manager, was not in favour of Garret FitzGerald's low fare policy: 'We used to have very vigorous arguments. Neil Gleeson had just joined and I brought him in. He was quite taken aback to find that price economics meant myself and Max Stuart Shaw banging the table at each other. . . . '

Results for the following year, 1952/53, were again disappointing: the number of revenue passengers increased by only 7.5 per cent and freight traffic on scheduled passenger and all-cargo services actually fell by almost 5 per cent. There was an equally serious drop in the load factor (the percentage of available seats actually occupied by passengers) from 74 to 69 per cent. A newly-fashionable concept, 'productivity', which, *Aerscéala* explained to its readers, is measured by dividing the traffic carried by the number of staff employed, also gave cause for comment: a staff increase of 11 per cent during the year was disproportionate to the increase in traffic. Another dark cloud on the horizon was discernible in the shape of a falling share of the total surface and air traffic across the Irish Sea.

It was not only in the airline that there was concern at the apparent reversal of fortunes. In January 1954 the Department of Industry and Commerce informed the General Manager that it was not prepared to take action for the provision in the Estimates for Public Services of the amount required to meet the Aer Rianta share of Aer Lingus losses in the year 1953/54: 'It is the Minister's policy to ensure that the operations of Aer Lingus should be carried on without loss, and he regards it as most undesirable that recourse should be had too readily to the facile expedient of covering losses by Exchequer subsidy. In the Minister's [Lemass] view the time has been reached when the Board of Aer Lingus should seriously consider measures to rectify the financial position, and he would be glad to have, at an early date, a statement from the Board setting out their views on the action taken and which might be taken to enable operations to be conducted without loss by increase in fares and freight charges, and/or by reduction in expenditure.' The deficit on the 1953/54 operations was £27,074 before charging the company's contribution of £34,218 to staff superannuation funds.

The chief problem facing the airline, as diagnosed by Patrick Lynch in his annual report, was the seasonal nature of the traffic, making it necessary to maintain an organisation and an aircraft fleet nearly twice as large as would be necessary to carry the same volume were it to be spread evenly throughout the year: 'It is a problem with no complete solution because Anglo-Irish traffic, with which Aer Lingus is mainly concerned, follows a fluctuating pattern which no transport company can hope to modify.' He saw a partial solution in the expansion to points on the European continent, and hoped for a profit in 1955/56. In this he was not disappointed. Passengers increased by 18 per cent to 398,141 and cargo and mail also showed substantive improvement. The year 1956/57 was even better: an operating surplus of £158,548 was achieved. Nor had the Government strictures of previous years fallen on deaf ears. Capital had until then been advanced to the airline by the Minister for Finance free of interest. The company now adopted a new method of financing its aircraft purchases; it sought and secured capital from the Ulster Bank (£1,500,000 for ten years at the current rate of 5.25 per cent) and from the Irish Life Assurance Company (£1 million at 5.50 per cent for thirty years with no repayments in the meantime, but with the option to repay after fifteen years subject to a fine). Both loans required a Government guarantee, and it was a condition of the Ulster Bank loan that all Aer Lingus business should be transferred to it from the Hibernian Bank. The latter had been given the opportunity to meet the company's requirements, Patrick Lynch told the Board but had been unable to do so.

Since 1950 Aer Lingus had not sought a Government subsidy in respect of operating losses (which application, it had now been made clear, would not be entertained) and was now planning also to relieve the Exchequer of the necessity to provide its capital requirements. 'Irish air transport', wrote the Chairman, 'must now set itself towards relieving the taxpayer of direct responsibility for its financial requirements on both revenue and capital account. It is fitting that this degree of maturity should have been reached in the year in which Aer Lingus celebrates its twenty-first birthday; and it is confidently expected that the progressive expansion of business will justify the steps which have been taken.'

Though there was considerable public rejoicing, the airline's own celebration of its coming-of-age was confined to staff, relatives and friends. To keep costs down there were no formal inaugural flights on the new routes to

Frankfurt, Düsseldorf and Rome — the company, the General Manager told the Board, would 'have difficulty in making ends meet in 1957/58'. 'I have asked myself why Aer Lingus should have selected their twenty-first anniversary as an occasion for celebration,' wrote Seán Lemass, again Minister for Industry and Commerce: 'There is, strictly speaking, no analogy between the twenty-first birthday of the individual, with all that it implies, and that of a company. Nevertheless, on reflection, it seems to me that the choice of occasion is peculiarly appropriate as it marks the emergence of the company as a strong, self-reliant, self-supporting body after those groping years which succeeded the long period of State fosterage. It is a characteristic of the occasion also that this anniversary year is the year in which the Company faces for the first time competitive working on its most important routes. For the Company, therefore, challenge accompanies the congratulations.'

The extent of that challenge was not being underestimated, but a potent new factor had been introduced. 'Aer Lingus', said the 1958 annual report, 'is already gaining from the passenger traffic generated by Aerlínte Éireann. . . . Aer Lingus has now been transformed from a company isolated from the main flow of American traffic within Europe to a company as well equipped as any to attract this type of traffic.' Westward look, the land is bright.

6

After the Wake
1948–60

EARLY in April 1948 the newspaper columnist Kees Van Hoek overheard a priest at Shannon Airport discussing the recent postponement of the transatlantic service. He was suggesting to his companion that the Constellations, already baptised in the names of Irish saints, should be renamed the Sorrowful Mysteries.

The mystery was not to remain much longer; though there must have been few in Aer Lingus or Aerlínte who would have had any doubt as to the outcome. A memorandum from the company restating the case for the service had been rejected by the Minister for Industry and Commerce, Dan Morrissey, who wanted a precise layout of the arguments, pro and con, on opposite pages. The Government was not unanimous — Seán MacBride, the outward-looking Minister for External Affairs, was not convinced by the simple economic argument — but it was that which prevailed and the announcement, when it came on 20 April, looked no further: 'in view of the present stringent financial conditions and the urgent necessity for more urgent social needs. . .' Most people, thought *The Irish Times,* would be bound to agree with the judgment whilst regretting its necessity. In this it was, of course, ignoring the views of the adherents of Fianna Fáil.

That it was a political decision pure and simple many had little doubt; and the accusations and counter-accusations continued for many months, both inside the Dáil and out of it. For Seán Lemass it was a particularly bitter blow: 'The abandonment of the US service was a very great shock to me,' he confessed in July 1947, pointing out that no Deputy on either side of the House had spoken against the proposal in 1946. 'Why should we develop the transatlantic air services?' he asked, and immediately answered his own question: 'because we have got here conditions which, if we utilise them, could make this country a key point in the conquest of the North Atlantic by civil aviation.' He urged a re-examination of the whole question. The Government held to its economic argument, announcing *en passant* that the new terminal building announced for Shannon under the previous administration would not now be proceeded with: the existing wooden structure, suggested Dan Morrissey, would continue to be usable for fifteen to twenty years. He spelt out the losses: £504,000 in respect of training and development for the planned Aerlínte service. His coalition colleague Con Lehane asked for an independent commission of investigation for the purpose of allaying any public unease that might arise with regard to the figures and with a view to ensuring that future aerial development would not be impeded. He was told that it would be borne in mind.

Whilst the politicians retired to prepared positions, the airline found itself in full retreat. J. F. Dempsey flew out to the United States to close down the newly-acquired offices in New York and Boston and sack the staff. 'Let go' had not yet acquired its cosmetic currency — the service of these people, in Morrissey's phrase, 'was found to be redundant'. 'It had a devastating effect on the airline as a whole,' said Dempsey: 'I went out there and conducted something that was rather like an Irish wake. I had no doubt that we would have been well able to take care of ourselves. It took us some time to convince the air travel people in the US that the Irish airline as a whole had not closed down.' What concerned Dempsey as much as anything was that many people in North America would continue to regard Ireland as a backwater. For him it was a great calamity, and a heartbreak.

More than two hundred people lost their jobs — people who had been attracted back from employment overseas by the challenge of a national trans-atlantic operation. One of those who survived was Captain J. C. Kelly-Rogers, who had been appointed Technical Manager of Aer Lingus in April 1947 and Assistant General Manager-Technical of Aer Lingus, Aerlínte and Aer Rianta in February 1948. There was still, fortunately, a worldwide demand for pilots, and many of the men recruited in this category found other jobs. Some, like Bill Briscoe, went to KLM: others went to Hyderabad to fly arms for the Nizam under the control of the legendary Sid Cotton. For others it was not so easy, and the airline had no inbuilt machinery for rendering assistance. A section was hastily set up in the personnel department, then under the control of Michael Dargan, who had joined in 1946, to attempt to place wherever possible those who had been made redundant. Jim Hughes was one of those who had transferred from Aer Lingus to Aerlínte and flew three proving flights as a radio operator. When the blow fell he considered himself lucky to be able to scramble back to a job in sales. A planned engine overhaul facility at Dublin Airport was also a victim of the retrenchment; though the official reason given was 'difficulties of securing materials'.

Very grave damage had been done to the commercial reputation of the country, Seán McEntee alleged at the time; and though the dust settled the debate was not stilled. Patrick Lynch felt that possibly 1948 was premature, and the fact that the service was postponed for a decade may have been an advantage rather than a liability. He had doubts, however, as to whether the Government of the day had not done the right deed for the wrong reason.

Lemass, in his belief, had been prepared to see losses incurred, but with a definite upper limit. Garret FitzGerald, interviewed in 1984, remained convinced that the undertaking would have had no hope of economic success. The decision, he believed, was absolutely untenable. As an Aer Lingus employee in 1948 one of the tasks he was given with a colleague was to examine figures showing a projected loss of up to two thirds of a million pounds and to attempt to adjust them downwards. He estimated that the Atlantic service would carry no more than eight and a half thousand passengers in its first year and lose a million pounds — a very large sum by 1948 standards. He felt that the decision to buy five Constellations instead of the two required to operate the service into the then foreseeable future was quite extraordinary; and that the decision, imposed on Aer Lingus by the Government, that it should lease three of them from Aerlínte and operate them on the London route, involved it in formidable additional costs. The closure of the Atlantic, he argued, was thus an enormous relief to Aer Lingus (as distinct from Aerlínte) in that it made possible a higher and more profitable Dublin-London frequency using smaller, though admittedly less attractive aircraft, and avoided the estimated loss of a million a year. That was the view of an economist and, of course, a Fine Gael politician. There were many in the airline at the time who profoundly disagreed with him, even if hindsight in time modified their stance. 'People found it impossible to understand', said Tom Kennedy, who joined Aer Lingus in New York in 1948: '— even those of us who were part of it. Even now [1985] you wonder at that particular decision — it was not a very far-seeing one. It affected every facet of the tourism industry — Shannon was more or less downgraded; the luxury hotels, Ashford Castle and the like, were thrown on the market. . . . We had quite a substantial amount of sales in the kitty and all of that had to be returned to the travel agencies. It was a pretty tough thing to do. . . . ' 'It wouldn't have been terribly different if 1948 had gone ahead', was the view, in 1985, of Dick White: but no admirer of Seán Lemass and the policy he promoted was convinced at the time that the cancellation was anything other than a major setback in the development of Irish civil aviation. This argument — and it remains a fascinating one — related more to what might have flowed from the early establishment of the transatlantic link rather than the link itself.

The argument runs that had Aer Lingus started flying to the United States' east coast in 1948 it would have been extremely well placed to extend even further afield, to the west coast and possibly onwards across the Pacific. Developments eastward from Ireland into Europe and the Middle East would then have laid the foundation of a world network. The comparisons most frequently cited were those of KLM and Sabena, both of which, from a base in a small European country, expanded their operations to all five continents. This projection, attractive as it may seem in retrospect, ignores some very fundamental issues. Firstly, Aer Lingus was unable to win any rights to serve the US west coast, either in 1948 or subsequently. It was the one route which Garret FitzGerald, otherwise very critical of the whole plan, later regretted: 'I would have thought that given the shift of population and the number of Irish there a west coast service would have been sustainable (sustainable, that is, in 1958 terms).' Without the west coast as a staging point to Australasia the KLM concept would have been stillborn. The real problem, in the view of David Kennedy, who became the airline's third Chief Executive in 1974, was that in any case Ireland lacked an empire with its associated worldwide trade. The Dutch had colonies in the Pacific and South America, the Belgians in Africa. And, as Dick White pointed out, Sabena had to pull back from world status following the loss of its overseas spheres of influence. Though Ireland had colonies in all but name in Australasia, Argentine and elsewhere, the enabling trade links were lacking that would have assured any kind of viable traffic.

Had it been tried, could it have worked? Financial resources apart, the will and the vision would probably have been found wanting. Ireland in 1948 was still a very small, isolated, inward-looking entity, in bad odour with many powerful associates on account of her wartime neutrality. 'I could never see us in the sense of having any ambition to girdle the globe,' said J. F. Dempsey: I hoped that we could build an airline that would stand up with the best but not in the sense of girdling the globe.' Even Lemass, in public, never projected his vision that far. Nevertheless it remained, for some time, an intriguing speculation.

'The whole thing was chopped. It was very, very sad. Although the way it was being run couldn't have made much sense — having a separate chief engineer and a separate chief pilot'. Bill Scott's criticism focused on one of the many curious consequences of the setting up of Aerlínte as a separate and distinct airline, not only in name but to some extent in fact. Perhaps more curiously still, the Government which had abolished its only reason for existence saw fit to preserve it, if only in a state of suspended animation. The expenditure it had incurred was to be treated as an 'operating' loss to be met from subsidy rather than capital, Morrissey announced, but in fact the final accounts showed, somewhat ironically, a surplus of £55,861. The five Constellations were sold in May 1948 to BOAC for £315,000 each — a clear profit — with spares and equipment at valuation. The premises acquired in New York were sold to the Department of External Affairs, the subsidy from Aer Rianta (£401,444) and capital (£1,425,005) repaid. The end of the beginning.

There matters rested. The transatlantic service had not been the only enterprise to fall victim to the economic axe wielded by the new Government: the Busáras in Store Street, Dublin, designed as a new CIE headquarters, became in its higher reaches the Department of Social Welfare, and Radio

Éireann lost its projected short-wave overseas service. More positively this period saw the establishment of the Industrial Development Authority, the signing of the Anglo-Irish trade agreement, and the beginnings of State economic planning which anticipated Dr T. K. Whitaker's White Paper on economic development of May 1958. Such planning did not include a transatlantic air service. 'If there is no case for state enterprise and State subsidy in the development of transatlantic air services then there is no case for State enterprise or State subsidy for air services anywhere,' Seán Lemass complained during the second reading of the Air Navigation and Transport Bill of 1949, which continued the subsidy to Aer Lingus for a further five year period. He entered a strong plea for the North Atlantic link on ethnic grounds.

In the meantime other airlines were reaping the benefits of the expanding traffic between Europe and North America. On 28 May 1949 a double-decked Pan American Clipper, registered NC1031V, touched down at what had by then become one of the busiest airports in the world, operating a round the clock service. It was the first of a new generation of aircraft and the future of Shannon looked bright. In September of the same year that future appeared to have been placed in jeopardy with the arrival of a party of United States officials who announced that it was their intention to operate through Dublin rather than Rineanna. Their subsequent discussions with Government representatives marked the first serious move in what was to prove a continuing campaign. Trans World Airlines were particularly anxious to secure Dublin as a transit point as they had their eye on the forthcoming Holy Year, 1950, in the context of their New York–Rome service. No one else was then operating on the Dublin–Rome route. The Chairman of Aer Rianta, in a letter to the Minister for Industry and Commerce, expressed the view that if transatlantic operators were allowed into Dublin they should not be granted Fifth Freedom rights to pick up passengers for points in Europe. If there were any question of granting rights of any kind he and his colleagues were anxious to be informed at the earliest possible moment so that they could consult the British Corporations in the light of the inter-company agreements and of the possible effects on Aer Lingus business. The Government, with an estimated three million pound investment in Shannon, stood firm, basing its case on the 1945 Bilateral Agreement with the United States which provided that all transatlantic aircraft utilising Irish air space must land at Shannon, which had been designated as Ireland's sole transatlantic airport. For the moment a tactical, if not a strategic advantage, had been secured.

With KLM, Sabena, Air France and BOAC joining the United States carriers at Shannon, the pressure on the airport itself under its manager Colonel P. Maher and on the Sales and Catering service under Brendan O'Regan, was intense. 'From dawn until sunset and into the hours of darkness passes an unending stream of people of high and humble status through Shannon Airport,' wrote Frank J. Roberts in *Shannon Airport Review:* 'landfall for the air traveller from the new world, springboard for those poised to leave the old. Now rated internationally as one of the major airports of the world, a variety of facilities, technical and otherwise, serve to maintain that reputation, but to the average traveller, none more than the service of its gigantic, smoothly-running catering organisation, of whose restaurant celebrities now speak as they would of dining at Claridge's, Sheppard's or the Waldorf Astoria. . . ' but with the difference that Shannon's excellent cuisine was available at any hour of the day or night. It was an experience to be eating dinner at 02.00 (the restaurant was open to the non-travelling public) a few metres from where the lumbering Stratocruisers were taxiing in and out, passengers peering sleepily through the portholes from their berths on the upper deck. The high romantic tone of Roberts' description was not inappropriate. This was the apogée of Shannon as an international gateway, and the procession of the rich and famous, the infamous and influential people passing through it day by day and night by night reads like a list of the incumbents of some privileged Valhalla. Arthur Quinlan, a long-serving Shannon correspondent, listed in 1954 some of those he had met: Tallulah Bankhead, Toscanini, Jeanette McDonald, Maureen O'Hara, Marlene Dietrich, Douglas Fairbanks Jnr., Danny Kaye, Cary Grant, eleven Princes of the Church including Cardinal Mindszenty, Marshal Smuts, General George Marshall, Dean Acheson, John Foster Dulles, Anthony Eden, ex-King Michael of Rumania, and Andrei Gromyko ('the only way I could break conversational ground was to sympathise with him on the death of Stalin who had died earlier that day. . . . The 45-year old snub-nosed Russian is not as friendly as his colleague Andrei Vyshinski. The latter once surprised me with his knowledge of Irish literature and quoted long extracts from Synge.') There were also the somewhat less rich and famous: the pathetic groups of 'displaced persons' as they were euphemistically described, moving uncertainly from a disastrous past to an unpredictable future.

Brendan O'Regan's achievement in establishing and subsequently expanding the Sales and Catering service from what was little more than a sandwich-stall at Foynes into the world's first duty-free airport has been widely and justly acknowledged, but it demands a full-scale study in itself. Though Aer Lingus took no direct part in the provision of these services and had been precluded from operating through the airport, its presence on the ground was by no means insignificant. In addition to flying the Dublin–Shannon route, it acted at this period as agent or general agent for all the international carriers, handling their aircraft, passengers, equipment and cargo. The operation was based on a four-shift cycle, each shift controlled by a traffic officer and a team of men and women who dealt with all the immediate handling problems. Other work, such as records and correspondence, was handled by a special day duty section. The key sub-section of each shift was the traffic watch. A description of the Aer Lingus duty room at this time offers an insight into airport control in the pre-computer era:

'Traffic Watch advises the Passenger Service Section of the Estimated Time of Arrival of a flight, also of transit stop time and the number of passengers, in transit and destined. The girls prepare arrival announcements, Transit Boarding Cards and Disembarkation Cards immediately. The embarking passengers are "checked-in", tickets sold to them and their immigration papers checked. This collated information is passed to the Cargo Section, who check out the bags and place them on a trolley for loading. If open weight space is available, transhipped mail and freight are checked out, manifested and the indicated weight passed to Ships' Papers. Ships' Papers complete all manifests and "run-off" sufficient copies for the next port of call and for local requirements. When the flight arrives, Ships' Papers check the Health Form and collect the Log. The girls lead the passengers to the terminal building and give them transit cards.

Cargo Section moves in the trolleys to load. Ships' Papers check inwards files and prepare Load and Trim sheets. If adjustments are to be made, a revised figure is passed to Cargo. This may necessitate an off-load of freight or an on-load of further freight. In the meantime, the Traffic Officer is keeping a close eye on equipment and loaders. Steps and chocks were positioned in time and now he is satisfied that there are sufficient men to load and clean the aircraft. But now another aircraft has arrived and another is, perhaps, just landing. The Traffic Officer is keeping a watching brief on all his subsections. Forty minutes after flight arrival Cargo report "Finished". The Traffic Officer makes a final check. Ships' Papers give the "all clear" and the flight is called. Passengers are conducted out through the exit door by the "girls in green". The log is put aboard. The steward checks his load. Then the "all-clear" is given — the signals "Steps Away", "Engines Running", "Chocks Away" — and another flight moves down the strip to the runway.'

In 1951, two years after it had formally declared a Republic, the coalition Government collapsed in the wake of the débacle occasioned by Dr Noel Browne's Mother and Child scheme. The election of May 1951 returned Fianna Fáil, ruling as a minority government with the support of independents, and Seán Lemass stepped back into his familiar role as Minister for Industry and Commerce with responsibility for civil aviation. By the following year negotiations were under way with Seaboard and Western, a United States cargo line which had been flying into Shannon since 1947, on the possibility of opening an Aerlínte service with chartered aircraft. Lemass, perhaps a little disingenuously, explained to the Dáil that this would not, in fact, cost the taxpayer anything: the profit from the 1947-48 attempt, which he now quoted as amounting to £457,005, would be enough to cover start-up costs and possible losses. The Opposition were, not surprisingly, unconvinced. They queried Lemass's arithmetic and Liam Cosgrave felt that the proposal was a bad one in the economic circumstances then obtaining. Seán McBride was in favour of providing the service if it could be made to pay: he was against a Government subsidy. He added that after the cancellation of the original proposals he himself had had discussions with regard to a joint service between an Irish company and an American company operating a world service. He believed that this new attempt would be too limited, and that if it failed it would be very difficult to come back with another new proposal. Gerard Sweetman, Fine Gael, feared that other airlines would seek to cut out the Shannon stop in consequence, whilst Jim Larkin, for Labour, could not see much prestige in 'putting a fur coat on a skeleton'.

All in all the Dáil was not impressed, either with the economic prospects or the nature of the service to be introduced. Ireland-US traffic for 1952, at 10,600, was nearly 100 per cent up on the previous year, and the new national festival, An Tóstal, which was planned for Easter Sunday 1953, was expected to provide further stimulus. But Cosgrave did not think that sentiment would attract passengers, and the fact that the service was to be operated initially with unpresssurised Skymasters — DC4s — pending the introduction of Constellations produced misgivings. 'A shabby entry into transatlantic air competition', said Deputy Collins: 'We are linking up with a charter company that has been doing tramp service across the country in freight', complained General Mulcahy: 'We are asked to gamble this £400,000 for the sake of a few hostesses, the green uniforms and the lick of paint on the machine.'

The agreement was planned to run until the end of 1956 — or earlier if there was a delay in the substitution of Constellations — and would provide three round trips per week in the high season on the routing Shannon-Gander-Boston-New York. The true genesis of the agreement, according to James Dillon, was a desperate and necessary step to prevent the operating licence granted in 1948 lapsing without prospect of renewal. And there were others closer to the scene of operations who were by no means happy with the projected service. At a special Aer Lingus Board meeting held to discuss it in December 1952, Lord Douglas said that in his view the British members (still owning 40 per cent of the airline) had been kept in the dark. It was true, he said, that Aer Lingus was nominally a separate company from Aerlínte, but it now appeared that the proposals circulated by the General Manager involved Aer Lingus to a considerable extent. He objected both to the Aer Lingus senior executives 'double-jobbing' and to a management fee for their labours for Aerlínte which would not, in the eyes of the British shareholders, compensate for the loss of their services to Aer Lingus. His objections, of course, went much deeper: the Aerlínte operation would represent serious competition for BOAC on its Shannon–United States segment. The big guns were brought into play. In the following March, Lord Douglas told the Board that BEA had authorised him to state categorically that they were in disagreement with the arrangements and requested their cancellation; and that the British Government was considering whether they should give the statutory twelve months' notice of the termination of the Bilateral Agreement.

This drastic response was not in the event to prove necessary. The United States' Civil Aeronautics Board took its time in considering the proposal and then placed an inhibiting limit on any agreement with Seaboard and Western. 'We sat around with the Norden brothers who were then in charge of Seaboard and Western', said J. F. Dempsey: 'and we worked out estimates based on some previous experience and set a timetable much in line with the 1948 edition, which provided for Aerlínte on the Atlantic between New York and/or Boston and Shannon; and then turning over to an Aer Lingus flight number and flying on to Dublin. Rather late in the day, I should say, the Civil Aeronautics Board said they would only permit the leasing operation to operate over a two year period and by that time we would have to have our own aeroplanes.' In the view both of the Government and Aer Lingus this would not have offered a realistic prospect of commercial success, and the project was once more abandoned. It is probable that the CAB's action was directed not so much against the Irish company as Seaboard and Western: they did not wish to see an unscheduled operator gaining a foothold in the prosperous North Atlantic market. In the first nine months of 1953, 5,339 aircraft carrying over 200,882 passengers landed at Shannon as compared with 4,933 movements involving 158,332 passengers in the whole of 1951. The airport, catering for nine scheduled airlines and a number of non-scheduled carriers, was now handling half of all the traffic offering between Europe and North America.

One evening in June 1954 Patrick Lynch, who had left the civil service in 1952 to become a lecturer in economics at University College Dublin, took a telephone call from John Leydon, Secretary of the Department of Industry and Commerce and former Chairman of the air companies. The new Minister, William Norton, had asked for a list of names for the position of Chairman of Aer Lingus which was now vacant following the death of E. T. McCarron and Leydon wanted to put Lynch's name forward. Patrick Lynch was surprised: he could think of no reason why he should have been considered and did not feel that he could make the decision in two hours, which was all the time allowed him. He succeeded, however, in securing the approval of his academic superior, George O'Brien, and that of the head of the College, Michael Tierney, who felt that the invitation represented a compliment to the institution. The General Manager of Aer Lingus, J. F. Dempsey, first learnt of the appointment when he heard it announced on the Radio Éireann news. 'It was not', said Lynch, 'a model piece of public administration.' The Fianna Fáil government had been replaced by another Fine Gael/Labour coalition in May 1954. The economic outlook was still depressing and attempts to improve matters under John A. Costello's second administration by cutting expenditure, imposing import levies and increasing taxation did little to lighten the general gloom. Writing on 'The Irish Economic Prospect' in 1955 Patrick Lynch referred to 'the cynic's complaint that Irish economic conditions alternate between being hopeless but not serious and being serious but not hopeless.' This did not inhibit him from putting to the Board of Aer Lingus the suggestion that perhaps the time had come to think again about the transatlantic service. He placed the results of the ensuing corporate thinking before William Norton. 'His objectivity was admirable: he said that in principle he had no objection, provided that it had prospects of becoming profitable. He accepted that in the short run there would inevitably be losses. He had no doctrinaire view.'

Negotiations were set in train with TWA but came to nothing, and another change of government in 1957 saw Lemass once more responsible for aviation. He quickly made it clear that his ideas had undergone no fundamental change whilst in opposition: 'I know that there still persists in the minds of many people in this country the idea that air transport is still something of a novelty or a luxury. I want to make it clear that the Government regard it as nothing of the sort . . . no intelligent plan of national development can fail to make provision for the growth of air transport.' In February 1958 he announced that operating agreements were being sought with Seaboard and Western based on the 1952 agreements updated.

One of the conditions imposed by the Government was that the service should route through Shannon. The negotiations in the Gresham hotel in Dublin lasted for three days non-stop. What emerged was an agreement for a 'wet lease' (aircraft and operating crews) of Super Constellations from

One of the Super Constellations leased from Seaboard and Western in 1958

AER LINGUS

Seaboard and Western pending the purchase by Aerlínte of Boeing 720s — the runways at Shannon were already being extended to take the first generation of jets. Aerlínte and Aer Lingus were to provide cabin service and hostesses, as well as office staff in the United States. At the management meeting at which J. F. Dempsey announced the decision to his colleagues there was, in the recollection of Mícheál Ó Riain, who had joined the company in 1957 and was acting as minute-taker, only one dissenting voice — that of the chief accountant, James Moran, who suggested that if the airline had not the resources to buy its own aircraft it should not get into the business. This time, however, Lord Douglas accepted the position on behalf of the British shareholders, provided that the transatlantic service was to be separate from Aer Lingus and that the latter was not to be at any loss in the matter. In fact, the inter-relation of the two companies was about to take on a complexity bordering on the Gilbertian. The Chairman of the Aer Lingus Board was to act on the Board of Aerlínte in the Aer Lingus interest. The Secretary of Aer Lingus, who was also Secretary of Aerlínte, was appointed to the additional post of Executive Assistant to the General Manager of Aerlínte, The resources of the Aer Lingus administrative and sales organisation were to be made available to Aerlínte on a fee basis and Aer Lingus divisional and departmental heads were to be named executives of Aerlínte where this had not already been done. There would, in effect, be no separate staff for the transatlantic operation apart from those employed by Aerlínte in North America. The Boards, nevertheless, in the words of the official record, would continue to remain 'distinct and separate' — an achievement, one would have thought, involving a considerable exercise in bilocation. Finally, the Aerlínte aircraft were to be re-chartered from Seaboard and Western to Aer Lingus for the Shannon–Dublin sector, employing a 'legal fiction' — as it was described by its critics — that was to draw the increasing wrath of United States interest in the future, even though they had themselves utilised the same stratagem on their internal services.

It was to be third time lucky. The first flight, by the Super Constellation *Naomh Pádraig*, was due to depart from Dublin Airport at 20.00 on 28 April 1958. At the inaugural dinner preceding the departure, the Taoiseach, Éamon de Valera, paid a generous tribute to his Minister for Industry and Commerce: 'I doubt if this undertaking would have come to fruition were it not that at the head of the Department of State concerned there was a man capable of conceiving bold enterprises with the ability to plan them and the resolution to put them through. It would not be regarded as detracting from the credit due to the directors, managers and staffs to say that, behind all their efforts and all their successes, had been the unflagging interest and determination of Seán Lemass.' The large official party, led by Lemass, included such veterans of civil aviation as T. J. O'Driscoll, now Director General of

Bord Fáilte; Captain J. C. Kelly-Rogers, now Deputy General Manager of Aerlínte; and the recurrent John Leydon, its Chairman. The flight got away at 20.20 and landed at Shannon at 23.00, from where it left at 00.10 for Boston and New York. Among those who joined the party there were Colonel P. Maher, the Airport Manager, and Brendan O'Regan, Chief Executive of the Shannon Free Airport Development Company. On the following morning in *The Irish Times* the 'By-Line' cartoonist, Niel O'Kennedy, showed two citizens peering up at the passing aircraft. 'It's marvellous all the same,' said one: 'only 39 years after Alcock and Brown, to get a service that is not all cock and bull.'

On the way over the Atlantic the Seaboard and Western captain, Bill Donoghue, sang all the verses of 'Kevin Barry' over the public address system. Delayed by headwinds and fog, the aircraft, after a stop at Gander, finally reached the New York area to find the whole of the eastern seaboard closed. It had to divert to Halifax, Nova Scotia, where, in addition to having to endure harsh winter conditions, the party — or that segment of it which included Tommy Dunne and Michael Twomey — found themselves in what they considered to be sub-standard accommodation: 'Sufferin' Jasus,' said Twomey as reported by Dunne: 'It's a temperance hotel!' On setting out into the snow to remedy the situation they met a policeman from Enniscorthy who directed them to an establishment in which they discovered the rest of the *Naomh Pádraig*'s complement, which had been dispersed amongst hotels of a similar complexion. The flight finally left Halifax just ahead of a blizzard, eventually finding itself in a stack of seventeen other aircraft waiting to land at New York's Idelwild airport — the future J. F. Kennedy. The passengers were greeted by the Irish ambassadors to the United States and the United Nations, civic dignitaries and the band of the fighting 69th New York Regiment. The celebrations, culminating in an official dinner, extended over four days. Of these ninety-six hours Tommy Dunne slept for just eighteen, and on his return 'was just taken out of the Viscount in London and stood up'.

Better late than never? Liam Boyd, who represented TWA in Ireland for many years, believed that Aer Lingus had lost a golden opportunity by not being on the Atlantic from 1948: 'They were the great years. They would have been one of the first transatlantic carriers — they would have been in before many European national carriers, and they would have been able to build up that experience over that ten year period.' Garret FitzGerald thought differently: 'Closing was absolutely the right decision at the time. It was opened at the right time ten years later when the traffic was building up to the point where it was possible to envisage an economic operation.' The argument was certainly not silenced by the band of the Fighting 69th. Barely a year later, in the course of the debate on the Estimate for the Department of Industry and Commerce and that on the Air Navigation and Transport Bill

1959 it was being phrased again in hard political terms. William Norton hoped, no doubt with little conviction, that when the story of Aerlínte was told it would be in sober language and that they would not be given the impression that it was a new wonder which was being established by Fianna Fáil. He asked for some appraisal of what the service was going to cost to maintain. We may have to face up to the fact, he suggested, that to stay in the air across the Atlantic would be an exercise which in the long run would involve a fairly substantial amount of money. 'It is fair to say from this side of the House that we have always opposed a transatlantic service,' said Sir Anthony Esmonde, Fine Gael: 'I think it is fantastic to say that it is a necessary adjunct of our position as a sovereign state to be in the transatlantic air transport system because it is manifestly untrue.' James Dillon went further: 'I believe the enterprise to be misconceived, to be reckless, and to partake of a character of a wholly improvident gamble with the resources of this country.'

More important, perhaps, than these ritual party polemics was the provocation they offered Lemass to restate his own position. 'We have no reason here to feel any need to apologise for the extent to which the State has already entered into the industrial field,' he told the Dáil: 'All these State commercial enterprises which have been set up over the years have been uniformly successful and represent a very substantial addition to the country's economic resources. Indeed they were themselves responsible for a large part of the economic progress which has been accomplished.' He was still, however, Lemass the pragmatist: there was nothing subversive of the prevailing order in his thinking on State involvement: 'The fact that the State has to act as the industrial entrepreneur does not alter in any way the character of our society and indeed we do not intend that it should.' He was equally emphatic in spelling out the practicalities as he saw them: that they were trying to attract only persons who wanted to travel from New York to Ireland and nobody else (the day of the Irish travelling the other way except on one-way tickets was in the future) and that he had no interest in prestige in this regard. 'The decision to proceed with the transatlantic air development, which had been pressed on me by the Board of Aer Lingus, was taken on hard, cold commercial facts and nothing else.' The amount of pressure required, it need hardly be said, had not been excessive. The Bill to which Lemass was speaking authorised Aer Rianta to increase its authorised share capital, all held by the Minister for Finance, to £10 million, of which £5,868,000 would be required to finance the jet fleet of three Boeing 720s, orders for which had been placed.

Criticism of the new service was not confined to the political arena, nor was all of it entirely unfounded. 'The staff employed in New York were of a very low calibre initially,' recalled Garret FitzGerald: 'There were two investigations and eventually a number of the senior staff were sacked and replaced. They terrorised the junior staff into not reporting what they were up to. In the early weeks they were quite incapable of putting on the plane a manifest — or any piece of paper — saying how many people there were on the flight. I was eventually reduced to sending someone down to Shannon to count them coming off.' At the time, however, he was painting a brighter picture. He wrote in his commercial commentary in the June 1958 issue of the staff magazine *Aersceála:* 'The initial difficulties of getting our service known to travel agents and the general public have been more readily overcome than had been bargained for. There seems good reason to believe that during the remainder of the summer our cautious estimates will also be reached and, perhaps, passed by a small margin. . . . So Aerlínte is finding its feet at last, more quickly, I judge, than some of its predecessors on this important but difficult route.'

If this was not quite the case, management moved quickly to remedy the situation. Michael Dargan, now Staff and Services Manager, reorganised the New York staff under Jim Leet, an ex-Pan American employee, with what proved to be a steady hand at the helm. The image of Aerlínte still left something to be desired: when Brendan O'Kelly, then a senior Pan American sales representative in Chicago, decided to join, most people thought that he was 'putting his career on the line'. Tom Kennedy, originally recruited by Major Eamonn Rooney, then in charge of Aer Lingus press and public relations, had lost his job together with all the other Aerlínte people in New York in May 1948: 'It provided me with an opportunity to go out and equip myself better to come back to Aer Lingus — though I didn't think that was what I was doing at the time.' When he was invited by J. F. Dempsey to return, he was at first hesitant: 'I suppose I was a bit gun-shy and it wasn't until they actually ordered the jets that I let it be known I was available again.' He rejoined on 16 March 1959 and on 18 March was seconded by the airline onto the retinue of Seán T. O Ceallaigh, who was paying the first ever visit by a serving Irish President to the United States. 'The Government at that time didn't have press representation in this country,' said Kennedy, 'and after a while it became more or less the thing that if they had a Taoiseach or anybody coming over I would slip to his side and work with him.'

Aerlínte published its first balance sheet in the summer of 1959. It showed that in the eleven months to 31 March it had carried a total of 14,781 passengers on the transatlantic service, as against the forecast of 13,000 which formed the basis for the decision to go ahead. The loss for the six months from April to September 1959 was £180,000, considerably less than forecast. An offer from Seaboard and Western during the year to invest in the airline was rejected since it was confidently expected that the B720 jets would effect a rapid improvement in the financial position. In the following year Packy Bourke went to Washington State as Senior Inspector to liaise with Boeing on the preparation and delivery of the new aircraft, and crew training began in earnest. The company were never parsimonious about spending money on training, in the opinion of former pilot Tommy McKeown: 'This is what stood to Aer Lingus and built up the professionalism and the safety standards in the company. Once we started buying Boeing we had American pilots train us . . . they trained us on the B720, they trained us of the B707 and they checked us out on the B747.' The prospects for pilots were bright, though the selection of those to be trained for the B720 caused something of a storm. Viscount selection had been made by a board of non-practising pilots, engineers and others, which tended to cause resentment among those actually flying. The highest possible standard was sought for the new jets, and five practising pilots were constituted selectors, each making a list of possible trainees. When the results were announced there were protests from the pilots and their union, IALPA. Training records were gone through but a case was made out for only one individual, and he was taken on. Captain Stanley Williamson became Operations Manager for the introduction of the Boeings — 'management, to my knowledge, never questioned a requirement for training' — and the job of Chief Pilot–Atlantic went to Dick White. It was a completely new organisation within the airline. 'Flying the Atlantic stamped us as an international airline,' said Tommy McKeown, 'stemming from that other countries began to recognise that we had something.'

. . . something that some other countries, notably the United States, were anxious to get their hands on. In April 1958 Pan American and TWA had sought rights to Dublin and onwards to European destinations not served by Aer Lingus. This — seen at the time to be a relatively modest request — was to develop into the acrimonious battle that was to become known as the 'Dublin rights' issue.

Frank Fitzpatrick, who joined the airline in 1946 and was working in the publicity department on print production, went to New York in 1960 to supervise the preparation of publicity material in connection with the introduction of the Boeings. Public relations was being handled by Tom Kennedy with a staff which in 1960 included Bill Maxwell, a Dublin journalist, and Anne Tolan, whose role in the successful promotion of Irish fashion and a general awareness of the country through the medium of her own radio programme had garnered considerable favourable publicity for herself, for Ireland and for the airline: 'Anne Tolan', said a woman who stopped Frank Fitzpatrick in the street on seeing his Aer Lingus pin — 'is she for real?' Fitzpatrick recalled going out to Idelwild airport to see the first B720 arrive prior to its delivery flight to Ireland. For the gathering of representatives of several other Irish bodies as well as Aer Lingus it was a memorable occasion: 'You saw for the first time', recalled Fitzpatrick, 'an Irish plane with a shamrock. There was a great deal of emotional pride in the thing.' Pride which Tom Kennedy immediately translated into practical terms. 'Isn't it marvellous', he said to Fitzpatrick, 'to think that we can now go out and sell something that is as good or better than anything else on the Atlantic?'

In this he had the wholehearted support of the entire official Irish community. 'The tourist board and the people in the consulate', he later recalled, 'worked with us like they were all members of Aer Lingus.' The same was true of the Irish community at large, particularly the very important travel trade sector: 'One of the remarkable things was that when we came back in 1958 the same people were the first on line to help us again — Paddy Grimes, Michael Sinnott, John O'Connor . . .'

On 18 November 1960 Boeing 720-48 EI-ALA *St Patrick* landed at Dublin, having been piloted from New York to Shannon by Captain R. N. White and from Shannon by Captain R. B. Seigne. It broke the existing record for the New York-Shannon sector by covering the distance in four hours fifty-seven minutes. 'And now', said a contemporary advertisement, 'a new era of Irish Air Travel begins . . . borne on the surging power of the Boeing Shamrock Jet. It is the only direct service from Dublin to North America. . . .'

The arrival of the first B720: (left to right) Jack Lynch; Maurice Dockrell, Lord Mayor of Dublin; Seán Lemass; Patrick Lynch

AER LINGUS

7

Men, Women and Machines 1945–60

DUBLIN in 1945 was an unreal city, half-celebrating a victory in which it had had no hand, act or part. In Jammet's back bar, in the Buttery, the Red Bank, the battleworn veterans of twenty-four summers rehearsed their wizard prangs and the pieces of cake, eyed the popsies and looked for new worlds — or any world — to conquer. Dick White, back from the Far East where he had been flying DC3s in the war between the Dutch and the Indonesians, ran into an old friend who told him to go out to Aer Lingus with his RAF logbooks. He was interviewed by Darby Kennedy and Bill Scott. You have more DC3 hours than anybody else round here, they told him: when would you like to start? Would Monday be all right? 'Open recruitment had stopped,' White remembered: 'I was lucky to get in.'

Not all the pilot intake were returning Irish, survivors of another man's war. 'There was a great exodus from the British forces,' said Aidan Quigley, 'foisting superior knowledge on ignorant Irish peasants. Quite a few of them were the greatest crowd of chancers that ever crossed the Irish Sea. The hallmark of a pilot and his ability to fly is his logbook. We got some characters whose logbooks were forged. There was no way of screening them so I thought it a good idea to funnel them in. But it got out of hand.' It was those who had not experienced service discipline in its full rigours who were the most difficult to handle, in Frank Delaney's recollection: the RAF intake accepted the rule of authority. They were all kinds, White recalled: Fleet Air Arm, flying-boats... there was difficulty in getting twin-engine pilots. As a bunch of people they must have been extremely difficult to manage: 'that was why', he suggested, 'they got J. C. Kelly-Rogers.'

There was the makings of an explosive mixture with, as one of the post-war generation remembered, 'the beautiful girls who were recruited at the same time — a very lovely and talented group of young ladies. With this rather wild pilot group and these young ladies it made a situation that was a little bit ahead of its time for Dublin.' The solution to that problem — apparently — was the recruitment of 'a very able woman called Pat Blake, a woman of tremendous authority. She did a very able management job in keeping some control of the situation.' B. T. O'Reilly, one of the wild men, was addicted to practical jokes: 'One of the tricks he pulled a couple of times before the hostesses got wise to it', said a former colleague, 'was coming back from London or somewhere and you couldn't get in — the weather closed and you went to Rineanna. The passengers are taken up by train. The aircraft stays overnight and flies back empty. O'Reilly's trick was very simple: he waited till they were up and cruising and the hostess was in the back — it had to be a new hostess and rather green. There were two luggage compartments at the back of the cockpit. He'd put the first officer in one, then plug in automatic pilot, then press the button and jump into the other luggage compartment himself.' The hostess would walk in to find nobody there!

'But you could always depend on them,' said Stan Williamson, himself ex-RAF. 'When I came into Aer Lingus', said Oliver Hone, (he was from BOAC) 'it was noticeable to me that the flying crew, particularly the captains, very definitely recognised themselves as part of an airline with a responsibility for the airline's success. They didn't aspire to the godlike image that some of the pilots in "the other airline" had.' The Boot Inn, at the back of the airport, was the crew room. Undoubtedly there was a cavalier attitude, and in some cases — for example the Birmingham crash — regulations were not strictly adhered to. 'There was great antagonism and in some cases bitterness between the two halves of the airline [operations and administration],' White remembered: 'A lot of distrust'.

Bill Scott had been with Imperial Airways before the war. When he arrived he was very impressed by J. F. Dempsey and John Leydon, both of whom interviewed him: 'I was very impressed also with the degree of enthusiasm.' When he was appointed Operations Manager in May 1946 Aer Lingus had three serving captains. Within a year the number had increased to thirty, and by March 1949 the total crew strength was 135. He had been a Mosquito pilot with the RAF, and most of the intake from that source consisted of twin-engine pilots like himself. Dick White, who joined in October 1946, had been trained as an RAF fighter pilot but flew DC3s ('a lovely aeroplane to fly') in the Burmah theatre in 1944. He had to wait less than a year to be made a captain. Many of the RAF people who came and stayed were, like Scott and White, Irish, or had Irish connections, and were given preference by the selection boards — though, as Stan Williamson recalled it, 'the number one was to get the lads from the Air Corps'. There were underlying tensions because there was then no structured promotional ladder. 'The RAF types were able to jump the gun,' said White. Some of them had a lot of flying hours and could claim twin and four-engine experience not readily available to Air Corps pilots, and this was considered very important in view of the projected transatlantic service. When Tommy McKeown joined from the Air Corps at the end of 1945 there were seven other ex-Army pilots like himself and perhaps eight or nine from the RAF. In early 1946, of a total of sixty-one pilots, engineers and radio operators, approximately twenty-nine had Air Corps service.

There were those both inside and outside the company who believed that there existed a very definite pro-RAF bias and what would then have been described as a West-British outlook. A letter from an ex-Army captain who had been elected a representative of the Federation of Irish Ex-Service Men alleged serious discrimination: 'Within a few days of my election I was called before the Staff and Services Controller and he informed me that he, acting on behalf of the Management, had to inform me that he could not, and would not, tolerate any such association within the Company.' He was threatened with dismissal but, he complained, an RAF association was allowed to flourish unimpeded. Robert Briscoe told the Dáil that control officers' jobs had gone to 'ex-RAF types' in preference to ex-Air Corps sergeant pilots on reserve. Whatever the truth of the matter — and Dick White claimed the situation was exaggerated — a certain amount of resentment was understandable as between those who had gained their experience in combat and those whose role during the Emergency had been somewhat more contained. Nobody questioned the quality of Air Corps training as against the RAF; but, as in many other spheres of life in post-Emergency Ireland, those who, for whatever reason, had seen active service were marked out from those who had not.

It was the Air Corps itself which had perhaps the chief cause for complaint since the products of its short service commission could not wait to leave to join the airline. 'As soon as these boys had finished they were out like bunny rabbits into Aer Lingus,' said Stan Williamson, himself ex-RAF. It left the Air Corps with a top and bottom but no body, and obliged it to introduce a medium service commission of ten years in place of the short service commitment. In the early 1950s Aer Lingus began discussions with the Army authorities and the Department of Industry and Commerce on the possibility of instituting a pilot training scheme. This went into operation and provided short-term commissions in the Air Corps for selected candidates. On their transfer to the reserve at the conclusion of the commission Aer Lingus agreed to offer employment to those considered suitable in accordance with the airline's needs.

Before this Air Corps pilots joined initially on secondment for six months. 'If we didn't like it we could go back to our Army job,' said Aidan Quigley, who flew as a first officer for ten months and was then, in October 1946, promoted captain, having been checked out by the three veterans Darby Kennedy, Ivan Hammond and Noel McAuley. There was prestige but little glamour. 'On a Saturday night we might fly two newspaper charters to Manchester in a DC3 starting at six o'clock in the evening and finishing about one or two o'clock in the morning,' Tommy McKeown remembered.

There were no restrictions then on hours and they put together their own operating instructions. 'When Kelly-Rogers came he brought BOAC instructions, which weren't suitable for us at all,' said Bill Scott.

J. C. Kelly-Rogers came to Aer Lingus as Technical Manager in 1947 with an international reputation as a pioneer flying-boat captain in the service of Imperial Airways. From Dun Laoghaire, County Dublin, he at first followed the sea and retained until the last something of the presence of the master mariner (his first office in a temporary building at the airport was known as 'the Admiralty'). The stories of his acting as Winston Churchill's pilot during the war were told and retold, both by himself and others, in infinite variations until they were crystallised in a book title: *I Flew with Kelly-Rogers,* by Winston Churchill. In the opinion of some, his experience was already dated by the time he joined the airline, but he himself certainly did not see it that way and he fought bitterly with anybody whose opinions did not coincide with his own: Darby Kennedy, J. F. Dempsey and, in particular, the equally immovable Max Stuart Shaw. To Oliver Hone Kelly-Rogers was 'one of the godlike captains of BOAC', together with Bill Scott. Both of them, he felt, could have brought with them the 'élitist' behaviour characteristic of that organisation, but it was to their credit that they didn't encourage it. They did bring with them a code of discipline and formality in staff relations that irritated some and put the fear of God into others.

Max Stuart Shaw joined in 1946 from Shannon where he had been Traffic Manager for BOAC. Originally on secondment, he stayed and eventually became an Irish citizen. He was the calibre of person, in the opinion of Niall Weldon, with the experience the airline needed at the time to set it on the right lines: 'We didn't have anyone to draw upon at that time from within Ireland. He played a very important part.' 'When one came to know him,' Weldon added, 'he was the salt of the earth, but in the course of one short discussion he could be charming, rude, humble and domineering. Underneath that veil of sharply contrasting moods he was a caring, warm-hearted and friendly soul. But he terrified people right, left and centre.'

With the exception, of course, of Kelly-Rogers. 'In any organisation', as G. P. Dempsey put it, 'the marketing side and the production side are always going to clash,' but in this case there was an element of personal friction. 'They were allowed to say rough words to one another,' recalled Frank Delaney, 'this created two conflicting groups and, unfortunately, it was allowed to percolate down onto the shop floor.' It was what they subsequently called 'management by abrasion', commented Arthur Walls, who joined in 1947. Garret FitzGerald worked under Stuart Shaw and his contemporary Gerald Giltrap under Kelly-Rogers. 'Each of them told us not to talk to the other,' said FitzGerald: 'but they frequently found themselves in the most surprising agreement on things, which they found very puzzling. The tensions were constructive.' It was healthy stuff, in Niall Weldon's opinion: 'Major disagreements were always thrashed out round the table.'

Away from the boardroom there was recourse to other methods. At one stage Kelly-Rogers introduced a new style of uniform featuring a double-breasted tunic in the manner of BOAC. It was also suggested that pilots might salute executives of the company. 'But', said Tommy McKeown, 'we soon disabused them of that policy. Then they decided that every pilot should have a psychiatric examination. I happened to be president of the pilots' association at the time so I said that would be quite all right provided all the management had a psychiatric examination and if they were going to read our reports we wanted to see theirs. But we never heard any more.'

Such personality and policy clashes were taking place against a background which both sides of the airline found fulfilling. The mechanics and engineers in the hangar were, according to Dick White 'very dedicated'. 'New routes were opening all the time,' said McKeown, 'new aircraft were coming into the system; and the Atlantic was in sight.'

At the end of March 1948 the fleet consisted of eight DC3 passenger aircraft, two DC3 freighters, five Vickers Viking Mark 1Bs and two Airspeed Consuls. The latter, EI-ADB and EI-ADC, had been acquired from the parent company Aer Rianta who had bought them for a charter project

One of the Airspeed Consuls (centre) in the hangar at Dublin

JACK COADY

which did not materialise. Aer Lingus used them for crew training and occasional charter work. One was disposed of to British South American Airways in 1949 and the other to the Karachi Aero Club in 1953, just after it had carried the official airline party to the scene of the DC3 crash in Snowdonia, Wales. In 1947 the company had disposed of its two oldest aircraft, the Supermarine Walrus Amphibian which was bought from the Air Corps but never registered, though assigned the letters EI-ACC, and the Lockheed L414 Hudson 1, from the same source, which was registered EI-ACB only for the ferry flight to Belgium in 1947 after its sale. The unfortunate Walrus, bought as an air-sea rescue aircraft, was sold for £150 but many years later was discovered in a derelict state in Britain and was bought for the Fleet Air Arm museum.

The contract for seven long-nosed Vikings, total cost £312,842, was signed in December 1946, the same month that permission had been obtained from the Department of Industry and Commerce to dispense with the weighing of passengers. The order was prompted not only by political pressure from the British Board members, but also by the acute shortage of DC3 spares which threatened to render the fleet inoperable. The situation improved somewhat in 1947, and that indestructible aircraft not only saw the luckless Vikings

Unloading a DC3. The aircraft is EI-ACI 'Aodán' (St Aidan), with the Irish name in Gaelic script.

BESTICK WILLIAMS

come and go, but continued to serve the airline well until the last one, EI-ACE *St Colmcille*, later *St Celsius*, was sold to Royal Nepal Airlines on 13 July 1964 after eighteen years' service. The Aer Lingus fleet embraced both conversions of the C47 cargo aircraft and several variations on the DC3 passenger theme. The original seating accommodation for twenty-one passengers was progressively augmented — to twenty-six and later to thirty two — but they remained maids of all work, readily adaptable to full or partial freight configurations. For the travellers of their day they possessed a personality all their own, which Francis Stuart caught successfully in his novel *Good Friday's Daughter*, published in 1953: 'He climbed up into the narrow, tilted nave of the plane with the high-backed Gothic seats upholstered in the same green as the girl's costume. He settled himself in one of them and looked out through the small window beside him that reminded him of one of the tiny windows let into the mud walls of cottages near his home.' And, after taxiing to the runway: 'The plane stopped. There was a short silence in which he imagined the blunt, tilted nose raised to the wind. Then a quickly-growing roar through the long cabin, rising to a moment of climactic vibration and subsiding again. A pause, a second of intenser, silent waiting as though for some signal he could not see, and then a forward movement that he recognised at once as more urgent than the gradual, exploratory ones that the plane had been making.' When the DC3 was flown in passenger/cargo configuration, as not infrequently on the Paris route, the atmosphere in the residual half-cabin was almost embarrassingly intimate, particularly in rough weather. An unsettling experience, on a dirty night out of Northolt, was to observe a pilot travelling off-duty in the seat in front suddenly tense and peer out the window into the rain at the throbbing Pratt & Whitney R1830-92 war surplus engine. But the DC3 more than proved its worth. Nineteen served with Aer Lingus between 1940 and 1964, forming the backbone of the fleet until the arrival of the Viscounts and Friendships. As late as 1983 six of those nineteen were still flying, in places as far apart as France, Portugal and Honduras. First flown in 1936, the aircraft proved itself to be probably the most durable design of all time, celebrating its own fifty years of active service in 1986.

Enter late, and already in bad odour, the Viking: an all-metal, mid-wing monoplane powered by two Bristol Hercules 130 engines and developed from components of the Wellington and Warwick bombers. The prototype first flew on 22 June 1945, but Vickers were unable to deliver the Aer Lingus order of seven V634 Viking IBs until September 1947. 'We more or less had to buy them through our relationship with BEA,' said Oliver Hone, who had joined in 1947 from BOAC and became Traffic Manager in 1952: 'they were a disaster financially'. 'Noisy and difficult to maintain', was Frank Delaney's verdict: 'the unserviceability was very high'. Arthur Walls remembered them as 'a very bad aeroplane in detail . . . bits and pieces of tinware fell off'. The delay in delivery (they were originally due in March), their excessive fuel consumption and the fact that in the meantime DC3 spares had become more readily available sealed their fate, though they proved almost as difficult to dispose of as to acquire. Two were eventually sold to the British independent Airwork, which used them on government troop charters; the rest, after protracted and somewhat exotic negotiations, went to the Egyptian airline Misrair. For Aer Lingus it was a mind-expanding introduction, via the Oriental arts of haggling, to a new role as aircraft salesmen on a large scale. The General Manager of Misrair, a sheik, came to Dublin to discuss details with J. F. Dempsey, General Manager, Major General Michael Hogan, Assistant General Manager, and P. J. Brennan, Assistant Secretary, in the Russell hotel. As negotiations proceeded the sheik began fingering his worry-beads whereupon Brennan, not to be outdone, produced his rosary beads. Bill Scott found himself included as part of the deal: his role was to go out to Egypt to train pilots in the operation of the Vikings, whilst Packy Bourke was assigned a similar role in respect of the maintenance staff. This was the first of what was to be a long line of Aer Lingus teams working with airlines abroad, and it did not at first have a particularly easy passage. The sheik promised Scott that he would be supplied with the finest belly-dancer in Egypt to perform just for him, but the first problem was to get within range of this delectable pleasure. The United Nations was at the time banning supplies to either the Israelis or the Egyptians, who were at loggerheads. Ireland was not then a UN member, but the Aer Lingus team had nevertheless to travel via non-UN countries and thought it best not to advise their departure in the normal way, with the result that they were detained in Catania in Sicily having passed safely through Spain. The Irish Embassy in Rome succeeded in extricating them and they proceeded to Cairo and a tremendous reception — but, Bill Scott maintained, no belly-dancer.

The Constellations, on lease from Aerlínte, also came and went, creating something of a sensation on the London route, for which they were unsuited, before their final withdrawal on 6 June 1948. Arthur Walls, who was Project Engineer at the time, recalled the aircraft in connection with the appointment of a 'civilian flying instructor, a man called l'Estrange. L'Estrange could fly Constellations and he and I would come up the road at six in the morning on our bikes. L'Estrange would then get into the cockpit, take off his bicycle clips, start the four engines and we'd go off down over the Azores for four or five hours doing performance checking. And then we'd come back, put on our bicycle clips and go home.' In their brief period of service to London and Rome, the Constellations set new standards of comfort: in January 1948 it was decided that a steward should accompany the hostess as an experiment on the London route but that passengers should not be relieved of hats and coats except by request. Full meals were provided on the short-lived service. 'Travel in luxurious comfort — via Aer Lingus', proclaimed an advertisement of the period which showed Collinstown terminal building dwarfed by the tailplane of the Constellation.

The humbler hospitality of the DC3 was dispensed by just one hostess. The relationship with the passengers, many of whom were regulars, was patently friendly, though it was against regulations to make dates with them and few, if any, marriages occurred. Pat Blake, ex-British army and not universally popular with the girls was responsible, in Oliver Hone's estimation, 'for setting the standard that carried on under its own momentum'. They had to pass a test in French and Irish every six months or forfeit an increment; but they had at least three days off a week, sometimes four. At this period the airport did not open on Sundays.

If from the passenger's point of view the DC3 was relatively spartan in comparison with the Constellation, the Bristol Wayfarer was flying at its most basic: 'The noisiest, most uncomfortable, roughest old crate we ever operated', in the judgment of Dick White. The first post-war British aircraft to enter commercial service — on 1 July 1946 — the Wayfarer was capable of operating from small airfields with a payload of over four tons and was in basic concept a freighter: the passenger version, with accommodation for thirty-four, was never more than a compromise. Its acquisition in 1952 involved a close relationship with the manufacturers, the Bristol Aeroplane Company, and Kelly-Rogers saw an opportunity for expanding the engineering and maintenance aspects of the airline's operation. Paddy Tierney and Packy Bourke were amongst those sent over to Bristol to work out details, as a result of which early in 1952 Aer Lingus received an order for the manufacture and assembly of Bristol 170 components. 'We set up a manufacturing unit in two Nissen huts and we manufactured the control columns, the control box, the rudder pedals and the stabilizer,' recalled Paddy Tierney. 'K-R [Kelly-Rogers] sent me round various places in the country to see what machines were available. He wanted someone like CIE to set up a central area with machines to be rented by various interests.' The scheme did not materialise, but the Bristol contract marked the real beginning of the machine shop and had a claim to be considered as the first development in what was to become the key sector of aviation-related ancillary activities.

There had been an earlier attempt to develop the engineering side of the airline on a significant scale. Towards the end of 1945 negotiations had been opened with Miles Aircraft, British manufacturers of the Magister trainer, used by the Air Corps, and others such as the pre-war Hawk-Major, to set up an engine and airframe overhaul facility based at Dublin. The company, Aeroint Teoranta, was to be operated jointly by Aer Lingus and Miles

Aircraft. In February 1946 J. J. O'Leary, J. P. O'Brien and Denis Herlihy of the Department of Industry and Commerce were nominated to its Board and it was proposed to interview eleven applicants for the post of secretary. But problems arose, not least in the matter of accommodation, since the No. 2 hangar which had been earmarked for the facility was now required for the expanding fleet. In May 1946 the Board was told that Aeroint was not likely to be in operation for some considerable time and that the proposed connection with Miles had been severed. A technical adviser was in fact appointed but the project never materialised. The setting up by Lockheed of a similar undertaking at Shannon and the signing of the Bilateral Agreement with Britain were contributing factors.

The Wayfarer manufacturing project returned a modest profit after six months, and the Bristol contract continued until the withdrawal of the aircraft from the Aer Lingus fleet. In 1953 the technical division, which was headed by Kelly-Rogers, set up a technical planning branch to separate from the day-to-day work the overall function of planning, cost analysis and control, method study and work measurement. With the decision to acquire what might be described as the 'permanent' new aircraft — the Viscounts and Friendships — the workload increased substantially, not least because staff had to spend considerable time with the respective manufacturers learning the ropes.

The decision to convert from a piston to a turboprop fleet fleet was, in the circumstances, a courageous one. It was, in the view of Arthur Walls, 'a much bigger gamble than buying the Boeing 720' — the first of the subsequent jet fleet. Aer Lingus was one of the first three customers for the Viscount, and the new aircraft offered a challenge to the airline's engineers to which they responded, in Wall's recollection, with both skill and enthusiasm. He recalled going up to Sweden for cold starting trials: 'if you wanted to discover how an aeroplane behaved in the cold you simply took it to somewhere like Stockholm in January. The Viscounts were very difficult to start at first — but that was largely because we were using Mickey Mouse equipment.'

The acquisition of the new fleets from 1954 also put considerable pressure on training facilities, both for air crews and ground engineering staff. When the first post-war DC3s went into service, American expertise had been called in to assist with pilot training — Aidan Quigley and Tommy McKeown, for example, were put through their paces by Ray Wells and a colleague. From the beginning the highest standards were aimed at — Stan Williamson believed that the airline's good safety record was entirely due to training — and when the Viscount fleet was introduced this primary concern was reflected in the number of foreign airlines which sent their people to Dublin for training on that particular aircraft. Aer Lingus crew and technicians who had benefited from facilities offered by BEA to obtain first-hand experience of Viscounts prior to their entry into service now found themselves passing on that knowledge 'on request and for payment', as the 1956 annual report put it, 'to a wide diversity of airlines from many countries: Central African Airways, Misrair, Indian Airlines Corporation, Air Austria and Fred Olsen Air Transport of Norway'. 'Not only did we do business with these emerging nations,' said Frank Delaney: 'we did business with the international carriers with whom we were competing on cost only.' Thus was laid the foundation for another airline-related ancillary activity which expanded steadily through the years and through sequential changes of aircraft types. It was at this time, too, that technical staff began to travel very far afield to make available to other operators at their own home base their rapidly developing expertise.

The arrival of the Viscounts also increased the level of activity in the hangars and workshops, much of the overhaul work being undertaken in Dublin and some components manufactured under contract from Vickers-Armstrong. The decision to standardise on the larger 800 model from 1957 followed a good deal of trouble with the smaller 707s (not to be confused with the later Boeing 707 jet). The Viscount 707 fleet was grounded on 16 January 1958 following a signal received from Vickers advising wing spar modification. This came at a very bad time since the Lourdes pilgrimage traffic for the Centenary Year was reaching its peak. Garret FitzGerald had broached the subject of Lourdes in 1954 to his boss Stuart Shaw, an Englishman and a Protestant 'who thought it was some kind of religious mania on my part. He

Viscount V800 'Ciarán' with, in the background, Carvair EI-AMP

AER LINGUS

asked him to be allowed to keep two V-707s for the summer (further outer wing modifications were notified in March and the Board expressed its 'grave concern with its experience of this type of aircraft from the point of view of passenger relations and cost') and guaranteed to fill them from May to October. In the event there were eighty-two pilgrimages from Ireland and Britain to Lourdes, 'the nearest equation of supply and demand ever achieved in the aviation industry, I think', FitzGerald stated modestly. The Viscount 707s were eventually disposed of in 1960, to Britain and Bermuda. Stuart Shaw, 'an extraordinary man, on whom I think the success of Aer Lingus largely depended', according to FitzGerald, resigned on 31 March 1958 to take up the position of General Manager of Central African Airways. 'I gave him a shillelagh when he left the country,' said Nuala Doyle, then in reservations in Dublin: 'I told him it might be useful for beating the natives.'

The Viscount 808, the first three of which were delivered in May 1957, proved a more acceptable and satisfactory aircraft. An engineer, George Bourke from Cork, designed additional bar capacity which he described as 'the goozle box'. 'In Cork when they're going home on Christmas Eve with their black paper bags they call it 'de goozle', he offered in explanation. It was alleged that the term became so widely accepted that it found its way into the KLM Viscount manual. Dick White, following a year's secondment to BEA flying Viscounts as a first officer, had come back to manage flight operations for their introduction to Aer Lingus. The original 707s he had described as 'tomorrow's engine with yesterday's airframe', but was a good deal more enthusiastic about their replacements. Having seen them operating satisfactorily he returned to regular flying.

Arthur Walls was Project Engineer for the introduction of the Friendships, for which Aer Lingus was the first non-Dutch customer, and for some time travelled to the Fokker plant in Holland on Monday mornings, returning on Friday. 'Fokker were most excellent technicians,' he remembered, 'terribly honest but unbelievably stubborn. We were their first customer, and we would say "there's a motor there and you can't get at it when you want to change it". And they would say "that's where the drawing says it's to be. Do you want us to quote you for moving it?"' But apart from some unexpected problems with the centre structure, necessitating modifications at the manufacturer's expense, the Fokker Friendships entered service in November 1958 with most of the teething troubles resolved. EI-AKA *St Fintan* was the first F-27 to go into service with the airline, and there had been a procession of pilots (headed by Captain P. E. Little), airframe and electrical engineers and other staff going from Dublin to the Fokker factory for instruction in its handling and maintenance. The forty-seater high-wing turboprop aircraft proved a popular and successful choice both with the airline and its passengers ('A nice aeroplane to fly,' was one pilot's verdict: 'but it did bounce around a bit — a bit rocky in rough air'). It was particularly useful on short-haul routes and the fact that it utilised the same power unit as the Viscount 808, the Rolls-Royce Dart engine, made for economies in operation. By March 1960 the DC3 fleet had been reduced to five, employed mainly in cargo duties and stretcher traffic to Lourdes.

The very rapid advances which took place in the 1950s had not been achieved without some stress and dislocation on the personnel side. Approval sought from the Department of Finance in the summer of 1946 for staff superannuation and insurance schemes had for a considerable period not been forthcoming, leading to a serious degree of dissatisfaction, particularly among the pilots. They and other groups were also pressing for more money, and in March 1947 general agreement was reached with the relevant unions on their demands in respect of clerical and traffic staff and of skilled and unskilled labourers. Staff at Shannon were given an eleven shilling (55p) transport allowance per week, but no meal allowance and no reimbursement for board and lodging except in the case of 'passenger service girls'. In the same month a labour consultant, D. O'Sullivan, was appointed to the three air companies and simultaneously to Irish Shipping. There was a brief maintenance strike in the following year, and in June the Irish Airline Pilots' Association was threatening strike action over the long-delayed superannuation scheme. In the absence of a Government commitment, Niall Weldon had been involved in the setting up of pre-superannuation funds for clerical and manipulative staff, radio officers and for pilots, but this latter key group took matters into their own hands and declared a one-day strike on 21 July 1949. A deputation of the entire Board immediately resolved to seek a meeting with the Minister for Finance. It was agreed that the striking pilots would forfeit a day's pay and that sixteen who had lost a rest day would receive payment in lieu. It was also resolved that in the event of further strikes, token or otherwise, where the strike was declared by a recognised union or staff association, the management would not counter it by declaring a lockout. The Board took cognizance of the Labour Court recommendation in respect of the pilots' claim for improved rates of pay and for a superannuation scheme. The Chairman and General Manager called a special meeting with the union and staff association representatives, as a result of which the principles of a superannuation scheme were agreed and an interim provident fund set up. Management was given wide authority to negotiate up to a limit of £50,000 as a contribution towards past service benefits. With this decision Aer Lingus became the first State enterprise to establish a funded pension scheme. One consequence of the superannuation arrangements was that staff now felt that they enjoyed greater security of employment.

Michael Dargan had joined Aer Lingus as personnel officer from a civil service background in 1946, becoming Staff and Services Controller — later

Manager — in 1947. He imposed his own structures and philosophy on the industrial relations area of the company and, in the opinion of Niall Weldon, made a major contribution to the generally harmonious relationship which prevailed in the airline's industrial negotiations for many years. 'He always said in disputes that the two sides were wrong.' Following Dargan's appointment as Assistant General Manager-Administration in 1958 he was succeeded as Personnel Manager by Eamon Murray.

The company's relations with trade unions and staff associations had continued to be harmonious, announced the 1955 annual report: 'In a world beset by discontents and unrest Aer Lingus has been fortunate in avoiding interruption of its business from these causes.' The report painted, for obvious reasons, a somewhat flattering picture. Difficulties with the pilots continued; air hostesses, recently unionised, demanded an increase ('The £450 maximum to be conceded only if found necessary under pressure', the Board agreed). Nuala Doyle was the victim of a new regulation banning hostesses with more than seven years' experience from further flying: following extensive newspaper publicity it was rescinded. As the decade neared its end the pilots again challenged the airline over what they claimed was non-adherence to seniority in selection for transatlantic training and served strike notice. A special Board meeting on industrial relations was informed on 10 October 1959 that the company would be unable to meet the latest union claims even in scaled-down form. The pilot question was settled amicably, but the Government told the airline that it was not prepared to subsidise it with either capital or revenue to meet wage increases. A limited move towards a 'union shop' was taken in February 1960 with an agreement in respect of clerical grades up to and including Clerk III.

'The number of bad managers in the period 1946-47-48 was very high,' Arthur Walls recalled: 'and Aer Lingus was frequently criticised for employing people who were either lazy or incompetent or had drink problems or anything. The reason was a very simple one: if you had to set up an airline at that time the only people you could hope to get were people who had been in the armed forces — there was no civil aviation. The talents required to be a squadron leader were very different from the talents required to manage a budget or handle union problems.' Michael Dargan was quick to recognise both the challenge and the opportunity. 'As the pace of our growth and recruitment were so high, I informed the heads of universities — Trinity, UCD, UCC and UCG — that I could foresee rapid management advancement coming for young people — men and women — of high ability, and I asked them if they would each communicate informally to me a group — say ten — of their outstanding students for selection for management trainee positions. The universities looked upon this as an unusual approach at that time.' Jobs were eventually offered on this basis to, amongst others, Garret

FitzGerald, Gerald Giltrap, Gerald Draper and Arthur Walls. Giltrap was subsequently, after a distinguished Aer Lingus career, to become Secretary of Trinity College whilst Draper rose to high rank in British Airways. Walls, a graduate engineer, found that the licensed engineers at first resented him, but Dargan's initiative was an overall success. 'At the same time', he said, 'we took extra care to give equally competitive opportunities to our own staff who showed ability on the job, whatever their educational background. So loaders on the ramp worked their way to become effective managers, as did learners on the administrative side taken on at sixteen years of age. Engineers who opted for a change became sales superintendents.' One of these was Walls. 'When the job came up for Assistant Sales Manager I applied for it and got it,' he recalled: 'though I didn't know one end of a ticket from the other. In those days sales consisted of four or five people who went around, chatted up customers and bought them pink gins. Donal Brennan, in charge of Paris, was known as a Commercial Representative — you would never use such a vulgar word as "salesman".' Walls was to become successively General Sales Manager, Assistant General Manager-Technical, Deputy General Manager and General Manager before leaving the airline to take up an appointment with Ryan's Tourist Holdings.

Many others who were to hold senior management positions joined at this period. James Moran came in 1946 from Kennedy Crowley as Chief Accountant — a man, in the recollection of Brian Skelly who joined in 1946, of the old school 'who struck fear into the hearts of all those who worked for him. He was a perfectionist, and spent a lot of time with trivial matters, such as whether lines were straight or weren't straight on forms. . . . ' He had been associated with the Electricity Supply Board which was then operating the first punch-card system in Ireland, and brought this new knowledge and expertise to the airline. Alf Donoghue also joined from Kennedy Crowley in 1948 as an accountant after experience with Irish Steel Holdings. He was to be Moran's deputy for many years, eventually succeeding as Financial Controller. Despite personality clashes, he shared Moran's insistence on perfection and precision: the old ways were slow to change. 'In those days', recalled Louis Slater, 'you would start preparing your draft of the annual accounts and you would produce thirty different versions. Eventually when you came to number thirty there was very little difference between it and number one.'

Louis Slater joined the finance department in 1947 at a salary of £4 a week — 'my first job was writing up the nominal ledger for Aer Rianta, because the two were together.' He recalled a degree of friction between James Moran and the other managers — Dargan, Kelly-Rogers and Stuart Shaw. 'He couldn't quite understand the *laisser-faire* attitude of people on the technical side whose business was to fly aeroplanes . . . the idea that if you wanted spare parts you rang up somebody and got them shipped over without an order was anathema.' Slater was to become Internal Auditor, Revenue Accountant and subsequently Assistant Chief Executive–Finance. 'I would regard myself,' he said in 1985, 'as being not only a finance man but an airline professional. The finance function in an airline is quite different from the same thing anywhere else, because it is so highly specialised. You're dealing with airline economics, which tends to be a volatile subject. We relate internationally with the world wide banking community. We are in the true sense an Irish international company.'

James Moran was a Kerryman, a politically-committed man who had been on hunger strike during the Civil War period. One of the strengths of Aer Lingus at that period, in the subsequent view of David Kennedy, was the diversity of background from which many of the important figures were drawn. A group of army men, which included Colonel Delamere, Colonel Micheal Hogan — a close friend of Kevin O'Higgins — Major Rooney, Donal Brennan and Seamus Kelly, later *Quidnunc* of *The Irish Times*, brought a concept of discipline and organisation which stood the non-flying area in good stead. J. T. (Jimmy) Ó Briain, on the other hand, joined in 1946 following internment in the Curragh during the Emergency. A man of strong nationalist and socialist convictions, he still found himself able to mix well enough with the other tradition as represented by Stuart Shaw, and rose to become Commercial Planning Manager and Manager–International Affairs. J. R. Leonard became Sales Manager in June 1947, Paget McCormack Chief Engineer. G. P. Dempsey, who had spent much time explaining that he was no discernible relation of the General Manager, joined in February 1954.

J. F. Dempsey had been appointed General Manager in August 1946. Eleven years later he was elected to the Board. He was, as one of his junior colleagues put it, 'God in our day'. On a more familiar level he was 'Uncle Jerry', and there were many stories of his avuncular concern for his staff and his uncanny ability to remember tiny but significant facts about individuals. He was a good chief executive, in Oliver Hone's view, because he was able to give him an impossible instruction whilst at the same time conveying the impression that he was conferring a favour. For many years he used to greet the crew of the last aircraft to arrive back at Dublin Airport on Christmas Eve, gathering the staff into informal groups in a hangar, in the restaurant or in other work areas to offer them his own personal account of the year's progress. This practice marked him out as a man of sentiment and sympathy as well as a shrewd financial operator, a wily tactician — particularly in his relations with Government interests — and a firm supporter of the international approach to civil aviation. This dated from his role in the Havana conference of 1945 and culminated in his election as president of IATA in 1962. Of the relationship between the State and its creation, the state-sponsored body, he said: 'I recognised that we were public servants, never recognised that we were civil servants. I recognised, of course, that in matters of major policy the Government would, as they did in the case of the Atlantic, say at the time stop that or do that or contract or develop, as the case may be. In that sort of broad sense the Government would operate through the civil service, but not in the particular ways of the day-to-day.' It was, he added, in his experience a situation that the civil service never accepted.

Whereas Dempsey's background and preoccupations would predispose him to distill theory from practice, Patrick Lynch, who became Chairman of the companies in 1954, approached the concept of his role from the standpoint of the academic economist. The dilemma involved in State control of an ostensibly independent body fascinated him, and in the first annual report produced in his term of office — that for 1955/56 — he included among the statistics and financial returns an *ex cathedra* statement on 'The Role of Aer Lingus as a Public Corporation in the Irish Economy'. He acknowledged the advantages of operating without undue interference but made the point that the rapid development of the public sector had left the fundamental questions largely unresolved: 'The efforts of a state-sponsored public utility to find a form and a structure in which, subject to public supervision, the flexible methods of private enterprise are employed can be defeated if its structure reproduces, perhaps to a heightened degree, the rigidities which are often ascribed to a Government department and which can be seen also in some large scale units of private monopoly. The Government Department, however, is directly responsible to the Oireachtas, and the private monopoly sooner or later becomes amenable to the pressures of public opinion. In the case of State enterprises it might be thought that even if these two controls are not always effective there still remain the criteria of the free market; but it is often not practicable to apply the criteria of the free market when in fact the free market in a particular field has been abolished or abridged. A public enterprise should be able to show that its pricing policies are not the result of arbitrary decisions . . . ' — a point that was to be well taken by subsequent critics of the Aer Lingus fare structure.

On the day-to-day level the responsibility of conducting the relationship between the Shareholder, as represented by the Minister for the time being, and the airline companies, lay with the Boards. 'Whilst the relationship has to be a warm one,' Michael Dargan commented, 'one recognises that each keeps his distance, so that the different responsibilities are clearly acknowledged. The Minister has his own needs and his own pressures: it is the task of the Boards, and particularly of the Chairman, to ensure that he gets no surprises.' The Minister should, he said, be alerted to possible developments well in advance, but at the same time the Board should take pains to ensure that he is not swamped with information. Dargan, who was himself to become

Chairman on 1 August 1980, carried over from his role of chief executive a high opinion of the quality and composition of the airline Boards and of their readiness to make decisions. More mistakes, he believed, were made by Boards who did not take authority than by those who did. Niall Weldon believed that Aer Lingus could consistently claim the best Board of any State company, pointing out that Patrick Lynch did not miss one meeting in his twenty-one years as Chairman. His commitment, in spite of his continuing academic responsibilities, was total and his relationship with his General Manager and his fellow Board members very close. Over the years long-serving members such as John Leydon, T. J. O'Driscoll, Conor Carrigan, J. J. O'Leary, Denis Herlihy and J. C. O'Connor had established, or were to establish, solid reputations in other spheres. Though there were undoubtedly some political appointments, the Board succeeded in preserving to a large extent the tradition of the individual approach exemplified in the person of Seán Ó hUadhaigh who, though having retired from the Chairmanship, was a serving member of the Boards of both Aer Lingus and Aer Rianta at the time of his death on 24 January 1959. At their meeting on 13 February his former colleagues recorded that 'he had, at great personal sacrifice, done more for Irish aviation than any other individual in the country'.

The winter of 1947 was the coldest in living memory. Garret FitzGerald began his service with Aer Lingus in a room in O'Connell Street, Dublin which fortunately boasted an electric heater and a telephone, but no other furniture whatsoever: the rapid expansion of the airline was putting very great pressure on available accommodation. By March 1956 four hundred people were housed in eight separate buildings in the city, rented piecemeal on an *ad hoc* basis. A city air terminal at Cathal Brugha Street, opened in 1946, quickly proved inadequate (baggage could be checked in here as well as at the airport) and the Government was asked to assist in securing a larger site. The response, particularly after the Coalition took office in 1954, was not overwhelming. The airport itself, operated by Aer Rianta but with an Aer Lingus Manager, Colonel W. P. Delamere, was largely occupied by the airline; the original terminal building had spawned a sub-growth of 'temporary' huts and other makeshift structures, occupied by hostesses, part of the accounts department and others, and was familiarly referred to as 'Nutt's Corner'. A timber passenger building, erected in 1958 by Aer Lingus at a cost of £12,000 for the Lourdes pilgrimage traffic, survived until 1980. A new cargo terminal, converted from an existing cargo hangar, was opened in 1958 to cater for this expanding area of business. But though working conditions were far from ideal, morale — in Niall Weldon's recollection — was high: 'You would almost pay to come to work.'

In May 1957 Garret FitzGerald was promoted from Assistant Commercial Manager-Planning to Commercial Research and Schedules Planning

Manager at a salary of £1,950, but without a car. It was the final step in a career which had its origins in his discovering an interest in air transport at the age of twelve. In Aer Lingus he began as assistant to P. J. Brennan, then Assistant Secretary, but succeeded in having himself transferred to sales, which department was at the time presided over by Ralph Leonard in rooms located above the Flowing Tide public house in Abbey Street, Dublin. 'My background', he confessed, 'was history and modern languages — it wasn't economics at all. I didn't know what economics was.' His interest was not so much in selling as planning. He toured Britain in 1948 and planned an ambitious route network but could not at the time interest the company in it. There was, he believed, a slowness to react on Irish Sea routes during the period of monopoly. FitzGerald devised the timetable layout which remained in use until the early 1980s and evolved the flight numbering system which was to last even longer. Scheduling at that time had to be done daily: 'In order to do a schedule you take your 17 aircraft, 100 air crew and 200 hostesses and allocate them for every day of the 180 days in the optimum way — which required considerable mental effort because there were no computers. You had to go right through 36 hours with no sleep or anything to retain all this.' Thekla Beere, subsequently Secretary of the Department of Transport and

Thekla Beere

AER LINGUS

Power, recalled his methods: 'He'd talk at such a pace that after he'd left we would all get together to make sure our recollections and notes were the same.' Neil Gleeson, who joined in 1952 and worked with the future Taoiseach, remembered him at that time as 'an extraordinarily intensive person who worked at a tremendous pace. He had an enormous capacity for figuring in his head. His written work was extremely scruffy, appallingly organised. He had very bad handwriting.' They both brought their work home to Milltown Avenue, where they lived close together. 'He had a great capacity for handling schedules. He found more than a little difficulty in communicating with his superiors at the time: he was always moving too fast. And his mind travelled even faster. It was quite an exciting business working with him.' When FitzGerald left on 30 September 1958 Brennan said of him: 'He has played a leading role in the commercial planning of the network and many innovations were adopted on his recommendation.'

Garrett FitzGerald was certainly the most prominent individual to experience both perspectives of Aer Lingus during its first fifty years. Commenting on this experience in 1985 he expressed a view that the problem of the responsibility for investment decisions had never been resolved and was perhaps unresolvable — this was before the Irish Shipping debacle sharpened his Government's attitude to its role in relation to state-sponsored bodies. There was also a need, he felt, for the State element where a national interest was at stake — an area which, for him, clearly included the national airline: 'I would be reluctant to see the whole Irish tourist industry at the mercy of private interests.' Still personally an air transport enthusiast, he wrote his last paper, on the overcapacity on the transatlantic routes, in 1972 for a conference in Trieste. 'We seem to need to rejuvenate the atmosphere in State companies', he suggested 'to get back to the atmosphere we had in Aer Lingus in the 1950s.'

'It is said that a lot of excitement has gone out of Aer Lingus,' said Niall Weldon in 1985: 'But the old excitements have been replaced by new ones. I have the same interest in my job today as I had 38 years ago.' In the 1960s these excitements were to be centred in the challenge of expansion and new technology in an era of soaring national confidence and prosperity.

8

Jets and Other Debts 1957–73

THE presidential election of 1959 which transferred Eamon de Valera from Leinster House to Áras an Uachtaráin marked the end of an era, not only politically but even more notably in the economic sphere. It may be argued whether the boom years of the 1960s were consequent upon or merely coincidental with the publication of *Economic Development* by T. K. Whitaker and others, but the seven fat years of Seán Lemass's government changed the structure and direction of Irish society more fundamentally than any period since independence. Lemass had waited a long time in the wings; and though he achieved much in the favourable climate of his eventual term as Taoiseach, many of his successes were built upon the groundwork laid during his long periods of tenure of the portfolio of Industry and Commerce. It was typical of the man, and expressive perhaps of his opinion of those following in his footsteps, that one of his first acts should be to hive off from his old Department a large section of its most important responsibilities. Aer Lingus found itself under the aegis of a new entity: the Department of Transport and Power. Its Minister was to be Erskine Childers who, on Irish Aviation Day 1936, was sailing from New York as secretary of the National Agricultural and Industrial Development Association on a voyage direct from Dublin on the *S. S. California* that marked a new, if shortlived, development in transatlantic travel.

The Minister lost little time in explaining the role of Transport and Power to the Dáil: 'The purpose of the Department is, first of all, to prepare legislation when it is required, to examine the demands for capital for future productive purposes and the promotion of various companies, to examine how capital already provided is being spent and whether or not it should be remunerated at any given stage in a company's operations, to examine the general policy of these companies in relation to the national economy as a whole, to see if they are contributing to the national economy, and to see if there are any elements in their operations which are hindering other companies or other interests.' Patrick McGilligan characterised the new Department's remit somewhat more succinctly as 'Jets and other debts'.

It was clear from the Minister's initial attitude that Transport and Power

AER LINGUS

Erskine Childers (centre) at the opening of the new Belfast office in Castle Street, 16 February 1967. Left to right (foreground) M. J. Dargan; Patrick Lynch; Brian Faulkner; J. F. Dempsey

was going to be no soft touch as far as the state-sponsored bodies were concerned. A further round in the great debate was signalled, and Patrick Lynch, now chairman of all three air companies following reorganisation, was not slow to respond. After the fall of the second Coalition in 1957 he had offered his resignation, to be told by Lemass: 'I'm not concerned about your politics, if you have any. I hope you have. Everyone should have political convictions.'

Lemass had taken the view that the operation of the airline was a matter for the Board and management and had not attempted to interfere, or encourage his Department to do so. Faced with a new dispensation and a possible alteration in this policy, Lynch moved to defend the airline's position. 'In my view', he wrote in the 1961 annual report, 'the first concern of the system as a public enterprise is to live within its means; then to expand output and sales, and by controlling costs, to improve earnings with a view to building reserves, thereby reducing its dependence on the State or other resources from fresh capital and new developments. By ensuring viability in the conduct of its business, a public enterprise can meet one of the most important of its obligations — the progressive reduction in the cost of its service to the community.' Having set forth the theory and suggested that the return on the nation's investment in the air companies ought not to be measured predominantly by the yardstick of cash dividends, Lynch became somewhat more specific and spelt out, in the year of its twenty-fifth anniversary, his assessment of the contribution of Aer Lingus to the economy as a whole: 'in the provision of an essential air service that is safe, efficient and economically priced; by the transport of tourists; by facilitating Irish economic development in establishing services to countries with which Ireland has increasing commercial relations and sometimes to countries where until the advent of the aeroplane Ireland had little direct trading; by providing good employment with security of tenure and satisfactory conditions for Irish men and women in Ireland and overseas; and by stimulating productive employment throughout the country in other industries.'

It was an impressive catalogue and one which was generally accepted, in this anniversary year, at its face value. The Dáil used the occasion of the debate on the Air Navigation and Transport Bill 1961 to pay its own tributes: 'I have never found any other airline to provide a superior service to that provided by Aer Lingus,' said James Dillon: 'The pilots of Aer Lingus seem to be able to bring down an aeroplane with less bumping than pilots of any other aeroplane on which I have travelled.' He could not, however, resist adding: 'I should not like to see Aer Lingus, which I believe has a great future, suffer because of the activities of its more profligate sister.' (The reference was, of course, to the new Aerlínte transatlantic service.) The codicil was not merely Dillon rhetoric: the operating surplus of Aer Lingus for the year ended 31 March 1961 was £276,838, the highest since the formation of the company; whereas Aerlínte, engaged in changing from hired piston-engine aircraft to its own jets, recorded an operating loss of £93,621 for the same period.

The revision of the Hiberno-British air agreement in 1957 had the expected effect of reducing growth on the airline's Irish Sea services which was not immediately compensated for by growth on the newly-opened continental routes via Manchester. 'Aer Lingus seems to be engaged in a more or less permanent obstacle race,' commented *The Irish Times* in its review of that year, and in 1960 the General Manager was attributing the slow development on the routes to mainland Europe to 'lack of basic support by way of a publicity campaign by Bord Fáilte . . . '. This question of the role of the airline in tourist promotion, clearly categorised by Lynch in his 1961 annual report, was one which had been and continued to be a source of some irritation between the two State bodies. In 1953 J. F. Dempsey had complained that the contribution of £1,000 a year offered by the tourist authorities towards the cost of the Aer Lingus office in Paris was insufficient, and recommended that it should be closed.

Premises in Paris — a basement and four storeys at 2 rue de Castiglione — had been acquired in 1946 and Michael Fitzgerald appointed Senior Representative, later District Manager. Fitzgerald, whom Patrick Lynch described as 'a very remarkable man', had served in the French army and married a daughter of the first French Minister to Ireland, who through her two brothers had close contacts with General de Gaulle. His position with Aer Lingus was only part time since he was attached to the Irish diplomatic mission in Paris as Commercial Counsellor. The Paris route had not been anything more than marginally successful, and the Board was fully in accord with their General Manager's view that the large office should be disposed of and future representation handled by Air France. The Government, however, made a direct request that the premises should be kept open, though offering nothing towards their upkeep. In 1955 Bord Fáilte agreed to pay 25 per cent of the running costs, but the relationship thereafter remained uneasy.

Donal Brennan, who had joined as a Traffic Officer from the army in 1945, went to Paris in February 1954 and took over as manager for France on the retirement of Michael Fitzgerald in 1956. A convinced Francophile, he moved in influential circles ('J'étais bien connu') and counted amongst his friends Dr Daniel Rops of the Académie Française, who had written extensively on Ireland. 'France was a very strange place to the Ireland of those days,' he recalled: 'You were trying to translate the France of Jean-Paul Sartre into the Dublin of John Charles McQuaid.' One Irishman who had little difficulty making the transition was the short-story writer Frank

A Lourdes pilgrimage flight

LENSMEN

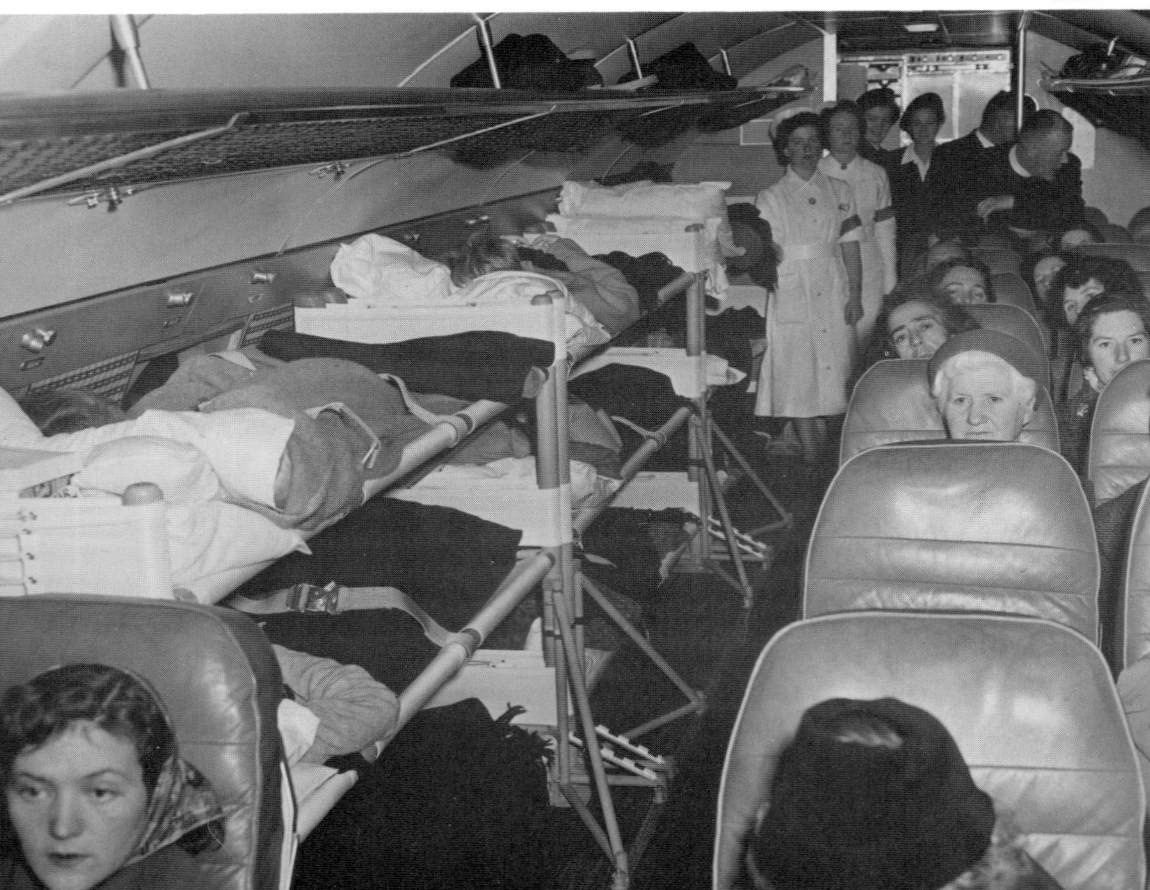

O'Connor who, on a solitary excursion to Paris in the summer of 1956, burst into the office in rue de Castiglione to fling his transport problems on the desk of Donal Brennan. The two men discovered a mutual interest in literature, particularly poetry, from which emerged a friendship which endured until O'Connor's death some ten years later.

The route from Dublin to Lourdes was introduced via Dinard on 14 May 1954, and re-routed via Rennes the following year. A service to Biarritz was inaugurated in 1955, followed on 10 June 1960 by a link with Cherbourg, providing — at £13 return — the lowest ever fare between Ireland and mainland Europe. This was seen as a major attempt to foster tourism in both directions, and large civic parties travelled in both directions *('Dans la capitale irlandaise la délégation cherbourgeoise a été magnifiquement reçue,'* wrote *Ouest France)*. The Lord Mayor of Dublin, P. A. Brady, TD, reciprocated the French visit and received an equally generous reception: '*Je suis devenue tellement français*,' he told the Cherbourg press, *'que j'ai été amené, ce matin, à dire "Madame" à ma femme.'* The tour was planned by Donal Brennan with the willing assistance of the municipalities of the Cherbourg district and the Abbé Goutière of the St Paul Institute in the town. 'Aer Lingus is indeed fortunate to have such an ambassador in France as M. Brennan,' concluded a French tourist director.

'It would be unforgivable if air transport failed to learn from the mistakes made when rail transport encumbered itself with an excess of branch lines,' warned the 1964 annual report, but some of the continental routes never really succeeded in avoiding that particular and, to the uncommitted public, rather appealing character. Dinard and Biarritz opened and closed, leaving — unlike the railway branch line — scarcely a trace. Rennes closed with the introduction of direct Lourdes services using Viscounts, only to reopen in 1961 via Jersey with Friendships. In the year 1962/63 it carried 518 passengers, a decrease of nineteen from the initial year of the renewed operation. Donal Brennan, who ran the Paris office with a small French staff, sent Anne de la Chevannerie O'Kelly de Gallagh to Brittany to oversee operations 'because she could be a little proud in the office over certain work she thought might be beneath her'. The city was served by a Friendship which landed in the rural solitude of Rennes-St Jacques military airport. Grass grew out of the cracks in the runway and the station manager also acted in the capacity of bus driver for the journey into town; his wife dispensed a warm welcome from the coffee stall whilst the few travellers waited for her husband to lock up the airport. Rennes was scarcely typical: but it did indicate an attempt on the part of the company to develop a traffic in areas where there was apparently no discernible pre-existing demand. It succumbed in 1970, to be reinstated for the second time in 1985 as a Commuter service from Cork.

When Desmond Fennell, the writer and critic, took up his position in Düsseldorf in 1958 as the first full-time sales representative in Germany he discovered that he was 'supposed to simply go and make both Ireland and Aer Lingus known — as usual in this sort of operation you were partly doing Bord Fáilte's job.' The Düsseldorf route operated over Manchester and continued to Copenhagen until the German authorities withdrew rights in April 1961, after which Copenhagen was served via Manchester direct. No one else at the time was very keen on operating from Manchester to the Continent said Norman Edwards, who in 1985 had been a public relations consultant to Aer Lingus in the north of England for twenty-eight years. The airline marketed its routes to the six continental destinations energetically 'and in fact did the groundwork and spadework until they became very viable indeed. This was a period when posters in Manchester carried messages from Aer Lingus saying 'Manchester is our second home', and 'Aer Lingus operate to more destinations from Manchester than any other airline.' The British Airways' policy of concentrating services on London-Heathrow rather than decentralising had deprived provincial airports of direct Continental services to a large extent, and the Aer Lingus routes were used intensively by British businessmen. At the time there were no duty-free facilities between Ireland and Britain, and Irish passengers were happy to avail of this courtesy as between Manchester and Dublin.

Desmond Fennell's experience in setting up the Düsseldorf office was probably not untypical of the pattern in several cities as the airline sought to establish its European presence. He had been a student in Germany and had

The Manchester message

AER LINGUS

just returned from a period in the Far East. 'The reason they appointed me was not that I knew anything about the airline business but that at the time people who knew German fluently were rather scarce.' After a few months' 'familiarisation' ('a great word at the time') he went to Düsseldorf with the task of finding both an office (on the Berliner Allee) and a secretary ('a German girl who turned out to be interested in Aer Lingus principally because she had a boyfriend in India and hoped that it might make it easier to get out to see him — which she ultimately managed to do'). He found the process of setting up the office 'very like what I believe it is like in the civil service: every step of the way you had to have somebody come out from headquarters to vet the office space, to look into the furniture, to transport out the furniture'. His territory was the whole of Germany, and he was principally expected to visit travel agents — five hundred to a thousand of them — for which purpose he was given a Volkswagen car. It was, he recalled, tedious work. 'It was difficult to explain why you should go to Ireland. It was regarded as rainy. . . . ' It was, however, Fennell discovered, a good place to be from. Heinrich Böll had recently published his *Irisches Tagebuch* and the German image of the country was that of a haven for the sensitive minority who wanted to get away from it all. Dublin didn't tell Desmond Fennell anything about the market he was working in — he was supposed to go and find out for himself. At the time all German advertising for airlines depicted well-dressed executives carrying briefcases: it was still considered chic to fly. Düsseldorf he discovered to be a wealthy, stylish city ('Tochter Europas', as it described itself), a city of fashion, great arrogance and confidence. The Aer Lingus representative was supposed to model himself accordingly, which posed for Fennell some personal dilemmas. But he looked back with enthusiasm on his eleven-month experience of the airline: 'I was proud to belong to it. I discovered what morale in a firm means. Everybody cared; everybody expected the highest standard. You had the feeling of belonging to an élite group.'

The Continental network acquired a further panoply of new routes with the opening, after years of frustration, of Cork airport on 16 October 1961. For a time the small airfield at Farmer's Cross had been considered in terms of development, but the site was too restricted. It was not until 1952 that the Minister for Industry and Commerce informed the Dáil that Cork was to be provided with a full-scale civil airport, and in 1954 it was announced that a site had been selected at Ballygarvan. The necessary area was finally acquired by the Land Commission in 1957 and construction involved the excavation of some million cubic feet of earth. The site, approximately eight kilometres south of the city, though in an elevated position with good approach clearance, proved to have an indifferent weather record and was frequently closed by fog — it was to become increasingly evident that the wrong choice had been made. The first aircraft to touch down, at 09.27 on 12 October 1961, was Aer Lingus Friendship EI-AKG *Fiachra* on a proving flight. Following the official opening, which was conducted in unpleasant weather ('All the staff worked the whole night through to have things ready for the next day,' said Thekla Beere) an Aer Lingus Viscount arrived carrying Seán Lemass and Dublin's Lord Mayor, Robert Briscoe. Aer Lingus, which had opened a Cork office in Patrick Street in 1955, immediately inaugurated routes to Dublin, London, Bristol and Cardiff, adding Cork-Paris on 20 October, Cork-Birmingham on 6 April 1961, Cork-Lourdes-Barcelona on 5 May and Cork-Jersey the following month.

Cork's troubles began almost immediately — troubles with which Aer Lingus was, of necessity, intimately associated. In the previous May, CIE had objected to the proposed Dublin-Cork fare on the grounds that it competed unfairly with the rail service. Negotiations followed, but in December the Minister wrote to the airline directing it to set its fare at a level which would 'remove the competitive element of the service vis-à-vis the surface transport'. The Board agreed that the company had no option but to accept the Minister's direction but wished it to be recorded that the fare did not represent its decision. In March 1963 the Minister said that he would exercise his discretion to appoint other operators besides Aer Lingus for internal services, the airline replying that it was prepared to operate internal routes when it appeared that these would be remunerative. 'From the beginning we did not hold ourselves out to be providing a service between Dublin and Cork,' argued J. F. Dempsey in June 1963. As the continental route system was consolidated (1962/63, the first full year of the Cork services had been 'somewhat disappointing') the need became apparent to provide shorthaul jets to replace the turboprop Viscounts and Friendships and keep pace with competitors. In December 1961 the Board decided to seek Government permission to buy three Sud-Aviation Caravelle VIRs for delivery in 1963-65. A meeting with the Minister took place on 1 February 1962, at which the airline was informed that the Government did not consider itself to be in a position to provide equity capital for the purchase of the aircraft whilst the company could not provide a direct return on such capital by way of dividend. The Minister had in the previous month made clear his view that State capital invested in the air companies should be remunerated directly 'to an ever growing degree'. The General Manager was left with no choice but to seek outside finance, and early in March informed the Ministers for Finance and Transport and Power that the Ulster Bank was prepared to provide the requirement — at a price. The proposed loan was £3.25 million, the interest on which would be met from operating surpluses and the repayment of which would commence in 1964/65 and be spread over a period of four years. However the repayment would have to be financed from State sources.

On 8 March 1962 Thekla Beere wrote to J. F. Dempsey informing him that the Minister for Finance considered that the purchase of Caravelles was not justifiable on economic grounds and that he was not prepared to commit Exchequer resources to such a purchase. She proceeded to outline the reasons for the refusal, as conveyed to her own Department, in some detail. Since this set in train a serious confrontation between the airline and its Shareholder which raised again the whole question of responsibility and control, it is relevant to quote it *in extenso:*

(i) The proposed investment of £5 million in Caravelles is large, both absolutely and in relation to the company's issued share capital. It compares with £7 million invested in the transatlantic jet service on a route where, in the year 1960/61, passenger revenue amounted to £2.12 million. By contrast, the passenger revenue during the same period from Aer Lingus's established continental routes was only £.85 million. The present issued share capital of Aer Lingus is £3.3 million. The purchase of Caravelles, even after the absorption of the available depreciation reserves, would be equivalent to doubling the share capital.

(ii) As regards the probable effect of the increased size and operating costs of the Caravelles on the substantial contribution to the company's overheads at present made by the continental routes, the Minister for Finance has noted in the Aer Lingus report for the year ended 31st March 1960, that the greater size of the new aircraft which by that time had been purchased by Aer Lingus had 'led to a temporary fall in load factors and the benefits of the lower unit costs can only be fully achieved as load factors rise up to and above their earlier levels'. The purchase of Caravelles might well again depress substantially load factors, before the full benefit of the lower unit costs has been reaped.

(iii) ... the airline industry everywhere has been suffering losses due to excess capacity. Unless financial considerations are to be entirely discarded, it would seem highly inprudent for Aer Lingus to increase its capacity substantially by three 86-seater aircraft. Unless encroachments by their competitors or potential competitors were more than matched by increased traffic, it is possible that, even with the existing fleet, load factors might fall. Furthermore, as Aer Lingus's continental traffic is largely seasonal, the danger of excess capacity (in the expensive form of jet aircraft) is to be particularly avoided.

(iv) The assumption underlying the proposal to provide jets for continental routes appears to be that these routes must be maintained at all costs. The Minister for Finance is not aware that the company's continental services are economic individually or even globally. Nor is it even clear that they are as essential as feeders of traffic to the transatlantic service as the routes linking Ireland and Britain. Finally, in so far as competition might be expected from other countries or on direct lines to this country, the Minister for Finance would not regard such an eventuality as necessarily undesirable since the operators concerned would then have an interest in the number of their own tourists coming here and would, of necessity, have to resort to promotional activities to make the routes pay'.

The strong objections of the Minister for Finance, Thekla Beere's letter concluded, were based both on the very doubtful economic merits of the proposal and on the wider financial considerations. 'Up to now, virtually all of Aer Lingus's equity capital has been provided by the State, and it remains a totally unremunerative investment. The Minister for Finance considers that the position should have been reached by now where fleet additions, etc. are not warranted unless Aer Lingus can finance them through additional earnings and/or economies.'

The letter was, in effect, seeking to direct the airline not only on financial matters but on policy decisions involving its fleet planning and day-to-day operations. A special joint meeting of the Boards of Aer Rianta and Aer Lingus on 12 March expressed itself concerned as to the serious issues of principle raised and to the relative functions of the two Ministers concerned. In a speech to the Institute of Public Administration three years previously Seán Lemass, dealing with the role of state-sponsored bodies, had stated quite clearly that 'in all cases the initiation and shaping of policy in the broadest sense is the prerogative of the Government. The method and degree of Government control over these boards and companies is, however, to some extent still a matter of debate and controversy.' He continued: 'The relationship between State Boards and the Ministers who are responsible to the Dáil for their operations is not always very precisely defined. . . . The Minister's main instrument is criticism. . . . As a general guiding rule the relations between the Minister and the Board should not be too cordial.' The reaction by Finance to the Caravelle proposal clearly went beyond criticism and, it would appear, policy in its broadest sense. The deadline for the signature of the contract with Sud-Aviation was 30 March. The joint Board meeting authorised the General Manager to continue to attempt to secure a favourable decision from Transport and Power before that date.

In the correspondence that ensued J. F. Dempsey set out to counter in detail the ministerial assessment, claiming that the size of the investment in relation to the issued share capital of the company was an inexorable feature of airline finance which arose every time new equipment had to be purchased; that the quotation from the 1960 report had been taken out of context; that excess capacity was a condition that Aer Lingus had hitherto successfully avoided; and that all the airline's traffic was seasonal, not only the continental routes. On the question of overcapacity he said: 'It is most unfair to argue from the airline industry to a particular proposal made by a company which is not involved in the industry's capacity problems.' Dempsey was particularly critical of the Minister's view that competition on continental routes would be of benefit to tourism — an argument that was to appear again in relation to competition on the Atlantic: 'There appears to be some very fallacious reasoning in regard to the effect on tourism through the efforts of foreign operators who may choose to take up their rights to operate direct lines from the continent to this country. Foreign competitors will not promote traffic to Ireland. They will leave that to us. But in Ireland they will do for their countries what we do in their countries for Ireland. To the extent that they are successful here a tendency to worsen our balance of payments position will develop.'

The concluding argument, spelt out in great detail, related to the proposed financing. Dempsey suggested that Aer Lingus had to date provided for capital expenditure, out of its own resources, nearly as much as the State had provided by way of equity capital; that it was unrealistic to expect the cost of modern and expensive equipment such as jet aircraft to be met exclusively from the company's resources; and that the Aer Lingus contribution to employment, tourism and the economy in general should be taken into account: 'because the extent of State investment and its direct remuneration are not the only factors by which the adequacy of the company's contribution to the national economy may reasonably be judged'.

The chain of communication was, to say the least, cumbersome: Dempsey had in the first instance to convince the Minister for Transport and Power, Erskine Childers, sufficiently to persuade him to reopen the case with the Minister for Finance, Dr James Ryan. In this instance he was unsuccessful. But the door was not completely closed. 'The Minister does not dispute that when it is necessary to replace the present fleet Aer Lingus will have to purchase jets,' Thekla Beere wrote on 20 March: 'In these circumstances, should the Company so desire, he will be prepared to re-examine the proposals later in the year when traffic figures on the Company's Continental routes for the Summer period are available, with a view to re-opening the matter with the Minister for Finance should he consider such a course to be justified. For this purpose it will be necessary to have detailed operating accounts for each of the routes involved.'

The airline had to be content with that, though J. F. Dempsey protested that the commercial value of a route or group of routes could not be correctly assessed by taking them in isolation: 'In a short-haul operation the services are closely integrated and the relative importance of individual routes is not determinable solely by the size of their contribution to the economy of the business as a whole expressed in the restricted terms of a profit and loss account.' Even that fell on deaf ears. 'I am glad to see that returns from the

Continental routes, showing revenue and costs, can be furnished by your Company in due course,' wrote Thekla Beere on 28 March. Later airline opinion agreed that Finance were right to refuse the Caravelles. In the view of G. P. Dempsey, who was Chief Accountant at the time, the refusal resulted in the airline being enabled to purchase a newer generation of jet aircraft which had not been available when the Caravelle decision was taken: on 6 December 1962 it was decided to place an order for four 74-seat BAC 1-11s. The Government again asked for an analysis of each route on which it was proposed to utilise the new aircraft, but relented and agreed to accept estimates on a regional basis.

The Caravelle episode, though its outcome could not, in hindsight, be said to have seriously disadvantaged the airline in respect of its planning and development, acted as a sharp reminder as to who was calling the tune. D. Ó Riordáin served in his time both as a civil servant with responsibility to Aer Lingus (Secretary of Transport and Power from 1945 to 1948) and subsequently as a member of the airline Board (from 1976–80). 'My own line', he

BAC 1-11 'St Mel' at Cork Airport

ROBERT ALLEN

said, 'was to make it known to all the companies I dealt with that if people outside nobbled the Minister on a proposition before the Department was aware and had an opportunity to brief him, then I personally would be opposed to that proposition no matter what its merits were ... I felt myself that a certain standoff in relations with a State body was a good one. Aer Lingus have always credited me with being a great friend of the company but up to the time I was on the Board I wasn't necessarily flattered by that description because that wasn't my role.' 'We left the companies alone as much as possible,' another Department Secretary, Thekla Beere, asserted, 'unless they wanted to go into something that was very expensive. Aer Lingus were very proud of their independence and didn't like interference. And naturally were very annoyed when they couldn't spend money they hadn't got.' 'As Chairman I found my position as a sort of buffer', said Patrick Lynch, 'to protect the management of the airline and guarantee its independence.'

The role of the Minister in the Byzantine relationship was spelt out in his characteristically didactic manner by Erskine Childers in the Dáil in November 1966. He was obliged once again, he said, to state very briefly (the latter adverb proving to be somewhat optimistic) his relations with State companies and to indicate the nature of his functions. The catalogue is interesting as an indication of how a deeply conscientious minister saw his function, a major element of which was his involvement with the air companies: 'I examine with the Boards of the companies, through my officials, the annual accounts of all the companies and all matters that seem to me to be of interest or significance in connection with the accounts. I sanction in most cases the expenditure of capital. I give sanction to that expenditure in relation to what I consider to be the Government's policy in relation to each State company and that means a very definite form of specific control of the general policy of each State company. I discuss at regular intervals with every State company all the important aspects of its administration ... I bring to the Dáil and Seanad at frequent intervals Bills for the enlargement of the capital of State companies and for other purposes ... I deal with every complaint of faulty services that comes to my Department and if faults are repetitive I discuss them with the Chairman and the General Manager or with the Board as a whole. I incidentally meet the chairmen, managing directors and boards of the companies regularly ... I get a detailed statistical picture of every company in all its main activities ... I ask for comparative productivity estimates, when these are possible, in order to compare the efficiency of one or other of our State companies with those of a corresponding character and size outside the country or with private enterprise within the country. I might add that it is not always possible because such an examination has a limited value ... I ask for long-term estimates or production or achievement of one kind or another ... I regularly inspect the premises of all State companies. I ask for information from the management of companies regarding their industrial relations . . . I also have always received from the State companies general statements of their wage levels and fringe benefits . . . I need hardly say that all that takes a great deal of time. . . . '

It was perhaps fortunate for the State companies that temporal exigencies restricted much of this involvement to the area of pious aspiration.

Whether or not the Caravelles would have proved themselves in service, there were few doubts about the performance of another new aircraft, the ATL-98 Carvair, two of which the airline acquired in February 1963. 'A pain in the neck from the word go,' was Bill Scott's memory of them, 'A bloody awful aeroplane — it really was'. The aircraft, EI-AMP *St Albert* and EI-AMR *St Jarlath,* had been ordered as a response to a licence granted by the British authority to Channel Airways to operate a car ferry service. The application had been supported in London by Bord Fáilte. The Carvairs were introduced on routes between Dublin and Liverpool, Bristol and Cherbourg and between Cork and Bristol, but proved themselves very uneconomic and very poor performers, with, according to Dick White, a very high unreliability of engines. They were still giving trouble in 1966 when, with the British Rail sea ferry on the horizon, they were withdrawn. Not surprisingly they remained unsold until 1968. In 1965, the year in which the first of the short-haul BAC 1-11 jets was delivered, it had been decided to sell the Friendship fleet and standardise on Viscounts to cater for traffic expansion particularly in the developing sun charter business. Nine Viscount V-803s were bought from KLM.

In that year the General Manager asked the Board for clearance to acquire two Boeing 737s for delivery in 1968 or 1969. The decision not to buy additional 1-11s arose from the inability of the manufacturers to produce a 95-seater model on time and the airline's need for a larger aircraft for the London route. Various options were studied, with the DC9 a serious possibility, but the B737 emerged as a clear winner. With 113 seats it was much roomier than the 1-11 and had the same fuselage cross-section as the B707. A further advantage was that a QC (quick change) version was available, enabling it to be employed as an all-passenger aircraft at peak times and to be converted to a freight configuration when cargo loads so demanded.

By the mid-1960s it had become clear that the entire fleet would have to be replaced with the faster jets if Aer Lingus was to remain a modern, competitive airline. Despite high capital costs an all-jet fleet would prove more economic in operation. BEA, the main competitor, was re-equipping with Tridents, but Aer Lingus was very happy in its choice of the B737. Following the decision to buy two for the London route the Board decided to replace the Viscounts and the 1-11s with the same aircraft, thus standardising the entire fleet on Boeing. In opting for the 737 the airline was ten years ahead of Air France and British

Airways, and it was to establish itself as one of the most successful short-haul aircraft ever built. 'We can divide the Aer Lingus half-century', said Antoin Daltún of Economic Planning, 'into three periods in each of which an outstandingly successful type dominated: DC3s in the piston period, Viscounts in the turboprop era, and the B737 dominating the jet era through to the late 1980s.'

On 18 April 1968 the General Manager was authorised by the Board to seek the Minister's approval for the purchase of seven B737s, of which four were to be the QC version. The intention to dispose of the 1-11s could not, in the event, be fulfilled. Their resale value dropped substantially as a consequence both of the success of the competitive short-haul jets and as a result of a devaluation of sterling which also had the effect of increasing the price of the B737 by 17 per cent. The 1-11s were retained and were to survive as a valuable component of the Aer Lingus fleet into the 1970s and beyond.

Relationships with BEA had been witnessing a steady deterioration following the revision of the Bilateral Agreement in 1956. In 1961 the British complained of what they saw as a serious imbalance between the two companies on the Irish Sea routes, though they were taking the major share of traffic increases. BEA had been handling Aer Lingus traffic at London since the resumption of services after the war, but the level of charges prompted Aer Lingus in 1962 to study alternative arrangements and to undertake its own handling from April 1963. Later that year the Chairman, Patrick Lynch, discussed with Lord Douglas the proposition that BEA should withdraw its remaining small holding from Aer Lingus. Lord Douglas agreed to the selling of the BEA shares to Aer Lingus at par; and he himself retired from the chairmanship of BEA on 31 March 1964. 'I take this opportunity of expressing my appreciation to him personally and to BEA for their valuable assistance to Aer Lingus,' wrote Patrick Lynch: 'Lord Douglas has a long association and close links with Ireland and many friends here.' The two companies continued to operate several pool routes, but the 'special relationship' was effectively at an end. A meeting with BEA was held in April 1966 to consider what was felt to be a deterioration in the association: the Belgians were withdrawing Aer Lingus rights between Manchester and Brussels following the entry of the British airline onto that route, and there was discontent with BEA over pool payments. The Aer Lingus position was that 'there were certain areas of commercial agreements where each company had to protect its own position and that scope for a special relationship should be built up in major areas such as traffic rights', and in the context of the free trade agreements between Ireland and Britain which were at that time close to formalisation. 'It was accepted', the Aer Lingus representatives at the meeting reported, 'that the non-participation of BEA in the capital of the company and the absence of any board representation on a mutual basis or otherwise necessarily changed the original basis for a special relationship... but that other circumstances now made it sensible for the two parties to get together in their mutual interest and to work as closely as possible on common problems'.

The Government had taken the opportunity presented by the withdrawal of BEA to bring in legislation (The Air Companies Bill 1965) aimed at re-organisation both financially and structurally. The Minister, Erskine Childers, described it as 'a tidying up process', and its most significant implication lay in the change it was to effect in the role of Aer Rianta, which was relieved of its functions as the holding company of Aer Lingus and Aerlínte so that the State investment in these companies could be held directly by the Minister for Finance. Both had reached a stage of development, said Childers, where their operation as independent companies, freed from the complexities inherent in their existing status as subsidiaries of Aer Rianta, was fully justified. There had been a good deal of confusion in the public mind, and a tendency to assume that the capital invested in the air companies was double the real amount because the same figures appeared in the Aer Rianta accounts and again in the Aer Lingus accounts. The role of Aer Rianta would henceforward be effectively confined to the management of the airports: it was clearly bad that this should be done 'by a company so closely identified with a particular operating company', said the Minister. This decision set in train the separate development of Aer Rianta along lines which were in some cases to lead to a conflict of interests with its former subsidiary.

The Bill incorporated into one measure all the relevant legislation relating to the control and financing of the air companies as embodied in previous Acts and, whilst it increased Aerlínte capital to £13 million, it made no provision for further share capital contributions from the Exchequer to either company. Both, in the Government's view, had reached a position in which they could reasonably be expected to meet their capital requirements either direct from their own resources or by borrowings serviced from those resources. Repayable advances of up to £1 million would, however, be available on terms to be set by the Minister for Finance. The Bill also introduced uniform conditions relating to the appointment of directors to apply to all three boards. The measures were welcomed by both sides of the House: 'We cannot be sufficiently proud, in words at any rate, of our air services, from whatever aspect we view them,' said Fine Gael Deputy Patrick Lindsay: 'they are extremely good, comfortable and safe.' Two years later amending legislation was brought forward to guarantee borrowings by Aerlínte consequent upon a decision to buy Boeing 747s. The Dáil was again in a congratulatory and self-congratulatory mood, and the Minister, Erskine Childers, permitted himself an optimistic forecast of the future, in which the B747s would rapidly give way to supersonic transport. 'The next phase after that will not be, I believe, until 1985 or 1990,' he concluded more cautiously, 'when we shall have the hypersonic plane which will fly at such speeds that it will take people from Shannon to New York in the space of a quarter of an hour'.

A vision of a boundless new world. But the momentum of the 'Swinging Sixties' was fast dissipating: in Ireland it was brought to a sudden and shocking stasis by marchers and demonstrators, bullets and batons, on the streets of Burntollet, Derry and Belfast. The old, sad euphemism of the 'Troubles' was dusted off again in an attempt to sidestep the brutal reality of civil strife. Aer Lingus had operated to Belfast and onwards to Glasgow and Liverpool for a period in 1947–48 and had opened its office in the city in 1960. In January 1968 it inaugurated a Belfast–Shannon–New York service which was warmly welcomed in Northern Ireland. Bill Yeoman, who worked with the Aer Lingus subsidiary, Enterprise Travel, in Belfast some ten years after the outbreak of the 'Troubles', still found a strong feeling of goodwill towards the airline from both sides of the community. He concluded that Aer Lingus was regarded in something of the same light as the Irish rugby team — uncontroversially Irish: 'They don't really see the direct Government connection.' Thekla Beere, on the other hand, discovered that the Northern ministers found her difficult to come to terms with: 'They couldn't understand how a Protestant woman got my job. They were always asking had I been gun-running or something.'

When the confrontation erupted, the airline was immediately affected in a number of ways. In August 1969 the Boards were informed that the unrest had damaged business system-wide, and that five of their senior press relations people had been recruited to the Government Press Office. Michael Dargan, who had become General Manager on 1 April 1967 in succession to J. F. Dempsey, had just been appointed to the Board. The Government decision, he told his colleagues, 'had been taken without consultation with us and the resulting publicity had been bad for us'. It had been possible to avert the call-up of fifty pilots on the Army reserve, but an equal number of other staff had been called to active duty. Loaders refused to handle the importation of British newspapers. Against this unpromising background, Aer Lingus was continuing discussions aimed at securing a financial stake in Air Ulster, a struggling Northern-based airline, both as a means of protecting its own interests and of particpating in the development of new routes out of Belfast and possibly Derry. As a project it did not appear to stand much chance of success, since the financial difficulties were formidable and the available traffic rights, from the Aer Lingus point of view, were of limited value. There were also suggestions of weak management, and in late 1970 an Aer Lingus executive was seconded to the embryo organisation for a period of a month. Negotiations had been based on the lease by Aer Lingus to Air Ulster of a Viscount for a period of three months with the possibility of an extension, though the latter were pressing for a capital investment of £200,000 represented by two Viscounts; but the reports of the seconded executive were such that the Board felt it had no option but to dissociate itself completely from the project in the form it had been presented.

Aer Lingus's interest in Northern Ireland stemmed not only from its strongly held belief that it should seek to serve the whole of Ireland but, on a severely practical level, from the evident fact that the small population base represented by the Republic afforded little scope for development. These considerations remained valid, as G. P. Dempsey confirmed in 1985: 'We had a hell of a problem in air transport because our base was so small. We looked not only at Northern Ireland but also at the UK and have continued so to look.' Following the collapse of the Air Ulster scheme in 1970 it was agreed that it was still in the interests of Aer Lingus to pursue the idea, and discussions commenced with a group of Northern businessmen under the chairmanship of Dr. H. Corscadden of the Ulster Bank. Negotiations progressed to the point where a committee of five was set up, consisting of three Northern businessmen; A. J. Walls, Deputy General Manager; G. P. Dempsey, Assistant General Manager–Finance of Aer Lingus with Brendan Casey, Aer Lingus Cargo Manager, as Chief Executive Designate. The outcome was agreement in principle that private business interests in Northern Ireland would subscribe capital to a joint company in which Aer Lingus would have an interest. 'We didn't think Aer Lingus should control the airline,' said G. P. Dempsey, 'but hold a minority stake and manage it. It was decided to raise the matter with Brian Faulkner, who became Prime Minister of Northern Ireland on 23 March 1971. Preparations for launching Northern Ireland Air Services continued through 1970, but the necessary Northern government support was not forthcoming, either directly or indirectly. It is hard to see the reluctance as other than political. Events in the North were moving towards crisis. The reintroduction by Faulkner of internment without trial on 9 August 1971 was followed by the events of Bloody Sunday in Derry on 30 January 1972 and the burning of the British Embassy in Dublin. Aer Lingus estimated that this latter event cost the company the loss of a handling contract with British Midland at London Heathrow and BOAC training operations at Shannon.

There was also an Aer Lingus involvement in 1970 in what was to become known as the Arms Affair. On 6 May Charles J. Haughey, Minister for Finance, and Neil Blaney, Minister for Agriculture, were dismissed by the Taoiseach, Jack Lynch, and arrested on charges of illegal importation of arms: Haughey was subsequently acquitted and Blaney discharged. On the previous 17 April the cargo department of Aer Lingus in Dublin had been approached by 'a Captain Kelly' with an enquiry regarding the transportation of arms from the Continent to Ireland. An earlier and similar enquiry had been made to the office in Frankfurt and refused, though subsequently and for reasons unexplained, clearance was given by the Department of Transport and Power to carry the arms. Brendan Casey, the Cargo Manager, decided that he would nevertheless not transport them without a signed document from the Minister or Secretary of either Transport and Power or Justice. The affair received no publicity at the time but attracted the attention of the Belfast and British press some three weeks later, which alleged that there had been new approaches to the Frankfurt office. The story was for a time given credence by Lufthansa, Aer Lingus handling agents in Germany, owing to a confusion of dates. A small consignment was in fact loaded by Lufthansa in contravention of a standing arrangement between the two companies, and reached Ireland on 27 May. After a good deal of nervous activity it was established that these were arms which had been sent to Vienna in 1968 by the Department of Defence for rectification and which were now being returned to the Director of Ordinance. 'They came in labelled GUNS,' Arthur Walls recalled. 'Just like the *Dandy.*' The whole situation was, in the circumstances, extremely delicate but the General Manager satisfied himself after extensive enquiries that no Aer Lingus staff member had been involved in any improper activities. A situation which could have been potentially very damaging for the airline had been averted, but it could not avoid the wider implications of the Northern disorders. 'We are doing everything possible to offset the significant effect on our business of the disturbances and unease in Northern Ireland,' the Chairman reported in March 1972: 'All business which depends on tourism either in the Republic or in Northern Ireland, or in our case in both, has felt very serious effect.'

Civil strife was, as it emerged, only a peculiarly Irish accretion to the difficulties that were besetting the airline industry worldwide: a wave of hijacking, bomb attacks and other acts of political violence had led to inordinate increases in security and insurance costs. In the case of Aer Lingus and Aerlínte special war risk insurance cost £500,000 in 1970/71 over and above the £800,000 increase in ordinary rates. A further specifically Irish problem was domestic inflation, which was beginning to climb above average European and United States rates, posing a severe problem for an airline which earned the bulk of its revenue abroad. Passenger numbers had fallen, and in the financial year 1971/72 the two companies incurred a combined net loss of £2,390,000 — the first for twelve years. Another loss, only marginally smaller, followed in the subsequent financial year. With little fundamental alleviation foreseen of the three besetting difficulties — the North Atlantic, domestic inflation and the Northern Ireland crisis — far-reaching measures were indicated. In 1968 the new General Manager, Michael Dargan, had recommended the legal merging of Aer Lingus and Aerlínte as a step towards rationalisation and economy. The Government agreed in principle in September 1971; also to a proposal to raise equity capital from private sources. In June 1973 the Board was told that the way was clear to a merger. Both proposals, however, continued to hang fire and had not been acted on as 1985 drew to a close. In January 1972 Dargan told his colleagues that talks had been taking place on a different type of merger — in this case with another airline. Quantas, Air New Zealand, Varig, South African and United (USA) had been involved in discussions on the concept of 'end-to-end' operation, particularly on a north-south axis. This idea, which was based on two airlines in different hemispheres agreeing to a connection of services at a suitable mid-point, was — and remained — of particular appeal to Aer Lingus. But, said Dargan, 'merging airlines in different countries was nearly impossible unless there was a broad political will'. The British, he told the Boards, had also been approached, but 'our value to BOAC would be in eliminating a nuisance to them'.

If these merger projects were at least temporarily stultified, another option — diversification into ancillary activities — was to prove more immediately practicable; in a climate of prevailing economic gloom as far as conventional airline operation was concerned, it was to provide the impetus for growth and development into the next two decades.

9

Rights and Might
1961–71

IN the autumn of 1961 there were 977 Aer Lingus staff, in Ireland and North America, directly dependent upon the success or failure of the transatlantic service. On 9 September Michael Dargan, then Assistant General Manager–Commercial, wrote to them concerning the request of the United States Ambassador to Ireland for negotiations on the subject of the right of American airlines to serve Dublin. As matters stood, he told them, three airlines — Pan American, TWA and Seaboard and Western — were licensed to fly into Ireland with full Fifth Freedom rights, which meant that they could pick up traffic at Shannon for any destination they served in Europe and beyond. Ireland, on the other hand, had one airline — Aerlínte — licensed to fly into the United States to serve Boston and New York, but with no rights to pick up traffic for onward destinations. Rights were also available to Chicago, but only via Montreal, a city which held out little prospect of economic traffic volumes for the Irish airline. Our airline also competed, he went on, not alone with the US carriers but with fifteen of the world's greatest airlines also holding Fifth Freedom rights at Shannon. Of these 'one US company this year found it convenient to serve Shannon with a limited frequency terminating service'.

The following day Dargan told an Aerlínte Board meeting that the granting of rights to operate into Dublin to any other transatlantic operator would have serious financial consequences for the airline. Management's examination of the position clearly indicated that there were no conceivable concessions from the US side that would compensate the company for giving up its exclusive position in relation to Dublin airport, which it enjoyed through the interchange arrangement with Aer Lingus.

This was the line that was to be held, with consistent tenacity, through a decade of confrontation with American airline interests backed by political pressures of varying intensity and the economic might of the most powerful economy on earth. If this presentation in David and Goliath terms seems simplistic, it constituted the ground upon which Aer Lingus, supported with fluctuating conviction by the Government, chose to fight. The actual line of battle was drawn at Shannon Airport, which had been designated Ireland's only transatlantic airport under the 1945 Bilateral Agreement and the future of which was the primary concern of the Government. With the arrival of the jet age it was becoming increasingly vulnerable. Aer Lingus, from an economic point of view, was less than enthusiastic about being required to serve both Dublin and Shannon. It recognised, however, that its Shannon stop could not be omitted without fatally weakening its argument, quite apart from losing the available traffic and utterly antagonising the powerful Shannon lobby and its political supporters. This stance, with minor temporary tactical adjustments, held good throughout the long sequence of bilateral discussions. It was the Americans, largely as a result of their own domestic pressures and conflicts of interest, who found themselves having to shift their ground. The Irish negotiators — for the most part officials of the Department of Transport and Power supported by airline observers — deployed their slender resources with no little adroitness; and it was only what was in effect an irresistible ultimatum from the United States side that brought the struggle to a final and compromised conclusion. 'We must hope', warned *The Irish Times* at the halfway point in the ten-year process, 'that by offering to conduct negotiations on what on the face of it looks like a false basis, we have not won a battle with the propect of losing a war.' If the war

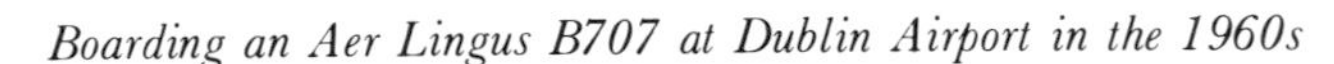

Boarding an Aer Lingus B707 at Dublin Airport in the 1960s

LIEF GEIGES

was ultimately lost, in that the United States gained their objective of access to Dublin, it was for them a pyrrhic victory, Aerlínte, on the other hand, succeeded in preserving its 'monopoly' (as the Americans liked to call it) through the bountiful and profitable years on the North Atlantic. What followed was another, and bloodier, story.

The first really serious, full-scale negotiations took place in Dublin in December 1961. Leading for the United States was Edward Bolster, Director of the Office of Transport and Communications of the State Department. In the green corner, to vary the metaphor, was Thekla Beere, holder, *jure officii,* of share number 2,073 in the company. Transport and Power, reflecting a firm Government commitment to the future of Shannon, were at this juncture very sympathetic both to the Shannon and the Aer Lingus case, and the negotiations yielded nothing to the Americans. In the second week the latter produced modified proposals: 50 per cent of US flights to serve Shannon; the foregoing of onward Dublin-London traffic except for pickup; and 'reasonable opportunity' for Aerlínte to compete. The airline urged rejection of these reduced demands also; and the Government held firm. The Americans withdrew and the issue simmered until September 1964, when Allen Ferguson, Aviation Co-ordinator, US Department of Commerce,

Cardinal Cushing greets President Seán T. O Ceallaigh on his arrival from New York via Aerlinte, 1963.

AER LINGUS

hinted whilst on a visit to Ireland that 'they wanted to terminate the Aer Lingus monopoly'. Michael Dargan wrote to Thekla Beere: 'We recommend that any request for resumption of negotiations should be refused as no developments have taken place since the last discussions which would warrant any resumption at the present time. This is an answer which the US authorities will be in a position to expect, having regard to their experiences with other countries with whom they have been negotiating. It will be in line with their own negotiating postures as shown as recently as August last in respect of the Japanese when having kept a Japanese delegation waiting in Washington for over a month, they indicated that even though Japan had a moral right to what they were seeking the economics of the situation were a stumbling block. In our case the US doesn't start off with any moral right.'

The Government again accepted the airline's position, and in October formally refused the American request for discussions. The morality of the argument did not, however, impact upon all Irish interests with equal force. The Second Programme for Economic Expansion, published in the same year, called for a doubling of tourist income by 1970, and private tourist interests were using this to support the case for US entry on the grounds that since Pan American and TWA served many more American cities than Aerlínte, the effect on tourist traffic could not but be beneficial. The obvious strategy was to attempt to drive a wedge between the interests of Aer Lingus on the one hand and the totality of the tourist industry on the other. 'We never felt bitter,' said Liam Boyd, TWA's representative in Ireland, 'But we were never impressed with the legality of the argument . . . Sometimes, I believe, Aer Lingus interests were not in complete conformity with the overall national interest.'

There was one aspect of the controversy which at the time caused those involved on the Irish side some little embarrassment. In November 1964 the US trade journal *Aviation Week & Space Technology*, in an article on the Dublin rights issue, pointed out somewhat mischievously the apparently contradictory positions of J. F. Dempsey, a member of the Boards of both Aer Lingus and Bord Fáilte: Brendan O'Regan, Bord Fáilte and SFADCo; and T. J. O'Driscoll, Bord Fáilte and Aerlínte. The multi-hatted manifestation was, of course, familiar in the Irish context, but the apparent conflict of interests cannot have encouraged the Americans to believe that they were simply engaged in an argument on moral rights.

In the course of a visit to Washington in April 1965 Michael Dargan was warned by Bob Murphy, Vice-Chairman of the Civil Aviation Board, that the subject of Dublin rights was once more 'very hot'. His reaction was that Aer Lingus should show no willingness to consider US carrier intervention, no matter what the circumstances, since this could be taken as a starting point for horse-trading. At the beginning of June the US carriers involved approached the State Department directly seeking action. On 29 June, in Dublin, the new United States ambassador, Raymond Guest, addressed the United States Chamber of Commerce. The greater part of his speech was couched in conventional terms and dealt with non-controversial issues. But the sting was in the tail. Irish tourist development, he told his audience, was inhibited by the denial of American flag airline landing rights in Dublin: 'Ninety per cent of the Americans travelling to Europe are bypassing Ireland, and largely because this capital city, Dublin, well-known to Americans in history, song, theatre and literature, is not a gateway city to Europe. My friends, this is not the way to build a strong tourist trade in an age when service is a major economic factor, especially in competitive tourism . . . we cannot honestly concur in an economic argument which holds that an airline is more important than a nationwide tourist industry.'

The speech, as it was intended to do, put the cat among the national pigeons. Bord Fáilte, which had decided a month previously to stay clear of the question, now found itself with a case to answer. The Government responded by intimating that it was willing to discuss the position. Guest had made the claim in his speech that US involvement would promote more traffic; but in the summer of 1965 Ireland was served from only two United States points, New York and Boston, out of a total of twenty-one serving Europe. 'Both the American airlines and their Irish rival', said the *Irish Independent*, 'are in the business to make money: the inference is that only Aer Lingus is directly concerned to make money for Ireland.' Seat days or seat nights for the national airlines are as much a part of tourist revenue as hotel bed nights, Patrick Lynch told Minister Childers. As the new round of talks opened, again in Dublin, the hard economic argument came to the fore. The Taoiseach, Seán Lemass, had experienced some difficulty in accepting the statement prepared by the airline on the estimated decrease in operating profit (the revenue loss was put at £7 million–£10 million over the five-year-period from 1966/67) should entry to Dublin be permitted even if only on a turn-around basis. 'There is no reason why the introduction of a second airline would in itself stimulate growth,' Childers now suggested to him: 'if a new carrier began to serve a route without increasing the total promotional effort being put into it, no increase could be expected in the rate of traffic development. Indeed, if a carrier commenced operations on the route and did nothing to promote it, it could, by reducing the business of the other carrier and its capacity for route promotion, effectively cut total route promotion and consequently the rate of growth.'

The argument, if lacking Erskine Childers' customary verbal felicity, was effective. Public opinion was generally in favour of Aer Lingus and the American cause was not served by the fact that they were at the time engaged in similar talks with many countries, a large majority of which were exhibiting increasing resistance to the American position, which was seen as an undesirable legacy of their near-monopoly of world air routes in the immediate post-war period. On 15 November 1965 J. F. Dempsey wrote to Thekla Beere expressing admiration for the manner in which the Irish delegation, under her leadership, had maintained such a firm defence. The United States delegation had weakened their case by pressing for multiple designation, that is, the right of more than one carrier to serve Dublin, whereas had they claimed on behalf of just one airline they might have held a better chance of success. Their domestic difficulties had, however, ruled this out, and all they could do at a late stage in the discussions was to offer what J. F. Dempsey described as 'a hastily compiled and inaccurate projection of traffic based on wildly optimistic levels of growth and stimulation'.

The American request was again rejected, the Government stating that it was its policy 'to give priority to the development of the Western tourist areas, for which Shannon airport is the natural gateway'. There was no immediate threat of retaliation, but early in 1966 both Pan American and TWA began a 'grass roots' campaign aimed at securing sanctions against Aer Lingus and cutting back its service. On 1 February, Charles J. Tillinghast, Junior, President of TWA, told the International Aviation Club in Washington of his deep concern over the outcome of the bilateral talks: 'For twenty years TWA and Pan American have been serving Ireland through Shannon. For twenty years the door to Dublin has remained shut while Irish International (Aerlínte) since 1958 has been privileged to serve three cities in the United States. Certainly we do not begrudge Irish International its fine load factors, which for years have been at or near the top of those of all North Atlantic carriers. But it seems a little naïve to suggest, as the Irish Government has done, that the area around Shannon is underdeveloped and needs more tourist spending and that US flag carriers should therefore not land in Dublin. It is somewhat akin to suggesting that, because parts of northern New England are economically underdeveloped, non-US-flag airlines should deposit their passengers at Skowhegan, Maine.'

Under United States law the final decision on the outcome of international route negotiations between the Civil Aviation Board and third parties was reserved to the White House. On 11 February 1966 the President, Lyndon B. Johnson, wrote to Charles S. Murphy, President of the CAB: 'I have determined that only one US Flag Carrier should be authorised to serve Dublin.' There followed a request for the Board's recommendation on the carrier to be selected.

This was a completely new situation and one which, Irish interests were quick to realise, would demand an entirely new approach. Raymond Guest was quickly on the scene, urging the Taoiseach to agree to admit one airline even before the CAB had made its choice. Transport and Power told Aer

Lingus that whilst the Minister felt that further pressure for access to Dublin should be resisted as long as feasible, he had decided that an examination in depth should be made of possible counter-proposals for mitigating the effects of a concession which might eventually be unavoidable. The airline itself, if outwardly still defiant, was privately preparing to make the best of the situation. 'Do not, yourself, read too much out of the dire consequences which I outlined should a US carrier be admitted to Dublin,' Michael Dargan wrote to Jim Leet in the Aerlínte office in New York: 'As we stand now, even this would not be a fundamental threat to our long-term prosperity. Obviously this is not a view that I will express to anyone else.'

On that side of the Atlantic the struggle between TWA and Pan American for the concession was fought in earnest. Pan Am cited its 'historic interest in Ireland' going back to the early days at Shannon, whilst TWA presented a case on United States balance of payment considerations. Americans were at the time being urged to 'fly American' in the interests of reducing pressure on the dollar, but TWA's basing its argument on the national economic interest did not seem, on the face of it, very convincing. In the autumn of 1966 the Civil Aviation Board announced that Pan American had secured their recommendation. 'We have to keep our shields and bucklers seasoned and pickled', J. T. Ó Briain, Aer Lingus International Affairs Manager, wrote to Transport and Power: 'to ward off the next onslaught from this hatchetry when it comes.'

President Johnson approved the CAB recommendation in January 1967 and in February the Americans were back in Dublin, again led by Edward Bolster, now Director of the Office of Aviation. There were three sessions of talks, each of two hours duration, between 28 February and 3 March. The United States delegation complained that the Irish side seemed to be without powers to negotiate, and advised them informally that in the case of failure they would return and recommend that the Agreement of 1945 should be formally denounced. Again the Irish Government stood out against any compromise, the press release which was issued at the conclusion of the talks declaring that 'the policy of the Government continues to give priority to the development of the Western tourist areas served by Shannon Airport and to the maintenance of that airport as Ireland's only transatlantic gateway. In all the circumstances the Irish Government decided that the entry of a United States airline to Dublin could not be authorised.'

The United States' reaction was vigorous. In June 1967 the White House received a recommendation from the CAB and the State Department that the Irish rights to serve New York should be withdrawn, and that the lobbying of Senators and Congressmen had produced a reaction from some normally favourable to Ireland which was not as might have been expected. Transport and Power now specifically requested the airline to reconsider its position in the light of the threatened development, and Michael Dargan, who had been appointed General Manager on 1 April, told his colleagues that this course was not being taken 'having regard to the emotional content of the issue for the United States and the risk that the Government would yield for considerations outside the aviation issues'. If rights were given, he said, profitability would be eliminated for a time but viability was not in question. It would now appear to be tactically better to negotiate and to seek additional rights for Aer Lingus to the West Coast and Fifth Freedom rights out of New York.

One of the prime factors influencing the decision to open a transatlantic service had been the introduction of an agreed economy class fare, announced for April 1958. This development, together with the introduction of jets, stimulated traffic growth to a marked degree: a situation had come about in which, as Patrick Lynch pointed out in his 1961 annual report, it was crucial that the company should enter the Atlantic route or forfeit what might be a last suitable opportunity. The decision, initially at least, would appear to have been justified. Aerlínte traffic increased by 57 per cent in 1959/60 over the previous year and by 51 per cent in 1960/61, and its share of the total Ireland-North America traffic from 38 to 45 per cent in the same period. In both these accounting years operations showed losses, since development, training and the acquisition of the new Boeing 720 aircraft were making heavy demands on resources.

In May 1961 the Government introduced the Air Navigation and Transport Bill under which the authorised share capital of Aerlínte was to be increased from £10 million to £13 million and provision made for the issue by the Minister for Finance of repayable advances to the company of sums not exceeding £1 million in aggregate. The prospect of the air companies remunerating such loans was not, however, immediate. 'It is my general policy to bring about a position where State companies should ultimately be able to remunerate at least the new capital invested in them,' the Minister for Transport and Power told the Dáil: 'It must be recognised, however, that there are special circumstances in the civil aviation industry.' This caveat did not appeal to his critics, and to the critics of the Aerlínte operation in particular. 'We have a luxurious transatlantic air service and we have not a bus shelter in Finglas,' complained Declan Costello, Fine Gael, putting the matter into an apprehensible domestic perspective: 'I think that there is a connection between the two. We are concerned with prestige matters and with these magnificent planes but we forget the real needs of the people. I want to say categorically with regard to the transatlantic airline that it is a luxury this country cannot afford. . . . '

He was speaking in November 1962. In the year ending the previous March Aerlínte had in fact recorded an operating surplus of £200,413 compared with a deficit for the previous year of £93,621, but this achievement failed to impress Mr Costello. 'There is an operating surplus because Aerlínte has not to pay interest on capital. If it had to pay interest, there would be no operating surplus.' Mr McGilligan explained: 'They take refuge in this, that they are built on what is called share capital — they say you do not pay interest, but you pay a dividend. Such items as capital and pensions liability are things which must be counted in the world in which we live, unless this Parliament says "we shall not ask them to meet these charges. We shall take it out of the taxpayer's pocket." '

James Dillon put his own gloss on it: 'It is wrong to say that a public company paying no dividend is involving the State in no loss because the State did not get the money out of the air. It borrowed it, and the Exchequer is paying £500,000 a year for it. Unless the company is able to pay the State £500,000 a year to meet that charge it is, in effect, losing £500,000 a year.'

This line of economic argument in respect of state-sponsored bodies was to continue to attract its adherents; but fortunately for Aerlínte the results in the early and mid-1960s were sufficiently impressive to disarm all but the most doctrinaire of critics. In 1962/63 revenue showed an increase of 26 per cent over the previous year and operating profits an increase of 129 per cent. There was, however, to be no financial honeymoon. 'For the future the Irish air companies will be expected to secure capital from their own resources and from commercial sources,' the Chairman reported in 1964: 'Since most of this capital will be obtained from commercial borrowings, the companies will be involved increasingly in heavy interest and repayment commitments. This will inevitably leave them with reducing amounts for ploughing back into reserves. One Boeing 720 which has recently been delivered and another, which is on order, will be paid for from Aerlínte's depreciation funds and from accumulated profits without making any demands on the Exchequer. This second Boeing will require some outside borrowing of a short-term nature.' In May 1963 J. F. Dempsey had suggested to the Minister that instead of requiring the company to borrow commercially, he should provide the required amount in the form of repayable advances at a rate less than the commercial lending rate and over a longer period of time that was possible in the market, but the Minister had failed to take the hint. In September of the same year the Boards were told of the Department of Finance's firm decision that repayable advances from the Exchequer would only be available to the air companies at a commercial rate of interest. In December the Chairman expressed the view that if the company went to the London finance market for its requirements it would be co-operating with public policy.

Robert Briscoe, Dublin's first Jewish Lord Mayor, was perhaps expressing the bewilderment of the average citizen when he complained that it was very difficult to appreciate that Aer Lingus and Aerlínte were commercial airlines and at the same time state-owned airlines: 'This', he confessed, 'has been confusing me for some considerable time.' His confusion could not have been materially lessened by the response of Erskine Childers: 'I approve of State companies on a pragmatic basis,' he told him, 'not on a philosophical basis.' In February 1964 the airline took a decision that might fairly be categorised as falling under both heads: it lodged a refundable deposit of $200,000 with the Federal Aviation Agency in Washington to reserve two delivery positions for supersonic aircraft.

In 1966 Dick Murphy went from Aer Lingus in Dublin to work for Aerlínte in New York. They were the boom days, he recalled; there were only some seven to eight thousand travel agents in the whole of the United States compared with three times that number twenty years later, and representing the airline was more in the nature of a public relations assignment. It was not policy as such to staff the offices with Irish men and women or indeed people of Irish descent, though this tended to happen since a fair number of Irish already working in North America were attracted to what was then a highly successful venture. Between 1961 and 1967 Aerlínte opened offices in Los Angeles, Cleveland, Washington, Dallas, Philadelphia, Chicago, Detroit, Montreal, Toronto and Vancouver. In June 1964 the airline took delivery of its first Boeing 707-348C, EI-AMW *St Laurence O'Toole,* capable of carrying 179 passengers in an all-economy configuration as against 115 for the smaller B720. Its cargo capacity of forty tons was also a significant improvement in the light of the growing importance of this traffic. On 2 May 1966 a new route was inaugurated to Montreal and Chicago. The Boeing 707, EI-ANO *St Brigid,* piloted by Captain Stanley Williamson, carried the Minister for Transport and Power, Erskine Childers, the Minister for Health, Donough O'Malley, and the Lord Mayors, Mayors or chief citizens of Derry, Cork, Limerick and Ennis. Thekla Beere retained a vivid recollection of walking up the tarmac at Chicago between Mayor Daly and Donough O'Malley with Irish bands performing both before and behind. (Inaugural flights, in the view of Tom Kennedy were 'one of the greatest dangers ever invented because you invite 120 people but you are making 240 enemies — those who weren't invited. I used to hate the goddam things.)' In May 1968 a scheduled transatlantic service was opened from Belfast, the Lord and Lady Mayoress travelling on the inaugural flight.

The spectacular growth in the North Atlantic traffic in the early 1960s had led to the major decision in 1965 to place an order with Boeing for two 747 'Jumbo' jets for delivery in 1971. The quoted price, with support equipment, was in the order of £20 million. With traffic growing at between 15 and 20 per cent per annum the move seemed fully justified, and, following Government approval, a firm order was placed on 10 January 1967.

In January of 1966 the Minister had requested the airline to provide a special service between Dublin and Shannon to connect with non-Irish transatlantic services. Pressure was being brought to bear on behalf of the United States airlines, and the company acceeded to the request. The service was operated at a substantial loss for the summer period and the Minister asked for its resumption in the following year. Aer Lingus again agreed, deciding not to pursue a suggestion made by Brendan O'Regan that SFADCo might be prepared to contribute to the cost. If it was hoped that this would reduce the pressure from Pan American and TWA to be allowed into Dublin the expectation was a vain one. Both airlines continued in their policy of trying to drive a wedge between Aer Lingus and the broader national tourist interest as they perceived them. In May 1968 the Lord Mayor of Dublin, Tom Stafford, officiated at the opening of a new Pan American premises in the city and spoke strongly in favour of that airline being permitted to serve the capital. There were no further formal moves, however, until the end of the following year, 1969, when on 11 November the Taoiseach, Jack Lynch, informed Michael Dargan that John Moore, the Unites States' ambassador, had formally called upon him to discuss the issue and hinted at the likely consequences of 'escalation' should he have no ray of hope to offer. Dargan was of the opinion that External Affairs, in the person of the Minister, Patrick Hillery, would hold firm but that Transport and Power was wavering. 'I foresee about two years of real difficulty,' he told the Secretary of the latter

P. J. Hillery, as President of Ireland, in the cockpit of a BAC 1-11 with Captain J. Brady

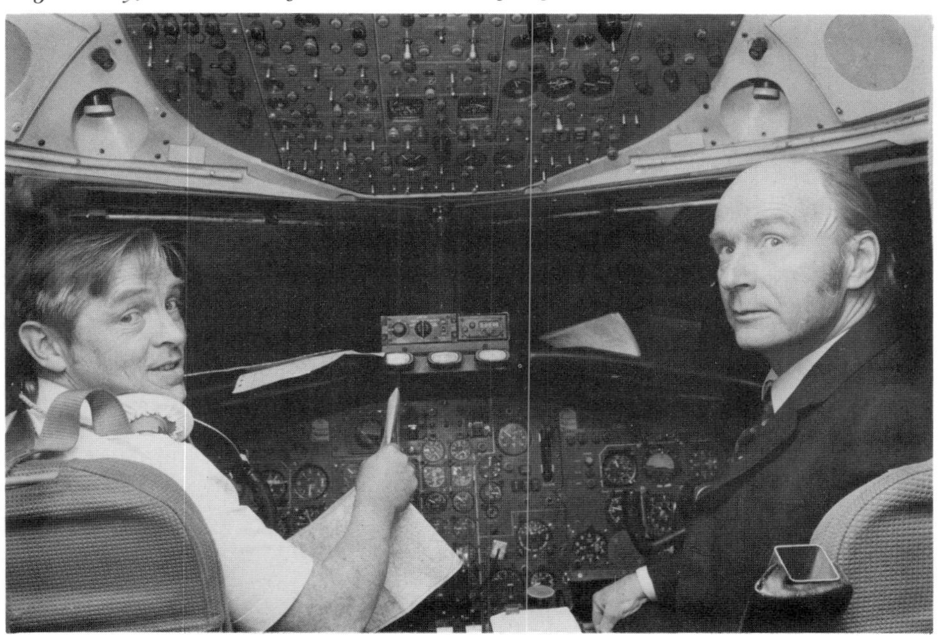

AER LINGUS

Department, 'probably with reduced profitability on the Atlantic for us, because we cannot escape the basic problems of the whole industry.'

His prediction was not inaccurate. Quite apart from the continuing argument over Dublin rights and the prospect of the financial stresses imposed by the massive investment in B747 aircraft, Aer Lingus, in common with all other transatlantic operators, was seriously concerned over the threat posed by 'supplemental' airlines operating charter flights in the peak season. With competition for traffic becoming more and more intense as the scheduled carriers sought to fill their big jets, the supplementals were creaming off a sizeable share of a market which was now growing only very slowly. In 1969 non-scheduled airlines operated sixty-seven charter flights into Ireland with the tacit support, as the scheduled carriers saw it, of the United States Government which adopted a somewhat different position when foreign carriers sought reciprocal rights. In 1970 Ireland permitted US carriers to perform eighty-three off-route charters whilst the Americans permitted Aerlínte to operate none at all. When it applied for a permit to fly a return 'off-line' charter to San Francisco in February of that year the CAB, having refused, was pressed for an explanation of its attitude. The Board replied that 'it appears that the Irish Government has approved very few applications of US supplemental air carriers involving charter flights between points named in Aerlínte's foreign carrier permit. In view of the continued actions by the Irish Government denying free entry of US supplemental air carriers into Ireland the Board does not find that it is in the public interest to approve the instant application.'

The Americans were clearly committed, as Neil Gleeson, then Assistant General Manager–Commercial, was to put it, to 'giving a living to supplementals. I recall being told in Washington by one of the CAB fellows that they wouldn't give us one single offline charter until their supplemental carriers could get rights from Boston, Chicago and New York into Ireland. Their attitude in general, I have to say, has been and continues to be extremely unreasonable.' Many of the supplementals had been established on the basis of a glut of cheap aircraft consequent upon the ending of the Vietnam war and they were regarded by the US Government as part of the strategic reserve to be called upon in the event of future hostilities. They were now operating a cut-throat policy in an attempt to gain and hold business. This factor, allied to the political confrontation in Northern Ireland, signalled the beginning of the end of the boom on the North Atlantic which had sustained Aerlínte through twelve years of profitable growth. As Michael Dargan put it: 'The airline industry tends to have cycles of euphoria brought about by rising markets and rising profits... followed by acute melancholia when the pendulum swings the other way.'

This particular oscillation was in no way tempered by the strongly aggressive stance now being adopted by the CAB in the matter of Dublin rights. The United States' view was based quite simply on the primacy of market forces. As the US *Business Week* put it in December 1969: 'At stake is a basic US policy that frequency of service and type of equipment should not be regulated by governments.' Non-US airlines, however, regarded this stance as fundamentally mercantilist, seeking growth for their own operators at the expense, if necessary, of their competitors. The attack on Aerlínte was only one element in a general campaign (Qantas, for example, were finding it extremely difficult to introduce their new B747s on the San Francisco service without granting the Americans new rights at Melbourne) but there was no doubt but that Dublin was high on the CAB's hit list.

'All our contacts were Irish Democratic politicians,' said Tom Kennedy, 'so we found ourselves, when the Republicans were in, in an extraordinarily vulnerable situation.' Fortunately, there were still some friends in high places. Patrick Carolan, Aer Lingus District Manager in Washington and a man very much in the front line of the renewed battle, was able to arrange a luncheon at the White House early in 1970 to enable Michael Dargan to put the airline's case to Peter Flanagan, aide to President Nixon. With Dargan was John A. Mulcahy, a strong Republican supporter and contributor to party funds. Nixon was planning what was to become the obligatory 'roots'

Richard Nixon on a private visit to Ireland with (left) Niall Weldon, Secretary, Aer Lingus. The hostess is Catherine White.

visit undertaken by Irish-American or pseudo-Irish-American presidents, and was not uninterested in the Irish vote. Dargan, for his part, realised that the game was probably up: 'I had sadly to recognise that economic might and single-minded pursuit by US authorities of Dublin might have to be taken into account at some time in the future,' he told Jack Lynch, who reaffirmed the Government's attitude. But entry would be disastrous at the present time, he warned, until 'we had digested our two B747s'. These were to be delivered in 1972. Dargan suggested that the airline would not object to the re-opening of negotiations in the autumn of that year.

For the moment a stay of execution had been won. Nixon warned off the United States' vested interests and the issue was allowed to subside until after his October 1970 visit to the land of his hastily-resurrected ancestors. 'It was your intervention that was the determining factor,' Dargan wrote to John A. Mulcahy. The respite was to be a short one.

Jack Lynch was in Washington for St Patrick's day 1971. Both he and the Irish ambassador, William Warnock, were briefed on the Aer Lingus position but the visit passed off without serious incident: 'The situation is contained for the present,' Dargan hoped. Then, in April, the airline appeared to play straight into the hands of the Americans. On the very day that Maurice Stans,

In the first class lounge en route to New York, 1960: (left to right) Alderman Garnet B. Boughton, Lord Mayor of Birmingham and the Lady Mayoress; Maurice Dockrell, Lord Mayor of Dublin; Alderman Stephen Barrett, Lord Mayor of Cork; and Alderman Robin Kinahan, Lord Mayor of Belfast

AER LINGUS

the United States' Secretary of Commerce, was in Dublin for talks with the Government on a range of issues, it was announced that the Shannon–Dublin feeder service was being dropped for economic reasons with the permission of the Department of Transport and Power. The arrival of the first Aer Lingus B747, EI-ASI *St Colmcille,* on 6 March 1971 had been greeted by the Minister, Brian Lenihan, with a speech which, in the view of *Business and Finance,* 'may have sparked off the full scale international row which is brewing between the Irish and American governments on the question of landing rights. . . . ' In a speech which surprised many, Lenihan told the national airline that it could not expect the State to come to its rescue if it got into financial difficulties. It is significant that a few weeks later Aer Lingus finally wrested from the Department of Transport and Power permission to axe its highly uneconomic feeder service which was introduced in 1966 as a sop to American airlines. Clearly Aer Lingus was saying 'if you want us to operate an uneconomic link you will have to pay for it.'

Brian Lenihan's words had not, however, come as a surprise to Aer Lingus, which had reached the conclusion that time was running out as regards the Dublin rights issue and was happy for it to be known that it was ready to stand on its own feet. 'Pan Am was the airborne CIA,' in the view of Tom Kennedy, 'it was Coca-Cola in the air. It was immensely powerful — it had the entrée to the White House no matter who was there.' He believed that Dargan had realised that there was no point in fighting it further and that his holding action had bought time for the airline 'to get ourselves in solid, reaching beyond a total dependence on ethnics'.

In the event, the Americans were quick to pounce upon the propaganda advantage offered by the Shannon–Dublin closure. 'US officials were taking a serious view yesterday of the abrupt cancellation' said the American *Aviation Daily* on 14 April, and quoted TWA comment: 'it is our understanding that cancellation of these flights violates commitments by the Irish government to the US government. . .'. Pan American drove the point home: 'This is a further distressing blow. It serves to worsen an already highly unsatisfactory situation whereby the US carriers are denied a fair opportunity to serve Irish tourist interests by flying directly to Ireland's capital.' The fact that, according to Michael Dargan, US airlines had provided an average of only ten passengers per BAC 1–11 flight in 1970 was not, understandably, alluded to.

Maurice Stans, in Ireland, also took full advantage of the opportunity that seemed to have been handed to him on a plate. Addressing the US Chamber of Commerce in Dublin on 20 April he told them that if Ireland wished to develop her tourist industry to its full potential, American carriers capable of developing huge new markets in the US should no longer be barred from the capital. 'These carriers', he continued: 'can swiftly fill the gap caused by the recent cancellation at no hardship to the Irish carrier which has, in fact, stated that it wished to abandon this service for economic reasons.' And he concluded in terms which he knew his audience would find hard to resist: 'In addition, the American service would be furnished at no cost to the taxpayer and to the great benefit of the Irish tourist industry.'

Why Aer Lingus apparently chose to play into American hands at this juncture is difficult to understand, particularly as there had been evidence from Washington that events were moving towards a climax. On 23 February 1971 Senator Howard W. Cannon, a Democrat and Chairman of the aviation sub-committee of the Senate Committee on Commerce, told the Aero Club in Washington that the situation in Ireland was deplorable. 'Pan Am has for years been denied the rights to exercise its certificate at Dublin even though the Irish carrier has substantial US rights. It's time to quit talking and take action. The US should renounce a portion of its bilateral air agreement with Ireland and the CAB should begin proceedings to delete New York from the certificate of the Irish flag carrier unless Pan Am's authority is established at once.' And Patrick Carolan of Aer Lingus had overheard Senator Cannon directing Deputy Under-Secretary of State Rains to move against the airline. In April the United States' ambassador informed the Taoiseach that there was agreement in all agencies and at all levels in Washington to denounce the bilateral.

A retreat was unavoidable. The Shannon–Dublin service was restored, with almost indecent haste, five days after it had been suspended, and on 29 April the Government informed the US ambassador that it was prepared, if formally requested, to have negotiations commence the following autumn on all aspects of the bilateral issue, including the question of landing rights at Dublin. The following month the Taoiseach told Michael Dargan that there were socio-political as well as airline considerations involved, and that he did not want an open row with the United States. Ambassador Moore intimated that Washington favoured giving notice of renunciation within the next month unless negotiations were set in train within a matter of weeks, and let it be understood that under consideration was a type of entry limited to one carrier only — Pan American had been nominated by the CAB — which would serve Shannon in both directions.

John Mulcahy was present at this meeting between the ambassador, the Government and representatives of the airline. His role, from the Aer Lingus point of view, had been invaluable. But in July he attended a luncheon at the St Regis hotel in New York in honour of T. J. O'Driscoll, who was retiring from his position as Director-General of Bord Fáilte, and found himself seated next to Somerset R. Waters, a management consultant to the tourist industry who had recently made a three-day visit to Ireland. On the strength of this brief experience, in the course of which he had meetings with the US ambassador, unspecified staff members of Bord Fáilte and representatives of private tourism interests, he had come to the firm conclusion that foreign airlines should be allowed to serve Dublin. 'If ever there was an opportune time for European and American carriers to seek landing rights in Dublin this is it,' his report stated — somewhat exiguously, since many European carriers already had full rights in this respect and several of them were exercising them, if not on the Atlantic route. He went on: 'The present position should not be considered a conflict between the Irish airlines and the Irish hotel industry but rather a struggle between a monopolistic airline and the public at large who are suffering from lack of employment opportunities and lack of foreign exchange needed to import essential foreign machinery and merchandise.' Waters proceeded to advocate the formation of a pressure group of Irish businessmen to work towards these ends. Aer Lingus was convinced, on strong evidence, that the Waters visit had been organised by the US competition, which had also arranged for him to be seated beside John Mulcahy; but it was far more concerned about the latter's reaction. He had requested a copy of the Waters report for forwarding to the Taoiseach and expressed the view that not only would Aer Lingus not suffer financial loss to the extent envisaged if US entry were permitted, but eventually they would gain. It appeared that the airline was confronted with the defection of a formidable ally.

In the shadow of this unsettling development the Board was preparing its case for the talks which were now scheduled to open in August. 'We want the present situation to continue,' Dargan wrote to the Secretary of Transport and Power, 'but if it became clear that this would not be possible it is absolutely essential that we get the best possible out of negotiations. It will be our last chance.' He recommended that if entry were permitted it should be on a basis on one airline only for all routes on a turnaround schedule only and with no onward rights; and that this should operate in the summer only. In return Aer Lingus would be seeking a comprehensive allocation of new rights which would include Dublin-Boston-Philadelphia-Washington and/or Baltimore; Dublin-Chicago-Los Angeles/San Francisco and onwards; Dublin-Philadelphia-Washington/Baltimore-Caribbean-South America: Dublin-Miami-Caribbean-South America and the right to serve a whole list of United States' internal destinations. 'Few if any of these rights could be economically exercised by us at present,' Dargan added, 'but they would be of long-term importance.'

The talks were to take place on 8 and 9 August 1971 in Washington. The delegation, led by Robert McDonagh of Foreign Affairs and including J. T. Ó Briain, Aer Lingus Manager-International Affairs, was booked into the Watergate Inn. The United States had indicated that a prior condition of the discussion was that Dublin entry would be accepted in principle. If the airline was tacitly prepared to accede to this, it was deeply concerned that it would be instructed to terminate its own service at Shannon. This, the Chairman, Patrick Lynch, told the Taoiseach: 'would damage our markets, reduce our revenue, gravely impair our opportunities for growth, impose substantial extra costs arising from large-scale feeder services and added maintenance, ground handling and other outgoings'. The replacement of Transport and Power by Foreign Affairs at the centre of the negotiations was causing the airline no little uneasiness, since it believed that the Shannon lobby had now secured a more powerful advocate.

The US delegation was headed by James S. Horneman of the CAB's Bureau of Internal Affairs. 'The sessions were friendly', said a spokesman, 'but we got absolutely nowhere. The Irish didn't budge.' The talks concluded with the Americans threatening denounciation of the bilateral. 'The move is obviously an exercise in brinkmanship,' was Michael Dargan's comment for public consumption: 'The threat, if carried out, would destroy the transatlantic airline. We are hearing again now of all the thousands of extra passengers that our competitors say they will bring into Ireland. Over all the years they have been operating into Shannon we have seen little evidence of their selling Ireland.'

On 18 August the United States' authorities announced that they were terminating New York landing rights for Aerlínte Éireann effective from 18 August 1972.

10

The Captains and the Kings
1960–71

WHEN Aerlínte went onto the Atlantic in 1960 with its own jets, the Boeing 720s, it involved a major move on the technical side. The transition from propeller to jet was very demanding on the air crews: 'Pilots had to learn their aerodynamics all over again,' as Dick White, appointed Chief Pilot-Atlantic, expressed it. The new aircraft exhibited characteristics very different from those of the Viscounts and Friendships and were much more demanding, particularly in the approach and landing phase. They required new disciplines, a change of habits — and, by modern standards, an enormous amount of conversion training in the aircraft. 'Most people did about 25 hours,' said White: 'nowadays you might do that in a simulator and three or four hours in an aircraft.' Crews went to Boeing in Seattle for ground school training and then to Tucson, Arizona for the actual flying, finishing off with proving flights up the American east coast. Initially it was hoped to operate the 720s with a three-man crew, replacing the navigator with the dual Doppler system which gave readings for drift and ground speed. But its performance was not consistent: the technology was too new and demanded a very high quality compass which was not then available. Navigators were carried until the arrival of the B747s which were fitted with the inertial navigation system.

'They made the wrong decision in buying the Boeing 720,' in the opinion of Tommy McKeown, one of the men who flew it: 'it was an intermediate jet, and very often on the way to New York we had to land in Goose Bay or Gander — which did nothing for promoting goodwill among the passengers.' The aircraft did not meet the payload/range projections which the airline had made and had to be returned subsequently to Seattle to increase fuel tankage: 'Once you got about a 65 per cent load factor you were in the stopping business,' Dick White recalled: 'each operation was an epic of navigation as to whether you should speed it up and go to Gander or fly much slower and hope to make it.' One solution was a high-speed cruise to Gander at Mach .85 (the normal cruise speed was Mach .82), a quick refuel and on to New York. Nor was the B720, in common with the B707 that was to replace it, an easy aircraft to fly. 'It was not very stable on approach,' said White, 'and we got things like

"Dutch Roll" which were quite difficult to handle.' The problems were partly due, he suggested, to a vehicle that wasn't quite up to it, but also to its commercial success: 'We got very much higher load factors and passenger numbers than were in the original study.'

The airline had opted for the B720 largely on the grounds that a relatively short sector (as compared, for example, with Paris–New York) indicated a short-range aircraft, but loads were so high that the number of enforced Gander stops became embarrassing. For a time the possibility was considered of re-engining the B720s, but on the recommendation of a special fleet planning committee of Neil Gleeson, Gerry Giltrap, George Bourke, G. P. Dempsey and Mícheál Ó Riain, it was eventually decided to re-equip with the B707–320C which also offered an improved cargo capacity. The first of these aircraft arrived at Dublin on 13 June 1964. It was somewhat less demanding to fly than its predecessor, more stable, with somewhat more efficient engines and no range problems. It was, in the view of Brendan McGann, 'a very sturdy aircraft'.

Since the Aer Lingus European fleet did not by then carry navigators, the airline was obliged to recruit them for the Boeing operations. Some came from SAS (Scandinavian Airlines), which at the time had a surplus. Brendan McGann joined in 1967 after flying experience with the Canadian air force and Canadian Pacific, the latter mostly in DC8s. He had also operated on a VIP squadron based in Ottawa which flew the Canadian Prime Minister. With an experience of five different airlines or air forces he found the cockpit atmosphere in Aer Lingus 'the best anywhere', technically very professional but very informal, with 'lots of humour in it'. From that point of view he found the Aer Lingus flight-deck 'a great place to work', but was less enamoured of the equipment with which he had to deal: 'I came back to Aer Lingus and discovered that the weather radar didn't really work on the B707s. For years, along with a few other people, I tried to get something done about it. The guys who were senior captains at the time had never seen a good working radar. We were really taking risks entering storm areas, and we had a number of storm incidents. I was absolutely astounded — and scared. But I made no impact.'

Though, according to Dick White, this experience would not have been confirmed by captains flying at the time, a similar view was voiced by a B737 captain: 'Year in year out the same mistakes keep cropping up. You can write reports till you're blue in the face but nothing ever happens.' Such reactions typify the fundamental division of interest that tends to develop between the flying and non-flying personnel of any other than the smallest airline. Dick White recalled that in his early Aer Lingus days the 'air crew versus ground-crew ambience', was 'quite militant and explosive'. 'We didn't know very much about management', said McGann, 'we saw them as a stodgy group of people who tried to interfere with everything we tried to do on the operational side. The bulk of the pilots in the view of Alistair Campbell, 'are not too impressed. They feel that the top men are good, but fall down badly in trying to motivate middle management.' Campbell, a senior B737 captain with a background of twelve years' flying with the British Fleet Air Arm, was 'one of the last of an era — I was an experienced pilot when I arrived'. This was in 1967 when the expatriate representation of the pilot strength was, in his estimation, 60 to 70 per cent. He characterised Aer Lingus as 'a very professional airline', from the operational point of view. With no Irish connections he chose it because it flew 'only to and fro', not in big circles like the big airlines', and after an upbringing as a son of a naval officer he wanted to settle down in one place. His view of the Irish was, after nearly twenty years, objective: 'They make good pilots. They're far more relaxed, for instance, than the British. The British are very much "by numbers" people. They don't like it done any other way and won't tolerate it any other way. Aer Lingus are not like that, and as a result they get more out of their aircraft and more out of their operation. It suits the Irish temperament, flying aeroplanes.'

A traditional cockpit confrontation, though one which has virtually disappeared with the introduction of new technology, was that between pilot and navigator. A former navigator with Qantas who flew the Sydney-London route in Constellations in the early 1950s recalled that at overnight stops the pilots exercised first choice of the air hostesses — a 'pecking order' apparently unquestioned . . . except by him. For Brendan McGann pilots were 'a difficult group to deal with. They tend to be conservative. Outside the cockpit they have problems they don't always know about — they don't know that they're no good at business and a lot of other things. As a group they can be very self-centred. . . . ' But then flying, he believed, was 'very much a club . . . if you fly you consider yourself to be a better person than anyone else. Once in that club your status is defined as accurately as your flying time: it's very, very structured.'

Another new factor which was introduced with the transatlantic service was the problem of transmeridian flying. Whilst serving as a navigator, McGann, who had graduated in economics from University College Dublin and studied psychology in Canada, undertook research into jetlag under operational conditions by having crews complete a record of sleep and by measuring performance on a set number of tasks after their return to Dublin — 'tasks which reflected as far as we could make them do so the kind of skills that would be required in the cockpit'. Transmeridian flying was very difficult: 'You had to be fit to survive. Some of the girls were never prepared for the transition from a village in county Clare to Manhattan.' The Aer Lingus minimum stopover of twenty-two hours was, in his view, 'about the worst possible thing — far better to turn around in twelve hours from the psychological point of view'. The stopover created its own tensions, though the group tended to constitute its own social support system in New York. There were those who had made their own private arrangements and developed local interests, emotional or otherwise, though McGann believed that the system constituted no challenge to any sound marriage. Many of the tensions arose from operating conditions at Kennedy Airport: 'EI 104 (the evening flight for Dublin departing around 20.00) was a disaster. You could be in line for as much as an hour.' In a non-airconditioned B707 the temperature would rise to an unbearable level: 'You begin to hallucinate; you get a diffused pattern in the brain.' Visibility was often bad, the lights after takeoff confusing and there were aircraft all round you, as commercial pressures led to everybody taking off at the same time. Scenes between aircrew and station managers nearly ended in fisticuffs on several occasions. McGann left Aer Lingus in 1971 and with the introduction of the B747 things improved considerably from the pilot's point of view, a development confirmed by Dick White: 'There could hardly be a nicer aeroplane to fly.'

The years of the B707s, whatever problems the aircraft may have posed for those who operated them, were the golden years with six 707s and two 720s on the transatlantic service. 'We were then a major carrier on the Atlantic, 'said White: 'we were bigger than Sabena, nearly as big as KLM and we were quite a force to be reckoned with.'

Following the Government refusal to agree to the purchase of Caravelles the European sector had to wait for its first pure jet aircraft until 25 May 1965, when EI-ANE *St Mel*, a BAC 1-11 series 20 AL was delivered to Dublin. It was an aircraft with an unfortunate test development history. The original model, with seats for only seventy-four passengers, had been considered by Aer Lingus to be too small for the key London route. 'We negotiated with Sir George Edwards in BAC (British Aircraft Corporation),' said Neil Gleeson, 'and got them to undertake that they would develop a bigger 1-11 that would have up to ninety-five seats.' BAC agreed, but it never materialised and delivery of the smaller version was delayed by six weeks over the agreed date, causing considerable problems. The matter was taken up personally with Edwards, who agreed to make certain allowances and contribute to a joint publicity campaign. Shortly after Aer Lingus finally took delivery, the DC9 and the Boeing 737 were announced by the manufacturers. 'There was no way we could get the 1-11 to look better than the B737,' said Gleeson, so the choice fell on Boeing. In May 1967 the Board discussed the feasibility of fleet standardisation; Michael Dargan, who had taken over from J. F. Dempsey two months previously, informed them that there would be an increase of 29 percent in productivity per technical group employee. 'We wouldn't have had the 1-11s if it hadn't been for the time the pound sterling was devalued vis-à-vis the dollar,' said Neil Gleeson: 'we would have got rid of them and had B737s only. With our size of fleet you just can't afford different aircraft types.' As it was the four 1-11s survived to become Aer Lingus veterans. The first of what was ultimately to grow to a fleet of fourteen was delivered in March 1969. 'The new 113-seater short to medium-haul jet has gone into service on the London route,' said the 1969 Annual Report, 'and is providing the highest standard of comfort for our passengers. The technical reliability of the aircraft has exceeded our expectations and is ahead of the standards achieved on previous aircraft.'

Before the large-scale introduction of B737s some measure of standardisation was achieved with the replacement of the F-27 Friendships by further Viscounts bought from KLM. It was a move largely dictated by the necessity for increased seat capacity, but one which some, in retrospect, believed to be wrong, since on some of the thinner routes load factors did not come up to expectation. This new batch of V803s, delivered in 1965 and 1966, was to be reduced in numbers by two fatal accidents. On 22 June 1967 EI-AOF *St Cathal* crashed near Ashbourne, county Meath whilst on a training flight, with the loss of the three crew members, an instructor pilot and two trainees. Niall Weldon, who was Personnel Manager at the time, had the task of conveying the news of the Ashbourne disaster to the relatives of the crew: it was the worst experience of his long career. On 24 March 1968 EI-AOM *St Felim* disappeared into the Irish Sea with sixty-one passengers and crew, none of whom survived. The aircraft, piloted by Captain Bernard O'Beirne, was on a regular flight, number EI 712, from Cork to London on a fine Sunday morning with no adverse weather conditions predicted. With the full cognizance of air traffic control authorities it took the normal 'short cut' from Youghal in county Cork to Strumble Head in Wales, where it was to pass from Irish control to that of London Airways. The plane had taken off from Cork at 11.32 Irish time (10.32 GMT). At 10.58 GMT London radar intercepted a call: 'Twelve thousand feet, descending, spinning rapidly'. At between 11.10 and 11.15. GMT, a seaman aboard the M. V. *Metric* saw a plane plunge into the sea near the Tuskar Rock off the coast of Wexford. Arthur Walls, 'at home in a sweater', was called and told the aircraft was overdue. 'I knew it was gone', he recalled. When he reached the airport 'the passenger list began to come through and I saw my brother's name the third one on it'.

Though a thorough investigation was carried out by the Department of Transport and Power following the recovery of part of the wreckage, there was no positive conclusion as to the reason for the crash of EI-AOM. The suggestion that it was struck either by another aircraft or by a missile of some description could not be ruled out; those who supported this theory pointed to the extreme promptitude of the British navy in appearing on the scene, and the modest bill which they furnished for their part in the search and salvage operations — a part which proved a major one since Irish facilities for mounting such an operation were at the time woefully lacking. The fact that an element of the tail assembly, which could not have floated, was found some eleven kilometres from the scene of the crash on a Wexford beach appeared to support the conclusion that an errant military aircraft or missile struck the Viscount, severing the tailplanes which were never found, and throwing it into a spin from which it recovered only at the cost of losing the complete tail assembly and sealing its fate — there was an interval of ten minutes between the last signal and the time of the crash. Evidence of the sighting of another aircraft in the vicinity was accepted as totally trustworthy, but the British authorities remained unforthcoming concerning the possibility of a covert operation of some description having gone astray, maintaining that the missile ranges at Aberporth in Wales were non-operational on the day in question. In the absence of any countervailing evidence the missile theory remained a possible hypothesis, though there were many, Arthur Walls and Dick White amongst them, who inclined to the view that the accident had been caused by structural failure.

The Tuskar Rock disaster was, in fact, the third accident involving an Aer Lingus Viscount in the space of nine months: on 21 November 1967 EI-AKK *St Aidan*, a freighter, crashed on landing at Bristol and had to be written off. There were no injuries but disciplinary action followed. In the wake of the Tuskar Rock crash the General Manager expressed the fear that the publication of conjectures as to its causes, following as it did so closely upon the loss of EI-AOM, could cause unnecessary public disquiet. One consequence was the decision to install voice recorders in the entire fleet.

The Viscounts were sadly conspicuous in their passing. The first of the B737s — EI-ASA — a reincarnated *St Jarlath*, was delivered on 2 April 1969 and by the summer of 1970 the airline was operating an all-jet service, the last of the total of eight, EI-ASH *St Eugene*, having been delivered on 25 April. Their predecessors proved largely unsaleable and lay out of use and deteriorating at Dublin Airport for an embarrassing length of time. At one stage there was a suggestion of offering them at a nominal price to underdeveloped countries under a foreign aid programme, but this came to nothing. In the end many of them went for scrap, several being broken up in May 1972. One aircraft — or part of it — led for a time a kind of hall-life as an Aer Lingus display unit at public shows. They had been overtaken, certainly before the end of their useful life, by the speed of aircraft development: 'The Viscount 800, with its four Rolls-Royce turboprop engines, cruises smoothly at 320 miles per hour high above the weather', the twenty-first birthday advertisement of 1957 had stated proudly: 'The cabin is pressurised and the air conditioning system keeps the atmosphere as fresh as a spring morning.' With the advent of the jets autumn was in the air.

Though the B737s initially incurred certain problems in relation to drag and thrust reversers, they proved both popular and efficient and were bought by many airlines. ('A great aeroplane', was one pilot's opinion: 'it just goes and goes. Eighteen hours in the air in summer is not unusual'.) Aer Lingus added a B737 simulator to those already installed at Dublin for the B720 and 1-11 and, as a result, secured a number of valuable training contracts. The question of *ab initio* training of the airline's own candidate pilots had been discussed with the Department of Defence in 1961 with a view to a programme being developed with the Air Corps, but in September of that year Aer Lingus adjudged the asking price too high and reserved ten places with Air Work Services Training at Perth in Scotland for 1962. The Department, in the meantime, agreed to prepare a modified scheme. This was advertised and attracted over eight hundred applicants. After twelve months at Perth, training was to be completed on Aer Lingus aircraft at Dublin. In the following year a further ten candidates were selected and went for initial training to the Air Corps base at Gormanston, county Meath. A parallel apprenticeship scheme for training ground engineers was inaugurated in January 1963 after discussion with the relevant trade unions, and was extended in the following year to cater for apprentice electricians.

'There, about two miles ahead, I beheld the magnificent terminal building. Even at that distance it was imposing. It seemed to rise out of the misty distance, tier upon tier, until it completely dominated the surrounding landscape with which, by the way it was in perfect harmony. Indeed, it seemed like a mighty land-beacon, with the sun-glint from its myriad windows beckoning all and sundry to its doors. . . . ' This was not Frankfurt or Kuala Lumpur or Chicago O'Hare, or even the new Dublin terminal opened in 1972 to accommodate the B747s, but Desmond FitzGerald's Collinstown observed from the standpoint of high romanticism by a contributor to the periodical *Wings of Flight* in 1951. By the end of the 1960s the airport had altered beyond recognition, as had indeed the surrounding landscape from which it was no longer possible to observe it in the 'misty distance'. New permanent structures — the North Terminal, new hangars and maintenance facilities, cargo and catering buildings — were replacing the jumble of Nissen huts and other long-lived temporary accommodation, some of it alleged to have pre-dated the airport proper.

Two significant additions to the growing complexity of structures, from the Aer Lingus staff point of view, were the church of Our Lady Queen of Heaven and the Aer Lingus Head Office building. By February 1962 the staffs of the three companies — Aer Lingus, Aerlínte and Aer Rianta — had raised £21,000 towards a projected building cost of £36,000 in respect of the church, the companies in their turn agreeing to contribute £5,000. The completed building was opened on 26 July 1964 by the Archbishop of Dublin, the Most Reverend John Charles McQuaid. The office block, for which Government approval had been finally forthcoming in September 1963, was declared open on 6 June 1966 by the Minister for Transport and Power, Erskine Childers. All aspects of the airline's administration including two IBM 1440 computers, the most powerful in the country at the time, could now, after thirty years of random location, be brought together under one roof. The actual numbers — about a thousand — represented, in fact, only a relatively modest proportion of the total airline staff at 5,360, of which some 4,600 were based in Ireland. It was in this year that the country commemorated the Easter Rising of 1916 — not only in the spirit of patriotic celebration but in the context of the tangible achievements of a still young State: it was a year which saw Aer Lingus at its apogee. 'Today', wrote J. F. Dempsey in the foreword to a brochure marking the opening of the Head Office building, 'the network of the national airline stretches from Chicago to Rome and from Copenhagen to Málaga, embracing 11 countries. Its sales offices are outposts of Ireland's economic effort in 30 cities in Australia, North America, Britain and Continental Europe. At £14m. the national airline's total of foreign earnings now represents a substantial contribution to the State's balance of payments. . . . Aer Lingus has had a part in the transition which marked the emergence of modern Ireland from the old introspective concerns onto the whole stage upon which she now takes her place among the nations. This year has seen the anniversary of one of the decisive moments in our history. The new headquarters of our national airline in its own way bears witness to the achievement of those who made that great act of faith in Ireland's future.'

No one had made a greater act of faith in the airline itself than the man who wrote these words and who, the previous 14 December, had announced his intention of retiring with effect from 31 March 1967. He was, by common consent of those who worked with him, the father figure: 'He had as a natural way the sort of things that modern management now preaches as gospel,' Neil McIvor said of him, 'listening to people, putting people first. What it did for Aer Lingus, and it lived after him . . . was that he developed the *culture* of the airline. He made you feel "I work here and I'm proud to work here and these are the things we stand for". He had charisma. There's nothing I wouldn't have done for him' — this from a man who was a colleague only in Dempsey's later years. Michael Dargan described him as 'the first man I met in business who had developed the ability to delegate broad responsibility, with the confidence to hand the whole job to you, to leave it to you and to back you up when you needed it'.

When Dempsey's planned retirement was announced, many others were quick to voice their appreciation: 'I do not think that in any of our State companies, or in any part of our private enterprise, is there a man to whom this country owes so much,' said Patrick Lindsay in the Dáil. 'He is not only a man of great administrative ability — all done extremely unobstru-

J. F. Dempsey wearing the presidential chain of office of the Irish Management Institute

MICHAEL O'REILLY

sively — but it can be said of him that he had a great labour relations understanding, the result being that during the thirty years there had been very little difficulty experienced in the running of these companies.' Erskine Childers praised 'his clear grasp of transport requirements, his business efficiency and his belief in the capacity of the Irish people to engage in highly technical services requiring tremendous efficiency and a very high standard of maintenance'. The Board of the airline passed a vote of appreciation 'not as a formality but as a warm expression of thanks'.

At a meeting in Sydney in October 1961 J. F. Dempsey had been elected president of IATA, the International Air Transport Association, for the following year. It was a signal honour both for himself and for the small airline he represented, and was in a sense the summit of his career. P. J. Brennan, Company Secretary at the time, recalled the IATA Dublin meeting of September 1962 as 'a great opportunity to put Ireland on the map'. 'Here we were,' said another participant, 'a little small airline hosting the airlines of the world'. The event was conducted with some style and panache. Delegates were treated to an outing to Powerscourt, a show-jumping competition featuring the highly successful combination of Tommy Wade and 'Dundrum', a cruise on the specially chartered mailboat out of Dun Laoghaire, a concert in the Gaiety Theatre with the pianist Charles Lynch, all assembled against the background of imaginative cuisine by Johnny Oppermann, head of Aer Lingus catering, with the emphasis on native dishes — including one described as *anraith neantóg* (nettle soup). 'From a national point of view the meeting created a fund of goodwill for the country and the national airline,' was the conclusion of Patrick Lynch . . . 'Mr Dempsey has worked energetically to promote the interests of the Association and in doing so had brought increasing international respect for the airlines for which he has so long been the chief executive.'

The fact that Aer Lingus in the 1950s and 1960s enjoyed an international reputation quite disproportionate to its size came to be accepted in Ireland as a fact of life, but, as Neil Gleeson pointed out, it could easily have been otherwise. He saw Dempsey's role as one of having laid down the ground rules and positioned the airline in Irish society. He was, as Niall Weldon saw him, the right man at the right time. And he acknowledged, in his decision to take a relatively early retirement, that his time was passing. To accommodate the jet era, the structure and direction of the airline would have to change and with it the style of benevolent paternalism which characterised his long tenure of the senior office. Those who worked with J. F. Dempsey recalled the formality — first names were not then common coinage; the assumption that one never arrived late for a meeting. One of his former colleagues recalled a management meeting at which one individual had plucked up courage to ask for a rise at the only permissible juncture — under the heading of 'any other business' at the very end. Dempsey, he said, received the request graciously and then proceeded to address the assembled company for some fifteen minutes on the theme of how fortunate they were to be working in Ireland and for Aer Lingus at that time. Afterwards the petitioner felt relieved to have escaped without having been persuaded to hand back a portion of his existing salary.

There was nothing of the 'management game' in this and similar incidents: they reflected an attitude which had its roots in a fundamental belief in the concept of service. 'Even what would have been unacceptable from other people was entirely acceptable from him, simply because he was genuine': the comment from a colleague expressed a feeling held by a large majority of those who worked with him. He was a man of genuine modesty, with a deep religious conviction and little obvious interest in material possessions.

J. F. Dempsey wrote on the eve of his retirement: 'This is a time for me, in particular . . . to reflect, in a spirit of fitting humility and gratitude, on what we owe to those daring pioneers who blazed the trails on which we now so safely operate. They are the people who have placed us in their debt, a debt which we can hope to discharge only if we recognise that the opportunities they created for us impose serious obligations also.'

'He's a man I admired a great deal', said Michael Dargan, 'and there's no stardust in my eyes about this, and never was.' Dempsey's qualities, in his view, were composed of his high personal standards, his feeling for people, his sense of communication and, above all, his integrity: 'The kind of integrity that affects an organisation, especially a young one.' The 'heart', as he put it, was his single greatest contribution to Aer Lingus. Any man who stepped into his shoes could expect comparisons of an exacting nature.

Micheal Dargan recognised himself to be a very different person and attributed to this difference the fact that he and Dempsey knitted well together: though he would not always have agreed with his conclusions they were, in his judgment, conclusions that were fairly formed. He would see Dempsey as the visionary, himself as the more empirical Sancho Panza, very well aware of the reality of the windmills in his path. Very shortly after assuming the general managership in 1967 Dargan spoke to a gathering of aviation people in Washington of the forthcoming crisis in the industry — a crisis which at the time few of them were prepared to envisage. 'When I took over things were going well,' he said, 'but it was bearing on me that they couldn't go well for long, that the whole industry was going to have a very sharp turnaround, and that we were badly equipped to deal with it. So I was looking at Aer Lingus and saying "what ark do we build for ourselves?"'

Michael Dargan's career began in the civil service, where he rose to the position of Secretary to the Minister for Posts and Telegraphs. Before that he had been involved in 'personnel work when it wasn't called personnel work', and it was this interest that he brought to Aer Lingus when he sought a change of occupation. He applied three times for various positions and on the third occasion was asked by J. F. Dempsey what he though he could do for them. 'I drew his attention to two areas I thought needed executive attention: one was personnel, the other was traffic and trading — the commercial side'.

This was 1946, with the operational side of the airline growing faster than the capability of the notional administration structure to keep pace with it. Max Stuart Shaw was given the traffic job, for which Michael Dargan had no specific qualifications, and he found himself as Personnel Officer in a company which had no personnel function — 'I tried to find out the number of people in Aer Lingus at the time and, literally, nobody knew' — and no relationship with the trade unions. His first task was to establish a recruiting system to deal with the growing intake, which had reached 150 a month, and the simplest of basic equipment to implement it. 'I had to start off by drafting an application form and then an interview form. The one that caused almighty murder was my third little form. It was a very simple little form. It meant that anyone who was taken in could be appointed by the head of the department after forms S1 and S2 had been filled in, but unless form S3 had been countersigned by me they couldn't be paid.' In other words, Dargan was removing the rights of the head of each department — people like Stuart Shaw and Kelly-Rogers — to run their own show: 'all those feudal kingdoms were in deep trouble'. The necessity for centralised control was quickly recognised by Dempsey, who backed Dargan against the petty kings. The next step was to establish conditions of employment and negotiate them with the unions, which were following the initiative of Jim Larkin in organising the clerks. It was routine but necessary work: the establishment of an internal postal system; the setting up of a departmental personnel function: and his abilities were quickly recognised in promotion to Staff and Services Controller in 1947 and Staff and Services Manager three years later.

It was in this capacity that he visited New York in 1958, shortly after the transatlantic service had opened. ('"The great emerald fleet" advertisement in the *New York Times* and we had one leased aircraft'). He was recovering from a serious operation and wanted both to recuperate and to see how things were going in his field of responsibility. The first day in the New York office he had an uneasy feeling. The second day, out at the airport, the feeling was redoubled: 'I couldn't put my finger on it, but there was something wrong'. Reservations had told him that that evening's flight was full. The next day he discovered that there had been forty empty seats. In the accounts de-

Boston, 1958: Seán Lemass; T. P. 'Tip' O'Neill; John Leydon; Liam Cosgrave

LENSCRAFT PHOTOS INC.

partment he came across cheques a fortnight old. 'I came to the conclusion within three days that we were in a disastrous situation of incompetency.' He rang J. F. Dempsey and told him of the state of affairs and that in his opinion the top man and the number two would have to go. 'If you think it has to be done you had better stay and do it,' said Dempsey. 'Is that a request or a command?', asked Dargan. It was a command, and he was given full authority to deal with a situation which ultimately involved changes in twenty-eight out of thirty-three supervisory positions. Dargan's philosophy was to turn defence into attack. He succeeded in convincing the Board that on top of an estimated £500,000 loss which had not been budgeted for and was a huge amount by 1959 standards, they would have to spend more in opening additional offices in North America and appointing people of real calibre. Both courses were agreed: San Francisco and Los Angeles were opened in 1960, followed by a presence in nine other cities over the following three years. And in the choice of Jim Leet, whom Dargan succeeded in attracting from a solid position with Pan American, the airline secured the services of a man who was to be largely responsible for the consolidation of its position on the North Atlantic through the 1960s.

In recruiting Leet, Dargan's motives were not entirely disinterested. He realised that unless he produced somebody of top quality he would be liable to be left with the job himself; and he had no ambitions to live and work out of Ireland. On his return, having completed the reconstruction of the New York operation, he was appointed Assistant General Manager–Commercial and moved into an area of work which really attracted him.

He was a man who had a great deal of management ability but was more distant, a later colleague said of him: 'He found it more difficult to communicate at a personal level. If he hadn't come in such sharp contrast to his predecessor he would have fared better.' But the airline was moving into a very different era: 'it needed more of a Dargan. He was an imaginative person. Exploring broader areas was his big contribution.' He had, in Niall Weldon's estimation, a natural business flair and business acumen: 'Anything I learned I would have learned from him. He was very demanding, but if you did a good job you were told — and if you did a bad job also. Dargan could be said to be the Lemass of the airline in the sense that he was prepared to take risks.'

The risks were carefully calculated, with their origins in the new discipline he introduced, that of economic planning. 'A number of people round the organisation weren't too keen on that because it looked like theory going mad or perhaps somebody looking for a concentration of power. It wasn't that. For my part the non-existence of it was what bothered me, because we were opening routes without really having a longterm plan, purchasing aircraft predominantly because they were recommended by technical people.' He found men of like mind and with more than adequate skills in Neil Gleeson, Jimmy Ó Briain and Mícheál Ó Riain, and succeeded in adding an organisation dimension to 'good commonsense management'.

When the crisis loomed in the aviation industry Michael Dargan was prepared for it: 'You didn't have to be brilliant to see it. I was tracing their cost curves and tracing their revenue curves and the crossing of the curves was already there to be seen.' The solution to him appeared to be self-evident: they would have to diversify. 'I spent a long time looking for the word to describe what I was at. Paddy Lynch found the word: ancillary.'

There remains the enigma of what might have happened had J. F. Dempsey not decided to retire when he did. 'It might have been even worse,' Neil McIvor suggested, 'because his time had run out, in a way. Dargan was more sharp-edged.' On the other hand 'he didn't have the charisma'. For that he substituted a very close working relationship with his Minister and the Department which was to prove of incalculable value when the move came towards diversification. 'Perhaps in retrospect we will regard the policy which he formulated of involving the airline in ancillary activities as being his greatest contribution to our long-term fortunes,' his successor, David Kennedy, wrote of him on his retirement in March 1974. Knut Hammarskjöld, then Director-General of IATA, saw in him one of the most outspoken industry leaders of the times, and a man who did not mince his words. In several respects the style could scarcely have been more different from that of his predecessor, but Dargan's tenure coincided with the ending of the honeymoon period for Aer Lingus, and indeed for many other airlines, the onset of crisis economics and the rise of an aggressive consumerism which began to see IATA not as a benevolent regulatory body, but as a price-fixing cartel. The stage was also being set for increasing difficulties in the area of industrial relations.

Several years earlier, in March 1960, disciplinary action had been taken by the company in the matter of certain pilots who, it was alleged, 'had broken the regulations which forbid drinking within 12 hours of the commencement of flying duties'. The pilots' organisation, IALPA, called a strike of its members which lasted for eighteen days, during which time services were maintained using executive pilots and chartered aircraft. A settlement followed from intervention by the Labour Court. In the following year a dispute took place involving the Electrical Trades Union, in which Father Molony SJ was called upon to mediate; discussions with six unions on the introduction of a special night shift in the production department, brought into focus the urgent need for permanent conciliation machinery. The company was not alone having to deal with the demands of the labour force: it was being pressed by the Department of Transport and Power to undertake prior informal consultation with Finance 'where salary claims are made in respect of groups of staff with counterparts in the civil service'. The Board felt, with some justification, that such a course would place them in an untenable position. In 1963 an agreement on permanent conciliation machinery was reached with the Civil Aviation Union group established under the auspices of the Irish Congress of Trade Unions, with Seán Ó Ceallaigh, principal of the School of Commerce Rathmines, Dublin, as the agreed independent chairman. In September 1963 the conciliation council recommended a reduction in working hours for clerical staff which was accepted by the company. In April 1965 negotiations commenced on productivity agreements with unions representing aircraft tradesmen, clerical workers and pilots. The agreement with the tradesmen, signed on 25 October 1966 covered some five hundred skilled workers belonging to eleven unions and involved salary scales, demarcation, shift flexibility and new methods and procedures based on work study techniques. It also provided or set out to provide for the avoidance of early settlement of disputes and was registered with the Labour Court. There was specific provision for the use of conciliation machinery and arbitration in the event of the failure of negotiations under the auspices of the conciliation council. In spite of a statement in the 1967 annual report that the agreement reflected 'a growth of mutual trust between the parties and the Companies', J. F. Dempsey had expressed concern in January of that year 'at the record of the Council whose recommendations had consistently gone against the Company, as compared with a contrary trend in the Labour Court'. The question of maintaining an individual Council of this kind was, he told his Board, 'under examination'. The productivity agreements were extended the following year to cover virtually all sections. In June 1968 the Workers' Union of Ireland brought in Senator Garret FitzGerald as a consultant to advise on the interpretation of the productivity agreement formula.

The 1969 annual report stated that continued success in competition with other international carriers should allow the airline to raise the wages and salaries in the foreseeable future at an annual rate of not more than 5 per cent 'taking one year with another, assuring continuation and full use of our productivity agreements'. In that financial year the company had been attempting to negotiate increases lower than those granted by other comparable organisations, but had been frustrated by the level of settlements already concluded by some of them — the Electricity Supply Board and the civil service in particular. At the same time the pilots were seriously dissatisfied with their pension scheme, a clause of which relating to widows' pensions was being objected to by the Department of Finance, and 'were now an agitated body'. Management, however, was not in pay matters entirely master in its own house. In 1970 the Government set up a review body on higher remuneration in the public sector, and the Boards expressed the unanimous view 'that the release of specific information as to the personal salary and other conditions of the chief executive would not be in the best interests of the airline'.

The national industrial relations situation in 1970 was a turbulent one; but Aer Lingus was to some extent distanced from the prevalent unrest and the general trend of inflationary wage settlements, as a result of its policy, adopted in 1966, of taking a course independent of the national wage rounds in the negotiation of fixed-term wage agreements. Most of the Aer Lingus agreements were, however, due to expire on 31 March 1971: new settlements would inevitably involve coming into line with the twelfth round awards and the 'status award' in the public sector at large for clerical and administrative grades. This inevitability was not immediately conceded, with the result that on 25 May 1971 production cleaners walked off the job, followed by ramp cleaners, loaders and drivers. Normal services were maintained with management involvement, but no cargo or mail was moved. The dispute, ostensibly over a proposal to employ female cleaners on B747 interiors whilst the aircraft were in the hanger area, was settled after two days, but was a presage of more serious confrontation to come.

At this stage in its development the airline had, nevertheless, good reason to congratulate itself in its industrial relations record and its success in establishing a successful working relationship with the unions. This, in the view of Mícheál Ó Riain, who in 1971 was Assistant General Manager–Personnel and Services, was in large measure attributable to the personalities involved: James Larkin, then Secretary of the Workers' Union of Ireland, was particularly influential, as were Gerry Monks and Joe McGrane, successively secretary of the Aer Lingus group of unions. The informing factor, however, — again in Ó Riain's estimation — was the personality of Michael Dargan, 'a man who wanted to avoid industrial conflict and believed it was not inevitable. "What is the issue?" he would ask: "is it important enough to take a stand on?" ' This was the countervailing view to that not uncommonly held by management that it was necessary to adopt a confrontational approach on all issues — to take the unions on. Dargan professed the belief that no strike was ever settled at less cost than would have been involved at stage one, and in Ó Riain's recollection this generated some irritation amongst his colleagues who resented the fact that, in the personnel area, he played his cards very close to his chest. 'Lose a bit of face,' he would tell them: 'you've plenty of it.' It was not, perhaps, the conventional wisdom of the management textbooks but, in the context of the successful 1960s, it had worked.

11

Another Way to Run an Airline 1960–85

IT was a small, empirical beginning. The big theories were to come later: the hotel sector as 'a counter-cyclical balance'; the concept of 'concentric diversification'. Somewhere in between, 'associated activities' became the more reverbatory 'ancillary activities'. At the outset, however, it was a matter of spare engineering capacity and expertise being put to good use. 'At a fairly early stage', recalled Patrick Lynch, 'J. F. Dempsey recommended to the Board that Aer Lingus should engage in aircraft maintenance, for itself and other airlines.' It was then regarded purely as a management matter and conducted without fuss or fanfare at a profit — until, in 1962, a development at Shannon threatened the livelihood of some two hundred Aer Lingus employees.

In that year a private company, Shannon Repair Services, was set up with the aim of engaging in engineering, maintenance and handling foreign airlines at Shannon — a facility already being successfully provided by Aer Lingus. The established role of the State company did not impress the Minister, Erskine Childers, who saw no reason why a state-sponsored body should be seen to be engaging in business capable of being undertaken by the private sector. In May 1962 the Board 'expressed disquiet at the implication that the Minister might propose to interfere with the exclusive responsibility of the Company for settling pricing policy in regard to its commercial operations.' It expressed incredulity that some part of its business might be transferred to subsidise a rival organisation at Shannon and recorded its grave concern that the Minister should assume that the Company would release certain operators from existing agreements otherwise than by the termination machinery provided therein. The Board also felt that any attempt by the Minister to apportion new business between the rival group and Aer Lingus would involve 'interference with the day to day conduct of the Company's commercial operations'. This uncompromising statement, uncommonly dogmatic in the context of the normal tenor of Board minuting, was provoked by a letter from Thekla Beere, Secretary of Transport and Power, to J. F. Dempsey informing him that all non-scheduled carriers would in future be handled by the new company: 'In the event of additional carriers using the airport on a regular basis, the Minister will assign them to either Company in such a manner as to preserve a reasonable division of work ... the Minister also intends that there may be competition between Aer Lingus and the new organisation as regards repair and maintenance of aircraft.'

The Board decided to inform the Minister, in their turn, that they could not instruct Management to release existing carriers from their contracts with Aer Lingus in advance of the formal expiry dates; but it learnt in March 1963 that the Department was bringing intense pressure to bear on certain operators to transfer their business to Shannon Repair Services. In June the airline was directed to relinquish the handling of the Flying Tiger Line and found itself 'with no option but to accept'; though the Chairman wrote to the Minister on 1 July pointing out that this decision had serious implications for Aer Lingus and 'respectfully advised' him against action in future 'that might amount to intervention in the day to day affairs of the airline'. It was a period, as G. P. Dempsey put, it, when Departments 'second-guessed' a lot of management and board decisions, 'which was a very wasteful way of conducting a public service ... if you hire a dog you shouldn't bark yourself'.

Shannon Repair Services, 1976. Jim Maher, Aer Lingus Manager, Shannon (left) with Peter Barry, Minister for Transport and Power, on the occasion of 'Expo '76' at Shannon

AER LINGUS

This was, however, more a matter related to the other extremity of the animal where the tail, in the Department's view, appeared to be doing the wagging. Later theory — and practice — was to take this phenomenon in its stride: 'It doesn't matter who is wagging the dog,' said G. P. Dempsey in 1984, 'as long as the dog is alive. To stay alive we have to expand our ancillaries even beyond the 50 per cent mark...'. This was, in 1960s terms, a long way down the road: for the moment the Shannon Repair Services (SRS) affair seemed to threaten any expansion even into the most obvious airline-related areas. As it happened, events were to play somewhat fortuitously into the hands of the airline. The rival organisation found itself in financial difficulties and was bought out by Aer Lingus, which in 1966 gained control of all the issued share capital and established it as a wholly-owned subsidiary. After initial difficulties it began to show a modest profit, but there were no immediate moves towards further diversification. In June 1968 the Chairman welcomed a study by the Economist Advisory Group on the economic value in money terms of indirect benefits to the national economy of the activities of the air companies as 'a pilot study which might lead to a headline of the role of

Working on the interior of a Viscount 800

JACK COADY

a public enterprise in a mixed economy', but two months later an enquiry from the Minister for Industry and Commerce as to whether Aer Lingus would have any interest in taking over the Potez factory at Baldonnel for use as an engineering base met with a negative response. The factory, which had been set up with substantial State assistance to produce light aircraft, and which had direct access to the Baldonnel runways, had never gone into production. After acquisition by Cement-Roadstone it was eventually to become the headquarters of the Aer Lingus subsidiary Airmotive: an example, perhaps, of what Michael Dargan described as the 'cyclical' nature of the airline business.

Before its acquisition of Shannon Repair Services the airline had, in fact, made a modest move in the direction of diversification with its acquisition, in 1960, of an interest in Irish Intercontinental Hotels. Its partners in this venture were Aer Rianta, International Hotels Corporation (a Pan American subsidiary), the Gresham Hotel of Dublin and other domestic and foreign interests. The aim of the company was to provide, at the urging of Bord Fáilte and other tourist interests, adequate accommodation of an acceptable standard for arriving air passengers, particularly those from North America. The move was not seen by the airline as diversification as such, but rather as a necessary investment in the tourist infrastructure: 'we wanted quality beds', as G. P. Dempsey put it — there had been no significant hotel construction since before the 1939–45 war. After initial difficulties the investment was successful, the ownership of the three hotels in Dublin, Cork and Limerick eventually passing to Jury's, with the airline retaining its 25 per cent stake. In April 1967 the incoming General Manager, Michael Dargan, recommended that management be authorised to explore further the area of hotel development in Ireland: he was apprehensive that the air companies would not be able to fulfil their plans in the years ahead unless there was an early and substantial increase in good class hotel accommodation at a moderate price. The Board was still a long way from seeing Aer Lingus in the role of hotel operator as such. It opted, after long negotiation, for an investment in Ryan's Tourist Holdings, approved by the Minister in September 1968. The relationship was to prove both difficult and controversial. The Minister expressed himself as 'concerned with the manner in which the Aerlínte/Ryan's linkup has broken into politics' and the investment — a 20 per cent interest — was attacked in the Dáil by Gerard Sweetman of Fine Gael, who claimed that it was a transaction 'with an enormous capital tax-free provided for one man'. On a more theoretical level he suggested that what the memorandum of association authorised a private commercial concern to do and what it was proper for a state-sponsored body to do were entirely different things. 'It was difficult', G. P. Dempsey admitted, 'for an institutional and state-owned company like us to become involved as a minority shareholder with a company essentially controlled by one individual.' The Board expressed its unease over the relationship on several occasions and the investment was finally liquidated, though not before the primary objective had been achieved: that of establishing a chain of modern hotels in key tourist areas. The experience was instructive; and when the possibility of Aer Lingus going into hotel ownership on its own account came to be considered it was decided that it would not be desirable to compete in Ireland with the private sector or, indeed, with Ostlanna Iompair Éireann, the State body which owned and operated the old Great Southern Railway hotels — this in spite of the conviction voiced by C. H. Murray, Secretary of the Department of Finance, at an Institute of Public Administration seminar that state-sponsored bodies should seek opportunities for profitable growth and not be deterred by competing with private enterprise. The Board was certainly not proposing, at this juncture, to grasp that particular nettle.

When the idea of diversification as a pragmatic strategy rather than an *ad hoc* tactic began to shape itself, the first serious signs of difficulty were appearing on the North Atlantic. 'The introduction of the pure jet aeroplanes faced us with a challenge,' said Frank Delaney: 'We found that we had reached a peak stage where we had a high productivity aeroplane, less maintenance and overhaul and a staff that was much too great for our five-year plan. It was at this stage I realised that the only alternative was contract work. I would never have accepted getting rid of the trained staff and the facilities. Now we were able to seek work abroad on a competitive basis. I looked upon Africa as one of our havens for the future, because they were starting up their own airlines and we had the experience of starting our own from a very small point. The larger carriers wanted to do the operation themselves and just supply a kind of feeder service.' 'Our first thought', G. P. Dempsey confirmed, 'was that we had to protect jobs. Consequently we took one decision which didn't require any great support from our Shareholder — that was to give an enormous push forward to the work they were doing in the production department on maintaining and overhauling other people's aircraft. Simultaneously we encouraged our stations at London and in the United States to seek aircraft-handling contracts from other airlines.' The aim was to retain the core of the airline, to avoid retrenchment, as well as to secure profit. Shortly after this it was realised that further diversification would of necessity have to take place outside the aviation industry proper. The advice of individual consultants was called upon and, with the example of Pan American and other airlines in mind, the hotel area was identified without too much difficulty as presenting an obvious target. The siting of the first venture also virtually suggested itself: London, the terminal of the airline's busiest and most profitable route, was an inevitable choice.

The General Manager, Michael Dargan, was in favour of a coordinated programme for hotel investment rather than a one-off venture but was very much afraid that if they were to await official clearance for such a broad programme, little progress would be achieved. He was commenting on a proposal before the Board on 13 January 1970 to buy a stake in the Kingsley-Windsor hotel group which, as well as hotels in Britain, owned the Hibernian and the Russell in Dublin, the Old Ground in Ennis and the Adelphi in Waterford. Because the family-controlled group was a public company the proposal had to be approved by the non-family shareholders at the insistence of the newly-formed London Stock Exchange takeover panel, which categorised it as a partial takeover bid. Conor McGrath, Aer Lingus General Manager in Britain, was conducting the negotiations with G. P. Dempsey, who went over to London in February both to watch Ireland play England at rugby and to close, as he hoped, the hotel deal. He was destined for a double disappointment. On the Friday afternoon Kingsley-Windsor received a total takeover bid from the Lyons group, and on the Saturday, in spite of the presence of A. J. F. O'Reilly making his last appearance for Ireland, England won. 'The whole thing', he recalled,' was a disaster of a weekend.' With the prospect of 'a messy takeover battle' which would not be in the interests of the airline, it was decided not to contest the much higher Lyons' bid but to look for a site rather than an existing hotel or hotels.

David Kennedy, then General Services Manager, was assigned as project leader and found himself spending three to four days each week in London between September 1970 and March 1971 negotiating planning approval against a tight deadline for a site which had been selected in Kensington, negotiating the building contract and initiating work on an 850-bedroom hotel which would be the largest in London at that stage in terms of bedrooms. The builders, McAlpines, took a minority stake in the venture which was financed by the flotation of a public debenture in London: in itself no small achievement since the continuing civil strife in Northern Ireland made the climate very unfavourable for Irish involvement in Britain. The site itself cost £1,487,500 or, at the then estimate, £1,750 per bedroom. The total airline investment was of the order of £7 million. The hotel, completed within budget, opened as planned in February 1973 in spite of a six weeks builders' strike in Britain. 'There was a certain amount of scepticism around at the time about this venture,' G. P. Dempsey conceded: 'at the time we opened our doors we hit a slump in the London market'. The London Tara opened on 1 February, 1973 and quickly found itself in difficulties: the first General Manager was asked to resign. In February 1975 trading results 'could only be described as calamitous,' the Board was told by the Chairman of the London Tara company, G. P. Dempsey, who was by then Chief Executive in charge of ancillary activities. Apart from a severe liquidity problem there was a more localised difficulty arising from the proximity of a busy railway line. In January 1976 it was recommended that £350,000 should be spent on measures to reduce noise. The problem was eventually overcome by a very ingenious combination of double glazing, air conditioning and a specially designed air brick silencer. With the appointment of Eoin Dillon, from the Dublin Gresham, as General Manager and the decision to revamp the hotel to bring it up to 4-star rating, the investment began to produce a solid return. Whilst it took longer than anticipated to achieve a profit, it was to more than justify the faith of those who had conceived and implemented it as the first major ancillary project.

The decision to build the Tara gave the impetus to the formulation of a positive policy towards diversification. 'Bearing in mind the requirement that

The greening of Kensington: the London Tara

AER LINGUS

we operate commercially, and in order to avoid the instability that seems to be endemic in the airline industry,' Michael Dargan, the General Manager, said in September 1970, 'it is my opinion that we should consider diversification in broad terms.' Three sectors were identified for evaluation: the leisure industry; banking and financial services; and the computer industry. In December of that year the company looked briefly at a proposed 'Eireoil' refinery in Cork to produce bulk petro-chemicals, but the scheme did not proceed. It was unlikely, in any case that it would have gained approval from a government and civil service which still saw Aer Lingus in terms of an organisation the business of which was to fly aeroplanes. It took a long series of meetings to achieve what G. P. Dempsey described as 'a rather grudging acceptance of the rightness of the strategy — grudging in the sense that they said "yes, you are right, you should do it, but don't come looking to us for the money".' There was certainly no possibility, in the early 1970s, of funding for non-airline related projects. Hence the primary focus on the leisure industry which at the period still looked attractive from an airline point of view in terms of creating extra business. The Aer Lingus decision to develop a golf course in Britain and a holiday resort in Tenerife was based on the conviction that the boom would continue, that the working week would get shorter and disposable income increase. It was also argued that a sizeable traffic would develop in consequence both between Ireland and the Canaries and in terms of North American golfers travelling to Ireland and onward to Britain.

'Very quickly we began to articulate to ourselves and to our staff that the only reason for being in ancillary businesses was profit,' said G. P. Dempsey. The objective given to management was to involve up to one third of the airline's total assets in profit-earning activities, a percentage which had received the explicit approval of the Minister, Brian Lenihan. At a special Board meeting on 14 December 1972, summoned to discuss what were stilll being termed 'associated activities', Michael Dargan told his colleagues that it was necessary to acquire 'quickly but shrewdly a business earning substantial profits... before continuing losses on the Atlantic would erode our credibility in our associated activities objectives and in order to hold the confidence of the community, of our staff and to retain our best management.' There were now two such possibilities under close examination.

The concept of a golf and country club at Foxhills in Surrey had been approved in principle some months previously, but negotiations with the principals — Sir John Borthwick, his mother and his wife — had proved frustrating. Sir John was now, however, ready to do business and Conor McGrath in London had been authorised to close the deal. The investment would be approximately £2 million. It seemed an ideal project: a golf club in the heart of the London stockbroker belt where such facilities were at a premium, set in four hundred acres of attractive countryside and centred upon a Jacobean-style manor house. Two championship courses were to be designed by a leading course architect and every kind of social amenity would be provided. Yet for some reason, and in spite of comprehensive market research and construction and equipping to a very high standard, local people failed to join in any numbers and the expected visitors never arrived. 'Foxhills was a disappointment,' G. P. Dempsey admitted: 'we never got anywhere near the number of golf rounds per year that had been forecast by the researchers.' It was disposed of in 1983 at more or less the price that was paid for it.

In the heady days before the 1973 oil crisis it seemed eminently sensible, when seeking an opening for profitable investment, to look for a place in the sun. The December 1972 Board meeting had before it as its second leisure project a hotel and golf course property development at El Paraíso, near Málaga in Spain, also calculated to involve an investment of some £2 million. The estimated rate of return did not, however, in this case appear to be satisfactory and El Paraíso was abandoned in favour of a site at Los Gigantes in Tenerife, though there was a concurrent if brief interest in a location in Corfu. The southern part of the island of Tenerife was, in the early 1970s, more reminiscent of Connemara than the Costa del Sol: an undeveloped littoral of little villages and black, unpromising beaches backed by a steep aclivity of mountain — it took imagination, and not a little faith, to see it in terms of a profitable leisure investment, particularly as the new southern airport was still on the drawing board together with the coastal *autopista*. To pace the volcanic

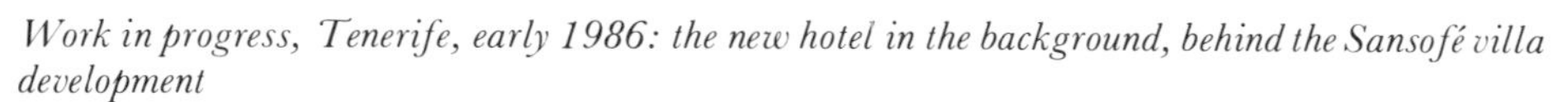

Work in progress, Tenerife, early 1986: the new hotel in the background, behind the Sansofé villa development

AER LINGUS

rock of the Aer Lingus site in company with Denis Rafter, who had been placed in local charge of the project, discussing a hotel here, a row of villas there and a marina where the rough Atlantic broke on inhospitable rocks, seemed an exercise in fantasy. And such, for a long time, it remained. The oil-induced recession made any involvement beyond simple acquisition quite impracticable; but from the Aer Lingus standpoint things could have been far worse — and would have been, had building commenced. 'All we had to do,' said G. P. Dempsey, 'was to sit on the acquisition of the land.' And sit they did, until in the early 1980s the climate improved and a joint development of part of the forty acre site was undertaken with the British firm of Wimpey and Beyre SA. The district name, Los Gigantes, was set aside in favour of the more mellifluous 'Las Rosas' and the scheme marketed on the newly-fashionable timesharing basis, together with 'whole ownership' sales. In 1984 Aer Lingus España Tourist Developments began building luxury apartments on the site: the complex was given the name *Sansofé,* the rough equivalent of *céad míle fáilte* in the old Guanche language of the island. It had always been the intention to build a hotel on the site when economic conditions permitted, and in 1985 a joint venture was negotiated with a local hotel company, Kurt Konrad, for an 820-bed establishment with full amenities and a four-star rating. Opening was planned for late 1986. Agreement was also reached with the same company involving the development of three more sites comprising villas and commercial zones — shops and restaurants. The total of these developments represented some 50 per cent of the land in Aer Lingus ownership, and in the autumn of 1985 the prospects for the eventual exploitation of the remaining area looked promising in the light of continuing tourist development of the Canary Islands as a whole.

Both the Foxhills and Tenerife projects originally aroused a good deal of criticism, on the part both of the media and Aer Lingus staff, which extended to the diversification programme as a whole. As the plan gained both in confidence and in authority, however, the doubters and the begrudgers, invariably present to point the bony finger at any new and controversial Irish enterprise, began, said Dempsey, to disappear. As the man in control of what had now become ancillary activities he was now charged with producing a significantly more rapid development over the whole area. In April 1974 he took his family on holiday to Florida to visit Disneyland. On the Sunday morning after his arrival he had a telephone call from Cathal Mullan, then in charge of Aer Lingus in North America, to say that an approach had been made to the airline by the Morgan Guaranty Bank which had a hotel company for sale. Whilst the Tara was being built it had been decided that New York was the obvious next move, but investigations revealed that the asking price of land was beyond the available resources and, as Dempsey put it, 'we couldn't find any hotel that wasn't so ghastly that we couldn't visualise how we could ever renovate it'. The Morgan Guaranty approach, therefore, was not without interest. G. P. Dempsey found he was discussing business with an insurance company, Aetna, which had become involved in real estate and had bought the Dunfey chain in 1970. Now, for various reasons, they wanted out and were looking for $60 million for their properties. Neither the asking price nor the hotels themselves made an immediate appeal — they were scattered about the map of the United States in such inappropriate locations, from an Aer Lingus point of view, as Connecticut, Vermont, Maine and New Hampshire, together with 'a couple of funny ones in Georgia and Texas that didn't seem to fit' — but the quality of the Dunfey management team, which came as part of the package, proved to be a decisive factor.

The Dunfey team was, to all intents and purposes, the Dunfey family. Mrs Catherine Dunfey presided like the Irish matriarch she was over a family firm run by six of her twelve children — Jack, Walter, Bill, Bob, Roy and Jerry — which was a precise simulacrum of the Boston Irish rags-to-riches paradigm. Part of the visit to the Dunfeys always included a sentimental journey to the waterfront at Hampton, New Hampshire where four of the brothers, back from the war in 1946, had opened a fried clam stand. Energy, initiative and Democratic politics had taken them to the ownership of Boston's Parker House Hotel, once the haunt of native poets and visiting celebrities including Charles Dickens and Sara Bernhardt, which had fallen on evil days but which they restored as the jewel in their corporate crown. It became once more the centre of Boston political life — which meant Democratic political life — and in 1976 was described by a local columnist as 'what the Vatican is to religion in Rome . . . a sort of Tammany Hall with room service'.

By a curious coincidence Aer Lingus had been approached in the late 1960s by the Dunfeys, who were at the time considering expansion into Europe. Nothing had come of it and now, with the position reversed, the proposal did not initially appear much more attractive. But G. P. Dempsey explained, 'as the deal began to evolve in our favour the financials looked very good'. Board members, on the other hand, expressed reservations. Who were the Dunfeys? they wanted to know. Why was Aetna selling? They could see no immediate spin-off for the airline and decided to spend £150,000 on research and investigation, voicing concern at what they described as 'our bad record' in hotels.

The negotiations with Aetna continued for some eighteen months. G. P. Dempsey, who was joined by Donal Downing, then hotels executive, and Colm Barrington, of ancillary activities division, believed that it was important for Aer Lingus to negotiate an acquisition that would not unduly burden its already strained balance sheet. Aetna, for their part, were under some pressure to get out of the hotel industry and clearly hoped for a total sale. The difficulties were compounded by the fact that the industry as a whole was in severe recession with a consequent effect on Dunfey's financial performance.

Dunfey's had at the time some twenty hotels, most of them located in the New England area. All had to be visited, structurally examined and appraised as potential Aer Lingus properties. At first Jack Dunfey, the company's founder and chief executive, represented G. P. Dempsey as 'an old friend from Ireland' who wanted to learn something about the hotel business rather than as a potential buyer, but in 1975, when it was made clear that Aer Lingus was interested in negotiating to a conclusion with Aetna, the visits became more open.

The deal as finally concluded in 1975 left Aetna as a property owner and Aer Lingus acquiring Dunfey as a management company with long-term leases and rent essentially linked to profitability — 'a masterpiece although of necessity extremely complex', was G. P. Dempsey's verdict. The complexity was such that it proved very difficult to explain just what it was that Aer Lingus had bought. 'Even today', said Dempsey in 1985, 'people are not sure if Aer Lingus controls the company (which it does) or whether the Dunfey brothers still retain equity (which they don't).'

The arrangement was in the event so favourable to the airline that Aetna

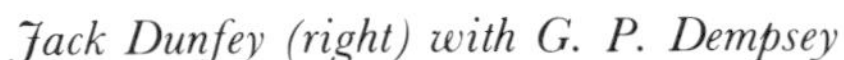

Jack Dunfey (right) with G. P. Dempsey

FAY FOTO SERVICE

asked to be freed from what they quickly came to regard as a burdensome lease. In 1978 Dempsey agreed to a revised deal by which Dunfey borrowed money from Aetna to acquire the leased hotels on terms similar to the previous rental obligations, thus enabling Aer Lingus to acquire them at a bargain price. The airline was now in hotel business in a big way. With the London Tara growing in profitability, with hotels in Chicago and New York shortly to be acquired by Dunfey, and with the Commodore in Paris having been bought from the British Lyons Group in 1980, the ancillary activities programme had blossomed in the leisure area in an impressive manner.

Reflecting on the development of ancillary activities in 1985 G. P.

The Hotel Commodore, Boulevard Hausmann, Paris

AER LINGUS

Dempsey categorised it as 'a shining example of enterprise in the public sector'. 'The support for our programme of diversification, once understood and accepted, has been very strong from successive governments,' he claimed: 'The concern and difficulties which have been expressed usually came from the civil service rather than from politicians and have been successfully and acceptably dealt with, either by Aer Lingus or by its sponsoring Department.'

In Dempsey's view no other Irish state-owned business, and indeed no other airline, had pursued its diversification objectives with such dedication and success. 'There are many lessons to be learned,' he said, 'but the most outstanding is that publicly-owned State companies can and should engender a spirit of enterprise which will flourish if the State leaves the Board to make commercial decisions and the Board in turn encourages management to be risk takers.'

At the Board meeting in December 1972 at which the proposals were outlined for the construction of the London Tara and the development of Foxhills and Tenerife, Michael Dargan had submitted that it would be necessary to break into the banking business as part of the long and short-term objectives. He told members that there was a proposal that he wished to put before them for an involvement in the new Guinness Peat Group formed by the merger of the merchant bank Guinness Mahon with the commodity brokers Lewis and Peat. 'We examined many banks but none seemed to fit,' G. P. Dempsey recalled; but this offer of an opportunity of purchasing a major stake in a new institution, which had reached Dargan only the previous evening and required a swift response, appeared to be what they were looking for. Guinness Mahon, one of Ireland's oldest merchant banks, had been founded in 1836 by Richard Rundell Guinness of the brewing family, and John Ross Mahon, a Galwayman. Its London company, Guinness Mahon Holdings, was now merging with Lewis and Peat to form the new merchant bank in which the airline was being advised by its London bankers, Warburgs, to invest. The proposal, Dargan told his colleagues, would involve a 10 per cent equity stake and would result in substantial commercial and banking benefits in the areas of the provision and cost of debt financing, passenger credit, freight forwarding and development, foreign exchange handling and other banking services, insurance brokerage and participation in opportunities with regard to associate activities. The stake would involve expenditure of some £5.5 million in ordinary shares or equivalent amounts of convertible loan stock.

The Board unanimously and enthusiastically supported the proposal, though there was some concern that the initial low return on capital, estimated as between 3.5 and 5.5 per cent, might give rise to public and staff relations problems. The Chief Executive was authorised to complete the deal, and on 18 December the Board gave its approval to the purchase of the shares, with the proviso that the transaction should not be publicly discussed for a period of six months. Guinness Peat, the Chairman wrote in the 1973 annual report, had invited G. P. Dempsey to join their Board and discussions were in progress 'to enable mutual benefit to flow from cooperation between the two organisations . . . the potential for cooperation between Guinness Peat and the airline is encouraging, not alone on the financial side but in international travel possibilities, in cargo/commodities business of worldwide dimensions, and the general area of associated activities.' These were brave words, coming as they did at the close of a year in which prospects for the airline had appeared uniformly bleak; but they were to be vindicated in the setting up in 1975 of a joint venture in aircraft broking under the unappealing name Guinair, quickly displaced by Guinness Peat Aviation.

The possibilities in this area had at the same time been recognised by T.A. (Tony) Ryan, a former Aer Lingus station manager in New York who was then in charge of leasing within the airline. He was proposing, in G. P. Dempsey's recollection, 'to set up a company along with a bank and prepared to offer us a minority share. We believed it preferable to have him as a minority partner and Chief Executive of the company we proposed to jointly own with Guinness Peat.' On 15 January 1975 Dempsey submitted to the Chief Executive of Aer Lingus, David Kennedy, an outline of the proposed joint venture in which he identified the key needs as 'high calibre personnel; introductions and high level contacts, access to back-up technical resources; ability to provide or organise financing'. The most important of the immediate steps to be taken, in his view, was 'the finding of key personnel. The success of this venture is as dependent upon the calibre of its executive personnel as on the strengths of its shareholders.'

The proposal had emerged from the examination of many possible joint ventures. 'The Chairman of Guinness Peat and I believe this to be the right one to pursue now,' said Dempsey: 'From our viewpoint, I feel it to be of great importance that substantial joint ventures of this kind are developed as they lie at the foundation of our investment in Guinness Peat.'

Guinness Peat Aviation was established in Shannon with a team of six people, including a secretary. 'Our role was primarily that of an agent,' said Tony Ryan in late 1979: 'For instance, we identified leasing or purchase requirements in the Southern Hemisphere and then matched them with surplus aircraft from the Northern hemisphere. This was a fairly easy task in '75 and '76 when we were still affected by a world recession — a lot of aircraft were around and a lot of airlines needed help in finding homes for them. When the recession ended in '77 the market changed and we had to go from an intermediary to a principal role where we acquired our own aircraft and leased and controlled them ourselves. This led to the formation of Air Tara, a fully-fledged airline with its own management structure, pilots and engineers — but without routes of its own.' After five years of operation Guinness Peat Aviation had already, said Ryan, become one of the country's major hard currency earners.

In 1957 Finbarr Donovan was lecturing in University College Cork when he saw an Aer Lingus advertisement inviting applications from graduates for a position within the company. He applied but was turned down because he had a science degree — the requirement was for a B.Comm. Michael Dargan was, however, keenly interested in the possible application of computer technology in the aviation field. 'Having seen my background in computers,' said Donovan, 'he wrote to me to come back to Dublin to discuss something of mutual interest.'

The outcome was an offer of a two-year consultancy assignment to look at the feasibility of introducing computers to Aer Lingus. 'I joined on October 1, 1957', Finbarr Donovan recalled, 'the week that the Sputnik was launched. It gave me my first nickname in the company'. After six months he was offered the permanent position of Systems Officer and began a feasibility study in the stationery stores area, 'a very messy operation in a basement in O'Connell Street'. After a year's work he had identified two areas in which he believed computers could assist the airline — general revenue accounting and the seat reservations system. 'I was lucky that when I was in the United States studying in 1956 I came across airline reservations as an application of computers', he said, 'so I knew a certain amount about it.'

The technology available in 1956 did not allow for what Donovan described as 'the alphabetical side of the business' — the recording of passengers' names and addresses. 'The reservations systems that existed then were primarily numerical. They had to match the list of passengers with the number of seats sold. This was quite tricky. They also had a lot of troubles insofar as they had to have "buffers" so that they would not oversell seats.' Since seats had to be available for sale at various points on the system for a given flight, this fear of overselling inevitably resulted in sub-optimum seat occupation. It was clear to Donovan that central control was the only solution.

In the late 1950s there was a breakthrough on the alphabetical side and American Airlines, with its SABRE system, became the first major company to computerise its reservations, marrying together in one transaction the numerical sale, the allocation of the sale to the particular flight and the name and address of the customer. Finbarr Donovan, who had been promoted Systems Manager in 1960, produced some two years later a computer feasibility study built largely around reservations. 'It was just prior to the announcement by IBM of probably the most significant thing that had occurred in the computer industry over the previous thirty years — the introduction of a series of computers called the 360 Family which meant that for the first time you could take a programme and bring it from one machine to the next. Up till then if you wrote programmes for one you couldn't transfer them to another. We were in the middle of designing a programme when I got word of this. I decided to cancel the project and put it on ice. This took a fair amount of courage because there was a lot of money spent at the time.'

Donovan had begun very much as 'a one-man band', as he put it, but was in due course asked to evolve 'some sort of minimum organisation. I identified three areas — computer studies, operations research and organisation and methods, and got one man for each area'. A steering committee, with Michael Dargan as chairman, was established to manage the whole enterprise — 'on it he collected the bright guys who were not at the top level of the business but at the next level' — men like Arthur Walls, George Bourke, Gerry Giltrap, Garret FitzGerald, Gerry Draper, G. P. Dempsey and Michael O'Shea, the early graduate group who were by now fully ready to assume key positions. 'They were my facilitators', said Finbarr Donovan, 'whenever I wanted to go into the lion's den — and there were a fair number of lion's dens — they made it easy for me.'

Donovan, whilst retaining his involvement with computers, was to become successively Sales Manager, Assistant General Manager-Administration and Assistant General Manager-Commercial before leaving the airline in 1967. 'I wanted to experience the private sector,' he explained: 'I had the opportunity of becoming chief executive of a company and I felt that I might never have got that in Aer Lingus for two reasons — I didn't think Mr Dargan would retire early and there was an enormous amount of competitive talent.' But in 1985 he looked back on his period with the airline as 'the best ten years of my life. I learnt an enormous amount. I had the best two professors of management in J. F. Dempsey and Michael Dargan.'

David Kennedy's first assignment with the airline, in 1962, was in operations research, for which he had been recruited by Finbarr Donovan. In the reorganisation that followed the retirement of J. F. Dempsey in 1967 he became Systems Manager and with the active interest and encouragement of the new Chief Executive, succeeded in getting a real-time computer system, as originally projected by Donovan, back on the drawing-board. In February 1968 a £2 million contract was signed with IBM Ireland for the installation of what was to be accorded an appropriately stellar acronym: ASTRAL, or Advanced System of Telecommunications and Reservations for Aer Lingus. It was the second of its kind in airline use in the world (one month behind that installed by BOAC) and its planning and realisation involved the recruitment and return to Ireland of many people with advanced technical skills acquired abroad — a development hailed as a timely reverse of the 'brain drain' that was a much-criticised feature of the contemporary social structure. ASTRAL's principal role was to provide a reservations service linking Aer

Lingus offices and agents initially in Ireland and Britain and subsequently further afield. The next step was to sell its spare capacity to other airlines. By the mid-1970s this had become a reality and Seán Braiden, on secondment to Air Siam, was fascinated to observe Bangkok–Los Angeles reservations for that airline being processed by the distant Dublin computer with an average delay of one and a half seconds. Michael Dargan had from the beginning seen it in terms of a marketing tool, and his act of faith in what was then a relatively unproven field of technology was fully vindicated. No computer expert himself, he placed his faith in his team, and David Kennedy remembered it as a very exciting period, productive of high team spirit and job satisfaction. For a small airline it represented a mighty leap into the big league of computer development; and much larger airlines, which in other fields would adopt the role of committed commercial rivals, were spontaneously generous with their cooperation and assistance: Pan American, one of the adversaries in the Dublin rights battle, being particularly forthcoming.

With ASTRAL up and running it was recognised that an opportunity existed to retain the assembled technical skill within the airline through the provision of a service to outside companies at a profit. This rationale, which involved a fuller utilisation of assets and capabilities which Aer Lingus had assembled for its own purposes, was to be employed again on a number of occasions in subsequent years in the context of an internal ancillary activities programme providing a range of airline-related services both at home and overseas.

Computer room at Dublin Airport

AER LINGUS

In December 1968 a unit was set up to sell computer skills to outside firms and a year later its progress was such that it was decided to hive it off as an independent subsidiary as from 1 April 1970. The Board was told that in the opinion of management it needed such freedom and independence in order to expand more rapidly and that the subsidiary should be seen as an enterprise standing apart from the main activities of the airline — an attitude of interest as much as an indication of the development of a distinctive philosophy with regard to ancillaries as marking a successful enhancement of existing skills. In 1971 the new infant was christened DATALINK, swiftly re-baptised as Cara Computing. The following year an existing business, Irish Computer Services, was acquired for £295,000, a deal negotiated by Mícheál Ó Riain, then Assistant General Manager–Personnel and Administration. Cara Computing, the name by which this ancillary business was eventually known, functioned successfully until the early 1980s when it began to encounter severe difficulties and the whole project was re-examined in the context of a further major investment. ASTRAL, however, continued to link Dublin Airport with a widening world in a manner unlikely to be replicated on the Aer Lingus route map; but if Aer Lingus aircraft were not to be seen on scheduled services to St Maarten, Lusaka, Bangkok, Maseru and Conakry, the airline was to establish a real, as distinct from an electronic presence in these and many other 'offline' locations. It had come a long way, in more senses than one, from the original biscuit-tin of spares at Baldonnel.

After-dinner conversation in Maseru, Lesotho, 1981. As in many a domestic Irish gathering the men and women, if not physically segregated, are conducting two separate social activities. Lesotho was identified as one of the prime recipients of aid under the Irish programme of assistance to developing countries, and this gathering is representative of many organisations and disciplines from both the State and the private sector. The men discuss agriculture, aviation, electricity supply, education, insurance, industrial development. The wives talk of the servant problem, where to send the children to school at home in Ireland, the places to shop over the border in South Africa. For a moment there is the illusion of the heyday of the Irish Raj, with the tricolour flying over Government House; but the reality is that of a small ex-colony making available its skills within the framework of its own aid programme and those of the United Nations and the European Community's Lomé Conventions where they can best be applied to a fruitful end. Aer Lingus, both on its own account and through its membership of DEVCO, the State Agencies Development Cooperation Organisation, was able through the 1970s and 1980s to make a significant contribution in its own sphere in many parts of the world.

The Lesotho contract, awarded in 1978, was a not untypical example. A five-man management team headed by Bill Cavanagh was given the task of developing a small, internal airline into an international operation. Though an element of prestige was involved, the fundamental motivation was severely practical: Lesotho, a multiracial state entirely encompassed by South Africa, desperately needed to be able to overfly that country to secure free passage for traffic not disposed to subject itself to the scrutiny of Johannesburg. Most contracts like this are in some sense rescue and stabilisation operations, the basic logic of which lies not in taking over but in working alongside the local people on training, organisation and finance, so that when the Aer Lingus team withdraws it leaves, ideally, an efficiently functioning airline with an enhanced infrastructure. No two contracts, of course, are exactly alike, no more than are the means by which they are secured. In Guinée, for example, Secou Touré, leader of a one-party Francophone state, found himself at odds with the former colonial power. The fact that both Air Guinée and Aer Lingus operated a Boeing fleet led, with a little prodding from the manufacturer, to the coming together in this instance of two unlikely partners. In the Netherlands Antilles a contract was secured from under the nose of the obvious candidate, KLM, by a combination of luck, reputation and the Aer Lingus business development people being in the right place at the right time.

The Zambia contract: David Kennedy takes tea with President Kaunda AER LINGUS

The real breakthrough in the securing of these overseas contracts had occurred in 1975 with the conclusion of an agreement with Zambia Airways involving more than fifty Aer Lingus staff. Oliver Boden became effectively General Manager and, with the strong support from flying, engineering and finance people, the contract made a worthwhile contribution both to revenue and to the deployment of potentially redundant personnel (there were a hundred applications for the initial twenty-five posts); although by the end of the year the Board was already hearing of credit problems with the African airline. The Zambian agreement was followed in June 1976 by a management services contract with East African Airways involving nine people headed by Donal Downing and including, in sales, Malachy Faughnan, formerly Passenger Sales Manager-Britain; Ed Kelleher from New York as Ground Operations Chief; Michael O'Shea as Finance Director, and Eric Jackson as Operations Director. Aer Lingus took over from a US carrier the task of running an airline owned by the three governments of Kenya, Uganda and Tanzania, and the contract was estimated to be worth $200,000 for three years. In the event, however, it was not to run its course. In

The Management of Kenya Airways, 1978: Donal Downing (centre) with (right) E. W. Mathu, Chairman

September 1976 the breakup of EAA was apparently imminent following serious disagreements between the partners, and Aer Lingus was approached by the Kenyans for assistance in setting up their own airline. East African ceased operations on 16 December, their principal supplier having refused to refuel their aircraft. In the following February a management agreement was announced with the newly-established Kenya Airways, Donal Downing becoming Managing Director and Chief Executive.

If there was a factor common to these wide-ranging contracts, from Kenya to Trinidad to Siam to Jamaica, it was the perception of Ireland as a small, neutral, ex-colonial country with no big power delusions of grandeur, and of Aer Lingus as an airline also without territorial ambitions or plans to stage a takeover under the guise of rendering assistance — though suspicions of this nature were from time to time encountered. 'You try to leave them better than you find them,' as one man with a wide and varied experience of such overseas commitments put it: 'You try to help them sharpen their skills, to

Trainee pilots from the Middle East in a classroom mockup of a B747 interior, Dublin Airport
AER LINGUS

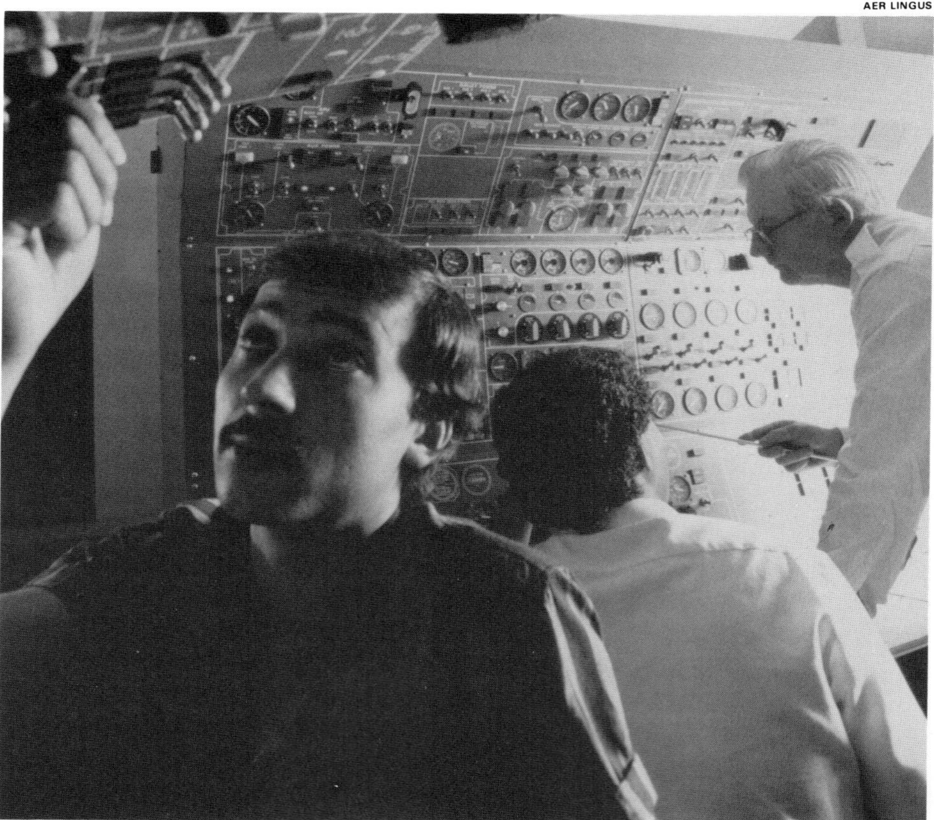

develop them to carry on after you go. By taking the pressure off them you give them an opportunity to develop.'

The teacher not infrequently learnt from the pupil, and the lesson was as much about perspective as anything else. Seán Braiden noted that most people in Siam had never heard of Ireland; or of those that had, one group had developed a somewhat untypical relationship with Belfast and as a result were confused on Irish domestic issues, as were the Swazis who, having only recently emerged from under British rule, found it difficult to distinguish the Irish from their former masters and were rather astonished at the idea of their killing each other. Swaziland was an interesting assignment in that the country had never had an airline before, and the people were very divided as to whether they really needed one or not. Aer Lingus arrived there in 1977 on the recommendation of other African states with a team of three — a commercial manager and acting chief executive, an accountant, and a pilot. Their task — or one of them — was to introduce modern technology into what was still basically a feudal society. The problems were not unlike those that had confronted Aer Lingus in its early days: 'starting from a zero base', as one of the team put it, 'with very little hope of going back for advice unless you could go back to the founding members of Aer Lingus who unfortunately were not around'. The population, as in the case of Ireland, was of a size which meant that most of the revenue from traffic sources would be generated outside the country. With no basic airline skills available they had to be created very quickly, a task involving a considerable work load and a concomitant weight of responsibility. 'When you are working abroad,' an executive with wide experience in the field explained, 'normally you are in a position of quite extraordinary responsibility and independence of action. To survive in that situation you have to develop into making decisions and making them quickly. So that when you return to a more formalised environment you begin to find that this irks considerably.'

For people like this, finding themselves suddenly transmuted from a bungalow with servants in Bangkok, Antigua or Maseru to a Dublin suburb and a desk in head office can be a totally unsettling experience, however many times it is renewed. Added to that are the customary preoccupations of outstations: how to convince the airline that the allowances are in need of revision, how to maximise the often considerable tax advantages. 'You never know how Aer Lingus judge you. Your criterion is how the people you are working with judge you.'

In such situations Aer Lingus personnel, in general, do not hold themselves apart. Terry McManus, on a LIAT contract in Antigua, West Indies, in 1984, made a deliberate decision to avoid the expatriate enclave and to make friends, as it might once have been said, with the natives. Such friendships not infrequently outlast the length of the contract: 'on a personal basis you tend to keep in touch', as one man put it. This relaxed interchange is assisted by the fact that the terms of many of these contracts stipulated that the Aer Lingus team work at each level with a local opposite number, so that in effect there were two chief executives, two financial controllers, and so on. Becoming chief executive of a foreign airline, however temporarily, posed its own problems since it immediately involved the individual concerned in local politics at a high level. In complex multiracial societies such as that of the Netherlands Antilles these could be initially daunting, particularly when, as Paddy McNamara discovered in Curaçao in 1983, the local reputation of the airline — ALM — which he was to manage stood at a very low level. In black Africa problems of race were not always entirely avoided. Donal Downing, as Chief Executive and Managing Director of Kenya Airways in 1978, faced a complaint that one of his team, in disciplining two captains for drinking within the prescribed time limits, had been guilty of racial discrimination. In other cases political manoeuvres frustrated attempts to secure promising contracts. Early in 1971 discussions on proposals for Aer Lingus management of Malta Airlines came to nothing, in spite of a very friendly relationship established with Dom Mintoff, then Opposition Leader who, on becoming Premier

Maintenance Base, Dublin Airport with a Sudanair B737, Aer Lingus BAC 1-11 and LTU Lockheed 10-11 Tristar

AER LINGUS

later in the year, renewed the contact. The fact that British European Airways owned 34 per cent probably proved decisive.

The range of services Aer Lingus was able to offer had grown considerably from the basic skills of aircraft maintenance and overhaul, though these fundamental disciplines continued to constitute the essential basis of the aircraft support offered to airlines throughout the world. This expansion was in the hands of Michael McGovern, who had joined in 1945 as a communications officer and become successively Production Manager and General Manager — Maintenance and Engineering. His policy concentrated on the offer of extensive training facilities to senior technical staff in the airlines of emerging nations. It proved very successful in that it led to the development of close links with Aer Lingus based on appreciation of the high quality of the technical service it offered, allied to a genuine understanding of their particular problems. Their range and capacity of aviation-related ancillary activities was increased with the acquisition in 1976 of Aviation Traders (Engineering), a company based at Stansted Airport near London, with additional investment in Shannon Repair Services and with the opening, in 1981, of Airmotive Ireland, a wholly-owned subsidiary specialising in engine overhaul. In 1974–75 some forty airlines worldwide were availing of Aer Lingus resources which included, besides engineering and maintenance, management, crew and hostess training, catering, ground handling, aircraft leasing, resources management and computer and financial facilities. Much of the training took place in Dublin, and shivering young Africans at the bus

The opening of Airmotive: the Taoiseach, Charles J. Haughey (second from right) with (left to right) Michael Dargan; Albert Reynolds, Minister for Transport; and Matt Donohue, General Manager, Airmotive

ROBERT ALLEN

stops on the airport road became an accepted feature of the landscape. Many of the overseas programmes, on the other hand, involved training both in Dublin and at the client airline's own base. British-centred operations, both at Stansted and Heathrow and in a smaller way at Gatwick, developed significantly, to the point where, at Heathrow, Aer Lingus secured the nomination as official handling agent of the British Airport Authority. Becoming 'a gentleman's gentleman to other airlines', as Conor McGrath described it in 1984, was the most exciting development in his area in ten years. The only other contender was British Airways, 'and they haven't got over it yet'. Aer Lingus supplied a wide range of ground services to some twenty airlines, the concession making a substantial contribution to its earnings. Ground handling was also developed with success in North America.

Airmotive, a major jet engine overhaul undertaking, was launched in 1981 following a number of setbacks and industrial relations difficulties. The object, the Board had been told in June 1979, 'Was to expand the most successful of our ancillary activity projects — namely the provision of maintenance services to other airlines. Maurice Foley, who had joined David Kennedy as an operations analyst, was appointed Project Manager and subsequently Company Chairman. It was being structured in such a way as to enable it to establish its own 'culture' and be separated physically and structurally from the airline'. 'Airmotive Ireland is built on the outstanding successes of the Aer Lingus maintenance organisation', the Taoiseach, C. J. Haughey, told his audience at the opening of the plant at Rathcoole in county Dublin on 9 April 1981: 'Aer Lingus maintains aircraft and engines for fifty airlines, and its engineers and managers are an advertisement for Ireland's technical skills all over the world. The plant is a good example of the type of State enterprise which we wish to encourage in Ireland. It is based firmly on the skills and competence which have been developed in the company over the years and apart from providing services which we need ourselves it also has the potential to contribute significantly to employment creation and to our foreign earnings.'

The potential was to remain for some little time unrealised. In October 1982 the Chairman, Michael Dargan, described the undertaking as 'an enormous business venture that was going seriously wrong', and told the Board that there was a substantial shortfall in revenue. Its establishment had unfortunately coincided with a fall in demand worldwide and the marketing of the service had been somewhat less than fully effective. In November 1982 Oliver Boden, who had returned from Zambia following the loss of a major portion of the contract to Ethiopia on political grounds, took over as Managing Director of Airmotive and a year later a further £2 million was invested by the parent company in the form of an interest-free loan. The following years were not without their difficulties for the subsidiary, but by 1985 the annual report could claim that 'it had become well known throughout the aviation industry as an efficient and dependable overhaul agency. In the past year the company earned increased profits and a further 60 employees were added to the workforce... The growth to date of Airmotive Ireland, an export company in a high technology business, against a background of intense international competition, represents a significant achievement.'

The depressed state of the aviation industry in the early 1980s also affected the subsidiary Aviation Traders (ATEL) at Stansted in Britain, which suffered in particular from a drop in the market for B707 maintenance consequent upon the phasing-out of the aircraft on economy considerations by many operators. On 9 October 1981 ATEL was informed by the United States Government that it must cease performing contract work for United Arab Airlines on B707 and CL44 aircraft and also on training. The company had contracts with UAA worth some $10 million over several years. This action, which had its roots in the United States' attitude to Libya, followed direct intervention to

Aer Turas DC8 PAUL DUFFY

prevent the sale by Aer Lingus of Boeing 737 EI-APG to UAA. 'We have been forced to call off the sale,' said David Kennedy, 'despite the fact that a binding contract had been entered into and a deposit received.'

In 1973 there was only one other licensed airline operating out of Ireland — the all-cargo Aer Turas which, the Aer Lingus Board was told in April of that year, was only marginally surviving. Far from being regarded as a serious competitor it was seen as a useful support service, and it was proposed to secure a minority stake in the company both to keep it alive and active and to avoid pressure on Aer Lingus to enter the bloodstock traffic in which Aer Turas was then specialising. Discussions initially proved unfruitful and it was not until 1980 that Mícheál Ó Riain secured an agreement as a result of which Aer Lingus acquired a 54 per cent stake at a cost of £360,000. In 1984 Aer Turas's DC-8-63F EI-BNA completed what was believed to be the first full around-the-world flight by an Irish aircraft, leaving Dublin on 5 August and routing via Stansted, Gander, Vancouver, Honolulu and Nandi to Auckland and Sydney, returning via Singapore, Penang, Taipei, Karachi, Calcutta, Dubai, Vienna, Milan, Dubai (again) and Katmandu, returning finally to Dublin on 16 August. In September 1985 EI-BNA became the first European-owned aircraft to be 'hush-kitted' to comply with United States' FAA noise regulations.

During this period total control had also been acquired of Irish Helicopters, a company which in 1969 had secured a contract from the Commissioners of Irish Lights to service lighthouses around the coast and which was to expand into the field of offshore oil and gas exploration. Under the Aer Lingus aegis and with Eiven Murphy as Chairman the operational base was moved from Dublin to Cork airport. In 1979 Irish Helicopters provided the internal transport on the occasion of the visit to Ireland of Pope John Paul II.

Other Aer Lingus aviation-related disciplines were the source of further innovatory enterprises. PARC was established in 1975 as a personnel and recruitment consultancy firm under the management of David Hanly, formerly of the airline's own personal department. Its range was worldwide, but it was to become particularly successful in the Middle East, where it was responsible from 1982 for the staffing and management of the new Ibn Al Bitar hospital in Baghdad, a development involving the recruitment of a large number of Irish personnel. PARC's role was in many respects a development from that performed in Africa, the Middle East and other developing areas by Aer Lingus technical management teams over the years, and it also became associated with Guinness Peat Aviation in the recruitment of airline crews and other personnel — 'A GPA for people'. Devtec, a small wholly-owned company offering a technical design service, was established in 1981 under Ciaran Mulhall, who had worked on leisure development projects following his return from the Boeing assignment in Seattle. In 1984 Devtec was

Bell 212 of Irish Helicopters on a gas rig off Kinsale, Co. Cork

AER LINGUS

Dublin Airport Restaurant in the 1950s

AER LINGUS

employing some forty people and had won an important European Space Agency contract. 'The idea', said Mulhall, 'is to use the depth of knowledge in Aer Lingus to allow manufacturers to produce hardware that would not otherwise be made.'

The tradition of Aer Lingus catering derived from the operation of a first-class restaurant at Dublin Airport which, under the guidance of Johnny Oppermann, created its own social and gastronomic milieu in the 1950s and 1960s and offered dishes such as Escalope of Veal Viscount and Crêpes Sláinte. The tradition was extended to the area of in-flight meals as longer routes and more sophisticated service became the rule. In 1968 a catering unit

Preparing meals for the First Class transatlantic service

AER LINGUS

within the airline was constituted to make this expertise available on a wider basis, followed in 1972 by the acquisition of the National Catering Organisation. This company supplied contract catering services to industry and institutions. It was also involved in the management of Tailors' Hall, the last of Dublin's eighteenth-century guildhalls, which had been saved from the developers and was operating at the time, though not particularly successfully, as a function centre. The investment proved unprofitable and National Catering was divested in 1976, though the airline continued to provide outside catering for many events in Ireland and to make its experience available to other airlines. In 1982 it acquired an interest in Swissco, a Cork-based manufacturer of specialised convenience foods.

Against the background of a severely seasonal pattern in operations on virtually all routes, charters and longer leases had come to figure significantly as sources of revenue to the airline, as well as absorbing temporarily surplus personnel. The most spectacular charter, from the publicity point of view, was that undertaken on 9 January 1963 by the Boeing 707 EI–ANO *St Brigid* which involved the first, and up to mid-1985 the only visit of an Aer Lingus aircraft to Australia. The Boeing had been chartered to carry stranded passengers from Malta to Australia following the breakdown of the P & O liner *Canberra* and was flown by two Aer Lingus crews. 'When we landed', Stan Williamson, who piloted the aircraft from Cairo to Sydney, recalled, 'we were very surprised to see a girl in complete Aer Lingus uniform at the steps.' She was not, as it happened, a representative of the local office, but an employee on holiday who had been told to take her uniform with her. The aircraft was opened to the public on the Sunday afternoon and attracted a large number of Irish-Australian visitors.

The Sydney office had been opened two months previously, largely to promote the Atlantic route and to take advantage of round-the-world economy fares: it reported to New York. Dorothy Peyton, who first took up duty for Aer Lingus in Australia in 1965, became in 1972 the first woman airline manager in the country, an event greeted by her colleagues with mixed emotions in what was then still a very male-orientated society. Her territory, which included New Zealand, was vast, and for many years she combined her airline role with that of representative of Bord Fáilte. Though Australia's population was ethnically one quarter Irish, Aer Lingus believed, according to Mícheál Ó Riain, that it had little opportunity of developing traffic and Dorothy Peyton's work largely centred upon bringing parties of travel agents to Ireland ('only one over the years didn't like it', she recalled in 1983) and arranging publicity events in Australia involving hostesses, shamrock and other appropriate trappings. St Patrick's Day, an event adequately observed in Australia, was an obvious focus, as were the prominent race meetings — there was an Aer Lingus Handicap run at Sydney's Randwick racecourse in 1982. The aim was limited to persuading Australians visiting Europe to make use of the Amsterdam or other gateway to Ireland as part of the customary grand tour and to this end packages were arranged with airlines operating the Australia–Europe routes. Though a possible direct charter was being discussed for the Australian Bicentenary celebrations in 1988, the airline in 1985 had no other immediate plans to capitalise on the rapidly strengthening links between the two countries.

In January 1966, following a confrontation between British and Russian aviation authorities, Aer Lingus was offered the opportunity to fly the Glasgow Celtic soccer team to Tiblisi, utilising the BAC 1–11 EI–ANE *St Mel.* In the years that followed the airline became very successful in securing British football charters, particularly in the case of the Liverpool team, which at one stage claimed that they always won European trophies when they flew Aer Lingus. The riot by Liverpool supporters in Brussels in 1985 and the subsequent suspension of English teams from European football brought this charter traffic temporarily to an end. Most charters, like most scheduled services, are of course a matter of routine, but Norman Edwards in Manchester recalled one in the 1960s involving what he claimed to have been the world's highest and fastest bingo school on a chartered B707 from Liverpool to New York carrying the Jim Beckett Old Folks' Club of Bootle, the members of which played the game throughout the trip. On 15 August 1977 the airline operated a 'flying ballroom' across the Atlantic, a Boeing 747 having a special dance floor installed for the Arthur Murray US School of Dancing, the members fox-trotting their way from New York to Ireland. The most consistent charter traffic, however, apart from that operated for the holiday tour companies, was that deriving from the Lourdes pilgrimages, particularly following the withdrawal of scheduled services on the route in the early 1980s. Dublin–Lourdes was opened on 14 May 1954, Aer Lingus becoming the first airline to operate scheduled services to the French shrine. On 3 May 1963 J. F. Dempsey was made a honorary citizen and presented with the Medal of Honour in recognition of the long and enduring connection.

The introduction of the larger and more expensive jet aircraft put the pressure on the airline to seek out ways of producing a year-round return on the costly investment. In the mid-1960s it pioneered the intensive use of off-peak leases to alleviate its particularly acute seasonality problems. 'Wet' leases (those involving crew and sometimes back-up personnel in addition to the aircraft itself) held an added attraction of offering valuable secondment opportunities, but some of these arrangements at times ran into trouble due to political, financial and other factors. A lease to El–AL in 1968-69 encountered insurance problems following incidents at Athens and Beirut related to the Israeli-Arab conflict, and the aircraft was repainted in Aer Lingus colours to minimise further risk. In December 1970 IALPA, the pilots' association, refused to allow their members to volunteer for a leasing operation which had been negotiated with Air Vietnam. The introduction of the B747s coincided with the slump in Atlantic traffic attributable to the Northern Ireland situation. With their greatly increased cost and capacity, this introduced a further urgency into the leasing programme and a pre-delivery charter of two of them was arranged in 1968 with Trans Caribbean to run from 1970 to 1975 during the winter periods. In 1970, however, Trans Caribbean was taken over by American Airlines, an event which caused Aer Lingus some concern since it suspected that the US carrier would not wish to take over the contractual obligations. Aer Lingus terminated the agreement in September 1970 on the grounds that Trans Caribbean were in default because of failure to make advance payments when due and failure to execute a lease for the first season within the stipulated time. It received the approval from the Court of New York to submit the issue to arbitration as stipulated in the contract.

The subsequent legal proceedings were both protracted and complex. The brunt of the Aer Lingus case was carried by Neil Gleeson who, as Assistant General Manager–Commercial, had been responsible for the signing of the contract with Trans Caribbean and who had, on the instructions of Michael Dargan, ensured that it was copperfastened. Though the American Arbitration Association ruled in favour of Aer Lingus, the issue dragged through successive courts of appeal, both at Federal level and in the State of New York, through 1973 and 1974. In January of that latter year indications that American Airlines might be prepared to negotiate a settlement proved illusory, and it was not until November 1974 that an invitation from its new Chairman, Al Casey, to David Kennedy to meet him in New York offered any possibility that the contentious issue might be resolved. At the first meeting Casey offered $3 million in complete settlement, a proposal which was rejected out of hand. Two days later the offer had risen to $7.5 million, a figure which was also rejected. Following the return of the Aer Lingus delegation and a series of almost daily transatlantic telephone calls, agreement was reached on 10 December 1974 that American Airlines would pay $9 million in settlement of the arbitration award. The Aer Lingus success in the case owed much, in David Kennedy's view, to the skill and tenacity of Neil Gleeson under intensive cross-examination. He also paid tribute to the impartiality of the United States' legal system: 'We had some concern going into the case against a major US corporation. However, in the event we felt we received full justice in what turned out to be a most complex and tortuous legal process.'

Early in 1973 Tony Ryan went to Bangkok to attempt to lease one of the B747s to Thai International. Thai International, however, were very much involved with SAS (Scandinavian Airlines) with whom they had a management contract, and quickly made it clear that there was very little likelihood of their taking an aeroplane from the Irish airline. Whilst he was trying to persuade them to change their minds Ryan discovered that a small local carrier, Air Siam, had a licence to fly across the Pacific, though its fleet at the time consisted of nothing more than a single BAC 1-11 and an antique DC3. Ryan established a cordial relationship with Mr Virachi, Air Siam's Chief Executive, persuading him not only to take up his Pacific option, but to lease an Aer Lingus B747, with crew and management team, to operate the route. The contract was planned to run from 1 October 1973 to 15 May 1975. It was a high risk option, the Aer Lingus Board was told in July 1973; but the risk was accepted (though a 'snatch squad' was constituted should it become necessary to take quick action to repatriate a major asset) since the only alternative was to keep the aircraft sitting on the tarmac at Dublin for the following two winters and most, if not all, of the following summer as well. The timing was good: the varied attractions of Bangkok were just beginning to register with the international tourist market, particularly the Japanese and the Americans, and soon Air Siam was operating an Airbus and a DC10 in addition to the B747. The latter flew the Pacific route to Los Angeles via Hong Kong, Tokyo and Honolulu, an operation which necessitated posting Aer Lingus maintenance teams at each of these ports of call. 'At one time we must have had 27 or 28 people in Bangkok as well as those posted down the line,' said Seán Braiden, who was there for the latter part of the contract. This was the airline's first introduction to South East Asia on this scale, and the Irish in

The Air Siam lease: the former EI-ASJ undergoing maintenance at Dublin

general found Thailand and its people to their liking and settled in relatively easily. Many, including the Braidens, embraced the Thai way of living, for financial reasons if none other. The social atmosphere, in certain of its aspects, was not unfamiliar: 'Once you set foot in town everybody knew it,' recalled Braiden: 'several people called you on the phone even before you had your suitcase on the ground.' Braiden's main task was to ensure that the lease payments were being made, 'which', as he said, 'they weren't'. Early in 1975 the treasurer of Aer Lingus arrived in Bangkok 'to probe further into their present and further financial positions'. The airline that had grown from nothing was beginning to run into difficulties. Thai International was govern-

The Air Tara delivery flight, with Tony Ryan (top right). Drawing by Rai Uhlemann from the cover of 'Cara', January/February 1980

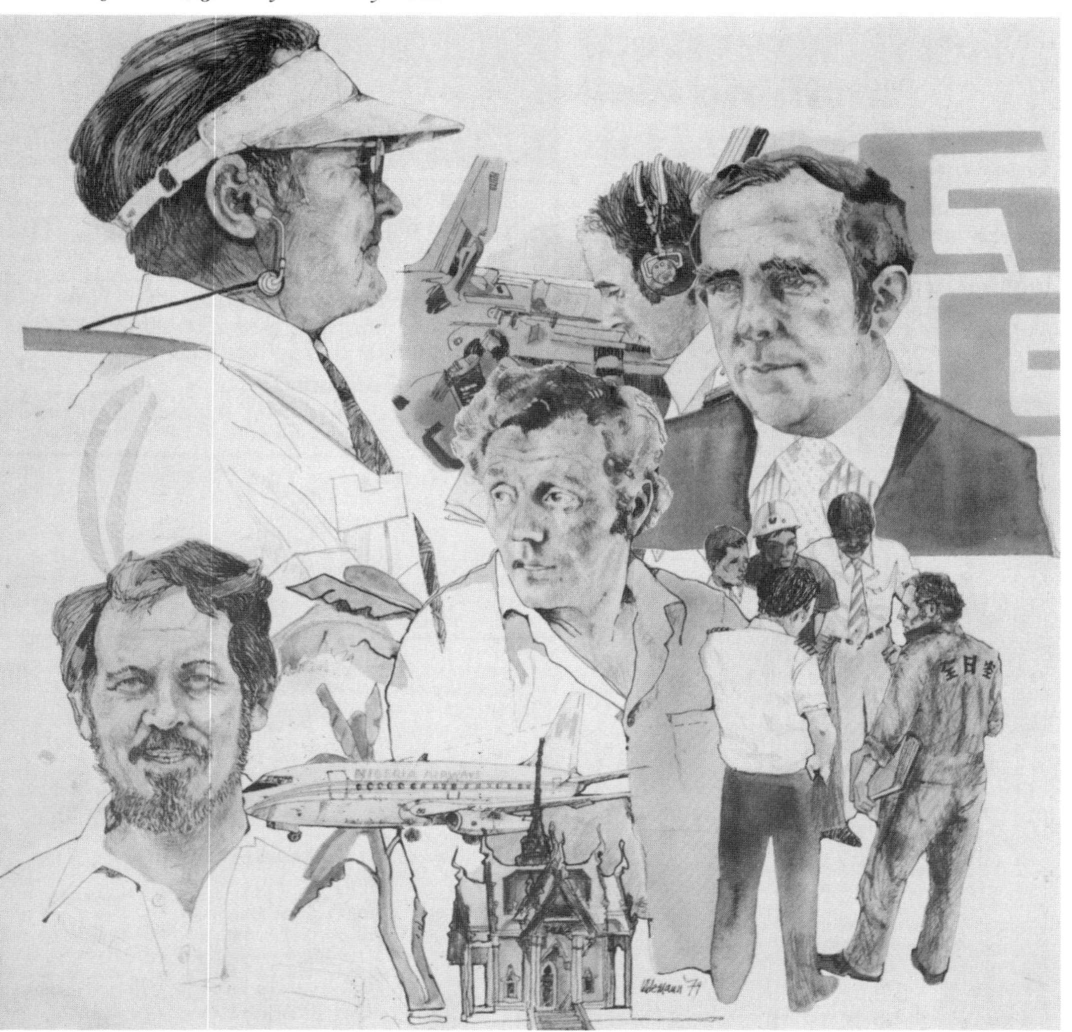

ment-owned and staffed largely, as was Aer Lingus in its early days, by ex-air force and military personnel who did not look kindly on an impudently independent rival. When the lease, which had been extended, finally came to an end in 1976 there were still $1.7 million owing which was to be paid off at the rate of $60,000 per week. It had nevertheless already yielded $6 million to Aer Lingus and had been, claimed David Kennedy, an outstanding success.

It was a success that was to be measured not alone in terms of revenue. During his period in Bangkok Seán Braiden was acting both for Aer Lingus and the newly-formed Guinness Peat Aviation, the prospects for which had been considerably advanced as a consequence of Tony Ryan's success with Air Siam. When that airline collapsed with much of the outstanding debt to Aer Lingus still unpaid, the prospects for recovery did not appear promising; but in October 1976 the Board was informed by G. P. Dempsey that 'Mr Ryan was now endeavouring to complete a sale (of the Air Siam DC10) to Korean Airlines which could lead to our receiving at least some of the money owed. If the deal was successful,' he added, 'it would place Guinness Peat Aviation among the world's leading aircraft broking firms.' The sale was concluded and the foundation laid for the most spectacularly innovative of all the ancillaries in which Aer Lingus had become involved.

On Monday 13 August 1979 a call came up from a ground station to the captain of Boeing 737 EI-BEF, somewhere over the Indian Ocean. 'Is that Mr Ryan's airline?' enquired the voice.

EI-BEF was an aircraft to prompt curiosity. En route from Osaka, Japan to Lagos, Nigeria via Hong Kong, Bangkok, Bombay and Jeddah, it carried an Irish registration, was painted in the colours and with the name of Nigeria Airways and was owned by Air Tara, the subsidiary of Guinness Peat Aviation, of which Tony Ryan was Chief Executive and Deputy Managing Director. The Shannon-based organisation had become a fast-moving operation in several senses of the term, with its executives flying up to 300,000 miles a year to all parts of the world to finalise deals. Niall Greene, who had joined Aer Lingus in 1961, becoming a Departmental Personnel Manager in 1970, went to Guinness Peat in 1976. 'Initially', he said, 'I was the sales guy responsible for South America. I was uniquely qualified for this in that I spoke neither Spanish nor Portuguese. However, once the first deal was done, I became hooked on aircraft leasing.' Greene was appointed Head of the Sales Organisation in 1980; three years later Maurice Foley joined from Aer Lingus as President and Managing Director. The same Aer Lingus view that to be successful in the aircraft leasing and broking business partners such as Guinness Peat Group were necessary now dictated that a North American partner should be invited to join. Air Canada acquired a 29.3 per cent shareholding, becoming an equal partner with Aer Lingus and Guinness Peat Group, with Tony Ryan holding the balance. Dick White, who represented Aer Lingus on the GPA Board and served as Chairman for a number of years, commented that not merely did Air Canada bring a strengthened North American perspective to GPA, it also changed its character from one with a Boeing emphasis into one which more clearly covered the total modern aircraft range. Bringing in new partners not merely brought strategic advantages to GPA, it also enabled Aer Lingus and the earlier partners to make a sizeable capital gain. The exercise was repeated in 1983 when General Credit Corporation paid $18 million for 22.68 per cent of the company — thus becoming an equal fourth partner with Aer Lingus, Guinness Peat Group and Air Canada, with Tony Ryan retaining 9.2 per cent of the equity. In 1983 Guinness Peat Aviation had a turnover of £55 million and a profit of £7 million; and in a review of the company in the following year by a London stockbroking firm was valued at $100 million. 'GPA provides a service where it is recognised as the market leader,' the review stated: 'Its knowledge of the market place and its ability to package a deal for a specific customer are widely recognised.' In December 1984 the company placed an order with McDonnell-Douglas for twenty-four new medium-range MD-83s at a cost of $600,000, forming a new company, Irish Aerospace, with the manufacturers for the purpose. In May, Guinness Peat Aviation raised $135 million in a loan facility, the largest financing package ever negotiated by the Irish commercial company on the London market. Tony Ryan told the United States Chamber of Commerce in Dublin in the same month that it was his ambition to see the growth of GPA's assets from the then level of $250 million to $1,000 million by 1990. In June of that year he became Chairman of the Guinness Peat Aviation group whilst remaining as Chief Executive. In August 1985, with a team which included many ex-Aer Lingus people, GPA was involved with a fleet of fifty-seven planes, forty-seven of which it either owned outright or leased in. The success of GPA lay, in the view of Paul Tansey, in 'the discovery and aggressive exploitation of a gap in the airline market; the realisation at an early stage that GPA was primarily in the finance, not the aircraft business; the benign tax environment in which the company operates at Shannon, and, most importantly, Tony Ryan, himself.' 'As co-founder of the entire enterprise', said G. P. Dempsey in 1985, 'Aer Lingus had some cause for pride in the manner in which the vision of 1975 had been not merely realised but surpassed.'

12

Do Chairde San Aer 1936–86

THE 1936 Aer Lingus summer timetable was a modest enough affair. In the square format favoured by the Great Northern Railway it set out the times of the services, details of the ground transportation and the necessary information that smoking was not permitted in or near the aircraft and that baggage over the free allowance of thirty lbs would be charged for at 6d (2.5p) a lb. The image it conveyed (though few would then have understood the usage of the word) was one of a businesslike operation — and, unmistakably, an Irish businesslike operation. The money, the pilot and much of the expertise might have resided with the foreign partner, but the name of Aer Lingus Teoranta was printed in type at least twice the size of that of its associate, and in the Gaelic script.

The first company letterhead, produced by Wood Printing Works, carried a shamrock upon which were superscribed, not very felicitously, the initials A L T, again in their Gaelic form. The first aircraft was painted silver with black outlines in a style which later earned itself the sobriquet of 'the mourning envelope' and, apart from the name IOLAR and the obligatory registration letters, was otherwise unadorned, as were the operating personnel. It was early in 1938 before designs for badges for caps and berets were submitted and approved, the Board thereupon deciding that the matter of publicity should be made the direct concern of a member of the staff and be controlled from within the company, and that the practice of employing a consultant on a retaining fee should be discontinued. In May of that year McConnell's of Dublin were appointed the company's advertising agents, with an appropriation for 1938/39 of £1,083.17s.0d. (£1,083.85). The insignia which had been in use until that point — a complicated arrangement of stylised wings surmounted by a harp which had the appearance of a committee revision of R. F. O'Connor's original concept — was abandoned and replaced by the shamrock, which was to undergo many transmogrifications in the course of its enduring association with the national airline.

Following its premature birth on the letterhead, the symbol emerged with a wing on one side only and it was not until 1939 that Seán O'Connell, the Publicity Assistant, suggested that when being used for stationery and advertising literature generally it would appear more complete by having a wing attached to both sides. The same Board meeting which approved this suggestion also agreed to provide uniforms for the traffic staff and to seek designs for a house flag. A publicity committee, consisting of Seán Ó hUadhaigh, J. P. O'Brien and T. J. Flynn, the latter later replaced by J. J. O'Leary, had been set up to control the publicity and advertising of both Aer Lingus and Aer Rianta, and had suggested that the description 'Irish Air Lines' should be appended to the Aer Lingus name: 'when operating into foreign countries', it explained: 'it was desirable that the name of the company should appear in a language additional to the Irish language.' The choice of English was, no doubt, entirely fortuitous.

On a broader level the *persona* was already well on the way to being characterised. James Dillon, in the Dáil in 1939, might have been speaking to an advertising brief: 'The ships are good; the schedule is well-kept; the accommodation at Baldonnel is perfectly reasonable; the personnel is admirable; every facility, convenience and courtesy are extended to people travelling by the airline'. It is doubtful whether McConnell's could have put it better.

The plaudits of statesmen were all very well but, more important from the company's point of view, was public awareness. The services had opened in 1936 in what could only be described as a flicker of publicity; and though the names of the passengers were for a period to be found in the daily Personal Column of *The Irish Times*, air travel could scarcely have been said to have stood high in the public consciousness. The establishment of an airline had come as something of a shock. 'The general problem was there, the problem of acceptance', in the estimate of J. F. Dempsey: 'There were cynics who thought that this was something not possible for the Irish people. The Irish had not the greatest reputation in the world for punctuality, were considered to be somewhat feckless and not capable of application to matters of any great precision such as the operation of an airline: and with that not overcome even after the war, the transatlantic service became one of the things they found it hard to comprehend. How would we find our way — even more so, our way back?'

The Emergency imposed its own drastic limitations in the matter of creating a public awareness, but the Board — and Ó hUadhaigh in particular — were not without resources. From the beginning, and mindful of their own origins, they had encouraged education in air-mindedness, making facilities available at the new Collinstown airport for the Irish Aero Club, the Irish Junior Aviation Club and the Model Aeronautics Council of Éire. In November 1941 Seán Ó hUadhaigh contributed to the catalogue of the First Exhibition of Inventions, Models and Aeroplanes, held in Dublin's Mansion House, an article 'An Eitilleóireacht in Éireann' [*sic*] which was also printed in an English version. In it he placed the role of Aer Lingus firmly within the national context: 'I think it right to say that the men who persuaded our rulers to go in for aviation as a major, large-scale National Activity, and here may I pay tribute to the members of the Government for their enlightened and prompt receptiveness, not only foresaw a great advantage to the Nation in general if we avoided playing second fiddle to anyone in the Air, but also aimed from the very beginning at securing well-paid employment for a large and growing section of our young men. . . . If our geographical position were not exploited to the full, it would be an act of treachery to future generations of Irishmen and women. . . . Finally I may say that one myth has been laid to rest in this country, namely that Irishmen cannot do these things. Irish National Aviation is manned by Irishmen. Whether we look at military or civil aviation . . . we see Irishmen making good as well as the best. Those who pioneered, both on the official and on the non-official ends, in this work can justly claim the credit for having rejected from the word "Go" that paralysing tendency to seek the "foreign expert" which has led so many promising enterprises in our country to an untimely demise. . . .'

The image of Ireland in the Emergency, as fostered both at the time and subsequently by interests to whom her neutrality was anathema, was one, in the words of R. J. Raymond, of 'economic stagnation during which the economic disasters of World War II were reaped in full: stagnating production, raging inflation, falling living standards, and declining real wages. The most significant and persuasive effect of the "Emergency", however, was a new consciousness that the Irish economy could be directed into the desired channels and the acquisition of some knowledge of how to guide it.' If this were true of the nation in general, it had particular application to Aer Lingus which, whilst continuing to plan vigorously for the future, was obliged to become fully self-reliant under the stress of economic and political circumstances. 'Your travel service of today and tomorrow', proclaimed the advertisement on the back of the 1941 Mansion House programme. The aircraft illustrated was the then unique DC3, unnamed and otherwise unidentified. The copy offered 'Week-day services to and from Great Britain with Speed, Comfort and Security'. Friendliness was for the future — and the introduction of the female element.

After the end of the war in Europe the writer Francis Stuart, who had been living and working in Berlin, made his way painfully back to Ireland via a French prison camp and a long series of humiliations and difficulties. This return of the native is mirrored rather than precisely recorded in his novel *Good Friday's Daughter*, published in 1952: 'When the air hostess opened a door in the glass wall and summoned the little group of travellers, adding "No smoking, please", Mark hung on each word and gesture. Her slight smile, her green costume that was not quite a uniform, her walk as she led them a few yards across the airfield, all had a peculiar significance. She was the shepherdess, leading him back to the fold out of which he had wandered, the first fellow countrywoman speaking his own language with the soft accent of home after an exile amid strange tongues, and only in a secondary degree an official making routine announcements.'

Some number of years later another returning literary exile, William Trevor, registered a similar reaction in *Fools of Fortune*: 'On the plane the pretty stewardess was attentive, smart in her green uniform. Her voice reminded me of Ireland.

"Yes, please", I said. "Yes, I think a little whiskey".

She smiled a soothing, airline smile.

"Jameson?", she murmured, caressing me with the familiar name.'

There was something about that 'soothing airline smile', it was widely agreed in the immediate post-war years, which created the 'friendly' image of Aer Lingus more than any other single factor: 'All the girls were ladies,' Nuala Doyle recalled, adding that they could not go into the centre of Dublin in their uniforms for fear of being mobbed because they were 'so unusual'. When they did go in, in civilian clothes, they made for Trinity College, for the museums and art galleries to 'learn off things to talk to the passengers about'. The passengers responded, or some of them: the Aly Khan, a regular traveller, invited a group of the girls to the races. Not all, however, were equally captivated. Peter Kavanagh, writing as John L. Flanagan in *Kavanagh's Weekly* in 1952, reported on a flight back from Manchester: 'I noticed that the hostess kept her money in a *cifleóg* — a little cloth bag, with a string around the top, which was a popular kind of purse with old country-women fifty years ago. It was the only bit of Irishness I noticed about Aer Lingus.'

Had he cast his gaze further, he would have seen that the DC3 was carrying not only the shamrock symbol of the airline in its current version but the name of an Irish saint. Throughout the Emergency there had been a good deal of Board discussion as to the names to be carried by the post-war fleet: *Iolar, Éire* and *Sasana,* it was felt, had not been altogether satisfactory in terms of projecting an image. In May 1946 a list of islands and birds was circulated by the Secretary, to be rejected in favour of the saints, and in July J. P. O'Brien and J. J. O'Leary were authorised to take the final decision. In July of the following year a somewhat curious ceremony took place at Dublin Airport. The first annual blessing of the fleet was performed by Rev. W. N. Henry, C.C., Swords, county Dublin, assisted by his brother from San Francisco and another priest from Oregon. The available fleet consisted of the DC3 *St Malachy* (EI-ACG) and Viking *St Ronan* (EI-ADF) which had been barely a month in service. The opportunity was taken, however, to bless and name eighteen other aircraft *in absentia*, all of them after Irish saints. Some of these must have been at the time little more than gleams in the eyes of the aircraft constructors. Thus was established the naming policy that was to rule thereafter, to be modified only by the addition of the name in the original Irish, followed by the dropping of the English version (and its subsequent re-introduction) and the omission of the celestial rank. The same names, in the course of the years, were applied to a succession of aircraft, many having carried during their period of service more than one, since it was the policy to transfer *Pádraig* and *Brighid* regularly to the most currently prestigious members of the fleet. A DC3 registered in November 1948 (EI-AFA) carried, for example, the names *St Kevin, St Laurence O'Toole, St Fergal* and *St Declan* in the course of its Aer Lingus career which lasted until October 1963. After a subsequent *St Kevin*, EI-AFL, had crashed in Wales in 1952 the name was not re-employed. The Friendships were all given names beginning with the letter F: fortunately the availability of saints proved adequate to cater for the full extent of fleet development.

A last word on nomenclature might fairly be left to Myles na gCopaleen, writing in *The Irish Times* in May 1948: 'the present writer (present, tense) has just returned by air from Paris where he has been acting as honorary valet and adviser to His Grace the Duke of Edinburgh. He takes leave at this stage to record that on alighting from the Aer Lingus aeroplane, an astounding and scandalous thing happened, viz. he was not met and "welcomed" by either Mr Seán Leydon or Mr J. J. O'Leary. Back to Ireland, land of insults! (But of course there may be a general sulk on over the gold-plated Constellations) One constellation — sorry! — one consolation about that particular business is that our eyes will not much longer be affrighted by the atrocity of the spelling *St Bridget*. Whoever thought that one up should be sold up with the planes and sent packing to Pakistan. . . . '

'Cushla mochree, and would you look what the Irish are doing! 'Tis a proud day that's coming for the Irish! It's a shamrock that's coming . . . the likes of which ye've never seen before. . . . And did you hear the news that's going round — the Irish are flying on St Patrick's Day' — Dr Noel Browne, speaking in the Dáil in 1952 on the occasion of the second attempt at a transatlantic service, was recalling the 1948 advertising in the *New Yorker* and elsewhere, with some distaste: 'There were the typical Irish caubeen and dudeen, and I think a pig came in somewhere. Positively shameful.' A Mr Harris of the American agency Foote, Cone and Belding had been appointed advertising and publicity manager for a period of twelve months from March 1947, but it is probably unfair to lay all the caubeens and dudeens at his door. The proposed transatlantic service was aimed very largely at the ethnic market and, for better or worse, this was the image of Ireland harboured by a high percentage of second and third-generation Irish. The caubeens did not reappear in 1958, but the image with which they were associated was slow to

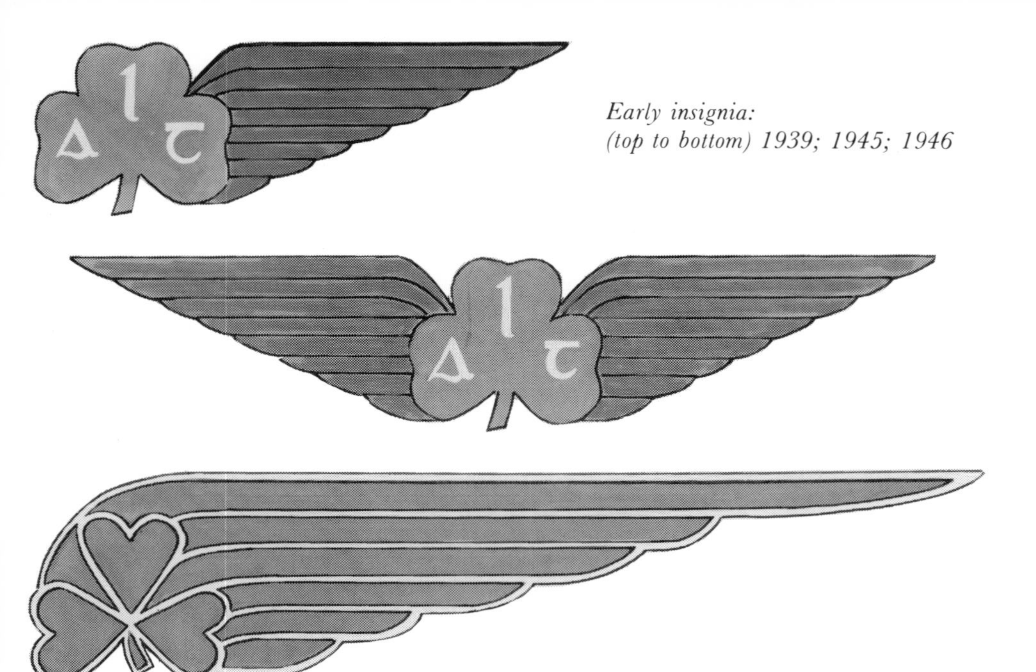

Early insignia:
(top to bottom) 1939; 1945; 1946

CLONTARF LOOKS DOWN ON SALLYNOGGIN

Remarkable the community spirit shown in those Sunday p.m. Scenic Flights, as, say, Clontarfites look down on Sallynoggin and other sections to compare notes. From the air each Dublin section stands out like your long-lost uncle's will, and is delightful to behold. Instructive, too!

10/-

Every SUNDAY at 4 p.m., BALDONNEL AIRPORT.

Free 'Bus From Office at 3.15 p.m.

AER LINGUS TEORANTA

39 Upr. O'Connell St.

'Phone 72872-3 for reservations

Fly to DUBLIN HORSE SHOW in 2½ hours

Just time to read through your newspaper before you step out at Dublin after the most luxurious 'armchair' journey you have ever experienced. Details and timetables from your travel agent, or phone.

- **LONDON** Croydon 5117/8
- **DUBLIN** Clondalkin 39 (day) Dublin 43533(night)
- **BRISTOL** Bristol 41165
- **ISLE OF MAN** Castletown 106
- **LIVERPOOL** Garston 64

IRISH SEA AIRWAYS

AIRPORT OF LONDON, CROYDON

Early advertisements:

British Media,
30 July 1938

Dublin 'Evening Mail',
13 May 1938

'A piece of design that tidied up something':
Kenneth Hollick's logo

dissipate. If Aer Lingus were not actually in the business of hand-feeding the pig over the years, neither were they over-hasty to show him the door, since there were positive sales advantages to be gleaned from the picture of a rural, technically innocent community where the concept of *mañana* was considered as something dangerously progressive. The roots were firmly embedded in the clay of a rural paradise, and one of the most successful Aer Lingus publicity items proved to be a large map of Ireland bearing all the family names — or as many as could be accommodated — displayed in the office window in Fifth Avenue, New York. There was nearly always a crowd round it, with people sometimes almost kneeling in snow and slush to attempt to identify the most southerly of their putative origins.

The fostering of this image — or the reluctance to do much to dispel it — was to lead in due course to some conflict of interest when the Industrial Development Authority began to sell Ireland as a home for high-technology industry with a full range of sophisticated resources and a modern infrastructure. The forty million Americans claiming Irish ancestry continued, nevertheless, to represent a significant segment of the traffic and their preconceptions were slow to change, both as regards the country and its airline. 'We still come across people', one of the New York staff acknowledged in 1985, 'who are surprised to find that we go beyond Ireland.'

The origin of this enduring ignorance of the European arm of Aer Lingus can be traced to the policy, introduced with the transatlantic service, of a diversified nomenclature. 'It has been found essential for commercial purposes, particularly in North America, to avoid distinguishing between Aer Lingus and Aerlínte. The trade name 'Aer Lingus — Irish International Airlines' is now widely used to denote all services,' the Chairman wrote in the 1962 annual report. What was used, in fact, on the transatlantic aircraft was 'Irish International Airlines — Aer Lingus', an indigestible mouthful which became attenuated on the American continent, first to Irish International and, subsequently, to Irish: the B747s, when introduced, carried the legend 'Irish — Aer Lingus'. Throughout the 1960s, when the transatlantic services were returning consistent profits, the New York office, and particularly its head, Jim Leet, resisted any attempt to market the airline under the name Aer Lingus, convinced that the American public would not accept it and that sales would slump drastically as a result. Thus there evolved, as Neil McIvor saw it, 'a different company with a different logo, a different style of doing business, very much involved with the ethnic market in a way not always of benefit to the long-term interests of the airline'. The only unifying feature, in terms of corporate image, was the shamrock on the tail of the aircraft, and a rather clumsy boxing of the two names set out on two lines, with Aer Lingus uppermost in Europe and Irish International in North America, which was used on display and other promotional material.

In so far as there was a corporate image at all, it had evolved in a haphazard manner. The stripes on the tail and the boxing were devised by Kenneth Hollick, a designer working for the airline's London advertising agency, Collet Dickenson and Pearse. It was seen as a graphic problem only and was not, as McIvor put it, 'an exercise with a great deal of integrity. As a piece of design that tidied up something it was reasonable'.

Aer Lingus moved to Collet Dickenson and Pearse in 1961 following objections from British Airways to both airlines employing Foote, Cone and Belding. CDP was a small and very new agency and Aer Lingus was only their second account. Jim Pearse, the founder and Managing Director, had some very positive ideas for his new client. Up to that point the airline's advertising in Britain had been something of a hit or miss affair, and apart from a major campaign run in conjunction with the introduction of the Viscounts, there was little policy or coherence behind it. Pearse advised Aer Lingus to forego this piecemeal approach and put all its appropriation into a new and as yet untried medium: the colour supplement of the London *Sunday Times*. The advice was taken; and there followed, as Neil McIvor described it, 'six or seven years of the most fabulous advertising promoting Ireland'. The approach was stylish, sophisticated, topical: 'Beatle off to Ireland' was the heading on a photograph of a currach with four legs protruding from underneath it — the shot had not yet become a tourist cliché. The advertising set out quite deliberately to sell the airline through the destination, and not vice versa. ('The Irish will give you plenty to do . . . and flying will give you an extra day to do nothing' was the theme of one of the double-page spreads that appeared in 1967). The extended campaign ran at a time when tourism from Britain was booming and its overt aim was to upgrade the image of the tourist product — and, by inference, the airline. It was continued until the confrontation in Northern Ireland produced an entirely new situation.

In the broader sphere the realisation was slowly dawning that what was coming to be described in the current jargon as a 'total communications strategy' needed to be devised if the airline were to continue to make an impact in an increasingly competitive field. From being in the 1950s one of a select group of European airlines that stood reasonably high in public awareness, Aer Lingus was being overtaken by small concerns that had grown in confidence and purpose. 'We need the strength of unity, the tone of voice that was going to be the same everywhere,' was Neil McIvor's evaluation of the situation as Head of Publicity: 'when you took a small thing and made it smaller you obviously suffered.' In 1971, after a lengthy investigation and a degree of heart-searching, the airline appointed the New York firm of Lipincott & Marguiles, design consultants, to report on the future 'look' of the operation. The appointment aroused strong criticism in Irish design circles which saw it as yet another example of calling in the foreign expert when there was ample talent deployable at home. In fact very few design consultancies in Ireland at the time had developed beyond house styles, essentially a graphic approach, to the formulation of a full 'communications strategy' — though it is quite possible that, given the opportunity, there would have been little reluctance to accept the challenge. Lipincott & Marguiles spent some months talking to everybody and anybody in Aer Lingus, from management to cusmer. Their report was presented in September 1971. They were good but they were, in Irish terms, very expensive and likely to prove more so, since they reserved the right to design every item as it became a candidate for replacement — from aircraft liveries to baggage tags. Ideally Aer Lingus would have liked from them a design manual from which they could have derived their own adaptations as the need arose. In the circumstances the relationship with Lipincott & Marguiles was not pursued and the task was given to the London firm of King & Wetherell. Arthur King had been running the London office of Lipincott & Marguiles and had recently set up on his own. He thus started with a considerable advantage, and proceeded to originate a strategy which was accepted and implemented from 1974 onwards.

In terms of what had gone before the 'new look' was revolutionary. Green was retained as the dominant colour — it could scarcely have been otherwise — but to the two shades of light and dark, strengthened from the 'Winchester Green' and 'Light Green' of Kenneth Hollick's scheme — was added, in the words of the promotional brochure, 'a clear, fresh blue, which "lifts" the whole effect and introduces a new, vital note'. What really caused a minor internal revolution, however, was the proposed treatment of the hallowed symbol of the shamrock. In Hollick's treatment it had been 'regularised and enclosed in a striped box which has five white bars'. This, he claimed, 'considerably strengthens and streamlines the shamrock motif'. But what G. A. Hayes-McCoy described in his book *A History of Irish Flags* as 'a very chaste vestige of the luxuriant growth of bygone years' was to be all but ravished by King & Wetherell. They produced a shamrock without a stem. It was regarded by traditionalists both as a botanical absurdity and an affront to a hallowed national symbol, but it was in fact based on an actual specimen and it worked — particularly on the tail fin of the aircraft where it appeared, in another affront to the conservative, in white on a green background. It proved to be strongly competitive with other airlines' symbols at international airports. Hollick's somewhat eccentric modified Egyptian upper-case lettering for the airline name was replaced by one of the new breed of sans-serifs: solid, legible and businesslike, if somewhat short on romance. The name Irish International Airlines vanished, without the predicted collapse of the North American market. The whole transformation was, in Neil McIvor's view, 'one of the things that the airline did rather well'. Arthur King was subsequently asked to produce the new image for the Bank of Ireland and for several other airlines.

Some people don't even know where Ireland is which is a very good reason for going there!

Dublin in the early morning. The city is still asleep. Only the river Liffey is on its way and singing as it goes. Lights are still flickering, strung like pearls on a string and a romantic evening ends as dawn peeps over the roof-tops. This is Ireland, the last unspoiled country in Western Europe. Here people who yearn for peace and tranquillity can escape from the rush and care of everyday live to another world. Here on this island country about 1/8 the size of France you will find wild unspoiled beauty, green valleys, white thatched cottages, placid lakes and peaceful villages. Here too you will find fishing and horse-riding and golf (more than 200 fine courses) and thousands of beaches. In Ireland you can explore wild picturesque mountains and moors without meeting a soul or mingle with the Irish at a colourful race meeting. Join the rousing singing in a pub or sit quietly listening to the waves washing the sand. Here you will enjoy good food, prime steak and fresh fresh seafood for instance and stay in friendly comfortable hotels. But you will look in vain for the hectic glitter of organised commercial tourism.

Not many holidaymakers know Ireland, this land of poets and dreamers, singers and storytellers, this year discover it for yourself. To get there is easy. By new swift Aer Lingus One-Eleven jet, the direct flight takes only a couple of hours. To find out more about Ireland and its airline send the attached coupon or talk to your travel agent or Aer Lingus at . . . . telephone . . . .

Coupon reply

Yes, I would like to know more about Ireland, so please send me your coloured booklet free of charge.

Name:

Address:

AER LINGUS

'. . . this land of poets and dreamers, singers and storytellers . . .' self-image, 1960-style

Not everybody was enamoured of the new look. Writing in the newsletter of the Society of Designers in Ireland in the autumn of 1984, some ten years after its introduction, a columnist, 'The Citizen', confessed that he or she 'conceived a deep hatred for this when it was first unveiled which the years have done nothing to moderate'. This dislike centred on 'the gross treatment of the shamrock which has nothing to do with plant forms but looks like an anatomical section. Someday, someone will mount an exhibition called "the poor bloody shamrock" showing the tortures the national weed has endured at the hands of designers. In general, aeroplane liveries are a vulgar lot heavily influenced by American design modes of the 1970s.'

On 22 July 1949 the Board agreed to spend £1,574 on hats, greatcoats, blouses, shoes, gloves and stockings — a sufficiency of the components of the hostess uniform, it was estimated to last until 31 March 1950. Over the years there were many changes of style, skirts ascending and descending in accord

Pre-Morton: Hostesses on parade, St Patrick's Day, 1968, in New York. The Fifth Avenue office is in the background.

AER LINGUS

with the dictates of earthbound fashion. 'Our regular passengers this summer will notice how our air hostesses and our girls on the ground at airports and booking offices are stepping into the seventies with a new touch of elegance,' Michael Dargan wrote in the April-June 1970 issue of the inflight magazine *Cara*: 'the new emerald green and St Patrick's blue uniforms are indeed easy on the eye'. In the same issue Vici Hainworth, a writer for the magazine *Harper's Bazaar*, described the genesis of the new uniform: '... hostesses and other uniformed girls were invited to take part in a design competition. A prize was offered for the best design and a selection of the entries was later used to brief the designer chosen. Having ensured a degree of practical participation by the hostesses themselves the airline sought out established couturiers in Ireland and in the international fashion world in New York, London and Rome. And happily, in choosing one of the top men in the London fashion scene Aer Lingus chose an Irishman. The man is Digby Morton.' Morton's ambition was to combine St Patrick's blue, which he remembered from his days as a choirboy in Dublin's Church of Ireland cathedral, with a true emerald green, achieved by borrowing and studying a friend's emeralds. 'He decided to dispense with the blouse and skirt,' wrote Vici Hainworth, 'to introduce a close-fitting pinafore dress worn over the new St Patrick's blue blouse, with a short jacket, simple flared coat, all saddle stitched and seamed in bold, definite lines, The perkily attractive new hat ... is distinctive without resorting to gimmickry and looks becoming over any hair-do.' 'A girl's dress is her armour,' the writer continued: 'a calculated reflection of her image, her personality. And on Aer Lingus this is her uniform. Not the anonymous mask of dreaded school uniforms, but a definite identity, a reflection of Ireland.'

The 'definite identity', in the Digby Morton version proved fairly rapidly to be found wanting, the 'spinach-shade legs', as one commentator described them, drawing a degree of unfavourable criticism from both the observer and the observed. In 1974 the Uniform Committee, chaired by Sadie Troy, then Manager-Passenger Services, circulated a questionnaire to all uniformed female employees. 'Nobody wanted pants,' reported the *Irish Independent* columnist Mary McGoris: 'Nobody wanted gimmicks. The overwhelming desire of Aer Lingus's uniformed ladies, expressed in consensus, was that their new uniforms should be classic. They also wanted to look feminine and as much as possible in current fashion. ...' The problem was on this occasion placed in the hands of Ib Jorgensen, the Danish-born designer working in Ireland and noted, said Mary McGoris, 'for designing clothes which never ignore the fact that a woman is a woman. He produced a design which is at least among the most elegant and charming among the airlines of the world and moreover suits at once the nature of the work and the wishes of the women. ... The basic ingredient is a suit. The skirt has two gored box-pleats in front and sways in three flat gored panels at the back, perfectly adapted to allow freedom of movement without any danger of unexpected indelicacy on windswept tarmacs.' The colour preference revealed by the questionnaire was for green, though with a sizeable minority in favour of blue. 'The blue and green factions were both satisfied,' reported McGoris: 'Jorgensen and his wife, Patricia, a textile designer in her own right, worked out a weave of green with blue which is especially made for the airline in two weights of tweed by Magees of Donegal.'

The Jorgensen uniform proved popular with both the wearers and the travelling public and was retained in its essentials through the early 1980s.

'Friendliaer Lingus': the play on the name was the essence of a campaign devised in 1974 by Iain MacCartaigh for McConnell's, currently handling the airline's domestic advertising. The 'friendly' image by then stood in some need of refurbishment, the 'reflection of Ireland' no longer always a reassuring one. 'At the end-user point there isn't a service tradition' said Brendan McGann, a navigator on the Atlantic between 1967 and 1971: 'there isn't a professionalism'. The style of the airline at that time, in his view, was 'hick', and he was equally critical of the hostesses: 'The girls are good in as far as they are allowed to do the job, but there was no upmarket, professional style about them — it's a village style.' If this was perhaps an extreme view, it was echoed within management in a concern over standards of service generally. Neil McIvor believed that the Dempsey philosophy of a small group of people being motivated because they saw the end product of what they were doing was in urgent need of being replaced. The standards of service were up and down, the standard of the individual, as he saw it, not what people expected. 'We got along in bumbling good humour — people forgave us a lot because we were so nice about it.'

James Dillon had put his finger on it as far back as 1962: 'It may be that with the development and growth of air transport, it is no longer possible to preserve the air of informality which was one of the great attractions of Aer Lingus. As people gained more experience of competitive airlines they were becoming less tolerant of the blend of charm and good humour masking deficiencies in standards'. 'We didn't have enough operating manuals,' complained McIvor: 'we paid lip service to staff training but we did not say "this is the standard that we operate and we will not compromise" '. After one particular acerbic management discussion over the cleanliness of the aircraft the Traffic Manager, Oliver Hone, was instructed to stop the flight if the plane concerned was not clean. He went close to it once or twice, McIvor recalled, 'but in fact he never stopped a flight. If he had, then we might actually have begun to establish the standards. But there was always the conflict with expediency, and expediency ruled as it rules a lot of Irish companies.' The aim, according to Hone, was to ensure that when passengers boarded the aircraft 'they were in a kind of envelope of Irish hospitality. A good meal served by an indifferent hostess was far less valuable than a good cup of coffee served with charm'. His recollection of 'the old days', when 'we had a percentage of people . . . who would not be satisfied and had to be told that if we did not satisfy them there were alternatives', was symptomatic of an attitude that was in some respects slow to change. The situation was judged to be critical enough, in 1963, to demand a new system of quality control 'to ensure', as the annual report disarmingly put it, 'that the standard of our sales service is maintained at a high level'. This took the form of special travel by selected staff who prepared analyses of their experience as passengers and of selling facilities in the countries they visited. The problem proved to be, as in most service industries, a recurring one — a fact recognised by the airline in a succession of internal staff relations projects aimed at heightening awareness and producing a constructive response. In 1984 a major campaign to raise standards was inaugurated when an internal programme dubbed 'Quality Quest' was announced as 'seeking to bring about a marked improvement in the product we deliver to our customers on all our services'. 'Aer Lingus has always demonstrated the strength of its selling efforts by consistently achieving market shares well in excess of fifty per cent against the competition,' said David Kennedy: 'The success of the "Quality Quest" campaign, with its emphasis on consistency of good service, gave the sales achievement another boost.' In the course of the first twelve months of the new programme the number of unsolicited complimentary letters doubled. In the summer of 1985 a major customer survey, covering 80,000 passengers and which was organised by IATA among the major carriers serving Ireland and Britain from the United States placed Aer Lingus clearly at the top in the category of satisfying its customers. In eighteen out of twenty-one elements of customer service it was judged either first or equal first among the airlines included in the survey. The traditional image of the 'friendly airline' was being refurbished through a more professional approach to service standards with tangible results.

In 1974 the Board heard a proposal for a club for regular travellers on the lines of those instituted by other airlines. It was agreed that commercial pressures would virtually compel its establishment, though fears were expressed on the dangers inherent in a practice that was to offer special privileges to regular customers. The name initially chosen was 'Corballis Circle', after Corballis House, once an isolated mansion in the countryside of north county Dublin which was acquired by the airline in 1953 for use by the personnel and training departments and had long been engulfed by the expansion of the airport. The name proved too localised and lacking in the necessary resonance, and was subsequently changed to the predictable 'Tara Circle'. It offered, in common with similar facilities offered by other airlines, a heightened degree of creature comfort at a limited number of airports and an element of ostentation in keeping with the expectations of the class of traveller for which it was designed to cater.

The multiplicity of passenger adjuncts which are now a commonplace of air travel for virtually all classes of passenger were in the mid-1960s concentrated, on Aer Lingus services, in a 'flight pack' which contained a bar tariff, a route map, a sick bag, and an assortment of promotional literature, the entirety of which was frequently scattered over the cabin floor by the impetuous or the uncaring. Neil McIvor had been attracted by Pan American's recently introduced inflight magazine and suggested an equivalent for Aer Lingus primarily as a means of bringing the diversity of printed material between covers, but with the secondary notion of promoting both Ireland and the airline. (The first element of this latter responsibility was being ably borne by Bord Fáilte's *Ireland of the Welcomes* which was carried on Aer Lingus flights with a special insert). *Cara* was first published, as a quarterly, in January 1968, the choice of editor having finally lain between Gordon Clark, who was successful, and Terence de Vere White, then Literary Editor of *The Irish Times*. 'CARA in its content and its production will reflect the high international standard which we set ourselves in all our endeavours,' Michael Dargan wrote in the first issue: some fifteen years later it was ranked by an international media publication with the magazines of Lufthansa and Air New Zealand as one of the three best in the field. *Cara* became bi-monthly in 1978. '*Certaines revues de compagnies aériennes ne sont, dans leur hâte à séduire le chaland, que la vitrine clinquante de leur pays d'origine paré et maquillé pour apparaître dans tout l'éclat factice d'une beauté hélas passablement dénaturé*', wrote *Études Irlandaises* in 1981: '*Cara . . . se garde bien de tomber dans de tels excès.*'

In its original memorandum of association Aer Lingus was empowered to 'support any charitable or public objects, and any fund, institution, society or club of a character conducive to the interests of the Company or its employees': and Aer Rianta, the parent company, was charged under the Act with the encouragement of aviation. These provisions were interpreted over the years as constituting a definite commitment to aviation education in its broadest aspect: a specialist education officer functioned within the publicity department. Aer Rianta, in as far as it operated a separate policy, concentrated on the area of sporting and amateur flying, gliding and aeromodelling, principally through the provision of grants and facilities at the airport; Aer Lingus was committed to the wider responsibility of making the country more air-minded, with particular emphasis on the younger generation. In 1954, for example, the education service produced an air map centred on the Shannon meridian and booklets on aviation in both Irish and English were circulated to schools.

In 1964 Father Tom Burke, a physicist at University College Dublin, paid a visit to a science fair in the United States and conceived the idea of a Young

Scientists' Exhibition. On his return he approached J. F. Dempsey, and the proposal was put before the combined Boards of Aer Lingus, Aerlínte and Aer Rianta on 27 February and approved. The first Young Scientists' Exhibition was held on a modest scale in Dublin in 1965. The winner was John Monaghan of Newbridge College, county Kildare, who offered a project on enzymes in the digestive system. He subsequently graduated in biochemistry from University College Dublin and when invited to be present at the Twenty-first Exhibition in 1985 was researching cell biology at the Roche Institute of Molecular Biology in New Jersey. He was joined on that occasion by a large number of former Young Scientists, many of whom had followed scientific careers with distinction subsequent to their winning the award. Many had also, following the Irish competition, gone on to achieve success in similar European contests. By 1985 the Exhibition had established itself as a major contribution to educational development in the scientific field. 'We are immensely encouraged by the steady growth . . . ' David Kennedy, the Chief Executive, wrote on that occasion: 'the increasing variety and complexity of

Young Scientists, 1986, with the Taoiseach, Dr Garret FitzGerald

AER LINGUS

the projects, and the extraordinarily supportive atmosphere in which the organisers work. As a physicist, I have a very personal interest in the Young Scientists' Exhibition. I am delighted that the enthusiasm I feel is so widely shared.' One particular source of satisfaction to the organisers was the support and involvement the event had consistently succeeded in attracting from schools and individuals in Northern Ireland: and many Northern names figured among the prizewinners.

Though this major venture was successfully maintained through the years of retrenchment, with some assistance in the form of grants from other bodies, the general education service fell victim to financial stringencies. Its residual function in the early 1980s was responsive rather than innovative: filling requests for informative material from school pupils engaged in projects and from journalists seeking background documentation. The activities of the airline in foreign fields continued to provoke similar requests: 'Wherever we have people in the world it tends to generate an interest in Aer Lingus,' said Margaret Coyne. The visit of a Chinese delegation to Dublin Airport in 1985 was followed within a week by requests from that country.

On 8 May 1936 Seán Ó hUadhaigh told two hundred children being presented with the Fáinne that the name of the new airline and its first aircraft would be in Irish only. He added that everything in their power would be done to have as much as possible of the business connected with the air service carried out in Irish. 'The use of the Irish language is encouraged by the Air Companies in a variety of ways,' the 1964 annual report asserted: 'We favour fostering the language in our affairs and we are at all times examining ways and means to ensure that those who wish to transact business with us in the Irish language may do so. In addition and apart from narrow business considerations, we recognise that in our position as a national enterprise we have a part to play in helping to foster a love of the language for what it should mean socially and culturally.' This attitude, which could be seen as stemming from Seán Ó hUadhaigh's initial commitment, was maintained with fluctuating degrees of intensity, from the formal '*cúpla focal*' uttered by the air hostess and frequently the subject of criticism by an assortment of linguistic watchdogs, to the wholehearted sponsorship of Slógadh, the language youth movement, in partnership with its originators, Gael Linn. 'It provides us with a most useful means of making a positive and practical contribution to fostering and developing the Irish language among teenagers and it fits in admirably with our other Air Education activities,' Niall Weldon told the Board in March 1973: it had approved an annual grant of £5,000 in 1970. The 'positive and practical' emphasis tended to guide the company's attitude to the use of Irish in general: timetables and other publicity material had at least a minimal bilingual content, with the first language considerably more in evidence in such prestige publications as 'Ár scairdeitleáin agus an tseamróg', produced in 1961 as an offering to passengers in a completely bilingual format. The booklet dealt with the naming of the fleet, the national symbols of shamrock and Tara brooch, and concluded on a note of visionary optimism: 'Tá trácht déanta againn ar an seamróig agus ar an seirbhís dár comhartha í. Le déanaí, tá Scairdeitleáin Sheamrógacha Bhoeing curtha le cabhlach Aer Lingus — Aerlínte Idirnáisiúnta na hÉireann, agus is comhartha eile é sin: comhartha ar an ndul chun cinn agus ar an meanman atá le brath inniú in Éirinn; agus comhartha is ea é ar ré na heitleóireachta atá tar éis cóngar cheithre rian a dhéanamh den oileán bheag so againne. Is í Éire úrphost deireannach na hEorpa . . . agus ó tá sí ina lúib cheangail idir an Sean-Domhan agus an Domhan Nua is maith an áirithe rathúnachais di é i gcóir an tsaoil atá amach roimpi.'

The Chairman's review in the annual reports appeared at different periods in both languages; but if certain aspects of the airline's language policy might be characterised as amounting to little more than lip-service, a positive contribution was the fostering of an awareness of Irish as a living tongue among non-Irish passengers and other customers. By contrast Aer Lingus appeared less committed to the development of a satisfactory expertise in other European languages, particularly as it related to passenger service: aircraft cabins, apart from the mandatory announcements, tended to remain monolingual in spite of the existence of language award schemes and the availability of a linguistic laboratory and other learning facilities. In 1985 perhaps 50 per cent of the cabin service personnel had fluency in a Continental language; though in this context it is fair to add that some 85 per cent of the airline's business derived from flights to and from Britain and the USA.

The airline had over the years intermittently demonstrated an awareness of its place in the historical context of Irish aviation history, but it was not until 1969 that an appeal was launched for material and records with a view to the establishment of an aviation museum. J. C. Kelly-Rogers, recently retired, was appointed honorary curator, and pending the development of a full museum, items received as a result of the appeal, together with some from other sources, were placed on exhibition in the new Dublin Airport terminal building in 1975. Plans for a permanent location in Castlemoate House, standing on airport property and owned by Aer Rianta, were subsequently announced and an appeal for outside funding planned. Kelly-Rogers wrote in an article commissioned for *Cara* magazine but not published: 'It was about 1950 that Michael Dargan, then a Departmental head in Aer Lingus . . . proposed the establishment of an Irish aviation museum. Under the pressures of post-war expansion some of his colleagues regarded the proposal as frivolous and nothing was done. More is the pity because it was nearly thirty years before interest in such a project was revived. In the meantime people and material of much historical interest had disappeared from the scene never to return. For it was in 1968, three years after I retired as Deputy General Manager of Aer Lingus, that I received a letter from the company which said, inter alia, "that many priceless relics of aviation in this country will be lost unless we form the nucleus of a museum" and invited my interest in preserving history — an example being the Alcock and Brown memorial at Clifden, Co Galway, for which I had been responsible. . . . I was also reminded that I had helped to make some history myself, flying the first scheduled air mail flights by a European operator to and from New York and Foynes, Co Limerick, in 1939 and the first passenger flights in 1940. . . . Now, in 1978, ten years after that Aer Lingus letter mentioned earlier, what is the score? It is quite good, as can be seen by the aeronautical exhibition at Dublin Airport.' Kelly-Rogers then proceeded to describe the range of exhibits, concluding: 'Over the last ten years the aeronautical collection, all of it having an Irish connection, has grown to a size much larger than can be accommodated in the present exhibition area and its value now runs into tens of thousands of pounds. A permanent and suitable home has been a necessity for some time and, happily, such a thing is now in the pipeline. . . . Buildings associated with the mansion will enable the historic collection of aircraft to be shown collectively, instead of singly, as of now: these include a De Havilland Dragon, a De Havilland Vampire and a Miles Magister. There is also a full size replica of Harry Ferguson's monoplane which I put together myself. I did so because I wanted people to see an example of how it all started and because Harry, a Co Down man, was the first to design, build and fly an aeroplane in this country.'

The Castlemoate House project — Kelly-Rogers' 'suitable home' — was to become a victim of the recessional economics and he did not live to see the collection properly housed. Aer Rianta needed the space it occupied in the terminal building, the exhibits were put in storage and whole scheme languished until Dermot Clarke, who had been a radio operator and subseqeuntly operations controller with Aer Lingus, retired in 1984 and was offered the post of museum curator with the initial task of finding both a site and adequate funding. 'It's crazy that a country like Ireland which has played such a prominent role in the history of aviation still does not have a proper aviation museum,' he told *The Irish Times*: 'every city in the world has one.' A new site at the airport was subsequently earmarked for development, but the project was slow to move and in the meantime, *The Irish Times* columnist succinctly put it: 'the aircraft the museum people have assembled sit twiddling their wings in a shed. . . .'

Supporter of the economy, fosterer of the language, neglecter of the aviation heritage, a 'hick' airline with the saving grace of a friendly presence . . . a corporate image is composed of many at times mutually contradictory elements and an almost infinite number of variables. In Britain, in the view of Conor McGrath, 'Aer Lingus seems to have had a separate image from things Irish and a very positive one'; even though, as Tommy Dunne recalled, the airline spent a lot of time selling Ireland before Bord Fáilte came on the scene. There was a problem, in that context, in that the level at which the promotion was pitched created an impression that Aer Lingus was only for, as he put it, 'top county people'. There was considerable concern as to how to attract other travellers whilst still retaining this valuable element. 'Then one day', said Dunne, 'a huge character climbed out of a hole in the road in Regent Street, walked straight into the office and said "I want to go home". He ignored the queue and the stares of the top county people, pulled out of his pocket a huge wad of fivers and tenners, took his ticket and got down into the hole again. So we did a promotion involving holes in the ground. If he was Irish you gave him a leaflet. Fellers were to be seen stopping their cars and talking into holes.'

Look up, as a later slogan was to put it: it's Aer Lingus.

13

The Troubled Air
1971–81

SEATTLE in early 1971 was a sad place. There were stories of Ph.D.s queueing for jobs in petrol stations, and at Boeing the long line of brand new B747s waiting for someone to come and collect them looked, for all the display of power and presence, somewhat forlorn. There was no room for intimations of mortality, however, among the resident Aer Lingus team which, under Ciaran Mulhall, had been superintending the preparation of the first Aer Lingus Jumbos: up to some three or four weeks before the scheduled delivery date arguments were still proceeding as to the interior carpeting and the use to which the upstairs lounge was to be put. Suggestions ranged from a children's crèche to a stand-up bar, which would almost certainly have resulted in the aircraft flying in a permanently genuflectory posture.

The first of the new aircraft, flown by Captains Peter Little and Gordon Wade, was delivered to Dublin Airport on 6 March to the accompaniment of considerable attendant publicity. The cover photograph of the April-June issue of *Cara* showing the Boeing 747 *St Colmcille* on the apron dwarfing a

'St Colmcille' at Dublin Airport, 6 March 1971, with a replica of 'Iolar' MICHAEL O'REILLY

replica of *Iolar* epitomised the magnitude of this latest addition to the fleet. It went into service on 5 April. Four months later the announcement by the United States' Civil Aeronautics Board gave notice under the US-Ireland Bilateral Agreement that Aerlínte rights at New York were to be suspended with effect from August 1972. On 27 May David Kennedy, described by the General Manager as 'a most promising man in head office' was appointed Senior Vice-President, Americas — or the head of operations on that continent — with effect from the end of the year, at which time the contract of Lou Marechal, who had succeeded Jim Leet, was due to expire. Kennedy, who had no experience on the sales side, went to learn that part of the business with Delta Airlines 'with the proviso', said Michael Dargan, 'that he was to be sent back and no temptations placed in his way to stay'. In November, the month in which he reported to New York, Dargan addressed his staff through the medium of *Aerscéala* on the Dublin rights issue. He warned that exclusion from New York would mean the virtual end of the North Atlantic operation, rejected the suggestion of a turn-round at Shannon, and laid heavy emphasis on the 'might is right' argument: 'The Irish negotiators have plenty of moral justification, but the physical strength lies with the opposition and they are accustomed to using it in airline rights negotiations round the world on which they keep a top level permanently employed.'

Further contacts took place in Washington on 23 and 24 November 1971 between the two governments, with Neil Gleeson present as Aer Lingus observer. 'They seemed to be completely convinced of the case and very annoyed with the way we had treated them over the years,' he reported: 'it was clear that the question of denunciation [of the Bilateral Agreement] was a somewhat traumatic experience for them and that they had put it off as long as they conceivably could.' The real motives behind the United States' action were variously identified as political and commercial, it being suggested, though subsequently denied, that Nixon wished to act against Ireland, Tunisia, Cyprus and Morocco as 'diplomatic traitors' on account of their failure to support Nationalist China's membership of the United Nations. The Taoiseach, Jack Lynch, detected a commercial motive, telling the Cork Rotary Club on 27 November that 'it is apparent that the United States expects all countries with whom she trades to make their contribution towards solving the US difficulties.'

The Taoiseach's namesake, Patrick Lynch, wrote to him on 2 December thanking him for his Cork speech. He recommended that the Government should be prepared to negotiate on the basis of one US carrier serving Shannon in both directions, that negotiations should be entered into only if the United States agreed to discussions on this basis, and that the delegation should be empowered to give notice of the withdrawal of American rights to serve Shannon from New York. 'We in Aer Lingus would urge with great respect', he added, 'that the time has arrived for positive decision by the Government, on the settlement which will be the best that our country can now achieve....'

If the formal notice of denunciation had been a traumatic experience for the Americans, it had also called the Irish bluff. It was, Neil Gleeson said later, 'an extremely unfriendly act and one which we did not think they would resort to against a friendly nation like ourselves'. The magazine *Airline Management* warned its American readers in its November/December issue: 'The Irish have a case, and if presented effectively next year it could make the Nixon administration wary of a public battle with Ireland'; and Dargan told John Mulcahy on 2 December that 'the whole Western lobby from Cork to Dingle is active — politicians, bishops, newspapers, hoteliers and all the rest are sounding off every day'. One of the most powerful voices was that of Bishop Éamonn Casey, then Bishop of Kerry. 'We simply cannot accept the validity of charges that the US is trying to push Ireland around,' a State Department spokesman complained on 4 January 1972: 'We hope to be able to find a negotiated settlement.'

The Irish Government were clearly embarrassed over the political consequences of an open rift, a situation which the airline was not slow to appreciate. 'Time is now running out very fast,' Dargan wrote to the Secretary of the Department of Industry and Commerce in January: 'unless a settlement is reached in the next three months, or some very clear pointers towards a settlement are visible to our market in North America, we look like facing a shortfall of several million dollars in revenue.' The consequences, he added, would be large scale redundancies, the sale of the longhaul aircraft, and a comprehensive scaling-down of the airline's structure.

The next move, a Civil Aeronautics Board pre-hearing conference in what was described by the US *Business Week* as 'the great Irish-American airline flap' was scheduled for the end of January. On 30 January British paratroopers killed thirteen civilians in Derry following a banned civil rights march. On 2 February, declared a day of national mourning in the Republic, the British Embassy in Dublin was burned. Violence continued throughout February and into March, and on 24 March, following the resignation of Faulkner's government, direct rule on the colonial pattern was imposed by the British on Northern Ireland. The consequences for Aer Lingus in North America were little short of catastrophic. 'Our market in April just dried up suddenly on us,' David Kennedy recalled, 'almost as if it had been turned off at the tap.' Travelling in on the train to the New York office in the morning he became accustomed to the same three issues dominating the headlines of his newspaper: the forthcoming presidential election, the war in Vietnam, and the war — as it was described — in Northern Ireland: 'If Northern Ireland was not on the front page it would be a good day for us.' Ethnic traffic continued to move, but the general tourist vanished, never to return in the same numbers in the decade that followed. Against this traumatic background the long drawn-out game involving Dublin rights seemed to be moving towards a final checkmate.

'The problem seems to be that the State Department, who now can see that the entry of one US airline to Dublin is at last within their grasp, want to push towards a tougher settlement . . . ', Michael Dargan wrote to Senator Claiborne Pell, who had supported a peaceful solution of the issue, on 10 April 1972. He warned that 'brinkmanship in holding off a settlement until the latest possible date before expiry of the August deadline may backfire. In that event we will all be losers and permanent damage to US-Irish relationships will have taken place.' Others were alive to this danger. On 30 March Senator Edward Kennedy had written to the Civil Aeronautics Board complaining that 'the State Department proposal is shocking in the impact it will have, not only on a foreign airline but also on an entire foreign nation. The economic hardship imposed by this ban on Irish Airlines would be crippling.' The effects were already being felt. David Kennedy, in New York, told Michael Dargan on 3 May that there was no doubt in his mind that they were currently losing bookings at a rapidly increasing rate due to the uncertainty as to the outcome and that 'our continued assurances that "all will be right" have an increasingly hollow ring.'

As the deadline of 18 August approached, Dargan became increasingly concerned over the apparent lack of action on the part of the Government and expressed himself as unhappy with the attitude of the Minister for Foreign Affairs, Dr Patrick Hillery. He wrote to him on 10 August, just a week before New York was due to be closed, repeating the view of the Boards that 'should the US Government persist in their attitude . . . the Irish Government should withstand that pressure for no longer than will involve the loss of New York to us for about six days'. Closure for a longer period, he said, would create a situation from which it would take the airline a long time, perhaps years, to recover. The possibility of operating without New York rights had been studied. 'The conclusion we have reached is that we might struggle along for a short time (maybe months) on the Boston and Chicago rights. We would have to ground our B747s, which at the present time are not saleable, ground or sell other aircraft as well, make some 1,000 to 2,000 employees redundant, and expose the Government on their guarantee of our very large loans from the Export/Import Bank of the US, as well as to other banks abroad. . . . Beyond a short time . . . we would be forced to recommend to the Government that the whole Atlantic operation be wound up. . . . '

On 15 August the CAB announced it had deferred the recommended closure of New York until the end of the year. The threat remained, however, until the beginning of January 1973 when the Taoiseach, Jack Lynch, met

President Nixon in Washington and secured from him an agreement to have the situation reviewed. The issue of charters was now joined to the main question of the Dublin operation, with the United States pressing for its supplemental carriers to be accorded the same rights as the scheduled services. On 8 March *The Irish Times* announced: 'US reduces demands for flight rights. Two airlines abandon Dublin landings bid.' These modified demands, which implied an indication that the demand for onward rights would also be abandoned, represented, said the paper, 'a considerable climb down by the Americans and are likely to be acceptable to the incoming Government'. A general election on 28 February unseated Fianna Fáil and installed an inter-party government under Liam Cosgrave. On 9 April the Secretary of the Department of Transport and Power read over the telephone to G. P. Dempsey the text of the new proposals from the United States' Government which stated that it was 'prepared to grant the Irish Government landing rights to New York in return for the Irish Government's acceptance of Dublin landing rights for one US airline with no beyond rights and with Shannon stops mandatory as long as all other airlines authorised to operate between Dublin and the US are required to do likewise . . .'.

The long-running confrontation, rich in aviation ironies, was drawing to a close. There remained to negotiate the question of charters, on which it was finally agreed to preserve the status quo, and on the question of the restriction on Aerlínte serving Chicago via New York or Boston, which was to be lifted in respect of the six winter months. At last, on 11 June the Minister announced that an exchange of notes had taken place amending the air transport agreement between the two countries, some twenty-eight years after the Americans had first raised the Dublin rights issue. 'We look forward with some curiosity to the bonanza in tourist traffic to Ireland which our US competitors said the admittance of a US carrier to Dublin would bring,' commented Michael Dargan: 'Should the chosen carrier be prepared to make a sustained promotional effort — not a one-shot, short-term promotion — in development of tourist traffic to Ireland, we will be the first to see it and even to welcome the competition. What we do not want to see happen is to have the US carrier live off our promotion in the US.'

Herein lay the final irony. Pan American were awarded the route, but decided not to operate it; TWA's brief tenure ended in 1979. 'They found that, given the level of fares, there was no possibility of their making a reasonable profit no matter what traffic there might be,' wrote Mícheál Ó Riain: the oil crisis of 1973 had decisively replaced politics on the North Atlantic.

When in that year Michael Dargan announced his retirement from the position of Chief Executive with effect from 31 March 1974 his obvious and natural successor was seen as G. P. Dempsey, who was appointed Deputy Chief Executive in the period between the announcement and its taking effect. At the same time David Kennedy was brought back from New York as Assistant Chief Executive-Operations. In October 1973 Dempsey decided for personal reasons to decline the offer of the position of Chief Executive-Designate and was placed in charge of the development of the programme of ancillary activities. The decision, he said, 'was related entirely to my own judgment of what Aer Lingus needed and what I could best contribute. In a sense you could say it was a very arrogant decision.' It was clear, he believed, that the area of ancillary activities was going to demand very concentrated direction from one person — it was no longer a secondary task. One immediate consequence of his move was a major reorganisation at management level with, as Michael Dargan observed, some able men suffering in the process of change. From this reorganisation David Kennedy emerged as Chief Executive-Designate: 'The Yom Kippur war was in October 1973. I was asked to take over about ten days later. I certainly did not appreciate what was ahead of us on the fuel side and the fact that in one year the fuel bill would jump from £2.5 million to £12.5 million and that we would have inflation at 20 per cent and a recession.'

As far as the Atlantic was concerned fuel, though a major factor, was to prove to be only one element in a universally disastrous situation. In a paper read to Lloyds International Civil Aviation Conference 3 in Paris in June 1981, David Kennedy, looking back on seven disastrous years for the industry and forward to a prospect no less inhibiting, identified the problem as partly ideological — a confrontation between 'the social objectives shared by the governments of most of Europe' and those of the United States, where 'a hire-and-fire system of employment still operates generally . . . and the range of social benefits financed through the tax system is more limited [than in Europe]'. The outcome of this clash of ideologies, he suggested, had been 'predatory and destructive competition, stimulated not by business initiative but by the missionary fervour of certain regulatory agencies. The important concept of public utility has been abandoned by these zealots and replaced by short-sighted consumerism. The recent sad history of the North Atlantic service shows where this leads. The carriers are in acute financial distress. The public finds that service is curtailed (US carriers have suspended service at fourteen European cities, while European carriers are dropping US cities more rapidly than new services are added) . . . and monumental confusion reigns with airlines offering a bewildering variety of fares which they change so often that not even their own sales offices can be sure what today's tarrif may be. Advocates of this "super competitive" regime admit this is true but claim that the bargain fares available to travellers are worth the trouble.' This assertion could not be sustained, Kennedy suggested, from the traffic statistics: 'The number of transatlantic travellers from the US actually declined in 1979 and again in 1980 and only the buoyancy of Europeanoriginating traffic produced any growth at all. The economics of the industry are being undermined in order to provide consumers with fares lower than they can afford and lower also than the value to those consumers of the service received.'

In his evidence to the 1980 Oireachtas committee, David Kennedy was firm in laying the responsibility for 'the financial debacle on the Atlantic' at the door of the United States' authorities. 'It started off with an attempt to find a niche on the north Atlantic for US supplemental carriers, as they were then called, who had prior to then earned most of their money on military charter work out to the Far East. US Government policy at that time wanted to ensure that these carriers continued to operate and were kept in being as part of the US strategic military reserve. That was the thinking behind the US Government policy of pushing these carriers onto the North Atlantic.' The supplementals, together with a small number of European counterparts, did perform the function of providing low-cost transport, and it was this availability, often from companies that were to prove financially unable to

Members of the Oireachtas Joint Committee on State Sponsored Bodies visit Aer Lingus on 13 February 1980. Front row (left to right) David Kennedy, Chief Executive; Barry Desmond TD; Senator Eoin Ryan; J. P. Hayes, Aer Lingus Chairman; Chief Operations Officer Dick White. Back row (left to right) Tom Ferris, Economic Advisor to the Committee; Senator Patrick Cooney; Liam Lawlor TD; Bill Kenneally TD

AER LINGUS

sustain a service on this basis, that attracted Bord Fáilte and other tourism interests and led to the sharp divergence of opinion on the role of the national carrier.

The core of the problem lay in the fact that, in Mícheál Ó Riain's estimation, 'the scheduled carriers faced the dilemma that even if they wished they were not allowed to compete on price basis with the charter operators... until 1977 the US Government agencies, on the one hand refused to discipline charters and, on the other, protected the charter carriers from retaliatory pricing by the scheduled airlines. Charter carriers were seen as being of strategic importance to the US....' When, however, Freddie Laker decided in 1977 to convert his established charter operation into a bargain-priced scheduled operation under the name Skytrain, the United States was forced in self-defence to change its policy, and embarked on a campaign to convert its own 'supplementals' into scheduled carriers and to force European governments, under a variety of pressures, to sign new bilateral agreements. These aimed at securing entry for as many airlines as wished to operate and represented a complete reversal of policy on the part of the United States which, throughout the 'Dublin rights' dispute, for example, had maintained entirely the opposite stance. One consequence of what was described by the London *Sunday Times*, perhaps not over-dramatically, as the Atlantic 'bloodbath' was the forcing of a confrontation with IATA which, in attempting to hold out for a policy that would not involve catastrophic losses for everybody on the North Atlantic, was cast in the perception of the public at large as a price-fixing cartel operating directly contrary to consumer interests — a view which the collapse of Laker, Braniff and others did little to modify. 'We believe that IATA was far too rigid and inflexible and was falling apart because airlines could not introduce without difficulty new fares which were related to individual requirements,' said David Kennedy in 1980: 'we were very anxious for reforms which have taken place. It is now much more flexible and responsive to market needs and we support that'. 'Apex' fares, in fact, pre-dated Laker's Skytrain by two years and began to make a real contribution towards some measure of reality on the Atlantic — a reality based on low fares which, from the airlines' point of view, were fully cost-justified. In the words of P. W. Reid of the British Civil Aviation Authority in evidence to the 1980 Oireachtas committee: 'It is by exerting a strict control of traffic, managing a particular inventory of seats and filling it right up that price is brought down.'

No amount of fare-juggling could, however, conceal the fact that the Atlantic was, in the climate of the 1970s, irremediably uneconomic and, for a small airline like Aer Lingus with no other longhaul routes to provide balancing profits, disastrously so. There was no clear commercial advantage to be gained by pulling off the Atlantic, David Kennedy told his Board in

September 1976; but the Montreal destination was abandoned on 1 November 1979, followed in 1980 by the closure of the Chicago service, on which the projected loss for the year would have been in excess of £1 million. In the spring of 1979 the fuel situation had become acute as regards both price and supply. There were serious problems at Dublin and Shannon which, together with London, accounted for 65 per cent of the airline's fuel uplift, whilst in the United States decontrol of prices by the Government led to an immediate increase. A specific effect on the fuel cost increase was to render the B707 aircraft completely uneconomical, and the consequent decision to phase them out and concentrate on the more thrifty B747 meant that the Chicago route, via Montreal, with its light loads, was no longer a feasible proposition. Though Boston was retained, New York was thenceforward consolidated as the principal Aer Lingus gateway for North America.

A new passenger terminal at J. F. Kennedy Airport, shared with Lufthansa, had been opened on 7 May 1971 by the Minister for Transport and Power, Brian Lenihan. It provided greatly improved facilities, but Aer Lingus, in common with other carriers operating into the airport, could do nothing to alleviate the appalling conditions in which disembarking passengers frequently found themselves, being obliged in many cases to queue for two hours to pass through immigration without, apparently, any concern whatsoever on the part of the authorities as to their comfort and convenience. 'The US authorities are totally oblivious of the whole question of passenger service,' said David Kennedy in 1985: 'The airline, and other airlines consistently over the years have been begging, cajoling, bullying, shouting, everything — it has no effect at all. The contrast between what the Americans expect when they go overseas and what they actually deliver themselves to visitors coming into the US is total.' In the autumn of that year there was slight evidence, in the shape of new paintwork and extra uniformed staff, that some attempt was being made to alleviate the situation.

If the atmosphere at Dublin's new terminal, opened on 31 May 1972, was somewhat less reminiscent of Ellis Island, it did not usher in an era of total harmony in the relationships between the airport's operators, Aer Rianta, and Aer Lingus: the previous March the Board had been told of problems over rental costs projected for the new facilities both at Dublin and Shannon. The setting up of Aer Rianta as a separate State body had been regarded with some diffidence by the airline. 'I hope the Minister for Transport and Power may thus be able to find satisfactory solutions to the organisational problems of Aer Rianta as a separate entity,' said Patrick Lynch somewhat patronisingly in 1967: 'I would look forward to seeing Aer Rianta evolve into an independent authority and with the autonomy and flexibility which would enable it to become responsible for the effective administration of Dublin, Cork and Shannon Airports.' The aspiration in the following year became the reality; but the outcome was not, perhaps, all that Professor Lynch and his colleagues might have anticipated. A 20 per cent increase in landing fees became effective from 1 April 1969 and in 1974 Aer Rianta again raised its charges, increasing passenger load fees by 100 per cent and landing fees by 30 per cent, resulting in an additional cost to Aer Lingus of £900,000 in a full year. In February 1975 relationships between the two bodies were described by the airline as 'generally good', but there had in fact developed a conflict of interest. Aer Rianta, whilst recognising that Aer Lingus was by far its biggest customer, was concerned with running its own business profitably, and criticised the airline for the scale of the charges it made for the handling of other airlines at Irish airports which, it maintained, was prejudicing its commercial relations with the foreign carriers. Aer Lingus countered with complaints as to the level of charges it was obliged to pay Aer Rianta. In 1980 Aer Rianta sent a submission to the Oireachtas Joint Committee claiming that it should have a degree of control over Aer Lingus charges but asserting that it had not been possible to reach agreement with the airline. 'There is an element of disagreement between us,' admitted David Kennedy: 'We would object to Aer Rianta having control in any definitive sense. Our response is that we are the people who provide these services and we could be placed in an impossible position if we handed over control of these charges to a third party.'

The conflict of interest between the two bodies may be attributed partly to their historic origin, partly to the normal tensions between landlord and tenant. Aer Rianta operated as the commercial arm of the Department of Transport and Power (later Communications) in running the airports but, in accordance with international practice, the Department reserved to itself, as the national aeronautical authority, the responsibility for air traffic control. In 1985 there arose serious problems involving deficiencies in equipment related to this function, with a section of the Official Secrets Act being invoked by the Minister, Jim Mitchell, to prevent air traffic controllers speaking to the media. In April of that year flights had to be restricted for safety reasons complicated by industrial relations issues. Delays resulted to Aer Lingus and other services, and the President of the Irish Airline Pilots' Association, Captain L. M. Smith, claimed that many regional airports offered better facilities than Dublin. Though Aer Rianta achieved a record trading surplus of £10.64 million in 1984 this was, under the terms of its remit, paid over directly to the Department. It was anticipated that the then urgent necessity for a new air traffic control building and a new runway at Dublin would involve a fundamental reassessment of Aer Rianta's status and responsibilities.

Whilst the situation on the Atlantic was going from bad to worse the airline was faced with a major disruption to its European network. In 1973 it was announced that services over Manchester to destinations in Germany, Belgium, Holland and Scandinavia would be phased out in the period to 1978 consequent upon the decision of the British authorities to withdraw Fifth Freedom rights. Manchester had become in many ways the airline's second home, and it had over a span of fifteen years developed profitable routes in which no other operator had until then shown any interest. Now the British, discerning the advantage, wanted to move in. The days of any special relationship with BEA which might have led to a bargain being struck were over, and Aer Lingus was faced with the prospect of restructuring its Continental system.

It confronted the challenge in a number of ways: one was the imaginative concept of the 'Amsterdam Gateway', offering convenient connections to worldwide destinations through a modern, efficient, one-terminal airport. The strategy was aimed at the regular, long-distance business traveller, who was appearing in increasing numbers as Irish industry strove to extend its export markets, but the ingrained habit of using London proved difficult to eradicate. Amsterdam offered many advantages over Heathrow as a transit stop: no identity or other checks — a source of embarrassment and delay to Irish travellers to Britain since the introduction of the Prevention of Terrorism Act; no customs formalities for transit passengers and no change of terminal. English-speaking staff and extensive duty-free facilities were an added attraction, though as late as 1985 the airport banks were curiously reluctant to display an exchange rate for Irish pounds. London, by contrast continued to treat passengers from Ireland as second class travellers, refusing to accord them full international or transit rights. Since Aer Lingus was relegated to the domestic Terminal 1, duty-free facilities were minimal, as was the normal airside convenience of a bar service, and security and immigration officials insisted that passengers arriving from Ireland should be denied access to an air bridge when disembarking and be obliged to travel by bus to the international arrivals building. This, said Conor McGrath, 'involves us in £80,000 per annum of needless expenditure which we would not have to incur were we allowed to disembark them at the pier'. At Heathrow, in his opinion, there was discrimination against Irish traffic and a deliberate withholding of facilities: 'We should be entitled to the full range.' Since Aer Lingus was scheduled to remain in Terminal 1 even after the opening of Terminal 4, this unsatisfactory situation seemed likely to remain indefinitely. The new Birmingham airport, on the other hand, found itself able to offer passengers for Ireland full international facilities.

The situation at Heathrow would appear to have originated not so much in operational convenience as in basic British attitudes — attitudes which were inevitably conditioned and reinforced by political events. With the onset of civil strife in Northern Ireland 'the business of being Irish in Britain involved a different relationship', in the experience of Conor McGrath: 'After outrages we have tended to pull our sales reps. off the road so that they won't be calling on travel agents in the immediate aftermath. They have run into static.' For the same reason he himself would tend to stay away from the golf club: 'My entering the room would cause conversation to stop.' Hate mail and abusive telephone calls were also to be expected, but as incident followed incident, these tended to diminish — the Brighton bombings of 1984 producing only two or three examples. Whether this could be attributed to increasing callousness or a realisation that Aer Lingus was not in any sense involved was difficult to evaluate, but McGrath perceived anti-Irishness over the years as having moved down the social scale. He suggested, however, that the possibility of a change of name from Aer Lingus to Irish International or Aer Lingus - Irish, actively considered during the period of prosperity on the Atlantic, 'could only have done us harm. To tag on the name "Irish" would have done us no good at all.' The repetitive violence, in particular the Dublin bombings of 1974, inevitably led to a fall in British tourist traffic, exacerbated by an ageing ethnic population and, until the mid 1980s, a minimal level of immigration from Ireland. Several strategies were adopted in an effort to reverse this trend, among them the establishment of the British-based Cara Tours and a short lived experiment with an 'Aer Coach' service involving a Dublin-Liverpool flight and a subsequent bus journey, but it was not until the mid 1980s that the market began to show any real signs of recovery. With the stasis in the tourist sector the ethnic market remained vital — and vocal in its continuing demand for special fares. 'We really do need to keep them as happy as possible,' said McGrath, 'but there is a continuing belief that we charge too much.'

Even after Ireland's accession to the European Community in 1973 traffic on the Continental routes was slow to develop. In 1970 the Board had noted that charters had been growing more rapidly than scheduled services, due to the rising popularity of inclusive tours to sun-destinations, and it was realised that this was a development that the airline could not afford to ignore. In January 1973 it acquired an interest in Sunbound, a wholesale travel agency, following this with the takeover of a similar operator, Blueskies, in November: both companies had been experiencing difficulties as private operators. G. P. Dempsey emphasised that the decision to move into the package tour business was seen by Aer Lingus as quite distinct from the concurrent expansion into ancillary activities — it was, he said, a market-related move involving the takeover of businesses which would otherwise have failed. The step inevitably led to criticisms of State involvement in a particularly sensitive area of private enterprise, the more so as the airline continued to operate charters on a normal contract basis for other tour companies. 'I used the expression in the Seventies that I thought they were daft even though at that stage there were only two subsidiaries . . . ', Joe Walsh, one of the most prominent private operators, said in 1985: 'I still think they are daft.' He said that Aer Lingus 'was both his provider of aircraft and his competitor six times over and this made business screwy', conceding, however, that 'when it came to flying an aircraft efficiently and safely Aer Lingus was the best in the business'.

There was nothing 'screwy' in the situation as far as the airline was concerned: its view was that it was entitled to maintain an interest in the distribution of its product to the ultimate consumer — the holiday-maker, and that virtually every other European airline was doing the same. Business was buoyant: Spain had been discovered by the Irish in large numbers, *paella* was appearing on provincial menus and Spanish arches proliferating through Connemara. With the acquisition of Sunbound and Blueskies Aer Lingus was able to establish a position in the sun charter business independent of the instability inherent in annual negotiations with a small number of wholesalers. In December 1976 David Kennedy explained to his Boards that the two companies were not set up in order to achieve high profits 'but with the specific aim of getting a grip on the distribution of our products in the market place'. In January 1979 it was announced that subsidiary companies of Sunbound and Blueskies were to be established in Northern Ireland, where the airline had already acquired a holding in Enterprise Travel. In 1980, Michael Walsh, a well-known Dublin travel agent who had pioneered tours to the Holy Land, decided to retire from business and invited the airline to take over his interests. It was being emphasised at the time that the subsidiary travel companies operated altogether separately from the airline — a claim that left some members both of the trade and the general public not entirely convinced, particularly as the situation was further complicated by the existence of holidays marketed on their own account by the airline under the name Aer Tours.

In September 1975 it had been decided to follow the lead of other major European airlines by packaging all-in holidays utilising normal scheduled services combined with specially negotiated hotel accommodation and offered at attractive prices through Aer Lingus offices. A long-running dispute with travel agents over the marketing of these holidays was resolved in 1977, members of their association agreeing to sell them through their outlets. This satisfactory conclusion of a potentially damaging disagreement was to a large extent attributable to Martin Dully, who had been appointed General Manager–Regions in February of that year and who was later to move to Aer Rianta as Chief Executive.

Whilst in acquiring its travel companies Aer Lingus was concerned with flying holidaymakers out of Ireland, it recognised that its main market still lay in the attraction of visitors from abroad. In this it shared a common purpose with Bord Fáilte, though the two State bodies had not always seen eye to eye in the matter of ways and means. A typical disagreement arose in 1984 when Bord Fáilte claimed that the country had lost 40,000 potential visitors between 1980 and 1983 on account of a decision by Aer Lingus to abolish GIT (group inclusive tours) fares from a number of European countries. The figure was firmly rejected by the airline which claimed that whilst its own inbound passengers had fallen to some degree in the same period, the major decline was in the numbers availing of surface transport and other airlines. Aer Lingus argued that it wanted to make its lowest promotional fares available direct to the public rather than solely to tour operators who would apply a mark-up. Bord Fáilte, it alleged, wanted the tour operator to retain his or her privileged position. The airline had, in fact, been selling its own packaged holidays in European markets since 1972.

The argument brought into focus yet again the equivocal relationship between the two organisations in Ireland: overseas they habitually found common ground and worked well together. David Kennedy during his term in New York maintained an extremely close relationship with Bord Fáilte's Joe Malone (a future Aer Lingus Director) to the extent of pooling budgets and undertaking joint promotional activities. At home the interests of the two bodies had not always been as closely identified.

The relationship was investigated in some depth by the 1980 Oireachtas Joint Committee on State-sponsored Bodies. Statistics supplied by the airline showed that 65 per cent of passengers on European routes and 88 per cent of those on the Atlantic were flying for non-business reasons and could thus be broadly classified as tourists. 'We are very conscious of the fact that every pound we spend in advertising Aer Lingus in any foreign market is advertising Ireland as a tourist destination,' said Mícheál Ó Riain in evidence: 'The only product we have to sell is a trip to Ireland . . . so we recognise that we have a very interdependent relationship with tourism.' David Kennedy made the point that no other airlines spent anything worth talking about in promoting tourism to Ireland: 'so we are promoting Ireland and promoting Aer Lingus'. He agreed that in the past there had been differences of approach with Bord Fáilte in relation to particular markets, 'but in my direct experience . . . it is very rare to have a serious difference of opinion'. The Bord Fáilte representatives who gave evidence tended to confirm this view, their Group Manager-Marketing Services, Noel Sweeney, agreeing that there was joint consultation at two levels: 'in the market place between local representatives, the tourist board and the airline, which is the first place where things begin to crystallise in terms of schedules or fares, and we have consultations at head office level. There are three areas where we have formal communication and dialogue — in terms of capacity and the volume of planes made available on particular routes; in the area of schedules, frequency of service and so forth; and in the area of fares.'

The latter area had in the past been crucial and, particularly in the area of the North Atlantic, the source of serious friction between the two bodies. In 1973 consultants had prepared a report for Bord Fáilte on 'An analysis of the choices open to Aer Lingus and Ireland under the impact of travel group rules on the North Atlantic' which Michael Dargan had described as 'a most dangerous document', containing 'basic misconceptions of a serious nature'. He told his Board that 'Bord Fáilte's action in commissioning a consultants' report on the activities and policies of another state-sponsored organisation was to be deplored'. In 1980 David Kennedy agreed with the chairman of the Joint Committee, Senator Eoin Ryan, that Aer Lingus had changed its fare structure in the course of the previous seven or eight years to one which was more likely to encourage tourism, but pointed out that tourism from Europe into Ireland had been developed by the airline largely on its own initiative on the basis of a wide range of innovatory fares: 'innovatory in so far as the entire industry is concerned, such as the fly-drive type packages which we have developed'. This policy had, he said, been responsible for increasing the inclusive tour business in the sector by 200 per cent over the period 1975–80. Noel Sweeney confirmed that the differences in the past had been largely related to the North Atlantic 'and that goes back probably to the mid-seventies. The mode of charter as a form of transportation on the Atlantic offered certain advantages for the development of tourism traffic such as very low seat cost and provision of capacity at times when the bulk of tourists want to travel. At that stage the policy of Aer Lingus was to develop scheduled traffic and to keep charters to a minimum.'

A problem of increasing significance in all aspects of the airline's operations was that of security. In advance of the unrest in Northern Ireland there was concern for the safety of passengers and crew following a serious increase in air piracy and bomb scares. 'Fortunately we have been spared from the first of these heinous acts and have had minimal inconvenience from the latter', said the 1970 annual report. In 1970/71 the cost of security was inflated by special war risk insurance at over £500,000 for which, contrary to practice elsewhere, no Government relief was forthcoming. In November 1972 the Board complained, following the introduction of additional measures, that there was no clear-cut decision at Government level as to the ultimate responsibility for security. 'The responsibility of governments in regulating and carrying out security functions at airports is being increasingly recognised,' the March 1973 report observed tartly. Following a recommendation by the airline and by Judge Finlay in his report on airport security, the Board complained again in July 1974 of the frustrating delay on the part of the Government in formally constituting a national aviation security committee: an incident on 27 July involving a British Airways' aircraft had invoked fears of a British reprisal. This time the delay was to be short-lived: a committee, chaired by the

AL 1371

Verstopfte Strassen sind ärgerlich. Wenn Sie in Irland ausfahren, so wird die hier gezeigte Situation wohl die einzige sein, die Ihren Wagen unfreiwillig zum Stehen bringt. Und darüber, so meinen wir, werden Sie sich bestimmt nicht ärgern.

Etwas vom Schönsten an Irland sind seine einsamen Strassen. Wenn Sie entlang der Küste, über Heide und Berge fahren, so werden Sie höchst selten einem andern Wagen begegnen — es wäre denn einem Pferdegespann.

Irland ist ein Paradies für Autofahrer.

Aer Lingus bietet Spezial-Arrangements für Autotouristen. Ein Beispiel: Komfortabler Hin- und Rückflug mit Aer Lingus Jet. Sechs volle Tage mit Zimmer und Frühstück in Erstklasshotels und ein moderner Mietwagen ohne Kilometerbeschränkung kosten sage und schreibe ab Fr. 680.—.

Ihr Reisebüro gibt Ihnen gerne Auskunft über Autoferien mit Aer Lingus in Irland. Wenn Sie uns den Coupon einsenden, erhalten Sie von uns kostenlos eine Dokumentation.

AER LINGUS · IRISH

AER LINGUS IRISH, SCHÜTZENGASSE 21
8001 ZÜRICH, TEL. 051 27 28 50

Adresse ______________________

____

____

Telefon ______________________

AER LINGUS

Encouraging German tourism

Department of Transport and Power and representatives of the security forces of the State and of aviation and other interests, held its inaugural meeting on 28 August.

In October 1974 there were two bomb attacks on public houses in the south of England which resulted in the death of seven people. Shortly after this James McDade was killed in the English Midlands by a bomb which exploded prematurely. On the morning of 23 November the Minister for Transport and Power telephoned the Chairman of Aer Lingus to ask him to explain the circumstances in which the airline had taken a decision to transport McDade's remains from Birmingham to Dublin, indicating that in view of the political connotations he was not satisfied with the decision and would be reporting on it to the Government.

An investigation by the airline revealed that at about 17.30 hours on the evening of 22 November the Captain of an Aer Lingus aircraft in Birmingham was approached by the British Airways' Station Manager who informed him that they had one of their aircraft on the ramp containing the remains and forty-one people, and that their ground staff in Belfast had notified their refusal to handle an incoming aircraft with the remains aboard. British Airways, who handled Aer Lingus traffic at Birmingham, had been instructed by the local police to get the remains away from the airport. The Aer Lingus Captain contacted the operations controller at Dublin who, not considering it to be a political decision, authorised him to accept the remains and the party of mourners. The flight was delayed until about 21.00 and in the meantime bombs planted by the IRA in Birmingham pubs exploded without warning, killing twenty-one people and seriously injuring many more. The British Special Branch boarded the Aer Lingus aircraft before it left and removed two passengers. The flight finally arrived at Dublin about 21.50 and the remains of James McDade were taken to the mortuary, to be removed the following day. The concern of the Minister in the wake of these events was understandable, but having had the circumstances explained to him, he decided against issuing a reprimand to the airline, requesting only that his displeasure be conveyed to the Boards and giving it as his opinion that Aer Lingus had failed to recognise the political implications of the decision. Following this incident and the Birmingham bombings, full security alert procedures were brought into force throughout the whole service network with increased surveillance for staff, fleet and buildings in Northern Ireland and in Britain, where anti-Irish feeling was at a new high level. In that country the Special Branch advised that as from 28 November 1974 and pending the introduction of the Prevention of Terrorism (Temporary Provision) Bill at Westminster, special security measures would be introduced at British airports for all passengers arriving from Ireland, north and south.

Early in 1976 Frank Stagg, an IRA prisoner on hunger strike, died in

Britain. It was eventually decided that the remains should be transported to Ireland. Following discussions between the airline and the Department of Transport and Power the Minister let it be known that no policy direction would be issued and that it was up to Aer Lingus to make its own decision. With British Airways, the other operator on the London-Dublin route, having already indicated their unwillingness to transport the remains, Aer Lingus accepted them for transport on the scheduled freighter service on the morning of Thursday 19 February. When the aircraft was some ten minutes from Dublin airport, a direction was received from the Government, immediately communicated to the pilot, to divert to Shannon. 'After landing', the Deputy Chief Executive told the Board, 'we had an anxious time until the Government officially notified us that they had taken custody of the remains. From a public relations standpoint we seemed to have emerged unscathed from the operation. We believed, however, that it could result in a residual threat to our security.'

At approximately 13.40 on Saturday 2 May 1981 Captain Foyle, piloting flight EI 164 from Dublin to London, reported to London Air Traffic Control that 'a fellow standing behind me smelling of petrol said he wanted to go to Teheran. Does not want to land in British airspace. On the way to Le Touquet in Northern France.' The aircraft landed at Le Touquet at 14.02, and within a short time negotiations were in progress between the hijacker and the French police and an Aer Lingus B737 was on its way from Dublin with airline officials and the Minister for Transport, Albert Reynolds. At 19.05 five women and six children were released, and the hijacker's demand for the freeing of the remaining passengers and crew was that he would be given confirmation that Aer Lingus would receive a telexed message which would be published in the *Irish Independent*. This assurance was given. At 22.08 French police succeeded in boarding the aircraft and arresting the man, following which the passengers were flown to London, their original destination, and the crew returned to Dublin, arriving in the small hours of Sunday morning. 'Their performance was truly exemplary,' said David Kennedy, '. . . their calm response to a most serious threat was transmitted to the passengers. Their ability to demonstrate that they were in total command of the situation was a critical factor in the overall procedure which led finally to the successful resolution of a very tricky situation.' The Taoiseach, Charles Haughey, commended the crew for their 'calm courage and care of the passengers'.

The incident, though ending happily, prompted an internal review of preventive and contingency procedures with a small working group being appointed to rewrite the security section of the Air Safety Manual in the light of experience gained. Each passenger on the hijacked flight was offered a complimentary return flight to any destination on the Aer Lingus network.

In a troubled decade another significant threat to the stability of the airline developed in the crucial area of industrial relations. Late in 1971 the Dublin District Committee of the AUEW (Amalgamated Union of Engineering Workers) withdrew from the Aer Lingus group of unions, precipitating the ultimate disbanding of the group some years later. 'This', said John O'Neill, the Personnel Manager, 'left the airline in the position in which it is today [1985] of unions on occasions coordinating their activities and on others moving in quite different directions and at a different pace'. In 1973 there was an outbreak of serious demarcation disputes between craft unions and in 1974 a threatened strike of WUI (Workers' Union of Ireland) members in the clerical, supervisory and allied grades. Following intensive through-the-night discussions, settlement was reached involving substantial extra payments and some fundamental changes in the salary structure, including long-service increments. An unofficial strike of mechanics and technicians in October suggested some deficiencies in internal communications. Groups of staff and management were in consequence set up within individual departments with the aim of improving contacts, but this and subsequent changes left the union side still critical of the staff development aspect of the personnel department.

The principal area of dispute involved relativities , anomalies and grading. With mounting payroll costs and marginal profitability, the Chief Executive met the airline unions on 8 December 1975 to put before them a four-point programme aimed at achieving, by 1977, a return to profit through a 25 per cent increase in passenger and cargo revenue; an increase of more than 25 per cent in revenue from ancillary activities; a substantial cutback in expenditure in other areas, and a nine-month pay pause from 1 April to 31 December, 1976 following the expiry of the national agreement. In return for acceptance of these proposals the unions were offered an 8 per cent payroll increase on 1 January 1977 with a guarantee of no planned redundancies in the meantime. Recruitment was, however, to be reduced to the absolute minimum, leave of absence and early retirement encouraged, and opportunities availed of to second staff to other airlines: an agreement with Zambia Airways provided the opportunity for fifty transfers of this nature. The unions were not enthusiastic, the first to reject the proposals being the National Engineering and Electrical (NEETU) in January 1976. The Government's policy on pay restraint posed additional problems for the airline in this connection in that, in the view of David Kennedy, 'it gave openings to the trade unions to bargain for additional awards for increased productivity. Our position was that we needed increased productivity and believed we were entitled to it without repeatedly having to pay for it.' In September 1976, following an approach from the FWUI, the Irish Transport and General Workers' Union and the Amalgamated Transport and General Workers' Union to honour the interim national pay agreement, the airline pleaded inability to pay, placing itself in a weak position in view of the fact that all other major State bodies, including Aer Rianta, had accepted. A Labour Court hearing rejected the plea and the agreement was subsequently implemented in full.

At the same time there had developed an important new initiative in the industrial relations field with an invitation to the unions from the Chief Executive to discuss the extension of worker participation in the airline. A union study group was set up with the airline providing facilities in terms of time off, secretarial help and assistance in securing outside consultants to work with the group in the development of its thinking. This anticipated action at Government level proposing the appointment of worker directors to the boards of State companies, but it was slow to achieve acceptance in the eyes of the workforce. 'We would like to see a greater involvement of our members at all levels in the decision-making process', Frank O'Malley commented in 1980: 'We may in some areas get an indication that this is happening but in the general overall situation that is not transmitted to all levels.'

What Barry Desmond TD, a member of the 1980 Committee, described as 'the hierarchical structure' of the company — was seen at the time by some groups within the airline as having a strong bearing upon a developing sense of alienation and of mistrust of the manner in which personnel matters were handled. 'There used to be a great sense of loyalty amongst the crews towards the company,' said one air hostess: 'That is very much on the decline because it's very one sided. The company expects us to break rules and regulations to facilitate them — but ask a favour in return, NO WAY. Out comes the rule book and it's a case of "It can't be done" and "it would be setting a precedent". No wonder everyone is becoming more militant and union-minded.' This viewpoint was based on evidence collected before the acrimonious 1978 strike. It was echoed in the wake of that event by Paul Boushell, subsequently to be elected one of the first Aer Lingus worker directors, in his evidence to the Oireachtas committee: 'My view would be that we have moved from a situation of the staff in general having a fierce loyalty to Aer Lingus, including the management thereof. They still have that loyalty to a thing called Aer Lingus, but it does not include management, who are roughing up their beautiful airline. The shift has taken place.'

The shift was seen by the unions as one largely involving middle management. As Christopher Kirwan of the ITGWU put it in evidence to the 1980 committee: 'We have some difficulty in persuading, certainly management on the shop floor, that they could be capable of making decisions to resolve matters of a local incidence and the general criticism that comes up within the operations sector is that far too often there is a tendency for middle management to refer problems which the staff think should be resolved there and then to a higher level.'

From the management viewpoint the growing militancy of the hostesses and their inclination to stay strictly within their union contract created problems: 'They seem extremely reluctant to give that extra effort which I believe at one time would have been willingly offered. Many of them seem to look for an opportunity to be difficult,' was one management attitude. 'This creates a problem in a number of ways but especially at airports where [the Aer Lingus ground] staff frequently go without meal breaks and work many hours over the normal time just to get the job done.'

There was apparently a problem to be tackled, and in the period September 1979 to March 1980 a comprehensive survey was undertaken of the attitudes and opinions of cabin crew with the aim of identifying it and formulating a remedial action plan. The survey, conducted by Terry Byrne, Head of Communications Development, and Geraldine O'Brien, Personnel Communications Analyst with assistance from Irish Marketing Surveys, involved a total of 548 questionnaires and a response of almost eighty per cent. It revealed continuing problems of identity ('There is no sense of individual contribution or feedback from our employers') and criticism of internal structures ('I think the big problem about being a hostess is the lack of communication between hostesses and people in management') but presented on the other hand, a very positive profile of the attitude of hostesses and stewards to their chosen occupation. Forty two per cent found it 'a little better' and thirty seven per cent 'much better' than most; fifty two per cent liked it 'very much'. The quality of Aer Lingus inflight service was believed by thirty eight per cent to be 'above average' and by an additional thirty two per cent 'one of the best'. The airline itself was viewed by twenty two per cent as 'one of the best' places to work in and by a further thirty nine per cent as 'above average': only three per cent felt it to be below average. 'Over the past year I feel I've gained valuable experience of life in general', was one response: '. . . having such a different lifestyle from what I've had before, I've become more aware of other people, their situations and more broad-minded generally'. 'I would like to see us rebuild the reputation of being "The Friendly Airline"', was another comment quoted: 'The memory that remains is not the food or drink, but the little word, gesture, etc. that makes the passenger feel special. We Irish have this gift by nature — if only we would use it more often'. The job was seen as physically very demanding and seventy three per cent of the cabin crew stated that they would like the right to retire at age forty-five.

A comprehensive action plan was drawn up to address the key issues identified in the survey — the need to improve internal communications with the cabin crew and to secure an adequate feedback on their performance. The outcome was reflected in a markedly healthier relationship and improved morale.

The marriage bar in respect of hostesses and other female employees had been removed in 1970. 'I took the decision that Aer Lingus was going to treat the marital status of any female employee the same way as any male employee,' said Mícheál Ó Riain: 'At the same time we didn't want a whole lot of elderly people in the flight cabin.' If the spectacle of green-uniformed grandmothers held little appeal for management, the action of the newly-established Employment Equality Agency in 1977 in taking the airline to task for advertising for hostesses and thus excluding male applicants was met with an equal lack of enthusiasm. 'It was the management's strong contention', the Chief Executive told the Board, that we should continue to have female cabin attendants only as we believed that our whole marketing strength was built up on the friendly image of our female hostesses'. The Agency failed to respond to this argument, and management reluctantly concluded that there was 'no realistic alternative but to open our present recruiting programme to male applicants'.

Elsewhere in the organisation women had made little impact: out of a workforce of 6,700 in the early 1980s, 1,950 were women, with only one in the top three management categories and only 14 out of 308 in middle management. There were 180 women out of 1,200 operatives, largely concentrated in the cleaning and catering areas. Out of 2,767 applications for apprenticeships in 1981 only 78 were women, a figure reduced to 58 after screening and to just one after a test in which 344 males were successful. Kay Garvey, an air hostess, was elected as a worker director in 1981 but few women had previously held a senior position. 'There was never any conscious decision to keep ladies out,' according to Niall Weldon; Margaret Coyne, who worked in accounts, sales and publicity before becoming education officer and public relations superintendent, believed that there was, in 1985, still some resistance to women progressing in the company, 'though women themselves are to blame in some part'. Josephine Walsh, formerly of Aer Lingus and in 1985 a Superintendent with the subsidiary Cara Computing, believed that the situation had improved: 'In the old days, women were pushed in the "dolly bird" areas — the *cailíní fáilte* and entertaining the VIPS. Once they ceased to be *cailíní* they got a gentle tap on the shoulder and found themselves with backroom jobs.'

The example of the women pilots would appear to contradict any suggestion of continuing discrimination: 'They are very successful, very capable and very confident' in the view of one of their male colleagues. Grania Cronin, then an air hostess, was selected for training on 27 September 1977, 'a choice which was virtually inevitable because', in the words of the same male colleague, 'she kept coming top of all the interviews. She was so bloody good she left all the lads trailing.' She and her successor, Maria Hetherington, who began training on 28 November 1978 were nonetheless confronted by a certain degree of residual sexism: They were really put through it when they joined, said a colleague. In training 'they used to fail engines on them and leave them hanging with one rudder full in for minutes on end. There were one or two of the older pilots who said "I'm never going to fly with a woman" — but they've been totally absorbed.' Less easy to solve were the social difficulties inherent in the new role: 'They have a fairly difficult problem because if they do get married they can really only marry another pilot.' Two, in fact, chose this solution to the putative problems consequent upon a high income level and a disruptive life-style, and they continued flying.

In March 1978 the airline found itself involved in its most serious industrial dispute to date, involving all members of the FWUI (Federated Workers' Union of Ireland) in addition to cabin crew. The Union had made an unquantified claim for compensation for past productivity and internal/external relativity issues as well as a cost of living increase demand. The internal relativity issue related to pay increases achieved by the skilled trades over the years 'which management', said Mícheál Ó Riain, 'conceded to the tradesmen as their due'. Notice was served on 1 March to take effect on 14 March, backed by an 80 per cent majority of FWUI members. On 4 March the Chief Executive represented to the Government, which had previously rejected the airline's productivity proposals, that some freedom to negotiate was essential, and the Department of the Public Service gave it clearance on 13 March to make an offer to the union through discussions which were proceeding at the Labour Court. An offer was put on the table representing a wage increase of 2–3 per cent in return for productivity measures. The union took the view that this was not a response to their 1976 claim and further raised issues of conditions of employment, maternity and other leave and similar matters. The airline agreed to look at these items but it was left with little room to manoeuvre, the Tánaiste having warned the Chief Executive that if the wage claims were found to be related to increasing airline profits the Government would look again at the request for further equity capital which was then before it. The strike began at 12 noon on Tuesday 14 March.

Members of all other unions (tradesmen, operatives and pilots) passed the FWUI pickets with the Executive Staff Association cooperating with management. Services were maintained using leased-in aircraft and some seven Aer Lingus Boeing 737s. Staff from many parts of the system, including North America and Britain, returned to Dublin to act as cabin stewards (the hostesses also having withdrawn their labour) and in other essential roles and worked in these capacities up to fourteen and fifteen hours a day. The attempts of the union to secure an all-out picket during the course of the dispute were unsuccessful, though there were mass pickets by the strikers on two days and some alleged cases of intimidation. Both sides finally agreed to accept mediation under the chairmanship of Dr Charles McCarthy and a range of proposals cleared by the Department of the Public Service was agreed to and accepted unanimously by the strikers on 5 May. These involved a lump sum of £450 to each striking member in relation to the previous productivity claim; a payment of 4.5 per cent per annum in relation to agreed future productivity measures and an additional 0.5 per cent for a short-term productivity measure relating to the year 1978/79, together with a lump sum of £125 to FWUI cabin crew and operatives who were on strike but not directly involved in the claim. The Chief Executive told the Boards on 25 May that a key element in these settlement terms would be their ability to achieve the future productivity measures and that it would provide a stiff challenge for management.

Work was resumed on 8 May in an atmosphere of some tension and hostility consequent upon the maintenance of operations through the dispute: executives returning to duty overseas were pointedly left to handle their own baggage. The cost of the strike was high both financially — some £5 million — and in terms of the airline's industrial relations, though it did result in a joint FWUI–Management working party being set up to examine methods of increasing productivity and sharing the benefits. 'Part of the reason for that strike,' Paul Boushell suggested to the Oireachtas committee, 'was a failure by Aer Lingus management to have any meaningful consultation on changes in work practices, changes in recruitment policy and a whole range of things.'

In the view of John O Neill, the airline's Personnel Manager, however, 'one of the main problems which negotiations encountered and which may have protracted the dispute was that the claim was never specifically defined so that when it was all over we still didn't know what figures we had been bargaining for'. David Kennedy, looking back on the event nearly eight years later believed that the strike had been unfortunate. 'The Labour Court had totally supported the Company's position and, expensive as it had been, the cost of acceding to the demands would have been even more expensive in the long term'. The Company, he added, had been prepared all the time to negotiate for future productivity benefits and this had been the main outcome of the eventual settlement.

The criticism of all the union members who gave evidence to the 1980 committee had focused on what they saw as the inability of management to delegate authority. They conceded, nevertheless, as Christopher Kirwan expressed it, that 'industrial relations in Aer Lingus will stand up favourably — for example, in comparison with CIE. . . . What we are saying is that within the industrial relations setup in Aer Lingus there should be the capacity to produce people who can take quick decisions on minor industrial matters as they occur on the floor.'

The second major strike, that of tradesmen on 30 May 1980, occurred over a substantial internal relativity claim arising from the grading and pay progression of operatives and clerks. It was referred to, and rejected by the Labour Court. A subsequent assessor's report had recommended only an increase of 3 per cent, finding no justification for a reduction in working hours. Subsequent negotiations broke down. The strike ended on 4 July on the terms of a revised Employer/Labour Conference formula of 27 June, again in an atmosphere of strained relations between the two sides and with follow-on claims from other areas. A subsequent and positive development was the final formalisation within the airline of consultative machinery under the title of the Central Representative Council, representing all in-house unions with the significant exception of the Executive Staff Association, which had taken the management side in both major strikes and which therefore found itself in a position of some difficulty. The Council was conceived, in the words of Terry Byrne, then of the personnel department, 'as a way of doing business with the unions that was a bit different from the knock down, drag out confrontational style . . . ' and was planned to extend from contacts at corporate level to individual departments. Under a joint memorandum of understanding the Central Representative Council was to deal with all aspects of the business of the airline as it affected worker-management relationships with the exception of pay and conditions of employment, which remained within the province of individual union negotiation. Though there were those on the management side who viewed the development as a further abdication of responsibility and those on the other who regarded it as a further effort to emasculate the unions and their power, roughly a third of the senior five hundred people in the company, in a poll in 1982, were in favour of greater worker participation, with one third against and the remainder expressing no opinion. One achievement of the CRC was to provide a second tier between the shop floor and the newly-elected worker directors.

The 1977 Worker Participation (State Enterprises) Act came into force the following year and on 30 April the Minister for Labour signed an Order increasing the number of Aer Lingus/Aerlínte directors to twelve, of whom four were to be elected by the employees. Elections were held early in 1981 and on 28 May the Board welcomed its first worker directors: Paul Boushell, Michael Costello, Kay Garvey and John Tatten. 'I think it would be fair to say that Board members were apprehensive about the outcome, but especially with regard to the issue of confidentiality,' said Niall Weldon: 'but it is also fair to say that no problems have arisen on that issue.' 'We don't claim to solve industrial relations problems,' said John Tatten in 1983, 'but we hope to create a much more positive industrial relations climate in which the old attitudes of "them" and "us" will disappear.' He was concerned over the role he and his colleagues were expected to play: 'We're primarily directors like any other although we also have a representative role. The problem is that some workers see us as super shop stewards which we are not . . . another problem is that real power does not lie in the boardroom but at managerial level. The real decisions are taken there.'

The view from the boardroom during the difficult decade of the 1970s was perhaps equally anomalous, the attitudes of 'them' and 'us' being perceived also as applying to the relationship with the Shareholder, particularly as represented by the Department of Finance. On 9 January 1969 the General Manager, Michael Dargan, had a 'vigorous' discussion with Dr T. K. Whitaker and Mr McInerney of Finance and Diarmuid Ó Riordáin of Transport and Power on the omnipresent topic of the airline's capital requirements. He put again to them the Board's view that an annual subsidy in lieu of additional equity would destroy the airline, quoting the examples of what had happened in the past to the boards and managements of BOAC, KLM and SAS when their economic viability could be sustained only by state subvention. After what he later described as 'very frank exchanges' an understanding was reached to the effect that such equity capital as might be agreed would be raised by the airline for the Exchequer outside the country; that Aer Lingus would in the course of 1971 engage consultants to report on its forward plans and programmes, commercial prospects and capital requirements, with particular reference to the question as to whether the airline should continue to exist independently or endeavour to link up in some way with another carrier. The Department agreed to review its attitude towards equity capital in the context of a new presentation from the airline reducing the amount required. Later that year the Government accepted the revised proposals and introduced the Air Companies (Amendment) Act 1969 under which the Minister invested £15 million in Aerlínte, £10 million in the form of shares and the balance as a non-repayable advance at full commercial rates of interest. The fact that the interest burden would fall on Aerlínte rather than Aer Lingus was of some concern to the General Manager, who wrote to the Department of Transport and Power on 7 April that 'it is our firm view that the £15 million should be invested in Aer Lingus. In the first place this is the company which has the requirement for this money because of its commitment to acquire eight new Boeing 737 aircraft during the course of 1969-70. Secondly it is the part of the airline which at present has the most difficult capital structure problem.'

The report of the consultants appointed by the airline — Smith, Barney and Company Inc. — circulated to Board members on 5 August 1971, recommended that the problems arising from the existence of the two nominally separate companies could best be resolved by a merger. It further recommended that the airline should be able to operate independently, if need be, of further equity participation by the Shareholder; that private equity capital should be raised at a suitable time; and that alternative methods of financing, such as leasing of aircraft or sale and lease back, should be examined. It also expressed the view that the diversification programme should be continued. On the basis of this report the Boards authorised the General Manager to seek Government approval both for the merger and for the option to raise equity capital from private sources or Government sources, or both, at the appropriate time. The report, Michael Dargan reminded his fellow directors, was a financial analysis rather than a commercial assessment based on management's own commercial judgments.

In the adverse economic conditions prevailing the commercial decisions of state-sponsored bodies were increasingly being brought under close scrutiny. Late in 1969 the Chairman, Patrick Lynch, reported that at a meeting of the heads of the commercial bodies in the public sector 'there was a unanimous view that there was a greater need for the setting of objectives . . . and also for the assessment of attainment of these objectives.' In February 1974, in an address to the Institute of Public Administration, the Fine Gael Minister for Finance, Richie Ryan, returned to the continuing dilemma: 'For public enterprise, however, where the need to pay its way is important . . . the overriding concern must be to fit into a total public policy. . . . Each commercial state-sponsored body must have its essential freedoms and at the same time be responsive to the needs of public policy. How to reconcile these requirements is the problem. The answer lies, I think, in the planning process and the institutionalisation of a planning function linking the Cabinet, Departments and the individual bodies in a common system.' In October of the same year the Minister for Transport and Power summoned the chairmen and chief executives of the state-sponsored bodies associated with his Department to a meeting to discuss capital expenditure, industrial relations, general matters of economic policy and the remuneration of chief executives, the latter an area of concern to the airline Boards following the appointment of David Kennedy the previous March. The Boards, Patrick Lynch told the meeting, agreed with the Government's decision that determination of a chief executive's salary was an internal matter but that decision was negatived by the statement that basic salary should be that suggested by the Devlin Report — a document which Perry Greer of Irish Shipping thought was 'a product of cloud-cuckoo land'.

Undercapitalisation and the consequent unfavourable equity/debt ratio remained a cause of serious concern and a request was made to the Government for a further reconsideration of the airline's capital structure. The response was not encouraging. At a meeting between the Chief Executive and the Secretary of the Department of Finance in June 1976 the latter said that the Exchequer was in serious difficulty and that prospects for the following year looked even worse, so much so that the Government would find it extremely difficult to raise the capital required or to service it even were the airline to raise it by its own borrowings. He requested Aer Lingus to re-examine the whole North Atlantic operation, to consider disposing of some of its major assets, to provide the Department with more information on the maturity of its debts and its ability to borrow more money either at home or abroad and to outline action being taken to reduce overheads. The Chief Executive agreed to respond as requested, but emphasised that without further equity capital investment it would be impossible for the airline to survive as a commercial organisation.

The following August David Kennedy told his Boards that there was an implication coming through from the Department of Finance that irrespective of the merits of their case it would be requiring the airline to sell some of its assets and that only then would it consider giving them any assistance. The Secretary of Transport and Power had undertaken to assume the initiative and recommend to his Minister that the latter should put the airline's case direct to the Cabinet, and a paper was being prepared which would contain a formal recommendation from the Minister for a £15 million equity injection for the airline.

Time passed. On 26 January 1978 Board members were expressing deep concern and dissatisfaction with the manner in which their case had been handled by the Government over the past two and a half years. 'Sometimes when major financial matters go to the Department of Finance we find ourselves running into a lot of delays,' David Kennedy told the Oireachtas committee in 1980: 'For example, we had discussions which went on for about three years, between 1975 and 1978, on the airlines' capital structure before a proposal eventually went to Government and was approved by the Oireachtas. Even on smaller matters we tend to run into delays there;' and the committee report itself was critical: 'We note that Aer Lingus projections of capital expenditure on a five year basis are regularly submitted to Government, that major capital expenditure requires Government approval and that Government also approves Aer Lingus' borrowing. The Government is thus fully informed of Aer Lingus' capital requirements and financing proposals well in advance. If the Government is satisfied that the investments proposed by Aer Lingus are well justified and has approved them we feel it should at the same time be prepared to commit its own contribution to their financing, including timely injections of equity finance when required.'

On 23 February 1978 the Chief Executive reported that the Department of Transport and Tourism (as was its latest manifestation) had been informed by Finance that the Minister would not oppose the case for increased equity 'on the scale already discussed' on the understanding that the North Atlantic problem be exposed to Government to enable the question of subsidy to be

ED
Padraig

'The most important single trip ever undertaken by an Aer Lingus aircraft', the Papal visit, 1979

considered and that the airline should review a number of its ancillary investments. Even though the new Fianna Fáil Government agreed, in December 1978, to the provision of a further £15 million of equity capital, bringing the total investment since 1936 to £43.6 million, Finance were still pressing the airline to realise some of its assets.

In the same year the formation of an independent Irish airline, Avair, forced Aer Lingus to confront once more the question of internal services. An economic study, circulated to the directors in March 1981, concluded that such services could not be operated profitably. 'We have submitted a copy of our study to the Government,' the Chief Executive told his colleagues in June, 'and informed them that while we would be prepared to consider taking a minority stake in any such enterprise it would have to be on the basis of an appropriate Government subsidy arrangement.' In December 1981 it was agreed to cooperate with Avair on the Dublin–Belfast route. 'On balance', said David Kennedy, 'it was better for us to cooperate with them on services that would be complementary to ours within Ireland', adding that Aer Lingus would object to competition both within Ireland and to Britain.

The following year, 1979, was to see what David Kennedy described as 'perhaps the most important single trip ever undertaken by an Aer Lingus aircraft'. When the idea of a Papal visit to Ireland was initially discussed in 1978 John Griffin, Aer Lingus Manager in Rome, was instructed to contact the Vatican and extend an invitation to the Pope to travel with the airline to Dublin, the established tradition being that he flew Alitalia out of Italy and onwards with the national airline of the host country. The visit was confirmed in the summer of 1979, followed by an intimation that the Pope would be delighted to accept the Aer Lingus invitation. 'We were conscious of the enormous publicity which would be generated,' said Kennedy, '. . . and were determined that Aer Lingus should be seen to play its full role on behalf of the Irish community.'

Some two weeks before the visit, in mid-September, Archbishop Marcinkus travelled to Dublin to meet David Kennedy and Seán Daly, responsible for the airline's role in the programme. His first words were that the travel arrangements would have to be changed. Alitalia had been in touch with the Vatican, furious over the choice of Aer Lingus, and the Archbishop wanted the invitation to be withdrawn in favour of the Italian airline. He was told very firmly that at that stage there could be no question of altering the arrangements, which had the full support of the Irish Hierarchy and had been widely publicised. The point was conceded and the arrangements went ahead.

Every precaution was taken against possible hitches, to the extent that a second B747 aircraft was painted with the Papal insignia and temporarily christened *St Patrick*. A B707 was placed on standby in Rome where the cabin crew, on their own initiative, insisted on being at the airport some three hours before the Pope's arrival on board to check on every detail of cabin equipment and food. The latter preoccupation was well rewarded, His Holiness remarking subsequently to a senior hostess: 'Now I understand why the Irish are so famous for their good breakfasts!'

Pope John Paul II left Rome for Dublin on 29 September on the Boeing 747 EI-ASI *St Patrick*, employing the call sign 'Aer Lingus One'. The crew comprised Captain T. P. McKeown, First Officer Richard Parkinson, Third Pilot Barry O'Brien and two senior hostesses, Sylvia Morrin and Annette Greenan. There were twelve other hostesses on board as well as a flight deck linguist, Captain Philip Russell. The flight also carried the Vatican Secretary of State, Cardinal Casaroli, and other Vatican officials, the Vatican press corps of some seventy journalists and a second press party of eighty-five Irish journalists and Aer Lingus personnel. During the flight the Pope insisted on going back through the aircraft to be interviewed by the journalists, who jostled him to such effect that he came close to being knocked down; but this was the only untoward incident on a highly successful flight.

The appearance of EI-ASI in the sky over Dublin constituted a moment of intense emotion, both for the huge gathering assembled in the Phoenix Park and for those on board. Between his arrival on 29 September and his departure on 1 October, Irish Helicopters carried the Pope to Drogheda, Maynooth, Clonmacnoise, Galway, Knock, Limerick and Shannon, with Aer Lingus hostesses flying as helicopter crew for the first time. On 1 October the Papal party left on EI-ASI from Shannon en route to Boston, the aircraft on this occasion being piloted by Captain Aidan Quigley, with First Officer Paddy Morrissey, Third Pilot Paul Plaistead and Captain Philip Russell. The Chief Hostess-Atlantic, Joan Camman, was assisted by Cabin Supervisor Breda O'Connor and senior hostesses Marcella Farrell and Geraldine Kealy. 'All of us who serve Ireland's national airline are grateful and proud to have been accorded the privilege of flying His Holiness and the Papal party between Rome and Dublin and between Shannon and Boston,' wrote David Kennedy: 'These routes, which are an integral part of our regular services, symbolise our role in linking the Old World with the New. The visit of the Holy Father has given that role new significance. We may regard this unique assignment as the crowning achievement of over forty years of service to the Irish community at home and overseas. . . .'

14

Function and Future 1981-86

'I AM directed to reply to recent criticisms of the fare policy of this company,' the Secretary of Aer Lingus wrote to the editor of *The Irish Press:* 'Our fares, if the distance is taken into account, compare very favourably with others.'

The date was 24 November 1936. E. T. McCarron continued: 'The full fare on Irish Sea Airways is less per passenger mile on our unsubsidised service than it is per passenger mile on most of the heavily subsidised services operating between London and the Continent.'

Some forty-eight years later John A. Bristow, a Trinity College economist, produced, with the encouragement of the airline, a report on *Aspects of the regulation of air fares in Ireland:* 'There is no evidence that regulation has allowed the efficiency and costs of Aer Lingus to get out of line with those of other comparable European airlines,' he wrote: 'nor are Irish fares generally higher than fares elsewhere in Europe. Indeed, the average fare per mile paid by Aer Lingus' passengers is lower than that paid on Major European airlines.

If the question, and indeed the answer, had changed little over the course of the half century, the context was very different. In the mid-1980s Aer Lingus was facing not only the greatest financial challenge it had had to meet in the history of its development, but also a fundamental reassessment of its role and function, with a concomitant effect upon its public image. 'Semi-State bodies in general don't have good public images and their problems receive little sympathy,' commented *The Sunday Press* on 1 July 1984: 'The fact that this perception is often unfair is neither here nor there . . . Aer Lingus can, and probably will, blind us with figures to justify their fare structure, but it doesn't cut much ice with travellers.'

If this could be said to represent a public attitude of 'my mind's made up, don't confuse me with facts', the same certitude could not be said to attach to more serious economic thinking on the subject of state-sponsored bodies in general. Though economists, most notably Patrick Lynch, had sought over the years to formulate some kind of pragmatic theory to define their role in the economy as a whole, there had been no real move towards any ideological consensus. 'A difficulty in Ireland is that neither political philosophy nor economic philosophy have had much impact on contemporary discussion,' wrote John L Pratschke in an examination of 'Economic philosophy and ideology in Ireland' in the summer 1985 issue of *Studies:* 'political parties (at least the two largest ones) still hold a wide cross-sectional, broadly-based rather than ideologically-committed support, and parties of the left are still pitifully small. Consequently, it may be that few expect economic policy suggestions to be ideologically based, especially suggestions emanating from the centre of mainstream academic life...' One of those in the mainstream, Ronan Fanning, in a contribution to *Economists and the Irish Economy,* a symposium published in 1984, pointed to the minimal role played by academic economists in influencing policy since the foundation of the State. Yet by this time there had emerged some evidence of a change. In June 1979 a Study Group Report on *Enterprise in the public sector* was presented to the National Economic and Social Council; and though there was only one academic economist (J. A. Bristow) amongst its membership, it made some attempt to address ideological issues before turning its attention to more practical matters. More significant, perhaps, was the welcome accorded to the Report by the Taoiseach, Charles J. Haughey, in his speech at the opening of the Airmotive plant on 9 April 1981. 'We have a mixed economy with great potential for enterprise and development in both our public and private sectors,' he said: 'We expect our state-sponsored bodies to operate in an enterprising and developmental manner. Without the state-sponsored bodies, much of the economic progress we have made would scarcely have been possible or would have occurred at a much slower rate.' In spite of this confident re-statement of belief, David Kennedy could speak in the following month, in the course of an address to the National Management Conference of the Irish Management Institute, of an 'increasing questioning of their [the state-sponsored bodies'] relevance, partly because of a reaction against the increasing role of central government in all our affairs... the charge is that state sponsored industry may have become irrelevant to today's needs and perhaps even parasitical in nature'. This theme was pursued by popular advocates of monetarist economics. In the transport sector in particular Seán D. Barrett questioned the role of the State in the provision of internal surface transport whilst conducting a sustained campaign in favour of de-regulation of air fares with particular reference to the Irish Sea routes.

'In theory the thirty years following World War II there was this rather wonderful thing about the Keynesian Revolution,' the economist J. K. Galbraith told the Commerce and Economics Society of University College Dublin in March 1985: 'there was a steady growth and increasing contentment and increasing satisfaction with the system. I might say very emphatically that these were wonderful years to be an economist: things worked and we took the credit.... One of the basic difficulties not foreseen by my generation was that inflation and not depression would be the problem . . . '. The discrediting of Keynesian economics under the impact both of inflation and the recession made way for a restatement of the liberal capitalist ideology which, according to Pratschke, had continued to characterise fundamental Irish economic thinking. On a popular level this manifested itself in the expressed disenchantment with the State sector in general, a reaction fuelled by some notorious deficiencies, and it was scarcely to be anticipated that in this new, bleaker climate Aer Lingus should retain a loyalty, rooted in both public pride and confidence, which had characterised its relations with its customers for the larger part of its operational history. Criticism was being directed not only at its fare structure but at the quality of its service, though, as letters to the newspapers revealed, there was still a strong body of opinion ready to defend it on the latter count. On a political level there was an increasing demand from politicians of all parties for tighter Government supervision of the State sector. Speaking in the Dáil in May 1985 the Minister for Trade, Commerce and Tourism, John Bruton, said that it should re-establish itself as a source of economic strength. 'Not enough attention has been devoted to a properly-structured relationship between the State bodies and central government. *Ad hoc* arrangements have continued for too long.'

There was scarcely anything new in this: Charles J. Haughey had announced in his Airmotive speech that he had 'initiated a review by the Government of the relationships between state-sponsored bodies and the Government with the aim of encouraging the full innovative and developmental capacity of the public sector and the removal of constraints which might inhibit greater enterprise in this sector.' By mid-1985 it appeared that little progress had been made. 'We have not properly defined the boundaries of responsibility for community-owned enterprises,' J. F. Dempsey told the Institute of Transport in Dublin on 17 April 1985, breaking a silence on transport matters of some twenty years: 'and in my experience the relationship between the public service and the so-called sponsored bodies has been a very uneasy one.' He remained, however, convinced of the validity of the basis upon which the State transport systems had functioned: 'My belief is that many of the concepts behind Irish transport policy over the years were not too far off the mark, but that the manner of the execution of these policies left much to be desired. For instance, I believe in State ownership of major national transport undertakings on the basis that it is only when the community is the shareholder that the best overall balance of transport development occurs, taking both economic and social objectives into account.'

As consumerist and monetarist attitudes become fashionable in the early and mid 1980s, the social role of bodies such as Aer Lingus came increasingly under scrutiny; and this, together with a hardening of Government attitudes under pressure of serious financial stringency, added to the complications of operating an airline on a commercial basis within the State framework. Whereas there was, on the one hand, a general view subscribed to by successive chief executives and chairmen, that relationships with the relevant Department and its Minister for the time being had been generally fruitful and productive, reservations were expressed on the handling of some day-to-day matters. J. F. Dempsey, looking back in 1985 on his early experience, was critical: 'Civil servants, the early ones anyway, were never trained with regard to their role in this field, with the result that their participation as professional bureaucrats tended to be, in my experience, one of damping down good decisions and encouraging decisions that were more expedient than wise. Due substantially to their own poor level of self-confidence and also a lack of clarity with regard to the responsibilities of their position, the civil servants found it very difficult to let the strings go, so to speak.'

Michael Dargan was generally satisfied with relationships at ministerial level and recalled in particular the interest in the airline expressed by Charles J. Haughey when Minister for Finance: 'He called me out of the blue to say that he considered it appropriate that the Chief Executive of such an important and fast-moving concern would be a member of the Board. He confirmed that the Government had agreed. While I never indicated to anybody my ambitions to serve on the Board, I deeply appreciated the confidence shown in me and felt that the decision to place the Chief Executive on the Board was the correct one.'

For David Kennedy relationships between the airline and its sponsoring ministers had, in his experience, been on the whole good — probably, he suggested, better than in many commercial State bodies. 'My principal source of dissatisfaction', he said in 1985, 'is the increasing tendency to centralise, particularly in areas of personnel management. Central government has tended to intervene more and more in this area in all State companies over the last ten years and I think that is an unfortunate development. It is based on the dangerous notion of the unity of the public sector. The real strength of the public sector lies not in its unity but in its diversity. This intervention makes it more and more difficult to operate on a commercial basis.' This view restated the conclusions of the Study Group Report of 1979: 'The concept of the unity of the public sector has begun to be interpreted more rigidly and narrowly than in the past. There is an increasing emphasis on centralised decision-making within the public sector and a tendency towards greater central control of the activities of state-sponsored bodies. These bodies are increasingly being regarded as forming a homogeneous group. They are not homogeneous and were not originally conceived as such. In our view, these efforts to introduce uniformity throughout the whole of the public sector are seriously impeding enterprise in the state-sponsored bodies.'

The restoration of commercial viability in the wake of the two oil crises of 1973 and 1979 was to constitute the major challenge of Kennedy's incumbency up to late 1985, and one to which he was to respond very positively. The response in the area of the airline's primary function, that of air transportation, was threefold: firstly to look for joint ventures with other airlines worldwide to reduce overheads and maximise the productive use of resources; secondly to increase productivity through cost reduction and improved efficiency; and thirdly through sector-by-sector marketing studies designed to relate the airline's services more closely and profitably to the perceived public needs. The introduction of executive class on the European routes and the Quality Quest campaign — the implementation of which lay with Michael Horgan, formerly Chief Pilot and now General Manager-Operations — were, David Kennedy suggested, obvious results of these studies. Though none of the attempts to establish joint operations on a continuing basis with other airlines came to fruition, the leasing of the B737 aircraft surplus to requirements in the winter months was largely successful: owing to international over-capacity the big B747s were more difficult to place. Cost-cutting measures involved a programme 'to get more staff to leave the airline', as David Kennedy put it in December 1982. A 500 man-year reduction had been achieved over the previous two years largely through voluntary retirement and natural wastage, but he now believed that target of 250 man-years in 1983/84 was not likely to be enough. In the event a thousand jobs in air transport disappeared between 1980 and 1985. 'There is a limit, however, to what can be achieved by cost saving and improved productivity in the absence of growth,' said Kennedy in the autumn of 1985: 'and it has been our dependence on a relatively stagnant market for air traffic to and from Ireland which has forced Aer Lingus to restructure itself in a very fundamental manner over the past ten years.'

In a statement of objectives first published in the 1971 annual report and subsequently re-endorsed (*see Appendices*), that of 'Growth' was defined as follows: 'To pursue maximum growth in air transport insofar as our profit position will allow us. To grow in activities related to air transport and in such other activities as may be desirable for reasons of markets, profit plans and the effective use of our resources.' The fundamental restructuring took place under these two headings of aviation-related activities and new businesses with some underlying airline affinity. 'We set up virtually every department within the airline not just as a cost centre but as a profit centre,' David Kennedy said of the internal ancillary activities programme: 'every manager and every senior supervisor was given not just a cost budget to control but a revenue budget'. The programme encountered some problems in the area of public profile. 'Aircraft maintenance is deadly boring,' wrote Jim Dunne in *Business and Finance* in August 1985: 'Most Irish people will never set foot in a

Dunfey Hotel. Neither Devtek nor Altek [*sic*] are destined to become household names. You begin to see Gerry Dempsey's problem: a lot of what he does is remote, difficult to present as a whole.'

In October 1984 Aer Lingus and Aerlínte had an interest in 103 companies — sixty wholly-owned subsidiaries, six subsidiaries involving minority interests, thirty-one associates (interest between 20 and 50 per cent) and six others. Those of the 103 actively trading (forty-three were holding companies or existed only for technical reasons) represented a book value of something between £60 million and £70 million. Inevitably there were suggestions in both public and private circles that some of these assets should be realised to set against the mounting losses, but the contrary view was given popular, if simplistic, expression by Pádraig Ó Moráin in *The Irish Times* of 23 September 1985: 'I don't suppose there are many entrepreneurs who would consider it a wise thing to sell off those interests which make a profit and retain only those which lose money? Indeed I don't suppose there are any like that at all. Yet this course of action is constantly urged on the State . . . Things are bad but if we are going to panic could we please not try to ruin ourselves in the process? When the theatre is crowded, and everybody is shouting fire, it is not wise to rush off and sell the fire extinguisher to the highest bidder.'

The struggle towards the restoration of the airline's profitability took place against the background of the worst ever business crisis in the history of aviation, with major airlines such as Braniff, Continental, Pan American and Laker being forced either into liquidation or major retraction. In the financial year 1980/81 the airline recorded a net loss of £11.21 million after four years of profit. In the annual report the Chairman's statement, detailing the 'concurrence of troubles' contributing to the loss was signed for the first time by M. J. Dargan, who had succeeded J. P. Hayes in August 1980. His appointment was coincident with the retirement of two directors, T. J. O'Driscoll and J. C. O'Connor, who had served the airline for twenty-two and twenty-one years respectively. In the light of the situation the correct commercial decision, David Kennedy told his Board in December 1980, would be to close down the Atlantic operation: there was no way, at that time, that it could be made viable. Dargan warned that the airline should not allow itself to be placed in a position where the Government would expect it to operate the service and at the same time not provide it with the means to do so. In May 1981 a submission was made for an increased equity investment of £40 million, but there followed on 11 June the first of three rapid changes of government which were further to complicate an already critical situation. The new Minister, Patrick Cooney, nevertheless expressed himself as sympathetic to the airline's case.

On 9 February 1982 the Government changed again, Charles Haughey replacing Garrett FitzGerald as Taoiseach. David Kennedy and Michael

Dargan met the Minister for Transport, now John Wilson, on 1 April 1982 and found him broadly in sympathy with their request for an equity investment which, due to continuing losses and mounting debt was now put at £60 million as well as an 'alleviation of costs' of the order of £5 million to £6 million in respect of the Atlantic. Kennedy was determined to return the airline to profit by 1984/85 and saw the investment of £60 million phased over three years as the only option to achieve this and the minimum required to enable it to carry out its mandate of operating to normal business criteria.

The Government took a decision to make an equity investment in 1982, with the implication that it would be taking a similar step in the two succeeding years, but before any long-term decision could be formalised the third general election in a period of eighteen months returned a Fine Gael-Labour coalition to power. This was on 24 November 1982. Some three months later it confirmed that an additional £15 million of equity capital would be provided before 31 March 1983 and a further £15 million before the same date in 1984. This brought the total equity invested by the State in the course of the fifty-year history of the airline to £73.6 million. Michael Dargan expressed his appreciation of the decision but hoped that Aer Lingus would be allowed to conduct its affairs 'on the basis of commercial criteria in the overall interests of the airline'.

In the meantime the Company's own measures directed towards achieving a return to profit had been markedly successful, the goal being reached ahead of schedule. 'It is my pleasant duty this year to offer my sincere congratulations to everyone in the airline,' David Kennedy wrote in the 1984 Staff Report, '. . . on our success last year in fighting our way back to profitability. . . . We ended the year with a net profit of almost £5 million after tax.' The results for the following year, 1984/85, were even more encouraging, with a pre-tax profit of £14.3 million, and it was confidently predicted that the 1985/86 figures would be even better. In mid-1985 Kennedy summed up his personal management style as 'a determination to be commercially viable and a refusal to accept that the shot may not be on'.

If three successive years of profit growth appeared to have vindicated this personal determination, the Chief Executive was the first to acknowledge that the precariously profitable organisation of 1985 — precarious, that is, in terms of the capital required for planned fleet replacement — was a very different animal from the Aer Lingus of a decade previously. Whilst continuing public debate was proceeding over the role and relevance of ancillary activities, the airline had in effect been fundamentally restructured to the extent that the original investment of 30 per cent of its resources in diversification, sanctioned by the Government in 1972, had by 1985 risen to some 40 per cent, underwriting, in Kennedy's words, 'the profitability and future of the entire airline'. The magnitude of this shift was exemplified by the fact that in the latter year Aer Lingus had become the largest supplier in the world of aviation services to the African continent and was maintaining on behalf of other airlines a fleet about four times the size of its own. It had also at that point provided senior management for more than twenty world airlines and owned or was managing over thirty major hotels in the United States representing a total of more than ten thousand rooms.

The airline's own aviation operations were, by contrast, continuing to experience difficulties. The traditional problems of acute seasonality and a small home market were compounded, said David Kennedy, by the depressed economic climate in Ireland and by increased competition. Jobs were shed, services on marginal routes such as Barcelona and Geneva suspended, and radical changes introduced in sales distribution policy. This resulted in a move from prestigious street-level offices in New York and Paris and the closing in early 1985 of a number of sales offices in Britain and North America. At the same time the airline invested heavily in computer systems which were designed to bring their product speedily and efficiently to the travel agent. Whilst some other relatively small airlines continued to place value on a continuing public presence, some of the major European carriers were adopting policies similar to that of Aer Lingus. In the event results on the North Atlantic in 1985 appeared to vindicate the move, with traffic growth in excess of 20 per cent. Cathal Mullan, Assistant Chief Executive–Commercial, forecast at the

Maintenance for other airlines: a United Arab Emirates 747SP at Dublin

AER LINGUS

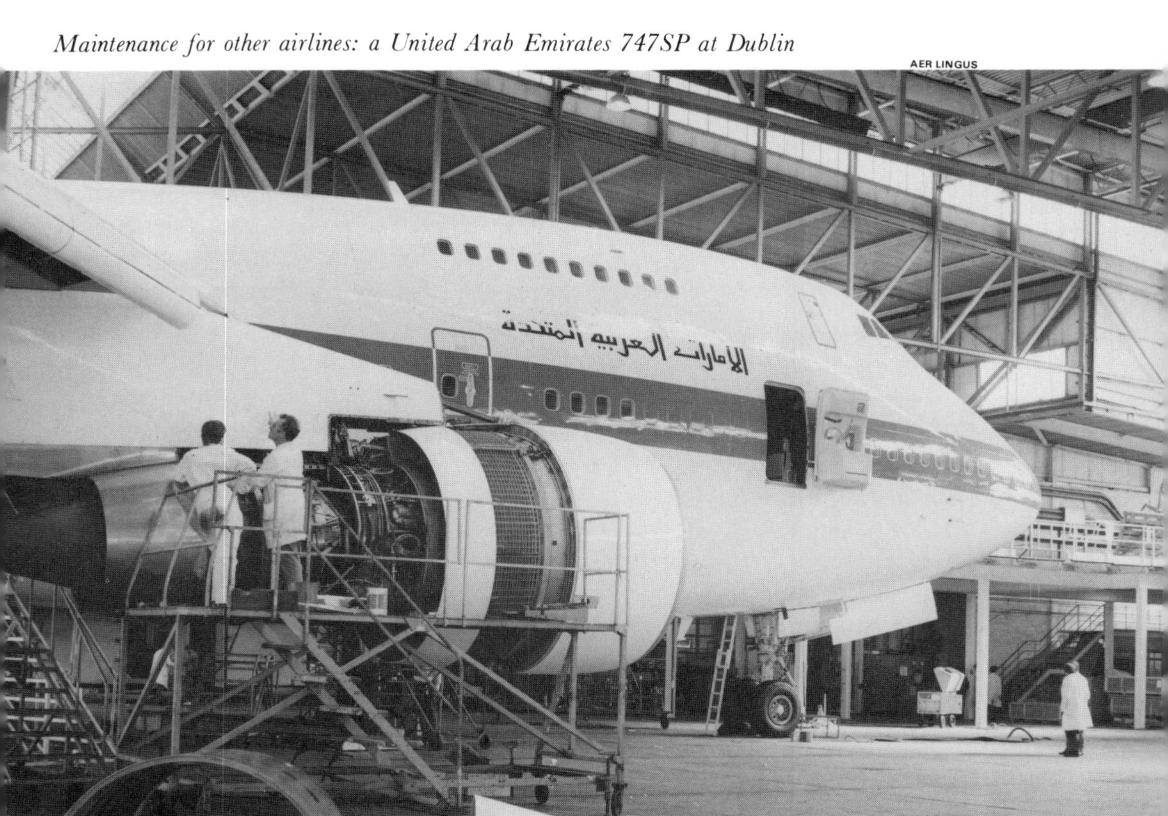

end of that year that Aer Lingus should return an operating profit on the Atlantic for the first time since the early 1970s.

Even the most optimistic future projection could, however, envisage little possibility of such growth being repeated on other sectors in subsequent years. 'I would tend to feel that at the moment it [Aer Lingus] has reached its optimum in terms of route structure,' David Kennedy concluded in mid-1985: 'There will always be marginal routes that one can look at but I think we are serving now pretty well all the natural markets to and from Ireland. I think the vision that might have been there in Jerry Dempsey's time of an around-the-world airline or a far east airline — I find it hard to see that becoming a reality in today's world.'

One of the most potent restrictions on traffic growth resided in the denial of access of Fifth Freedom rights to carry passengers on routes anywhere other than to and from Ireland, on which in 1985 Aer Lingus was carrying some 70 per cent of the traffic and which therefore offered little prospect of significant further development. 'For some years now the airline has recognised that the industry would face an increasing level of competitive pressure,' the 1985 annual report stated: '. . . Firstly, they [the pressures] exist in the market place where carriers . . . seek to increase their market share at the expense of Aer Lingus. . . . But pressures are also evident in the debate on the regulation by governments of the air transport industry, primarily overseas, but echoed strongly at home. In this context the airline, during the past year, has been communicating its own strong objections to certain practices currently applied . . . within the European area. We have pointed out that, over the past twenty years, European governments have systematically deprived Aer Lingus of operating rights where we have initiated and developed air services. Since the access of Ireland to the EEC this process continued. . . .'

This analysis — that deregulation, if carried to its logical conclusion, should lead to the restoration and expansion of Fifth Freedom rights — was restated in the airline's response to a policy paper developed by the Association of European Airlines for submission to the European Commission which proposed greater freedom to set innovative fares and greater latitude to increase the number of flights and seats on any given route. 'In any reform of the European Air Transit System Aer Lingus would want greater access to the major routes and not to be restricted to those serving Ireland directly as at present,' David Kennedy said on 2 October 1985. It was a position which opened up intriguing prospects, the first of which, under investigation in late 1985, involved a joint venture with a small Spanish airline, Hispania, which offered some prospects of gaining a foothold in the sun holiday traffic out of Northern Europe.

In the early 1980s Aer Lingus had instigated an examination of its smaller, thinner routes — mainly those between Dublin and provincial British cities.

'The economics had got very poor indeed,' the Chief Executive told a Northern Ireland audience in March 1985: 'with the traffic falling, the service then being cut back and this leading in turn to the traffic falling again. We were in a spiral and effectively were looking at a situation where we had either to make some drastic changes or else pull off these routes altogether. The only way of keeping these routes alive was to set up an entirely new kind of operation with much smaller, commuter-type aircraft and with major changes in working practice.' The airline decided to approach its staff seeking such changes and, following a seminar, the pilots set up a working group which recognised the seriousness of the situation and agreed to new work practices. The new Commuter Service was inaugurated on 1 May 1983 between Dublin and Liverpool and Dublin and Leeds/Bradford using a thirty-seater Shorts 330 built in Belfast. 'One of the things which has given us a lot of pleasure is that for the first time we are flying aircraft which are

Jim Mitchell at an Aer Lingus Executive Staff Association dinner, 1985, with (left) Una Kennedy, wife of the Chief Executive, and Mrs Mitchell

actually manufactured in Ireland,' David Kennedy told his Northern audience in March 1985.

On 24 February 1984 the independent airline, Avair, collapsed in an atmosphere of some hostility between it and Aer Lingus. When the independent obtained licences to operate services to Britain, the national carrier had advised it that it would not sell its international services through the Astral computer system. Avair responded seeking a court injunction and damages for breach of agreement but the application failed. Following Avair's being put into receivership its Managing Director, Gerry Connolly, accused Aer Lingus of attempting to put him out of business, an allegation that was to be given renewed currency in 1985 with the publication by *The Sunday Tribune* of an Aer Lingus internal memo purporting to favour opposition to all independent operators in Ireland. This implication was strongly refuted in a subsequent letter to the editor from the Aer Lingus official involved, but the 'confrontation' with Avair had given rise to many public misconceptions regarding the role of Aer Lingus which were slow to dissipate.

Avair at its peak had been operating services to Belfast, Derry, Sligo, Cork, Waterford, Jersey, the East Midlands, Blackpool and the Isle of Man. Following its collapse the Minister for Transport, Jim Mitchell, gave Aer Lingus permission to operate on the East Midlands route and to augment its Dublin–Cork service. It also added a Commuter service between Dublin and Shannon, a route which had previously been served by another independent, Aer Arann, acquiring two further Shorts aircraft for the expanded network. Though the new venture started well and was popular with the public, there was some internal dissension on the part of the pilots. 'At the end of the first year', said one of them, 'management were putting no input into it at all. The engineers were very anti — there were tremendous scenes with engineers refusing to service the aircraft, refusing to turn it around . . . they killed the one thing they had going for them which was enormous goodwill.'

Though this militant view may not have been typical, it served to indicate a degree of disenchantment among the pilot body which was to declare itself in the first week of July 1985 in a four-day strike over the failure of Aer Lingus to make a pay offer against a Government directive that no twenty-fifth round offer was to be made. Relationships with the pilots were, in David Kennedy's view, absolutely critical: 'more so than with any other group in the Company. If the whole culture of professionalism, of which our pilot body is rightly proud, starts to decline for whatever reason, it would be potentially very damaging.' One of the sources of the difficulty lay in the changing status of the profession — a 'deglamourisation' had taken place worldwide, accelerated by deregulation in the United States which had made the $150,000 Boeing 747 captain virtually a figure of the past. Aer Lingus had proved no exception:

AER LINGUS

The Shorts 330, the first Commuter aircraft, on its arrival at Dublin, 4 November 1983 (below); and Shorts 360 'St Senan' (above)

AER LINGUS

and the pilots' awareness of their own change in status was perhaps illustrated by their acceptance of the more self-effacing silver in place of the traditionally authoritative gold braid on the uniform sleeve.

The Commuter service apart (it was set up as a wholly-owned subsidiary in 1984 and added summer schedules from Cork to Jersey and Rennes in 1985), there was little prospect, as the airline approached its half-century, of new worlds to conquer on the operational side. One investigation did produce what appeared a feasible opportunity for a new route: 'The increased involvement of Irish people working in the Middle East makes it one of the more likely openings for Aer Lingus service. A thousand Irish people located in one place, returning home twice yearly, would justify a weekly B737 round trip.' In the meantime the airline appeared likely to be obliged to face renewed competition on its established network, both in Europe and from the reappearance of Pan American on the Atlantic, announced for the spring of 1986. In early October 1985, Delta, the third largest United States' airline, also announced its intention of operating into Ireland in the fiftieth anniversary year. Traffic on the Atlantic was benefiting from the effects of the strong US dollar. Commenting on the decision of Pan American to return to the route in a special 'Shannon' supplement in *The Irish Times* of 24 October 1984, Cathal Mullan, Aer Lingus Assistant Chief Executive-Commercial, said that the airline 'had lived with a very high level of competition for a long time and after increasing [its] market share could take them on. What they were worried about was that in any one year there might be a major increase in overall capacity which tended to force airlines into even more lethal pricing.' He said that one of the elements in the Aer Lingus recovery of the North Atlantic route was the contribution from cargo operations, which could have been even better but for a long-running dispute with Aer Rianta, the airport authority, who had prevented Aer Lingus from building a new cargo terminal at Shannon. The dispute was referred to the Minister for Communications who, in November 1985, indicated that the building of a new cargo terminal should proceed, subject to its being funded by Aer Lingus and a ground rent paid to Aer Rianta.

In 1984/85 Aer Lingus carried 72 per cent of the scheduled Atlantic passenger traffic through Shannon, the services benefiting from increased activity at the airport on the part of the Soviet airline Aeroflot, with regular transfer of New York–Moscow passengers to and from Aer Lingus. At the end of November 1985 an inter-governmental agreement gave Aer Lingus permission to operate to Moscow and Leningrad, with onward rights via Tashkent to South East Asia and Australasia, but there was little immediate prospect of such rights being taken up and in spite of press speculation as to a possible link-up with the Soviet airline, the formation of Aer O'Flot seemed a remote possibility. Nearer home, the economic prospects were regarded as little more positive for the Connacht Regional Airport at Knock, Co Mayo, which saw its first revenue services on 25 October 1985 with the arrival of three Aer Lingus charter aircraft — a Boeing 707 and two 737s, to carry a party of pilgrims to Rome.

In the closing months of 1985 the question which perhaps more than any other engaged the attention of the airline management was that of fleet replacement. 'Given the average [age] of the existing fleet (BAC 1-11, nineteen years; B737 twelve years; B747 fourteen years),' an internal study stated, 'it is reasonable to expect that most of them will have to be replaced within the next ten years or so. Because the capital involved is very large, it is realistic to expect to phase the replacement. With lead times of 2 to 3 years on new aircraft this could mean that relatively early commitment would be justified if circumstances were right. This in turn means showing as soon as possible the kind of profit performance which would make it possible to raise the necessary funds by equity financing, borrowing or lease.' In the course of 1985 a major financial study was being undertaken in cooperation with Goldman Sachs of London. 'We are coming to the point where the lines are beginning to converge,' said Louis Slater, Assistant Chief Executive-Finance, in October of that year, 'one being the outcome of the fleet replacement study and the other the line of the financial studies — looking at numbers. The great problem is that once you start bringing in new units of fleet you generate

Loading a cargo container into a B747

AER LINGUS

additional expenditure in terms of interest and depreciation. The numbers are gigantic.'

The studies concluded that, for the foreseeable future, the question of replacing the Atlantic fleet of B747s would not arise. The aircraft were still relatively young, and the possibility of acquiring a newer version which might achieve lower operating costs was virtually ruled out by the prohibitive price — some $100 million at 1985 figures for a stretched-upper-deck B747-300. The balance of the fleet, operating on the European sector, was another matter. The ageing 1-11s, though still a very cost-efficient aircraft on Aer Lingus routes, would have to be 'hush-kitted' at a cost of £1 million sterling before the end of 1986 to comply with International Civil Aviation Organisation (ICAO) noise regulations. Some of the B737s had been in service since 1969 and would also be obvious candidates for replacement.

A number of options were identified: to acquire 'newer' B737-200s; to move to the B737-300, a larger version with 130 seats; or to opt for one of the new types in course of development, notably the Fokker 100, due for initial service in 1987, and the Airbus A320 which would not be flying until the spring of 1988. In all cases the costs appeared formidable — from $17 million for a 99-seater Fokker 100 to £31 million for a 153-seater Airbus A320. There were many technical factors to be considered, including costs related to performance and the likely level of European traffic, and the strategy was further complicated by the probable availability in the mid-1990s of new technology prop-fan aircraft — in effect a return to the propellor powered by a new generation of fuel-efficient engines. It was not considered desirable to be found with 'all-new' jet fleet just before the prop-fan (or some other new development) arrived on the scene and caused its early economic obsolescence. The study concluded that there were 'myriad combinations in respect of timing, aircraft types and numbers'.

There were also a number of options being examined with regard to finance. The study alluded to the possibility of attracting equity from non-governmental sources and David Kennedy did not rule out the feasibility of leasing-in aircraft which might be required for limited periods of time. In view of the major expansion in the Guinness Peat Aviation fleet there was some speculation that the airline might choose to become a major customer of its associate company. It appeared unlikely, however, that decisions, whilst ultimately unavoidable, would be made precipitately. 'We can be relatively relaxed about the timing of fleet replacement,' said David Kennedy: 'our present fleet is admirably suited to the Aer Lingus network. We will probably do it on a phased basis.'

In the spring of 1983 Neil Gleeson, then Assistant Chief Executive–Finance and with a record of thirty-one years' service with the airline, was nominated as Managing Director–Designate of IATA, the International Air Transport

Association, with headquarters in Geneva. As he was in the course of taking up the appointment the following autumn, David Kennedy was elected President of the same organisation at its thirty-ninth annual meeting in Delhi — the second Chief Executive of Aer Lingus to be thus honoured. 'If you look at the size of Aer Lingus in the international aviation scene on the one hand,' commented Kennedy, 'and on the other the influence it possesses, there's just no relationship between the two. Aer Lingus is recognised within the aviation community worldwide as being a very professional airline.'

IATA had been evolving somewhat painfully from what was, in the popular view at least, a cartel-orientated body agonising about matters such as the competitive contents of airline sandwiches to one prepared to take unto itself more far-seeing responsibilities. It had changed its focus since the 1960s to concentrating upon broader trade activities, safety standards and the lobbying of airport authorities and government agencies to achieve lower costs. Aer Lingus and its Chief Executive were to the forefront of this development, Kennedy in his term of office being at the heart of a programme for promoting national airlines in the developing world. His initiative was recognised in his being accorded, in January 1984, a major United States aviation award. In a letter to the editor of *Air Transport World*, which sponsored the award, he pointed out that his interest in the project stemmed very largely from the extensive Aer Lingus involvement with airlines in the 'Third World', particularly the African continent, over the previous ten years. 'During that time we have worked with many airlines in different parts of the world, not merely in providing services but perhaps more importantly in the provision of training facilities to enable these countries to become self-sufficient as quickly as possible. As a relatively small airline in the world scene, which is not competitive with airlines in the underdeveloped world, we have perhaps found it easier to develop an affinity with these airlines and a better understanding of their problems.' Aer Lingus had been since 1975 a member of the State Agencies' Development Co-operation Organisation (DEVCO) which co-ordinates the interests and promotes the activities of its members in development co-operation and in the supply of their services to developing countries.

If any conclusions are to be drawn from the evolution of Aer Lingus in the course of its first fifty years they must derive from the tangible contribution it made to the influence and standing of Ireland in the world at large and to the country's own self-image which demanded initially an act of faith in the proposition that the country was capable of running its own international airline. For the inculcation and sustenance of this informing belief J. F. Dempsey must to a large degree be held responsible. His role as founding father both in the practical and the ideological sense remains undisputed by his former associates as well as his successors, and accounts perhaps for the remarkable degree of cohesion brought to the management and direction of the airline by the three post-war chief executives of which he was the first. Of his many qualities, it was perhaps his humanity that was most pervasive in building the aggregation of attitudes which resolved itself into an Aer Lingus 'culture' — the simple proposition that the public comes first: the 'friendly' concept that has largely survived the advertising cliché. The style, naturally, has changed: it used to be said that on arrival off a flight at New York Dempsey would enquire as to the health and welfare of the local staff man's wife and family, whereas Michael Dargan would request details of the load factor — but the underlying attitude remained. 'I think of the concept of serving the public, of looking after the customer, as something that is central to Aer Lingus,' David Kennedy was to say: 'That goes right back to Jerry Dempsey and Michael Dargan.' When that is said it is probable that only a small airline, based in and intimately integrated into the fabric of a small country, could hope to retain and build upon a human dimension that has demonstrated its practical as well as its ideological value in the wider world.

'I have always felt', said Tom Kennedy, in retirement in New York in the autumn of 1985, 'that there is more to Aer Lingus than running an airline for profit. I feel that it is an essential badge of our nationality.' He recalled the time when Ireland had as yet no transatlantic airline; when for the emigrants streaming westward out of Shannon the foreign aircraft were simply a mid-twentieth-century version of the nineteenth-century coffin ships. With the start of the Aer Lingus service all that, he said, changed. There were still the agonising farewells, but amid the tears the growth of a new awareness. 'These people', said Kennedy, 'had a different sort of feeling. The feeling that they could always come back.'

Forging the link: J. F. Dempsey in Boston, 1947 AER LINGUS

Appendices

APPENDIX I

AER LINGUS/AERLINTE EIREANN

OUR OBJECTIVES

During the year, we set down and published our function as we saw it and the objectives to which we in the airline are working. These are:

Function. To provide and develop an air transport service which will be safe, efficient, reliable and profitable. In carrying out this function our objectives will be:

Standards. To achieve standards of excellence in our operations and to provide a high and distinctive quality of personal service to our customers in all our activities.

Profitability. To earn a profit which will provide a realistic return on capital employed, relative to air transport experience. This is essential so that we may survive in our competitive environment and expand in our primary role as an air transport operator, while providing stable productive employment for our staff.

Growth. To pursue maximum growth in air transport insofar as our profit position will allow us. To grow in activities related to air transport and in such other activities as may be desirable for reasons of markets, profit plans and the effective use of our resources.

Community Benefit. As an international airline we will seek to contribute to all the communities we serve. Particular objectives relative to Ireland will include:

National Development: As a contribution to economic development, to provide a high standard of transport to the community, for passengers and cargo, at lowest possible cost;

Tourism: To engage in tourist promotion to Ireland to the limit of our ability, directly and in co-operation with others, and at a standard that will earn international respect;

Employment: While providing steady productive employment, to afford maximum opportunity for the personal development of our staff, and to expand that employment as the growth of our activities permits, striving continually for the highest standard in staff relations;

Balance of Payments: So to order our affairs as to maximise our earnings from abroad;

Educational, Social and Cultural: To contribute to the enrichment of the community in its educational, social and cultural affairs.

These objectives will be reviewed from time to time to ensure that they respond to changes in our environment.

(Source: Annual Report 1971 and reconfirmed 1980)

APPENDIX 2

AER LINGUS/AERLINTE FLEET LIST 1936-86

Aircraft Registration and Type	Registered	Cancelled
EI-ABI DH 84 Dragon 2 *Iolar*	26.5.36	16.2.38
EI-ABK DH 86A *Eire*	16.9.36	Oct 1946
EI-ABP DH 89 Dragon Rapide *Iolar II*	24.2.38	10.2.40
EI-ABT DH 86B *Sasana*	14.10.38	Nov 1946
EI-ABV Lockheed 14 WF-62	23.6.39	25.5.40
EI-ABW Lockheed 14 WF-62	23.6.39	25.5.40
EI-ACA Douglas DC3-268B	1.4.40	
Damaged beyond repair near Shannon, 18.6.46		
EI-ACB Douglas DC3-268C		
Reserved but not delivered		
EI-ACB Lockheed L414 Hudson 1	24.5.47	
Purchased from Air Corps 28.8.45 but registered only for ferry flight to Belgium after sale		
EI-ACC Supermarine VS 236 Walrus 1	Not taken up	
Purchased from Air Corps 28.8.45. Sold Nov 1946		
EI-ACD Douglas C47 DL *St Patrick, St Gall, St Senan*	17.12.45	15.6.63
EI-ACE Douglas DC3-D *St Colmcille, St Celsus*	27.2.46	13.7.64
EI-ACF DC3-D *St Kieran*	1.3.46	
Damaged beyond repair near Elmdon Airport, Birmingham, 1.1.53		
EI-ACG C47-DL *St Malachy*	15.4.46	31.10.60
EI-ACH Douglas C47A-25-DK *St Brigid, St Mel*	30.1.46	6.5.59
EI-ACI Douglas C47-DL *St Aidan*	8.4.46	2.12.60
EI-ACK Douglas C47A-80DL *St Albert*	29.6.46	9.2.60
EI-ACL Douglas C47A-1DK *St Declan*	13.8.46	2.6.58
EI-ACM Douglas C47A-20DK *St Fintan*	21.7.46	2.6.58
EI-ACR Lockheed L749 Constellation *St Fintan*	17.9.47	15.6.48
EI-ACS Lockheed L749 Constellation *St Patrick*	17.9.47	15.6.48
EI-ACT Douglas C47A-10DK *St Colman, St Conleth*	4.10.46	31.10.60
Replacement for EI-ACA		
EI-ADA L749 Constellation *St Bridget*	17.9.47	15.6.48
EI-ADB Airspeed AS 65 Consul	7.7.47	15.6.49
First registered by Aer Rianta. Registered by Aer Lingus 2.4.48		
EI-ADC Airspeed AS 65 Consul	24.9.47	27.4.53
First registered by Aer Rianta. Registered by Aer Lingus 13.4.48		
EI-ADD L749 Constellation *St Kevin*	8.10.47	15.6.48
EI-ADE L749 Constellation *St Finbar, St Enda*	24.10.47	15.6.48
EI-ADF Vickers V 634 Viking 1B *St Ronan*	4.6.47	10.3.48
EI-ADG Viking 1B *St Senan*	17.6.47	18.11.48
EI-ADH Viking 1B *St Celsus*	23.7.47	1.11.48
EI-ADI Viking 1B *St Mel*	28.7.47	Mar 1948
Sold early 1948		

Aircraft Registration and Type	Registered	Cancelled
EI-ADJ Viking 1B *St Flannan*	2.8.47	8.12.48
EI-ADK Viking 1B *St Jarlath*	9.9.47	27.8.48
EI-ADL Viking 1B *St Felim*	5.9.47	27.8.48
EI-ADW Douglas C47B-5DK	4.6.48	14.9.48
Leased from BOAC to replace Vikings		
EI-ADX Douglas C47B-15-DK	4.6.48	late 1948
Leased from BOAC to replace Vikings		
EI-ADY Douglas C47B-20DK	4.6.48	6.10.48
Leased from BOAC to replace Vikings		
EI-AFA Douglas C47A-80DL *St Kevin, St Laurence O'Toole, St Fergal, St Declan*	26.11.48	29.10.63
EI-AFB Douglas C47A-90-DL *St Brendan, St Cillian, St Jarlath*	26.11.48	9.1.58
EI-AFC Douglas C47A-90DL *St Enda*	26.11.48	25.6.64
EI-AFL Douglas C47B-35DK *St Kevin*	13.5.50	
Crashed in North Wales, 10.1.52		
EI-AFP Bristol 170 Mk 31E	14.3.52	23.10.52
Leased from Bristol Aeroplane Co.		
EI-AFQ Bristol 170 Mk 31E *St Finbar*	10.6.52	26.10.55
EI-AFR Bristol 170 Mk 31E *St Ronan*	17.7.52	10.6.55
Subsequently to Aer Turas as EI-APC		
EI-AFS Bristol 170 Mk 31E *St Senan*	5.12.52	28.12.56
EI-AFT Bristol 170 Mk 31E *St Flannan*	23.1.53	Oct 1956
Subsequently to Aer Turas as EI-APM		
EI-AFV Vickers V707 Viscount *St Patrick, St Ciaran, St Colmcille*	5.3.54	1.2.60
EI-AFW V707 Viscount *St Brigid, St Jarlath*	5.3.54	4.2.60
EI-AFY V707 Viscount *St Brendan, St Cathal*	25.3.54	19.1.60
EI-AGI V707 Viscount *St Laurence O'Toole*	2.4.54	29.1.60
EI-AHG Douglas C47B-25DK *St Ronan*	9.5.55	17.2.64
EI-AJI Vickers V808 Viscount *St Gall*	21.5.57	
Sold as scrap, 13.4.72		
EI-AJJ V808 Viscount *St Columban*	21.5.57	
Sold as scrap, 13.4.72		
EI-AJK V808 Viscount *St Cillian*	21.5.57	4.11.69
EI-AJV Vickers V745 Viscount	26.3.58	20.6.58
Temporary lease from Vickers to cover capacity shortage. No fleet name		
EI-AJW Vickers V745 Viscount	26.3.58	3.6.58
As EI-AJV above		
EI-AKA Fokker F27 Friendship 100 *St Fintan*	10.9.57	13.6.66
EI-AKB Friendship 100 *St Fergal*	10.9.57	14.1.66
EI-AKC Friendship 100 *St Finbar*	10.9.57	24.3.66
EI-AKD Friendship 100 *St Flannan*	10.9.57	10.1.66
EI-AKE Friendship 100 *St Felim*	10.9.57	8.6.66
EI-AKF Friendship 100 *St Finian*	10.9.57	10.1.66
EI-AKG Friendship 100 *St Fiacra*	10.9.57	10.1.66
EI-AKJ Vickers V808 Viscount *St Colman*	14.6.58	18.2.59
See EI-AKO below		

Aircraft Registration and Type	Registered	Cancelled
EI-AKK Viscount V808 *St Aidan*	14.6.58	
Damaged beyond repair at Bristol, 21.9.67		
EI-AKL V808 Viscount *St Colmcille*	14.6.58	21.8.70
EI-AKO Vickers V808 Viscount *St Colman*	18.2.59	7.9.70
St Colman was re-registered on 18.2.59 due to call sign confusion between AKJ and AKK		
EI-ALA Boeing 720-048 *St Patrick, St Pappin*	28.9.60	18.10.72
Cancelled twice from register and restored following lease to Braniff and sale to Transpolar		
EI-ALB Boeing 720-048 *St Brigid*	28.9.60	18.9.64
EI-ALC Boeing 720-048 *St Brendan*	28.9.60	10.8.72
Cancelled four times and restored following leases to Braniff, BWIA, Trans Caribbean and sale to Transpolar		
EI-ALG Vickers V805 Viscount *St Ciaran*	26.3.60	
Sold for scrap, 13.4.72		
EI-AMA Vickers V805 Viscount *St Canice*	31.10.61	
Sold for scrap, 13.4.72		
EI-AMP ATL 98 Carvair *St Albert*	5.2.63	29.5.68
EI-AMR ATL 98 Carvair *St Jarlath*	5.2.63	16.2.68
EI-AMW Boeing 707-348C *St Laurence O'Toole*	25.1.64	23.6.72
Restored as EI-AMW 28.11.77 to GPA/Air Tara. Cancelled 19.5.79		
EI-ANE BAC 1-11 Series 208AL *St Mel*	31.3.65	
EI-ANF BAC 1-11 *St Malachy*	31.3.65	
EI-ANG BAC 1-11 *St Declan*	31.3.65	
EI-ANH BAC 1-11 *St Ronan*	31.3.65	
EI-ANJ ATL 98 Carvair *St Senan*	17.4.64	16.2.68
EI-ANO Boeing 707-348C *St Brigid*	24.2.65	19.5.81
Cancelled and restored twice following leases to Flying Tiger		
EI-ANV 707-348C *St Enda*	22.3.66	16.6.81
EI-AOE Vickers V803 Viscount *St Dymphna*	29.10.65	22.3.69
Cancelled for lease to SATA, 12.3.69–3.11.69. Not restored and scrapped 24.7.72		
EI-AOF V803 Viscount *St Cathal*	3.12.65	
Crashed near Ashbourne, Co. Meath, 22.6.67		
EI-AOG V803 Viscount *St Finian*	15.3.66	
Scrapped 24.7.72		
EI-AOH V803 Viscount *St Fiacra*	18.5.66	
Scrapped 29.12.72. Nose to Irish Aviation Museum		
EI-AOI V803 Viscount *St Fergal*	16.6.66	
Scrapped 29.12.72		
EI-AOJ V803 Viscount *St Flannan*	27.9.66	
Scrapped 22.1.73		
EI-AOL V803 Viscount *St Fintan*	29.11.66	10.3.71
EI-AOM V803 Viscount *St Felim*	29.11.66	
Crashed off Tuskar Rock 24.3.68		
EI-APD V803 Viscount *St Finbar*	28.10.66	
Scrapped 29.12.72		
EI-APG Boeing 707-348C *St Senan*	24.4.67	7.9.82

Aircraft Registration and Type	Registered	Cancelled
EI-ASA Boeing 737-248 *St Jarlath*	23.6.67	
Cancelled and restored following lease to Zambia Airways		
EI-ASB 737-248 *St Albert*	23.6.67	
Cancelled and restored twice following leases to Egyptair and VASP		
EI-ASC 737-248QC *St Macartan*	5.8.69	
Cancelled for lease to VASP to 31.3.86		
EI-ASD 737-248QC *St Ide*	1.9.69	
EI-ASE 737-248QC *St Fachtna*	1.9.69	
EI-ASF 737-248 *St Nathy*	9.10.69	
Cancelled and restored twice following leases to Eastern Provincial Airways and Bahamasair		
EI-ASG 737-248 *St Cormac*	5.1.70	
Cancelled and restored three times following leases to Egyptair, Frontier and TAN Airlines		
EI-ASH 737-248 *St Eugene*	5.1.70	
Cancelled and restored seven times following leases to Transair, Frontier, Air Florida, Pacific Western and TAN Airlines/SAHSA		
EI-ASI Boeing 747-148 *St Colmcille, St Patrick*	20.7.70	
Cancelled and restored following lease to Air Siam		
EI-ASJ 747-148 *St Patrick, St Colmcille*	20.7.70	
Cancelled and restored twice following leases to Air Siam, British Airways and British Caledonian		
EI-ASK Boeing 737-222 *St Laurence O'Toole*	30.5.74	30.9.74
Leased on two occasions from United Airlines	9.5.75	1.10.76
EI-ASL 737-248QC *St Killian*	14.10.74	
EI-ASM Boeing 707-351C No name	5.7.75	24.2.76
Leased from Zambia Airways		
EI-ASN Boeing 707-349C *St Eunan*	27.3.69	24.3.75
EI-ASO 707-349C *St Canice*	1.4.69	
Cancelled and restored five times following leases to Qantas, British Caledonian, Zambia and Bangladesh Biman		
EI-BCR Boeing 737-281 *St Oliver Plunkett*	19.1.77	
EI-BDY 737-2EI *St Eithne*	31.3.78	17.10.78
Leased from Eastern Provincial Airways		
EI-BDY 737-2EI *St Brigid*	28.3.82	
EI-BEB 737-248 *St Eunan*	15.3.79	
EI-BEC 737-248 *St Fiacra*	15.3.79	
Cancelled and restored following lease to Eagle Air		
EI-BED Boeing 747-130 *St Ciaran*	5.1.79	
EI-BEE Boeing 737-281 *St Cronin*	2.5.80	
EI-BEG Shorts 330 *St Ultan*	30.3.83	25.5.83
Re-registered EI-BEH		
EI-BEH Shorts 330 *St Ultan*	25.5.83	8.11.84
Leased from Shorts		
EI-BEK Shorts 360 *St Eithne*	22.2.84	
EI-BEL Shorts 360 *St Aoife*	22.2.84	
EI-BEM Shorts 360 *St Senan*	15.6.84	
Damaged beyond repair near East Midlands, 31.1.86		

Aircraft Registration and Type	Registered	Cancelled
EI-BER Boeing 707-331C No name Leased from GPA	5.5.78	6.10.78
EI-BLC Boeing 707-347C No name Leased from International Air Leasing	26.7.81	2.11.81
EI-BSM Shorts 360 No name Temporary lease from Fairflight	28.2.86	
EI-BSP Shorts 360 Planned for delivery early April 1986		
EI-ABI DH84 Dragon *Iolar* Reissue of original marks to EI-AFK for use in Golden Jubilee Celebrations	12.8.85	

The following aircraft were leased from Seaboard and Western at commencement of the transatlantic service in 1958

	Lease commenced	Lease terminated
N1009C L1049H Super Constellation *St Patrick*	24.4.58	21.10.60
N611C L149G Super Constellation *St Brendan*	17.5.58	17.11.58
N1005C L149E Super Constellation *St Brigid*	-.5.58	22.12.60
N1008C L1049H Super Constellation *St Brendan*	3.6.59	27.9.60

(Note: The registration date is that on which each aircraft was placed on the Irish register. In some cases this was a considerable period in advance of delivery of the aircraft to Aer Lingus. The date of cancellation from register does not necessarily coincide with disposal of aircraft. Where no cancellation date is shown aircraft was still in service as at 10 March 1986, unless otherwise indicated.)

APPENDIX 3

ROUTE INAUGURATION 1936-86

1936

May 27	Dublin-Bristol
May 30	Dublin-Isle of Man
Sept 14	Dublin-Liverpool
	Dublin-Bristol-London

1940

Aug-Nov	(Manchester used as English terminal when Liverpool was unavailable owing to war conditions)

1942

Aug 12	Dublin-Shannon

1946

June 17	Dublin-Paris

1947

July 7	Dublin-Manchester-Amsterdam
July 26	Dublin-Brussels
July 29	Dublin-Belfast-Glasgow
Aug 1	Shannon-London
Aug 14	Dublin-London (all cargo)
Oct 6	Dublin-Shannon-Paris
Oct	Dublin-Belfast-Liverpool
Nov 28	Dublin-Rome

1949

May 2	Dublin-Birmingham
June 4	Dublin-Jersey

1952

April 22	Dublin-Edinburgh
June 11	Dublin-Cardiff

1954	
May 14	Dublin-Dinard-Lourdes
1955	
May	Dublin-Biarritz-Lourdes-Barcelona
1957	
April	Dublin-Manchester-Amsterdam-Dusseldorf
	Dublin-Manchester-Brussels-Frankfurt
June 27	Dublin-Zurich-Rome
1958	
April	Dublin-Lourdes- Rome
April 28	Dublin-Shannon-New York
Oct	Dublin-Shannon-Boston
1959	
April 4	Dublin-Manchester-Dusseldorf-Copenhagen
	Dublin-Paris-Zurich-Rome
May 15	Dublin-Blackpool
June 4	Dublin-Lourdes-Lisbon
1960	
April 2	Dublin-Leeds/Bradford
June 10	Dublin-Cherbourg
1961	
April 29	Dublin-Rennes
Oct 16	Cork-Dublin
	Cork-London
	Cork-Bristol
	Cork-Cardiff
Oct 20	Cork-Paris
1962	
April 6	Cork-Birmingham
May 5	Cork-Lourdes-Barcelona
June	Cork-Jersey
1963	
May 8	Dublin-Liverpool car ferry
May 11	Dublin-Bristol car ferry
May 12	Cork-Bristol car ferry
June	Dublin-Cherbourg car ferry
Nov 2	Dublin-Lourdes-Malaga
1965	
May 31	Cork-Manchester
	Shannon-Manchester
1966	
May 2	Dublin-Montreal-Chicago
1967	
Jan 8	DublinMunich
May 30	Dublin-Madrid
June 13	Belfast-Shannon
1968	
May 23	Belfast-Shannon-New York
May 25	Shannon-Dusseldorf
1975	
May 6	Dublin-Liverpool-London Aercoach service
1976	
Nov 1	Dublin-Milan
1978	
Oct 11	Cork-Amsterdam
1979	
June 3	Cork-Zurich
1980	
May 16	Dublin-Hamburg
1981	
April 2	Shannon-Amsterdam
1984	
May 24	Dublin-East Midlands
1985	
June 2	Cork-Rennes
1986	
May	Dublin-Guernsey

APPENDIX 4

FINANCIAL RESULTS

All figures are for Aer Lingus and Aerlinte combined. Operating profit is profit before interest and tax.

	Operating Revenues IR£	Operating Profit (Loss) IR£	Net Profit (Loss) IR£
1936/37	4,697	(5,147)	(4,824)
1937/38	15,040	(7,796)	(7,313)
1938/39	9,462	(14,779)	(14,779)
1939/40	15,015	(24,062)	(24,062)
1940/41	18,774	(32,040)	(32,114)
1941/42	17,649	(29,405)	(28,853)
1942/43	N/A	N/A	N/A
1943/44	25,439	(23,887)	(21,822)
1944/45	21,079	(27,015)	(25,775)
1945/46	N/A	10,813	9,797
1946/47	377,345	(139,476)	(76,656)
1947/48	1,002,438	(891,188)	(891,188)
1948/49	1,150,540	(281,227)	(281,227)
1949/50	1,142,617	(16,996)	(16,996)
1950/51	1,302,052	10,020	14,646
1951/52	1,619,667	83,692	72,405
1952/53	1,732,267	(91,123)	(83,718)
1953/54	1,835,129	(62,861)	(62,663)
1954/55	2,207,804	25,428	25,428
1955/56	2,612,623	51,495	51,495
1956/57	2,891,406	77,061	77,061
1957/58	3,023,551	(43,674)	(60,513)
1958/59	4,847,113	(668,926)	(768,846)
1959/60	5,605,556	(507,459)	(657,498)
1960/61	7,297,923	183,217	102,403
1961/62	9,853,486	259,774	218,886
1962/63	11,438,894	402,923	344,834
1963/64	13,031,519	1,157,553	1,156,000
1964/65	15,393,345	1,233,054	1,248,000
1965/66	17,977,141	1,015,281	890,000
1966/67	21,589,198	1,105,925	883,000
1967/68	24,038,131	1,195,661	898,000
1968/69	28,473,790	1,714,319	1,452,000
1969/70	33,509,000	1,510,000	664,000
1970/71	37,501,000	1,564,000	815,000
1971/72	42,766,000	(580,000)	(2,379,000)
1972/73	43,249,000	(327,000)	(2,304,000)
1973/74	53,910,000	3,903,000	1,249,000
1974/75	63,359,000	(2,597,000)	(5,251,000)

	Operating Revenues IR£	Operating Profit (Loss) IR£	Net Profit (Loss) IR£
1975/76	73,209,000	(1,976,000)	(5,260,000)
1976/77	129,258,000	4,325,000	117,000
1977/78	163,000,000	8,225,000	4,615,000
1978/79	190,000,000	7,316,000	4,019,000
1979/80	238,000,000	11,210,000	5,449,000
1980/81	272,000,000	(2,316,000)	(11,458,000)
1981/82	360,000,000	4,273,000	(7,418,000)
1982/83	404,000,000	13,660,000	(1,741,000)
1983/84	457,353,000	21,027,000	8,524,000
1984/85	502,693,000	26,558,000	14,343,000

Note: In the years 1936/37 to 1944/45 the operating losses were covered by subsidies (Aer Rianta Teoranta Orders).

APPENDIX 5

PASSENGER TRAFFIC

Total passengers as per annual reports of Aer Lingus and Aerlinte Eireann — scheduled and charter combined.

	European Services	Transatlantic Services	Total
1936/37	892	—	—
1937/38	2,908	—	—
1938/39	3,810	—	—
1939/40	5,002	—	—
1940/41	5,507	—	—
1941/42	5,297	—	—
1942/43	6,168	—	—
1943/44	6,537	—	—
1944/45	5,601	—	—
1945/46	21,235	—	—
1946/47	74,734	—	—
1947/48	148,705	—	—
1948/49	160,892	—	—
1949/50	191,141	—	—
1950/51	210,800	—	—
1951/52	258,464	—	—
1952/53	277,350	—	—
1953/54	284,970	—	—
1954/55	326,810	—	—
1955/56	383,909	—	—
1956/57	441,643	—	—
1957/58	426,176	—	—

	European Services	Transatlantic Services	Total
1958/59	483,619	14,781	498,400
1959/60	533,249	21,733	554,982
1960/61	685,381	33,160	718,541
1961/62	744,462	51,694	796,156
1962/63	774,425	74,723	849,148
1963/64	868,319	83,559	951,878
1964/65	948,023	121,297	1,069,320
1965/66	1,015,963	137,427	1,153,390
1966/67	1,167,211	169,100	1,336,311
1967/68	1,113,181	204,543	1,317,724
1968/69	1,141,577	219,790	1,361,367
1969/70	1,207,755	256,769	1,464,524
1970/71	1,355,215	275,817	1,631,032
1971/72	1,473,308	295,773	1,769,081
1972/73	1,401,327	278,738	1,680,065
1973/74	1,533,090	274,860	1,807,950
1974/75	1,462,269	241,266	1,703,535
1975/76	1,590,078	198,328	1,788,406
1976/77	1,684,251	214,330	1,898,581
1977/78	1,790,885	228,718	2,019,603
1978/79	1,942,180	295,702	2,237,882
1979/80	2,154,719	329,602	2,484,321
1980/81	1,869,618	266,389	2,136,007
1981/82	2,089,668	322,654	2,412,322
1982/83	2,036,179	322,516	2,358,695
1983/84	1,933,569	279,394	2,212,963
1984/85	1,903,113	291,513	2,194,626

APPENDIX 6

CARGO AND MAIL
(Short Tons)

Total cargo and mail as per annual reports of Aer Lingus and Aerlinte Eireann — scheduled and charter combined.

	European Services	Transatlantic Services	Total
1936/37	3½	—	3½
1937/38	N/A	—	—
1938/39	N/A	—	—
1939/45	N/A	—	—
1945/46	27	—	27

	European Services	Atlantic Services	Total
1946/47	295	—	295
1947/48	869	—	869
1948/49	1,291	—	1,291
1949/50	2,435	—	2,435
1950/51	3,082	—	3,082
1951/52	5,177	—	5,177
1952/53	5,417	—	5,417
1953/54	6,689	—	6,689
1954/55	7,755	—	7,755
1955/56	8,485	—	8,485
1956/57	7,776	—	7,776
1957/58	8,334	—	8,334
1958/59	8,966	112	9,078
1959/60	10,497	114	10,611
1960/61	14,146	293	14,439
1961/62	16,243	636	16,879
1962/63	18,976	1,037	20,013
1963/64	20,268	1,282	21,550
1964/65	21,851	2,500	24,351
1965/66	24,809	3,648	28,457
1966/67	30,907	4,721	35,628
1967/68	31,696	5,163	36,859
1968/69	37,227	8,321	45,548
1969/70	39,217	10,080	49,297
1970/71	42,509	10,468	52,977
1971/72	42,716	12,997	55,713
1972/73	47,425	15,494	62,919
1973/74	52,222	16,209	68,431
1974/75	52,278	15,390	67,668
1975/76	42,175	12,867	55,042
1976/77	46,911	14,214	61,125
1977/78	47,065	16,578	63,643
1978/79	42,984	16,693	59,677
1979/80	47,542	18,385	65,927
1980/81	39,964	16,092	56,056
1981/82	38,848	15,251	54,099
1982/83	38,826	15,128	53,954
1983/84	38,400	19,887	58,287
1984/85	40,787	20,131	60,918

APPENDIX 7

AER LINGUS DIVERSIFICATION PROGRAMME

Year	Operating Unit	Business Activity	Sphere or Location
1966	Aer Lingus Training	Airline Staff Training	International
1966	S.R.S. Aviation	Aircraft Handling and Maintenance	Shannon
1968	Aer Lingus Maintenance and Overhaul	Aircraft Maintenance	International
1968	Aer Lingus Engineering	Aircraft Engineering	International
1968	Aer Lingus Catering	Catering Services	Ireland
1968	Aer Lingus Systems Services	Airline Computer Systems	International
1969	Cara Data Processing	Computer Services	Irish & International
1970	Aer Lingus (Airline Support Services)	Aviation Management Consultancy	International
1972	Irish Computer Bureau Services (merged with Cara Data Processing)	Computer Services	Ireland
1972	National Catering Organisation (divested 1976)	Catering	Ireland
1972	Cara Ireland (Tours)	Tour Operator	UK
1972	Sunbound Holidays	Tour Operator	Dublin
1973	Blueskies	Tour Operator	Dublin
1973	London Tara	Hotel	London, Kensington
1973	Roy Bowles Handlers	Ground Handling Services	London, Heathrow
1973	Enterprise Travel	Tour Operator	Northern Ireland
1973	Aer Lingus Espana Tourist Developments	Holiday Properties	Tenerife
1974	Irish Helicopters	Helicopter Services	Ireland
1975	Foxhills Golf and Country Club (divested 1983)	Leisure Centre	London
1975	Guinness Peat Aviation (G.P.A.)	Aircraft Brokerage	International, based at Shannon

Year	Operating Unit	Business Activity	Sphere or Location
1976	Dunfey Hotels Corporation	Hotel Chain	USA
1976	Aviation Traders (Engineering)	Aircraft Maintenance	International, based at Stansted
1979	Hotel Commodore	Hotel	Paris
1980	Cara Holidays (formerly Michael Walsh Travel)	Tour Operator	Dublin
1980	PARC	Personnel Consultancy	Ireland
1980	Aer Turas	International Cargo Services	Ireland
1981	Airmotive Ireland	Aircraft Engine Overhaul	Rathcoole, Dublin
1981	A.L.D. Commercial Services	Equipment Leasing	USA
1981	Dirnan Insurance	Re-insurance	Bermuda
1982	Swissco (divested 1986)	Convenience Foods	Cork
1982	Devtec	Engineering Consultants	Dublin
1983	Alpex Trading	Aircraft Components	International, based at London
1983	PARC Hospital Management	Hospital Management	Iraq
1983	Omni Hotels	Hotel Chain	USA
1984	Altek Automation	Robotic Systems	UK
1985	Automation Tooling Systems	Robotic Systems	Canada and USA

In addition to the above programme, Aer Lingus made investments in the Irish hotel industry to assist the building of new hotels in Ireland.

Year	Operating Unit	Sphere or Location
1960	Irish and Intercontinental Hotels (subsequently changed ownership, becoming Jury's Hotel Group with Aer Lingus investment continuing at 25%)	Hotels in Dublin, Cork and Limerick
1968	Ryan's Tourist Holdings (20% investment subsequently divested)	Hotels in Killarney, Galway, Limerick and Sligo
1973	Dublin International Hotel (25% stake)	Hotel at Dublin Airport

APPENDIX 8

CHAIRMEN

Seán Ó hUadhaigh	Aer Lingus	May 1936-November 1941
John Leydon	Aer Lingus	December 1941-March 1949
	Aerlinte	March 1947-March 1949
	Aerlinte	January 1958-July 1960
E. T. McCarron	Aer Lingus	March 1949-May 1951
	Aerlinte	April 1949-May 1954
Patrick Lynch	Aer Lingus	June 1954-July 1975
	Aerlinte	June 1954-December 1957
		July 1960-July 1975
J. P. Hayes	Aer Lingus	August 1975-July 1980
	Aerlinte	August 1975-July 1980
Michael J. Dargan	Aer Lingus	August 1980-present
	Aerlinte	August 1980-present

APPENDIX 9

GENERAL MANAGER/CHIEF EXECUTIVE

Dr J. F. Dempsey	August 1937-March 1967
Dr M. J. Dargan	April 1967-March 1974
D. M. Kennedy	April 1974-present

APPENDIX 10

AER LINGUS DIRECTORS

PERIODS OF SERVICE

Seán Ó hUadhaigh	May 1936-March 1944 July 1957-January 1959
Augustus Percy Reynolds	June 1936-November 1941
John Joseph O'Leary	June 1936-November 1941 September 1943-July 1974
William Henry Morton	May 1936-November 1941
Thomas Joseph Flynn	May 1936-July 1945
John Leydon	November 1941-March 1949
John Patrick O'Brien	December 1941-December 1949
Seamus Fitzgerald	December 1941-June 1943
Gerard John Regis Leo d'Erlanger	July 1947-March 1949
Sir Harold Hartley	March 1947-June 1947
Conor Carrigan	March 1947-July 1969
Eamon T. McCarron	April 1949-May 1954
Lord Douglas of Kirtleside	April 1949-March 1964
Peter P. Wilkinson	December 1950-June 1958
Patrick Lynch	July 1954-July 1975
Jeremiah Francis Dempsey	July 1957-July 1976
Anthony Patrick McClafferty	July 1958-July 1967
John Christopher O'Connor	March 1959-July 1980
Denis Herlihy	July 1964-November 1976
Kenneth P. O'Reilly-Hyland	December 1967-July 1974
Michael J. Dargan	July 1969-present
John Patrick Hayes	August 1974-July 1980
Donal P. Flinn	August 1974-July 1985
Diarmuid Ó Riordáin	August 1975-July 1980
David M. Kennedy	August 1976-present
Frank J. Boland	February 1977-July 1982
Patrick Noel Hanlon	August 1980-July 1985
Joseph N. Malone	August 1980-July 1985
John B. McGuckian	August 1980-July 1985
Paul Boushell	May 1981-present
Michael Costello	May 1981-April 1984
Kay Garvey	May 1981-April 1984
John Tatten	May 1981-present
Edward Anthony MacRedmond	June 1981-present
John Desmond Traynor	August 1982-present
John Judge	May 1984-present
Eithne MacManus	May 1984-present
Martin A. Lynch	August 1985-present
Enda Marren	August 1985-present
Eileen O'Mara Walsh	August 1985-present
Brian A. Slowey	August 1985-present

Alternates	
Denis Herlihy	March 1947 subsequently a full director
J. W. S. Brancker (alternate for Sir Harold Hartley and d'Erlanger)	March 1947-June 1947
Lord Amherst (alternate for d'Erlanger and Lord Douglas)	July 1947-March 1964

AERLINTE EIREANN DIRECTORS
PERIODS OF SERVICE

John Leydon	March 1947-March 1949 January 1958-July 1960
Denis Herlihy	March 1947-April 1950 July 1960-November 1976
John Patrick O'Brien	March 1947-1951
John Joseph O'Leary	March 1947-December 1957
John Philip Reihill	March 1947-July 1954
Eamon T. McCarron	April 1949-May 1954
Peter Paul Wilkinson	July 1954-December 1957
Patrick Lynch	June 1954-July 1975
Timothy J. O'Driscoll	January 1958-July 1980
Conor Carrigan	July 1960-July 1971
John Cecil Kelly-Rogers	April 1965-July 1971
John Christopher O'Connor	July 1966-July 1980
Jeremiah Francis Dempsey	March 1967-July 1976
John Patrick Hayes	August 1971-July 1980
Donal P. Flinn	August 1971-July 1985
Diarmuid Ó Riordáin	August 1975-July 1980
David M. Kennedy	August 1976-present
Frank J. Boland	February 1977-July 1982
Michael Joseph Dargan	August 1980-present
Patrick Noel Hanlon	August 1980-July 1985
Joseph N. Malone	August 1980-July 1985
John B. McGuckian	August 1980-July 1985
Paul Boushell	May 1981-present
Kay Garvey	May 1981-April 1984
John Tatten	May 1981-present
Edward Anthony MacRedmond	June 1981-present
John Desmond Traynor	August 1982-present
John Judge	May 1984-present
Eithne MacManus	May 1984-present
Martin A. Lynch	August 1985-present
Enda Marren	August 1985-present
Eileen O'Mara Walsh	August 1985-present
Brian A. Slowey	August 1985-present

APPENDIX II

GOVERNMENT MINISTERS RESPONSIBLE FOR AER LINGUS 1936-1986

Sean F. Lemass, T.D.	Minister for Industry & Commerce	9/3/1932-16/9/1939
Sean McEntee, T.D.	Minister for Industry & Commerce	16/9/1939-18/8/1941
Sean F. Lemass, T.D.	Minister for Industry & Commerce	18/8/1941-18/2/1948
Daniel Morrissey, T.D.	Minister for Industry & Commerce	18/2/1948-14/6/1951
Sean F. Lemass, T.D.	Minister for Industry & Commerce	14/6/1951-2/6/1954
William Norton, T.D.	Minister for Industry & Commerce	2/6/1954-20/3/1957
Sean F. Lemass, T.D.	Minister for Industry & Commerce	20/3/1957-23/6/1959
Jack Lynch, T.D.	Minister for Industry & Commerce	23/6/1959-25/7/1959
Erskine Childers, T.D.	Minister for Transport and Power	25/7/1959-2/7/1969
Brian Lenihan, T.D.	Minister for Transport and Power	3/7/1969-2/1/1973
Michael O'Kennedy, T.D.	Minister for Transport and Power	3/1/1973-14/3/1973
Peter Barry, T.D.	Minister for Transport and Power	15/3/1973-30/11/1976
Tom Fitzpatrick, T.D.	Minister for Transport and Power	2/2/1976-5/7/1977
Padraig Faulkner, T.D.	Minister for Tourism and Transport Minister for Posts & Telegraphs	6/7/1977-12/12/1979
George Colley, T.D.	Minister for Tourism and Transport	13/12/1979-24/1/1980
Albert Reynolds, T.D.	Minister for Transport Minister for Posts & Telegraphs	25/1/1980-29/6/1981
Patrick Cooney, T.D.	Minister for Transport Minister for Posts & Telegraphs	30/6/1981-8/3/1982
John Wilson, T.D.	Minister for Transport Minister for Posts & Telegraphs	9/3/1982-14/12/1982
Jim Mitchell, T.D.	Minister for Transport Minister for Posts & Telegraphs Minister for Communications	15/12/1982-

Select Bibliography

Manuscript sources

Aer Lingus/Aer Rianta/Aerlinte board minutes, reports, correspondence and miscellaneous papers
Department of Defence archives
Fitzmaurice, J.C.: Unpublished autobiography
O'Connor, Richard F.: Personal papers and correspondence

Printed sources: periodicals

Administration, Vol. 3, no. 4, Airlines special issue
Aersceala, 1946-
Anon: 'Look up, it's Frank Fitzpatrick'. *Irish Printer,* Feb. 1985
Browne, Kevin J. (ed): *Shannon Airport Review,* 1954
Butler, Kathleen: 'Kildonan 1933-1936: a memory', *Dublin Historical Record,* xxxvii, 3&4, 1984
Cara, 1968-
Check List, Journal of the Hibernian Aviation Historical Society, 1982-
Dargan, M. J.: 'Aer Lingus — a prognosis'. *Administration,* Vol. 17. no. 2, Summer 1969
Flarepath, the Irish Journal of Aviation, 1964-
Galbraith, J. K.: 'Did we have it too easy?' *Business & Finance,* Vol. 22, no. 1, Sept. 1985
Griffith, John Purser: 'Galway a sea and air port', *Studies,* xviii, Sept. 1929
Irish Air Letter, 1975-
Keating, Michael: 'A history of Shannon and the Atlantic route', *Aviation Ireland,* 1978
Kelly-Rogers, J. C.: 'Aviation in Ireland 1784-1922', *Eire/Ireland,* Vol. 6. no. 2, Summer 1971
Kennedy, Kieran A.: 'The role of the State in economic affairs', *Studies,* lxxiv, no. 294, Summer 1985
Lynch, Patrick: 'Economics and public policy', *Studies,* xlii, 1953
Lynch: 'Escape from stagnation', *Studies,* lii, 1955
Lynch: 'The Irish economic prospect', *Studies* xliv, 1963
McAteer, Desmond: 'Suggested airport for Dublin', *Studies,* xxiv, 1935
McElhatton, Shane: 'Diversification — the world is a shrinking oyster', *Management,* June 1984
O'Brien, Geraldine: 'Negotiating order in the workplace: the case of the air hostess', *Journal of Irish Business and Administrative Research,* Vol.5, no.2, October 1983

O'Donoghue, Martin: 'A cost-benefit evaluation of Irish airlines', *Journal of the Statistical and Social Enquiry Society of Ireland,* Vol. 22, 1968-9

O'Driscoll, T. J.: 'Tourism and transport', *Administration,* Vol. 16, no. 4, 1968

Ó Riain, Mícheál: 'Survival in a bloodbath', *Aersceala* special supplement, April 1983

Pratschke, John L.: 'Economic philosophy and ideology in Ireland', *Studies,* lxxiv, 1985

Raymond, Raymond James: 'The economics of neutrality: the United States, Great Britain and Ireland's war economy 1937-47', (Abstract of thesis) *Irish Economic and Social History,* Vol X, 1983

Ryan, R.: 'The role of the State-sponsored body in the new public service', *Administration,* Vol. 21, 1973

Roberts, Frank J.: 'Shannon catering — a gigantic smooth-running organisation', *Shannon Airport Review,* 1984

Taylor, J. W. R.: 'The British civil air fleet', *Meccano Magazine,* Vol. xxx, no. 12, December 1945

Wings of Flight, Non-technical review of Irish Aviation, 1951(?)

Printed sources: books and reports

Anon: *Aviation on the Shannon,* Dublin, 1985

Bew, Paul and Henry Patterson: *Seán Lemass and the making of modern Ireland, 1943-66,* Dublin 1982

Bristow, J.: *Aspects of the regulation of air fares in Ireland,* Dublin 1984

Brophy, Seán A: *The strategic management of Irish enterprise 1934-1984,* Dublin 1985

Butler, P.H.: *Irish aircraft,* Liverpool 1972

Byrne, Liam: *History of aviation in Ireland,* Dublin 1980

Carrigg, Bernard & others: *25 years a-growing,* Shannon 1968

Chubb, Basil: *Source book of Irish government,* 2nd ed. Dublin 1983

Cohen, S. Ralph (ed): *IATA, The first three decades,* Montreal 1949

Corlett, John: *Aviation in Ulster,* Belfast 1981

Coyle, P.: 'Public enterprise in Ireland', in *Public enterprise and the Community,* Brussels 1975

Crean, Patrick J. & others: *Cork airport, the first twenty one years 1961-1982,* Cork 1982

Dempsey, J. F.: *Harmonising civil aviation,* Brancker Memorial Lecture to the Institute of Transport, Dublin 1965

Farrell, Brian: *Sean Lemass,* Dublin 1983

FitzGerald, Garret: *State-sponsored bodies,* 2nd ed., Dublin 1963

Hayward, Richard: *Where the River Shannon flows,* London 1940

Joint Committee on State-sponsored bodies — 14th report, Dublin 1980

Jones, Ivy Frances: *The rise of a merchant bank. A short history of Guinness Mahon,* Dublin 1974

Lemass, S. F.: *The role of the State sponsored bodies in the economy,* Dublin 1959

Lynch, Patrick: 'The Irish Free State and the Republic of Ireland', in *The Course of Irish History,* ed. T. W. Moody and F. X. Martin, 2nd ed., Dublin 1984

Lee, J. J. (ed): *Ireland 1945-1970,* Dublin 1979

McGann, Brendan: *Psychological aspects of transmeridian flying,* Dublin 1971

Matthews, James: *Voices. A life of Frank O'Connor,* Dublin 1983

Mondey, David: *World's airline registrations,* Shepperton 1974

Murphy, Antoin E. (ed): *Economists and the Irish economy,* Dublin 1984

Murphy, John A.: *Ireland in the twentieth century,* Dublin 1975

O Broin, Seoirse: *Scéal na h-eitleoireachta,* Baile Atha Cliath 1972
O'Donnell, James D.: *How Ireland is governed,* 2nd ed., Dublin 1970
Report of the National Economic and Social Council Study Group on Enterprise in the Social Sector, Dublin 1980
Quigley, Aidan: *The story of an Irish jet pilot,* Dublin & Cork, 1976
Quigley, Aidan: *Green is my sky,* Dublin 1984
Share, Bernard: *The Emergency. Neutral Ireland 1939-45,* Dublin 1978
Swann, John W.: *Forty years of airtransport in Northern Ireland,* Cultra, 1971
Viney, Michael & others: *Record of service. The story of J. F. Dempsey,* Dublin 1967
Walsh, Dermot: *Tragedy at Tuskar Rock,* Dublin & Cork 1983

Index